# Language Development

## A Reader for Teachers

Second Edition

Brenda Miller Power

University of Maine

Ruth Shagoury Hubbard

Lewis & Clark College

Merrill
Prentice Hall

Upper Saddle River, New Jersey
Columbus, Ohio

**Library of Congress Cataloging-in-Publication Data**

Language development: a reader for teachers / Brenda Miller Power, Ruth Shagoury
Hubbard, [editors].—2nd ed.
    p. cm.
  Includes bibliographical references and indexes.
  ISBN 0-13-094063-1
  1. Children–Language. 2. Language acquisition. 3. Sociolinguistics.  I. Power, Brenda
Miller. II. Hubbard, Ruth

LB1139.L3 L3239 2002
401′.93–dc21

2001044255

**Vice President and Publisher:** Jeffery W. Johnston
**Editor:** Linda Ashe Montgomery
**Production Editor:** Mary M. Irvin
**Design Coordinator:** Diane C. Lorenzo
**Project Coordination and Text Design:** Clarinda Publication Services
**Cover Designer:** Linda Sorrells-Smith
**Cover Photo:** superStock
**Production Manager:** Pamela D. Bennett
**Director of Marketing:** Kevin Flanagan
**Marketing Manager:** Krista Groshong
**Marketing Services Manager:** Barbara Koontz

This book was set in Times by The Clarinda Company and was printed and bound by Phoenix
Color Corp. The cover was printed by Phoenix Color Corp.

Pearson Education Ltd., *London*
Pearson Education Australia Pty. Limited, *Sydney*
Pearson Education Singapore Pte. Ltd.
Pearson Education North Asia Ltd., *Hong Kong*
Pearson Education Canada, Ltd., *Toronto*
Pearson Educación de Mexico, S.A. de C.V.
Pearson Education—Japan, *Tokyo*
Pearson Education Malaysia Pte. Ltd.
Pearson Education, *Upper Saddle River, New Jersey*

10  9  8  7  6
ISBN: 0-13-094063-1

For our children

Meghan, Nathaniel, Cory, and Deanna

Who taught us the rules of language and schools,

and then cheerfully broke most of them.

# Preface

There is something fascinating, almost magical, about the ability to speak. Though it is a common miracle played out each day, we are a long way from understanding the mysteries of language. Linguists have spent decades trying to unlock the codes of communication and have determined that human speech has very special properties that allow us to communicate at a rate 3 to 10 times faster than we could otherwise.

There is more to language than speech, however, and anthropologists have spent as much time considering the links between culture and perception. Teachers must have the skills to both understand and build on the language of their students. Through understanding students' language, teachers hold the key to understanding their learning.

## TEXT FOCUS

This reader is designed to take teachers into the domains of linguists and anthropologists. We believe it is important to read the studies of researchers who have shaped our understanding of how we develop language and use it to communicate meaning. But it is equally important to take that knowledge into the classroom, exploring how language can be used for genuine learning, for sharing understanding with others, and for delighting in the magic of language. We have included many studies of language from classrooms, written by teachers. These stories help us all understand how language develops and changes over time—and how this knowledge can help us change classroom practice for the better.

To take the dialogue further, we invited three language researchers to tell us more about the process of their work—and, beyond their published research, what they are working on now, what motivates their research, and how they link it to their teaching lives. Our interviews with Shirley Brice Heath, Deborah Tannen, and Karen Gallas challenge us to engage in a "passion for the ordinary," exploring closely what is occurring all around us.

In *A Map of the World,* (1994; New York: Doubleday) Jane Hamilton writes about a two-year-old child, Lizzie, who is just learning to speak:

> She was just beginning to speak in short sentences. She was at the juncture in her babyhood when it was possible she knew everything worth knowing. She understood the texture of her family; she understood the territory and rage and love, although she couldn't say much more than *ball* and *moo, I want, pretty girl,* and *bad dog.* As her language shaped her experience and limited her ideas, she would probably lose most of

her wisdom for a time. . . . Lizzie, at two, was on the brink, between stations. It was tempting to think that if only they could speak, infants could take us back to their beginning, to the forces of their becoming; they could tell us about patience, about waiting and waiting in the dark. (p. 27)

The pieces in this reader can help give us a language to speak about language. We can understand that feeling a toddler has of losing knowledge for a time. Some of these readings will challenge you—as they have challenged us—to rethink some of your most cherished beliefs about language, learning, and culture. Learning about language has taught us much about patience, about waiting and listening closely to students so we can grasp multiple meanings beneath the words they use.

## TEXT ORGANIZATION

Throughout this book we invite you to become a researcher of language in classrooms. We give guidance and many examples of teachers researching the language of their students. We've peppered the text with examples from novice teacher researchers who, like you, are just learning to analyze language—everything from purchasing tape recorders to coding tape transcripts to noting the way a head is held when someone laughs. We believe passionately that teachers can understand most deeply the lives and learning of their students if they are researchers within their own classrooms.

After the introduction, the book is divided into three parts. These sections represent different "stations" of knowledge classroom teachers need to move through as they work with their students. Part I, Historical Perspectives and Landmark Studies, highlights major theorists who have shaped our understanding of how language is acquired. Teachers need to know the wide range of language development that is normal. Too often, differences within this wide range are equated in schools with deficiencies.

Part II, Talk in Schools, is filled with examples of how teachers can change curriculum to support oral language development, as well as link oral language development to written language. In this section, teachers will see ways to listen carefully in the classroom, delight in the language communities they are a part of, and also learn to assess talk in the classroom in careful, systematic ways.

Part III, Sociocultural and Personal Perspectives, tackles some of the complex issues of language and culture. Language is indeed a social construction, and does not exist in a vacuum. As our society becomes more diverse, it is even more important for teachers to understand how that diversity will be expressed in students' language.

Sprinkled throughout the text are "Teacher Research Extensions"—examples of teachers applying the theories of language in the book to their own classrooms as they complete research studies.

We hope you learn important concepts and theories about language within these pages; however, we know the best learning, about your students' "territories and rages and loves," can come only as you learn to listen to them closely and patiently. We hope you enjoy this reader as much as we enjoyed putting it together. Our aim is to bring us all to a new place in understanding, awareness, and celebration of the language our students use.

## ACKNOWLEDGMENTS

We are indebted to the many teachers in our language development classes over the past decade, who bring such passion, humor, and integrity to their work every day in classrooms throughout the country. Their research and insights are infused throughout this book. Special thanks to Andie Cunningham, Joan Ellis, and Leeanne Larsen, who work alongside us teaching university language courses, and contributed useful ideas about language and teaching for this edition. James Whitney provided continuous friendly technical advice about tape recording and transcribing. Linda Montgomery is a smart, patient, and kind editor who measured her own words carefully in helping us improve the book.

The reviewers for this second edition did an amazing job—they gave the best feedback we've ever received in terms of specific, concrete advice for making the book better. Many, many thanks to Carol Gilles, University of Missouri; Lola J. Ferguson, University of Wisconsin–Madison; Beth Berghoff, Indiana University–Indianapolis; Heidi Mills, University of South Carolina; and Betsy Rymes, University of Georgia. We value you all.

B. Power
R. Hubbard

# Contents

## Part II   Talk in Schools    89

# Learning How To Research Language In Your Classroom

We hope the studies and stories in this collection come alive as you work with colleagues and students to make sense of them through your own experience as a teacher. The root word of theory is the Greek word *theoria,* which means "to see and contemplate." The visions of language in this book can provide many new insights into your students and your teaching, but only as you test them out in your classroom, and talk about what you are seeing with the colleagues around you.

The best way to learn more about the theories of language in this book is to become a teacher researcher—to systematically collect and analyze data from your own classroom. While the experience of doing research in your classroom will teach you much about language, it might also change your role in the classroom. As Alaskan teacher researcher Terri Austin writes:

> Being a teacher researcher keeps me alive intellectually—it tugs at me when I'm apt to settle in and feel too comfortable. It's so much a part of what I do that I can't imagine what life was like before I had data to examine, tapes to transcribe, articles to read, writing deadlines to meet. I don't do teacher research because it's the latest thing to do. I do it because I want to be the best teacher I can be.
>
> Terri Austin (The Well-Dressed Teacher Researcher, pp. 66–80
> in *Teacher Research,* Vol. 2, No. 2 Fall 1994)

As more and more teachers like Terri find the power in researching language in their classrooms, the teacher research movement grows. In addition, our professional understanding of language in classrooms becomes deeper, richer, and more personalized. In this introduction, we want to show you how to get started with language research in your own classroom—how to naturally integrate questions about language into your teaching day.

## FROM QUESTIONS TO DATA COLLECTION

Teachers begin their work as language researchers by asking, "What types of communication exist in my classroom? How can I create the best learning opportunities for *all* the children I work with?" These questions are at the heart of how teachers can strengthen their understanding of language development through research in their own classrooms.

"Research" is an ominous word for many teachers. It shouldn't be. Examining language theory through the lens of your own students—and through self-examination—can be enlightening, eminently practical, and even fun.

You probably already keep some form of anecdotal records, and this is a good start. But taping and transcribing audio and videotapes will add a powerful tool to your repertoire, helping you to come to understand the language interactions in your classroom in new ways.

Kindergarten teacher and noted writer Vivian Gussin Paley describes turning on her tape recorder in the classroom as a turning point in her teaching. In a recent interview, she recounts how "the tape recorder, with its wondrous ability to replay," allowed her to really hear her children. Her transcripts show what she calls "high drama" in the kindergarten: "philosophical discussions about God, fairies, and robbers, as well as speculative discussions about whether stones melt when they are boiled" (*Classroom Crusaders,* Edited by Ronald Wolk and Blake Rodman. Jossey-Bass: San Francisco, CA.1994, p. 20).

Paley also wanted to look at how she responded to children. She claims that pushing the record button changed her teaching—and her life.

"Like a rabbi who spends a year pondering one line of the Torah, Paley would analyze the things she said to children" (Wolk and Rodman, 1994). Listening to the tapes helped her understand her own language as well as her children's—and the messages about communication that were a part of her classroom life.

We believe that, like Paley, you will find your understanding of language transformed by pushing the record button. Of course, it isn't feasible or necessary to add many hours onto your teaching day with taping and transcribing. You needn't record every exchange in the classroom. But if you are going to do any kind of analysis of talk in a classroom, you will need to purchase a tape recorder and think about how you will use it. Without some verbatim recordings, there is a danger that much of your students' dialects, phrasings, pausing and interruption patterns will be lost. This is certainly true in much published research. Regardless of where the study was completed, the students' voices seem to rise from the page in a strange homogenized Midwestern radio-announcer style of speech. This often happens when researchers jot down children's speech without transcribing, inadvertently changing the dialect and speech patterns of the speaker.

One of the most important aspects of taping and transcribing classroom language is the gift it brings teachers—the gift of time. You have the leisure to listen carefully to interactions and hear things that you might miss if you heard them only once. And the tapes can help break down some of the solitude of teaching: you can share your transcripts with others and get new insights, talking through possibilities and courses of action.

In order to make the most of this tool, it helps to give careful thought to *how* you will incorporate it into your teaching life. It's easy to become overwhelmed at first. You will almost surely end up collecting more information than you can productively analyze when you record students at work. As you're collecting, label the tapes carefully, so you have easy access to them as you need them.

We've seen researchers leave tape recorders running at all times in different parts of the room. It's also become common practice to leave a video camera running from one classroom corner. But an accumulation of raw tapes like these, with no thought or function to the taping, will lead to too much data, too little focus—and lots of frustration.

The quality of your recordings can affect the ease of transcription, too. Teacher researcher Lynne Young reflected on the unexpected interference on her early recordings:

> I placed tape recorders in our teachers' lounge [with teacher permission] in two different locations and all we got was static and conversations I could not decode. Then I decided to tape two groups of children in my classroom at opposite ends. Part of the two conversations overlap each other and on one of them, we got lots of coughing from one of the girls who had a bad cold. Not much else could be heard.

Over time, Lynne adjusted the placement of the tape recorder. She narrowed the focus of the study and the number of audiotapes collected as she continued to collect data. It helps to try out different placements in your room for using your equipment. Fluorescent lights and aquarium motors are among the kinds of interferences that might affect your ability to hear the conversations you've recorded when you play them back.

## EQUIPMENT[1]:

Human beings are equipped with phenomenally good audio processing systems. We have the ability to selectively zero in on conversations in noisy environments, screening out much of the background interference and focusing on what we really want to hear. Not so for the lowly tape recorder; it faithfully records *everything*. The trick—or the art—of making your recordings sound as good as what you are able to hear real-time in the classroom is to practice with the equipment you will be using. It should not take much time to figure out what your recorder's electronic strengths and limitations are, and you can, in turn, make the necessary adjustments.

Your first step is to find a tape recorder. The ideal would be to purchase one that meets the needs of recording that will allow you to capture quality recordings with a minimum of effort. But first, we need to talk about how to get the best results from a wide variety of recording devices. We realize that many of you will be borrowing recorders from friends or using school equipment, and that finding the "perfect piece of recording equipment" does not head your list of priorities. However, at the end of this section, we have included advice for those of you who find yourself in the enviable position of helping your school select new equipment, writing small grants for teacher research, or investing in your own equipment.

## GETTING STARTED:

1. **Find a piece of equipment; thoroughly familiarize yourself with how it operates.**
   - Does it still have an operator's manual? If so, read it carefully.
   - What is the power source: batteries, electricity, or both? Are the batteries rechargeable? If so, it should say in your manual how long it takes to charge the

[1]The authors wish to thank videographer James Whitney for the explanations and insights, as well as the purchasing and recording suggestions included in the technical sections of this reader.

batteries. You can also look on the batteries themselves—they usually list the recharge time. How long can you record on a set of batteries? As the batteries in the recorder wear down, does the motor also begin to slow down during recording? This is very common occurrence in many recorders and you won't really know you have a problem until you plug in the recorder at a later date or play the tape back on another machine, only to hear your kids sounding like Alvin the Chipmunk. (If this does happen, don't panic. Many tape transcribers or tape recorders have a knob that varies the playback speed, and will allow you to correct a slowly recorded tape.)

- Recording levels: Almost all recorders are equipped to automatically adjust the recording level. Your recorder may have both a manual and an automatic level setting. Locate the switch that controls the automatic/manual setting and set it to automatic. Manually setting the record level will give you a better recording, but like everything else, it takes quite a bit of practice—and a set of headphones.
- Sound pick-up: The microphone. Chances are, your tape recorder has a built-in microphone. Where is it on your recording device? Try a number of test recordings to determine how to best position the recorder for clear audio. The general rule of thumb is to position the microphone as *close as possible to your informants*— within three to four feet *maximum*. It also helps to place the recorder on a piece of foam rubber if you find you're picking up a lot of surface noise from the table.

## 2. Tape stock
- Use name-brand, high quality tapes. Many of the generic brands *will not* withstand the rigors of many fast forward/rewind functions that are part of the transcription process.
- Avoid using anything longer than a C90 cassette (45 minutes per side).

## 3. Before you go out and record . . .
- Are your batteries charged? Do you have spare batteries?
- If your power source is electricity, do you have a cord?
- Do you have spare tapes and material to mark them?

## 4. On site set-up and test
- Go to the area where you will be making the recording. Set the recorder up and conduct a test recording. Talk into the recorder in a normal tone of voice, stating the date and any other pertinent marking information. Rewind and play back the tape. If possible, conduct a short test to make sure that the microphone is positioned to pick up all of the participants' voices.

**Table I–1**
New Equipment Selection: What to Look For

Good recording systems have three basic components: the recorder itself, microphones, and a way to clearly hear what you have recorded.

**The recorder**
There are many models and brands of recorders to choose from, with many different specialty features or functions. Prices vary from $40 to $500. You can buy a very good recorder for $200–250. We would recommend that you look for a recorder that offers the

following features: A sensitive built-in microphone; an external microphone jack; automatic and manual record level; an external headphone jack; a rechargeable battery; 2-way power (either plug in the wall or run on battery); direct connect telephone jack (to make recordings of phone interviews); a good built-in speaker.

### Microphones

Often, even with a good built-in microphone, you will not be able to position the recorder to clearly pick up all of the conversation. We recommend purchasing an additional external microphone to help you out of these dilemmas. There are as many different microphones as there are recorders, from shotgun mics to choir mics. Check with local vendors to find out what type of microphone best meets your needs. We can tell you from past experience that the use of the right external microphone can make an enormous difference in the quality of your recordings.

### Playback

You need to be able to hear what you have recorded clearly in the field in order to make the necessary adjustments. A recorder with a good built-in speaker will be able to faithfully reproduce what you have recorded, but it may affect the flow of activity in the classroom. Everyone will hear what you are playing back. A better alternative is to use headphones. Headphones will also allow you hear the recording much more clearly in a busy classroom. They are relatively inexpensive; a good pair will cost $35–45. A note of caution: make sure that the plug on the headphone matches the plug and stereo or mono playback capability of the recorder.

## TRANSCRIPTION MARKS

The goal in adding transcription markers to your texts should be to enhance understanding of the language used (see Table I–2, Key to Transcription Conventions). Most teachers we've worked with prefer to use these conventions sparingly. Depending on what you are researching, it can be very useful to be aware of pauses, or overlapping sentences, or even volume. You may even find that you need to create a marker for the particular needs of your study. But using **all** the possible transcription conventions can actually serve to hinder a reader's sense of language in the classroom. Because of this, most classroom researchers choose only a few when they transcribe.

**Table I–2**
Key to Transcription Conventions

. . noticeable pause or break in rhythm (less than 0.5 second)
. . . half-second pause, as measured by stop watch
an extra dot is added for each half-second of pause, hence,
. . . . full second pause
. . . . . second-and-a-half pause, and so on
<u>underline</u> marks emphatic stress
CAPS mark very emphatic stress
musical notation is used for amplitude and appears under the line:
        *p* piano (spoken softly)
        *pp* pianissimo (spoken very softly)
        *f* forte (spoken loudly)
        *ff* fortissimo (spoken very loudly)

*acc* spoken quickly

*dec* spoken slowly

The above notations continue until punctuation, unless otherwise noted

/?/ indicates transcription impossible

/words/ within slashes indicate uncertain transcription

[brackets] are used for comments on quality of speech and context

⌈ Brackets between lines indicate overlapping speech

⌊ Two people talking at the same time

Brackets on two lines ⌉

⌊ Indicate second utterance

latched onto first, without perceptible pause

---

*Source: The Art of Classroom Inquiry: A Handbook for Teacher-Researchers* (p. 44) by R. S. Hubbard and B. M. Power, 1993, Portsmouth, NH: Heinemann.

Here is an example of how Martha Pojasek used transcription markers selectively in her work. If you do use markers, you should always begin your text by defining these markers, as Martha does:

| Transcription Key | |
|---|---|
| - | false starts |
| . . . | pauses |
| ___ (underline) | emphatic stress |
| CAPS | very emphatic stress |
| /?/ | unintelligible word |
| [ ] | comments |

**Kara and Harry**
Tracing pictures from *Eyewitness Book of Birds*

1. K: This is an interest - interesting book. Look at these big bones from birds Harry. . . .
2. H: I see.
3. K: You didn't see it. . . . These <u>are</u> bones.
4. H: I know, I know, I know, I know.
5. K: Eeew!
6. H: What!
7. K: [makes noise of disgust with tongue]
8. H: UGH!
9. K: These are GROSS! Let's see what's at the end.
10. H: Well?
11. K: This is the end.
12. H: WOW!
13. K: /?/ OH!
14. H: What?
15. K: This is how they start out, yech! [Looking at a series of pictures on chicks' development inside the egg]
16. K: This is how they start out, yech!

**Figure I–1**
Martha Pojasek's tape transcription with markers.

There are three markers that teachers find the most useful. The period, denoting pauses in speech, helps readers gain a sense of the rhythm and pace of conversation. As teachers, we're often curious about wait time and pace of instruction, and these transcription marks convey a sense of time and pace.

Another transcription marker frequently used by teacher researchers is the [, or marker denoting conversations overlapping. This mark shows when a child is interrupted, frequently leading to a change in topic.

The # or /?/ denotes words that are indecipherable on tape. This marker helps readers know that some of the speech is missing. It doesn't let you know if it was because the person speaking mumbled, the tone of voice wasn't picked up by the recorder, or a toilet flushed in the background, but it reminds the researcher, and any reader of the transcripts, that something important may be missing.

One of the purposes of the transcription markers is to give more dimension to the communication in the classroom. The more you can record a sense of the context surrounding conversations in your classroom, the better you will be able to understand the interactions on the tape.

## TOPIC ANALYSIS

Topic analysis is a transcription technique that is less time-consuming than a detailed rendering of every word spoken. Some research questions don't require verbatim transcription of each conversation. You may be looking instead at who controls the topics, or an analysis of when one student, or one particular group of students, enter into conversations.

In topic analysis, you note who is speaking when, and who controls when the topic changes. Teacher researcher Karen Achorn found it most helpful to note who controlled topic change in her transcription analysis. Ronnie is clearly in control of introducing topics that relate to discussions of his goals, as the transcript shows (see Figure I–2, Achorn's Topic Analysis).

You'll come to understand these tools as you test them out. If you are planning to attempt some language research, it will also help you to read some of the examples of classroom language research from the next section of the book before you begin. But it's never too early to try to find the equipment you need and to test it out with students in your classroom. Like Lynne Young, you may find you need to experiment with placement and times of day before you get clear recordings.

## ALL THINKING IS SORTING: LENSES FOR LOOKING AT LANGUAGE

Analyzing language you record or note within the classroom is the key to really understanding many of these language theories. You may choose to begin with your own students, although many teachers also find it practical to analyze talk from a colleague's classroom.

We've found it often helps teachers to start with a few simple activities that can give a sense of patterns in language use in their own classrooms. As you begin to analyze language in your classroom, find the questions or issues around language use that are

| Digital Counter | Topic | Participants | How it came up |
|---|---|---|---|
| 001 | Goals | All | R: I want to be a toxicologist |
| 020 | Decision to become a toxicologist | All | R: mentions Tim Landry and "Auntie's" influence |
| 040 | Dinosaurs | All | R: Most third graders "don't know it yet" |
| 060 | How to prepare to reach goal in Gr. 3 | All | R: "teach others" |
| 080 | Experiments | All | R: talks of mixes |
| 100 | Rotten wood experiment | All | R: "magnifying, chlorophyll" |
| 120 | Other goals | All | R: interested in writing, would write all the bad things about Mike 0 |
| 140 | Brother | All | R: hits, kicks "really not a good kid," must be something about being seven |
| 160 | Self-esteem | All | R: dissected then ate a sunfish to improve himself |
| 180 | Taking Chances | All | R: risk is good, "I'm a lucky guy!" |
|  | Most Exciting Event in Life | All | R: I climbed Mt. Katahdin |

**Figure I–2**
Achorn's topic analysis: Flow of topics in discussion of Ronnie's goals.
*Source: The Art of Classroom Inquiry: A Handbook for Teacher-Researchers* (p. 70) by R. S. Hubbard and B. M. Power, Portsmouth, NH: Heinemann.

intriguing to you; only then can you find a research or assessment question that will sustain your interest.

## Analysis Through Anecdotal Records

Analyzing talk can begin with something as simple as keeping consistent anecdotal records of oral exchanges in the classroom. One way to begin this is to choose a time to keep records in your classroom when there is a lot of peer interaction. Pat McLure does this during her daily small reading groups. She writes a brief, one-page analysis of the talk around the books children bring to share at these groups (see Figure I–3).

Pat's records are a large part of the language analyzed in *Telling Stories* by Tom Newkirk, in Part II of this reader. Keeping these records each day takes only a few minutes of Pat's time. More important, as Pat writes, the students spend less time looking to her as the teacher to mediate the talk and more time speaking with each other. By the end of the school year, Tom noted that Pat had over 60 individual notations about each child's language in these records.

If you choose to keep records during informal or formal discussion periods in your classroom, try to be consistent. Set aside ten minutes every day when you will note what is said and who says it. After you have a few weeks of notes, you will begin to notice

| Name/Book | Comments          Date: 12/10/87 |
|---|---|
| Caitlin<br><br>The Terrible Thing That Happened At Our House | Caitlin summarizes the first part of the book. Kim says she is glad Mast Way Cafeteria isn't like that—it's nice and clean. Caitlin reads about ten pages, then stops (her favorite part).<br><br>Kim:      shows Caitlin her favorite part (big buildup of "No one cares, no one listens")<br><br>Peter:     I like the part where the dog ran into the table. |
| Kim<br><br>Funny Bones | Picks a favorite part. Reads well, much better than she read it when she first read it on Monday. Asks for help with four words.<br><br>Pat:      Why did you pick that as your favorite part?<br><br>Kim:      Because I could read it. And I also want to show you something. The book starts with almost the same words as it ends with (shows two pages).<br><br>Pat:      It comes back with the same words.<br><br>Peter:     I've heard that book before and I like the frighten part.<br><br>Caitlin:    I like when the dog bones and the "woofs" are all mixed up. |
| Peter<br><br>Caps for Sale | Reads this well. Explains other parts of the book as he reads. Talks about unusual arrangement of words on the page—"you have to move the book around to read it."<br><br>Pat:      I like the way the words and pictures are on the page in different spots.<br><br>Peter:     And they kinda make you guess, and the answer is on the next page. |
|  | [Group reads well, and is fairly attentive. Good questions; details pointed out.] |

**Figure I–3**
Pat's book-sharing conference form.

patterns. You might look for who controls topics, what causes you to intercede, when children seem to hold the floor longest. After you see these patterns emerge, you will have a sense of what you might want to explore in depth in your classroom.

## Tape Analysis

Tape recording and analyzing one small piece of language in a classroom rather than a series of conversations, is a good place to start in finding a focus for classroom language research. But even with a transcribing machine, tape transcription is time-consuming. We estimate it takes about one hour to transcribe every seven minutes of tape. (And the time you need for tape transcription multiplies if you don't have a transcribing machine.)

| Questions to consider | Thinking about classroom discourse | Responses for my classroom |
|---|---|---|
| 1 Purpose: | What was the purpose for talk in this session? In which context did it occur? | |
| 2 Structure of the lesson: | Did the lesson follow the<br>   I) teacher initiation<br>   R) student response format?<br>   E) teacher evaluation<br>Find some examples from your tape/transcript which show either this format or some alternatives. | |
| 3 Talk ratio: | What was the ratio of teacher talk to student talk during the lesson?<br>75:25?   50:50?   25:75?<br>How might this change? | |
| 4 Elaboration: | Were there opportunities for more talk about the same topic for either students or the teacher: How was this made possible? | |
| 5 Peer/peer talk: | What opportunities for students to talk to one another for specific purposes were actually set up by the teacher in the lesson? | |
| 6 Silence: | Did any longish periods of silence occur in the lesson? What was the purpose of silence? Who cut it short? How long did it continue? How do you feel about silence between talk? | |
| 7 Negotiations: | Was anything negotiated during the lesson? Procedures/meanings? Ideas? How did you know when agreement was reached? Or was it? | |
| 8 Feedback: | Who gave whom feedback during the lesson? What form did it take? Was it effective? Could it have been more effective? | |
| 9 Student reactions: | What form of talk did student reactions take? Did they have any role in structuring the way the talk occurred in the lesson? | |
| 10 Differential treatment: | Did you treat students differently? What differences in talk can you find which are evidence of this? How might you change this? | |
| 11 Talk as scaffold: | Can you find examples of teacher OR peer talk which acts as a temporary support for student learning? How can you provide opportunities for this to occur? | |
| Organization changes I could make to allow other comments for more effective classroom talk: | | Other comments |

**Figure I–4**
Thinking about classroom discourse chart.
*Source: The Literacy Agenda* (p. 33–34) by E. Furniss and P. Green, 1991, Portsmouth, NH: Heinemann.

We encourage you to start with a tape recording of a one-half hour segment from your own classroom, or that of a colleague, with an analysis that *doesn't* involve transcription. After you have tape recorded the segment, listen to it two or three times without any transcription. (It helps to listen to the tape in a car as you commute to work, or run errands.) As you listen to the tape, ask yourself, "What surprises me? What topics might I want to explore further?" After you've listened to the tape repeatedly and jotted down some of these initial reactions, you may want to try the "Thinking About Classroom Discourse" exercise developed by Elaine Furniss and Pamela Green (Furniss and Green 1991). *The Literacy Agenda* Portsmouth, NH: Heinemann, p. 87)

This chart is a good beginning because it doesn't require a full transcription of the tape. You can work your way through the questions, making rough estimates of classroom talk rations, and listening for examples of markers like "silence" or "negotiation." After you've completed the chart, you may want to star a few topics that are most interesting to you. For example, you might discover you're interested in looking further at your pattern of questioning students, or peer-to-peer talk.

Another starting point for analyzing language is an analysis of verbal and non-verbal behavior. Susan Pidhurney uses a "double entry" transcription strategy, which is both easy to do and can be adapted to an individual teacher's needs. Sue always puts a transcript on the left-hand side. Then, the right-hand side is sometimes used to note non-verbal behaviors, and sometimes is used for analysis (see Figure I–5).

None of these activities is enormously time-consuming. By structuring your anecdotal records in new ways, charting verbal and non-verbal behaviors during discussion activities, or attempting focused analysis of one small sample of language from a classroom, you'll notice different patterns beginning to emerge—and you'll discuss new questions as well. These questions will frame your continued language research agenda.

## BUILDING AN UNDERSTANDING OF LANGUAGE FROM THE STORIES IN OUR CLASSROOMS

> Rarely is it possible to study all the instructions to a game before beginning to play, or to memorize the manual before turning on the computer. We can carry on the process of learning in everything we do, like a mother balancing her child on one hip as she goes about her work with the other hand or uses it to open the door of the unknown. Learning and living, we become ambidextrous.
>
> Mary Catherine Bateson, *Peripheral Visions: Learning Along the Way,*
> 1994, New York: Harper Collins, p. 9.

The tools of teacher research can help you balance the learning, living, and teaching that make up the daily fabric of teachers' worlds. The starting points for research into language in the context of your classroom are as varied as the readers of this book. Here is a sample of the range of questions teachers we know are pursuing as language researchers. Consider them as possible starting points for your language research:

What is my language pattern in talking with students?

How is the classroom talk during a science experiment different than the talk during a literature circle?

| Verbal | Nonverbal |
|---|---|
| Josiah: [raising hand] Mrs. Pidhurney? | |
| Mrs. P.: Josiah? | |
| Josiah: We could make a book. | |
| students: Yeah, we could make a book! | |
| Mrs. P.: A book? | |
| John: Yeah, our own creepy sheep book. | |
| Mrs. P.: How would we do that? | |
| Ethan: We could draw scary things. | |
| Megan: Scary things! | |
| Mrs. P.: OK. With sheep? | |
| some students: Yeah! | |
| some students: No! | |
| Linda: I don't know how to draw sheeps. | |
| Mrs. P.: We could look in the book. | |
| John: No, we could just make things that scared them. | *lots of wiggling* |
| Mrs. P.: OK. Who will read your book? | |
| Shannon: The morning class! | |
| Several students: Yeah! Yeah! | |
| Mrs. P.: OK, that sounds like something they would like. Where do we start? | |
| John: With a title. | |
| Mrs. P.: A title? | |
| Melissa: For the book. | |
| Mrs. P.: OK, any ideas? [chatter . . . chatter . . . chatter] : Any ideas? | |
| Josiah: It could be about scary things. | |
| John: Scaring kids! | |
| Shannon: Scaring everyone! | *all hands up* |
| Mrs. P.: Everyone?! | |
| Ethan: Mr. Shaw! | |
| Several students: Yeah! Scare Mr. Shaw! | *students out of their spot* |
| Shannon: How about scaring the teachers?! | *in circle, crowding around my* |
| Several voices: Yeah! | *chair, hands raised in cheers* |
| John: We'll scare 'em all! | |
| Josiah: We need paper. | |
| Ethan: And crayons. | |
| Shannon: Let's go. | *Everyone heads for work table.* |

**Figure I–5**
Susan Pidhurney's double-entry manuscript.

Where do students choose to sit during writing workshop and how does that affect the talk that takes place?

What is this particular student's language with peers? How does it affect her socially?

How does my students' language change as they move from the classroom to the playground to the cafeteria?

What happens when students investigate their own register changes in different contexts?

What are the differences in talk in small groups between same-sex groups and mixed-sex groups? What are the benefits and drawbacks for each gender?

How do my students' questions change over the course of the year?

Once you have narrowed your focus to one specific question that reflects your language needs and interests, the starting point for your research may be as simple as making a commitment to look closely at students for ten minutes a day in your classroom, thinking carefully about the issue. Keep in mind Deborah Tannen's suggestions, too, to start by looking for tensions you'd like to explore further, or trying to understand things that are going well. You might also find it helpful to commit to writing in a log or teaching journal about what you're noticing for a few minutes each day.

Cindy Edgecomb, a reading specialist in northern Maine, found her focus when she looked at the quality of her talk with a child she was tutoring daily. She wanted to look at the ratio of student : teacher talk. The theoretical lens she was applying to this work came from Vygotsky (in Part I in this reader). Cindy wanted to know see if she was supporting her student in his "zone of proximal development," nudging in a way that both supported and challenged him. She chose to tally her utterances and the student's, and then analyze the kind of talk taking place. This analysis led to changes in her practice, as she writes:

> The talking I did that promoted active learning (proximal development) was minimal. I filled in the silences with remarks such as "Great!" or "I like the way you did that!" At times I just confirmed his work with vague words like "Yes" or "Okay" that weren't really necessary at all. Now I realize I need to step back and listen to what I say, in order to encourage more independence in my students.

Once teachers listen to tapes of themselves working with students, their practice is often changed forever. Teachers acquire a new perspective on their role with students. Wait time, questions, even the dominance of the teacher in conversations with students changes and shifts, usually toward more talk from students.

Over the years, we've worked with many teachers who have sustained their interest in language in their classrooms—and we've worked with many who have not. We thought it would be useful to close with what we have learned from the teachers who have been able to sustain an enthusiasm for language research over many years. The following principles guide the work of teachers who are able to build an understanding of language in their classrooms over time:

1. **Remember, you are the research instrument.**
   It's easy to get caught up in equipment and analysis constraints. Not having a quality tape recorder, or the time to record, becomes an excuse for not considering how language patterns are developing in your classroom. Keep Shirley Brice Heath's advice in mind: You are the research instrument, and you must learn to keep the instrument on all the time.

## 2. Begin small and build.

Too many teachers leave a graduate course with grand plans of how they will systematically collect masses of data in their classrooms. All of us have developed ambitious plans, only to have them dissolve in the dailyness of teaching—the literature corner that needs to be rearranged, the report cards that need to be sent.

Good teachers are adept at finding teachable moments, and they are developing the ability to see researchable moments as well. Look for those small details—the way a head is turned during a whole-class discussion, the instant a child is able to change the topic of conversation with peers—and think about how you might look more closely at the issues those moments raise.

Carry famed language researcher Courtney Cazden's questions with you as you watch students talk.

- What kinds of thinking and talk do you want around this subject matter?
- Is there evidence of learners having a chance to do this kind of talk?
- What's the distribution of participation?
- Who's getting a turn? Who's not?
- Who's silenced?

Much teaching is not systematic—it is a series of small interventions and shifts in thinking that happens in the midst of students. The same can be true of language research.

## 3. Integrate the research into what you are already doing in your classroom and school.

Additional responsibilities are always hard to fit into the school day. Think about your professional goals and try to find some way to incorporate language analysis into these goals. For example, if you are going to add an oral language component to your oral assessment system, develop a language analysis agenda that will lead to new assessment tools. If you are changing from a basal to a literature-based reading program, you might choose to analyze the talk that takes place in literature discussion groups, comparing it to the kids of written chatter that appears in students' response journals.

## 4. Enlist colleagues and students as co-researchers.

Interest in language issues can be sustained only if you have colleagues who share your enthusiasm. It is clear from reading all of the interviews that these lifetime enthusiasts are all part of a network of teacher researchers. These networks can be close to home, in your school, your district, your classroom—and can also be national and international communities. An added benefit of being involved in these larger internet communities is the ability to use written communication as a tool for helping us learn and make sense of what we are exploring.

We also encourage you to reclaim some of the required in-service days in your district as research discussion days. In work with different school districts, we have found administrators are almost always excited when teachers want to try new things in their classrooms. Teachers who work with their colleagues developing a plan for investigation in their classrooms are often surprised at administrators' willingness to allow teachers to use in-service days to continue their work. As part of your plan, you will need to decide upon collective readings and discussions for the group, as well as research activities. You may want to read one of the articles from this collection and discuss it. Your group might also decide to do one of the initial language analysis activities we describe in this introduction. For example, you might do the Literacy Agenda chart for 20 minutes in your individual classrooms, and then discuss your findings at a research meeting. You may want to take turns bringing in a tape excerpt to listen to and analyze together. It is important for these meetings to have a clear focus and agreed upon tasks, so that they don't wander too far away from the group's language research goals.

## FINAL THOUGHTS

The greatest benefit of researching talk in your classroom may be far beyond what it is you learn from the experience to share with colleagues. Talk is fleeting, yet so essential in forming and expanding the learning communities in our classrooms. Tom Newkirk, author with Pat McLure of *Listening In,* spent a year of studying talk in Pat McLure's first grade classroom. He eloquently describes his last quiet moments in Pat's classroom, after every-one has left on the last day of school in June:

> If I learned one central lesson, it was the importance of keeping track of talk. . . . The talk, virtually all if it, is gone, and for a few minutes I feel the poignancy of this loss. The life of this class was the talk—Billy's craziness, Abby's cat stories, Michelle's brother stories, talk of mousetraps and Mexican jumping beans and Tic-Tacs. . . . But we caught a sliver of it, however stripped of sound and gesture, and from that sliver we wrote this book. It is offered not as a model to be followed but as an invitation to listen in, to record, preserve, and reflect on those wondrous vibrations in the air. (p. 152, *Listening In*)

Newkirk's words are also a perfect invitation to new teacher researchers. Throughout this book, you'll see many examples of teachers recording, transcribing and learning from their students. We offer the work of these teachers not as models, but as invitations. May you grasp onto your own "slivers of talk" in your classroom, and in doing so expand and extend your understanding of the language of your students.

# Historical Perspectives and Landmark Studies

# Children's Language Acquisition

**Mabel L. Rice** *University of Kansas*

## EDITOR'S INTRODUCTION

We begin with this essay because it is a comprehensive overview of landmark research in language development, the issues that continue to challenge language researchers, and implications for instruction in language. Mabel Rice presents all the terms and major findings that are informing current research in language, even as she highlights theories that are the most contentious in the field. The themes she presents are woven throughout all the readings that follow.

One of the most remarkable achievements of childhood is also one of the most commonplace. Sometime during their second year, most children begin to talk, and in apparently little time they are adept at using language to address their needs and carry on social interactions. What is remarkable about this achievement is that little or no explicit teaching seems to be necessary.

Although this observation has long fascinated philosophers, it is a relatively recent topic of major interest for developmental psychologists. The contemporary literature began to appear in the 1960s but emerged as a strong area of inquiry only during the 1970s and 1980s. The study of child language sits at an interface among linguistics, developmental psychology, sociology, anthropology, and education, and it links basic questions about the nature of human intellectual competencies to applied questions of how best to teach young children.

The purpose of this article is to provide an overview of the current questions and findings regarding children's acquisition of language so as to highlight some fundamental issues and to suggest guidelines for educational policy. It must be recognized at the outset that this area of study is among the most contentious in the developmental literature. There is little consensus about the most fundamental issues. The debates are lively, and the data base, although growing rapidly, is far from complete. Therefore, the interested reader is encouraged to consult more comprehensive treatments of the literature (e.g., Berko Gleason, 1985; Fletcher & Garman, 1986; Ingram, in press; Rice & Schiefelbusch, 1989; Wanner & Gleitman, 1982).

The article is divided into four sections. In the first, the language acquisition literature is summarized according to some of the major current questions. In the second section, consideration will turn to children who do not master language readily. The third section will address how to teach language to children. In the final section, suggestions for educational policy will be presented.

*Source:* "Children's Language Acquisition" by M. L. Rice, 1989, *American Psychologist, 44:2*, pp. 149–156. Copyright 1989 by the American Psychological Association.

# OVERVIEW OF LANGUAGE ACQUISITION

Language acquisition entails three components: One is the language to be acquired, or, in other words, the task to be mastered; another is the child and the abilities and predispositions that he or she brings to language acquisition; and the third is the environmental setting, that is, the language that the child hears and the speaking context. Each of these components has generated considerable attention. The biggest problem, however, is to characterize how all three aspects fit together to account for the spontaneous appearance of language.

## The Nature of Language

**Dimensions of Communicative Competence.** Language consists of four major dimensions: the sound system (phonology), the system of meanings (semantics), the rules of word formation (morphology), and the rules of sentence formation (syntax). The phonological dimension is evident in such contrasts as *bat* and *pat,* where differences in sounds constitute linguistic distinctions. Semantics refers to the expression of meanings in language and is differentiated from underlying concepts or categories, a distinction to be discussed more fully later. Morphemes are the minimal units of meaning, either words (free morphemes) or meaningful parts of words (bound morphemes). Syntax refers to sentence patterns and the arrangement of words to represent relations between them.

In addition to these dimensions, language has important social aspects. A speaker is ill-equipped to use language effectively if all he or she knows is how to formulate a grammatically correct sentence. The social setting requires adjustment of both the topic and the style of language used, and it also determines how language is interpreted. For example, in some contexts, "Is that my coat?" might be a request for information, whereas in other circumstances it might be a request for the coat or an accusation of theft.

All these aspects of language must be, and are, mastered by children. The entire package of skills is referred to as *communicative competence* (Hymes, 1972).

## Theoretical Models

Linguists have focused much of their attention on the grammatical aspects of language, the morphology, syntax, and, more recently, semantics. Their goal has been to arrive at a satisfactory description of linguistic structures, both at the level of individual languages and at the level of universally shared features. They emphasize that languages do not appear in all possible forms, but the variation across human languages occurs within highly constrained bounds. Linguists hypothesize that these constraints correspond to those provided by a specialized biological program for language acquisition that is an isolated realm of competence not accounted for by more general cognitive abilities (cf. Chomsky, 1965; Goodluck, 1986; Wexler & Culicover, 1980).

Linguistic theorists have attempted to model the outcome of language acquisition, that is, the linguistic knowledge of the mature speaker. Although several models have been proposed, there is currently no consensus of support for any one of them (cf. Newmeyer, 1986). Instead, the field is in a period of rapid development, with emerging linguistic models competing with existing accounts and continual revision or updating of old models to meet new challenges, such as the emerging evidence about language growth and change over the life span.

Among the theoretical models applied to child-language data are transformational grammar, which is now several generations removed from the original model proposed by Chomsky (1957, 1981; Wexler & Culicover, 1980), case grammar (Brown, 1973; Fillmore, 1968), and lexical functionalist grammar (Bresnan, 1982). These models differ from one another in many ways, but one dimension of particular importance for studies of language acquisition is the extent to which syntax is seen as independent of semantics. The early transformation models assumed that syntax, or grammar, is an abstract, rule-governed system independent of the meanings of individual words. Case grammar, on the other hand, introduced semantic roles for noun phrases. This distinction allowed the case grammar model to capture important differences between syntactic constructions that appear to be highly similar in form. For example, in the sentences "John opened the door" and "The key opened the door," *John* and *key* are both nouns and both subjects. Yet the sentence "John opened the door with a key" reveals that there is something very different about these two subjects: *John* is an agent, and *key* is an instrument.

In the more recent lexical functionalist and government binding models, the meanings packaged in individual words are seen as carrying rich syntactic information. Verbs provide necessary information about the kinds of relationships that can be expressed and how they can be expressed in sentences. The following example, with asterisks to indicate ungrammatical sentences, is from Pinker (1989):

John fell.

*John fell the floor.

John devoured something.

*John devoured.

John put something somewhere.

*John put something.

*John put somewhere.

*John put.

A current hot issue is how children learn to avoid the ungrammatical sentences. The problem was pointed out by Baker (1979), and it rests on three observations. One is that there is no negative evidence available to children; that is, adults do not explicitly state such constraints while conversing with their children. Second, children tend to overgeneralize linguistic rules and make mistakes similar to the ungrammatical sentences listed earlier. Therefore, they must somehow learn to retreat from such errors. Finally, the constraints in a language are quite arbitrary and not readily predictable and thus seem not to be easily learnable.

## What the Child Brings to Language Acquisition

The answer to the problem, as well as to other unresolved questions, lies in information about what children know about language, the sequence in which they come to learn language, and how they use language. In turn, these observations lead to inferences about the means by which children master language. Ultimately, any satisfactory model of language development must be compatible with how children learn; their ability to perceive, conceptualize, store, and access information; and their motivations. What remains unresolved is the extent to which children draw upon general learning mechanisms or language-specific learning strategies and capabilities.

Much of the literature focuses on the conceptual and social processes that bear on language development and, to a lesser extent, on the cultural influences. Of primary interest is the ability of children to form linguistic categories, abstract rules for relating the categories, and learn to adjust language to social settings.

Because language emerges when children are very young, around one year of age, and because children this age do not answer direct questions, the major source of information about children's language learning comes from what children say. Investigators carefully transcribe exactly what children say, along with the utterances of other speakers conversing with children. The advent of audio- and videotape records has been central to the contemporary literature,

allowing for permanent records and careful data analysis. Most of the available transcript data are from White, middle-class, English-speaking children, usually with no or few siblings, although there are data from children learning non-English languages. The value of such data is evident in the formation of the Child Language Data Exchange System (MacWhinney & Snow, 1985), which serves as an international data exchange and transcript analysis center.

The transcript data capture children's production of linguistic forms and the settings and circumstances in which targeted forms are used. In addition, investigators explore children's comprehension of linguistic forms and grammatical rules and, as children become old enough to do so, ask children to make judgments of grammatical correctness.

**Cognitive Underpinnings.** Much of the work of the 1970s focused on the earliest stage of language development, the emergence of first words and word combinations, in the belief that the beginnings of language would be most revealing of the origins of communicative competence. The findings were striking and amazingly consistent across children and languages. In effect, young children first talked about what they knew, primarily the world of objects and actions upon objects, favorite things, and people and their activities. Children's first words were not about objects of no interest to them, such as refrigerators, but instead they named bottles and favorite toys and indicated recurrence ("more"), nonexistence ("all gone"), and negation ("no"). Furthermore, English-speaking children's first sentences were simple combinations of content words, such as "more juice," "Mommy sock," and "big ball" (Bloom, 1970; Bowerman, 1973; Brown, 1973). Conspicuously absent were words without obvious content, such as the linking words or functors, for example, *is, to,* and *will.* These simple early sentences were characterized as "telegraphic." This feature has not turned out to be universal, however, but instead varies as a function of the language to be acquired (cf. Slobin, 1985).

Brown (1973) noted that the kinds of meanings that seemed to be central for young language learners indicated strong parallels with Piaget's model of young children's cognitive achievements during the sensorimotor period (birth to around 18 months of age). Piaget emphasized the salience of objects and actions upon objects, a salience supported by children's first words. He also proposed that toddlers formulated an abstract knowledge about the world, with a system of mental representation that included knowledge that objects exist when not in view (object permanence) and that one object can be used to obtain another (means-ends).

It was a small inductive step to hypothesize that general cognitive growth accounted for the emergence of language, a position made appealing by its congruence with the transcript data and by accounting for why children the world over, who presumably share cognitive universals, were able to learn language in a similar fashion. For the past 15 years, investigators have collected linguistic and cognitive data from children in attempts to work out the relation between cognition and language.

Contrary to Piaget's prediction, the subsequent pattern of findings did not support the model of abstract cognitive precursors to language. There is not a clear temporal order of cognitive insights first, followed by linguistic achievements. Instead, language and related non-linguistic competencies tend to appear at the same time. For example, toddlers begin to say "all gone" at roughly the same time they are solving advanced object-permanence tasks. The conclusion has been that there are very specific, rather than broad and pervasive, relations between cognitive developments and semantic developments (cf. Bates, Bretherton, & Snyder, 1988; Gopnik & Meltzoff, 1987). Furthermore, the direction is not one way. Instead, children can use words to search for *or* solidify general understandings as well as to search for words or word combinations to express what they have already worked out nonlinguistically. It remains, however, that at the earliest stages of acquisition, most of the successful nonlinguistic predictors of language are cognitive measures (Bates, 1979).

Even good predictors do not, however, account for all the variability. Part of the unexplained variance may be due to the fact that nonlinguistic concepts are not isomorphic with linguistic categories or rules. Instead, there is a mapping, a translation from nonlinguistic to linguistic, that is required (cf. Rice & Kemper, 1984). The world and a child's understanding of it do not come prepackaged in a manner that transparently corresponds to language. For example, even a category as apparently obvious (to adults) as that of "cup" is not clearly given by the properties of objects. What is called a cup may or may not have a handle, may or may not be made of glass, may or may not be small. The styrofoam object that has no handles and looks like a glass is nevertheless called a cup. The repackaging of information needed for linguistic categories is apparent when considering the variability evident across languages. For example, in Dyirbal, an aboriginal language of Australia, there is a classifier category that includes women, fire, and dangerous things, a linguistic category unlike any in English and unlike any obvious nonlinguistic category of things (cf. Lakoff, 1987).

The point is that semantics refers to meanings expressed in language, a mapping established by the conventions of each language.

Furthermore, not all linguistic categories or rules have obvious parallels with meanings. Instead, they seem to fall outside the sphere of the mapping problem. An example is provided by the law of particle movement in English, wherein we can say "put the hat on," "put it on," or "put on the hat," but we cannot say "put on it." Such constraints are of a formal, grammatical nature not captured in the meanings expressed. Another example is from the English question-formation rule. We can say, "Mary threw something" and transform that into the question, "What did Mary throw?," or we can say "Mary threw stones and something," but we cannot transform it into the question, "What did Mary throw stones and?" (from Goodluck, 1986). It is not likely that children could master these rules on the basis of general nonlinguistic knowledge.

The relation between cognition and language seems to be strongest at the earliest stages of language development. Even at the beginning, however, it is not the case that prelinguistic conceptual knowledge always precedes and accounts for language development. Instead, the two domains seem to develop synchronously. By school age, children are adept at using language as a way of solving conceptual problems, as a mnemonic device, and as a way of organizing mental spaces. In other words, children at first draw heavily upon concepts as a way to master language and later use language to learn new concepts.

The acquisition of word meanings is a matter of great interest given the prominence accorded to the mapping of meanings and the centrality of meanings in current linguistic models. A well-known phenomenon is the rapid spurt in number of new words learned that usually appears somewhere around 18 months, at the time of early word combinations. This is followed by an impressive rate of new word acquisition throughout the preschool years. It has been estimated that during this time children learn to comprehend more than 14,000 words (Templin, 1957), or an average of about nine new words per day. Obviously, children manage to do this without explicit word-by-word tutoring. Instead, they seem to absorb, or "map," new meanings as they encounter them in conversational interactions. They draw on an ability to "fast map" new meanings, forming a quick, initial partial understanding of a word's meaning involving a restructuring of the known word-storage space and a restructuring of the underlying conceptual domain (Carey, 1978). They are able to fast map on the basis of only one or very few encounters with a new word in a meaningful context (cf. Rice & Woodsmall, 1988). Although the phenomenon of fast mapping has been replicated across several studies, the process by which children accomplish this apparently sophisticated feat remains undetermined. It is most likely that they draw upon a quick sense of likely meanings as well as their knowledge of word-formulation rules and grammatical contexts, although the relative contribution of these variables remains to be determined. At any rate, this rapid word-learning ability is central to a preschooler's overall language development and serves as an important foundation for later reading skills.

**Social Skills.** Just as the early meanings of emergent language show remarkable similarity across children, so do the early social uses. From the outset, language emerges as a social tool. Toddlers use language to get the attention of others, to request actions by others, to greet, to protest, and to comment, among other functions. Children have social as well as intellectual motivations for learning language.

Language skills emerge from prelinguistic communicative needs. The social dimension controls early uses of language, and the social setting in turn provides validation and confirmation of the child's effectiveness as a communicator. Children do not use their first words in a vacuum, as an intellectual exercise. Instead, in our society their earliest vocalizations, even cries, are interpreted as meaningful and are regarded as an important indication of the emergence of a new person. Parents actively shape the social aspects of language in the explicit teaching of polite forms such as "please" and "thank you" and appropriate ways of speaking to different individuals.

The social contexts of children's development are not universal but instead demonstrate enormous variability. Therefore, there is reason for caution in espousing a strong causal role for social input in language development. Any such factors would have to be consistent with what is known about different cultures and be able to account for how various cultural practices can lead to the general similarities in emergence of language skills (cf. Heath, 1989).

**Individual Variability.** At one level of description, there are striking commonalities across children in language acquisition. Among them are the following: Language tends to appear at about the same age; the same sorts of meanings are encoded in early words and sentences; and basic meaning relations are mastered before formal grammatical devices. Such consistencies suggest a universal language-making capacity (Slobin, 1985).

At the same time, on another, more specific level, there is considerable variability from one child to another in the rate of language acquisition and in the manner in which particular aspects of language are mastered and combined with one another (Ferguson, 1989). For example, toddlers vary in their preference for nounlike words versus other words. Children who prefer nouns, and later expand their number of verbs, have an advantage for early mastery of grammar (Bates et al., 1988).

Universal propensities and a child's idiosyncratic style interact in the language-acquisition process. There is no one formula, pattern, sequence, or gradient applicable to each child. Instead, each child draws upon a unique mixture of biological, psychological, social, and environmental factors to arrive ultimately at the shared conventions of formal language.

## What the Environment Contributes to Language Development

Obviously, children must hear language in use in order to master the system. Furthermore, it must make sense to them and somehow be important for them to acquire. Beyond these general requirements, it is difficult to specify essential features of input that must be present for a child to learn language. On the other hand, there is evidence about which features can enhance or facilitate a youngster's language development (cf. Snow, 1984).

Much has been written about the "motherese" style of adult input in White, middle-class, Western societies, in which adults and older children adjust their language input to young children. These adjustments consist of simplifications that correspond to youngsters' comprehension levels and interests. Among the features of motherese are an emphasis on the here and now, with a restricted vocabulary and much paraphrasing; simple, well-formed sentences; frequent repetitions; and a slow rate of speech with pauses between utterances and after-content words. It must be noted, however, that these features of "motherese" are not universal but instead reflect cultural practices for addressing infants and young children (Pye, 1986).

Central to the package of facilitative input style is semantically contingent speech. *Semantic contingency* refers to an immediate matching of the adult utterance to the topic or content of the child's utterances. In this scenario, a child may comment on a toy of interest, such as "ball." The adult may then repeat the child's utterance or use the child's word in an expanded comment, such as "that's a ball," or use the child's word in a question, any one of which demonstrates semantic contingency. The effectiveness of this interactive style has been replicated across a number of studies. The combination of linguistic encoding of what is of immediate interest to the child with the child's own utterances maximizes the matching of language form to communicative intent by means of joint attention.

Social interactive routines, such as book reading, are strongly supportive of language development, especially for vocabulary. Joint adult-child book reading is an activity appropriate for a wide age span, from toddlerhood through the elementary grades, and it bridges the development of oral language skills and the emergence of print literacy.

On the other hand, there are indications that some input styles may not be helpful for a child's language development. One widely cited finding is that a directive adult style, consisting of many commands, requests, directions, and instructions, is associated with a slower rate of acquisition of naming words (Nelson, 1973). There is reason for caution in interpretation, however, insofar as it is unclear whether the input style led to the delay, or delayed onset influenced the parental input patterns.

## How Do the Three Factors of Language, Child, and Environment Interact?

Ultimately, the question becomes how do children extract or induct from the language they hear or see the conventional linguistic rules of their native language(s)? To argue that children call upon cognitive or social underpinnings or innate linguistic devices only introduces an intervening layer and does not resolve the basic question of *how*.

At this relatively early stage of inquiry, investigators have rightfully concentrated their efforts on the description of children's linguistic abilities and patterns of acquisition. Contemporary attempts to account for how children acquire language tend to be narrowly defined, with an exclusive emphasis on one of the three components (specific linguistic rules, child variables, or input variables). One of the more comprehensive psychological models available was proposed by Nelson (1989). He argued that language can be mastered by a general cognitive mechanism, the rare event learning mechanism (RELM), which is applicable to all complex, symbolic, rule-governed systems. He concluded that language learning is based on rare events, or isolated moments of understanding. He emphasized the cognitive processes of attention, comparison, categorization, and memory as central to language acquisition, with localized "hot spots" of intellectual realignment. In this model, language acquisition does not proceed in a steady linear progression of increasingly accurate responses but, instead, encompasses four phases: preparation, analysis, assessment, and consolidation. These phases occupy unequal and sometimes overlapping times during the acquisition process. Language acquisition is a consequence of child-constructed experience.

The RELM model deals with the interface of what the child brings to the task and what the environment offers, in terms of what we know about children's general cognitive mechanisms. What is relatively neglected is the language-specific dimension of language acquisition. It is unclear how cognitive mechanisms, powerful as they may be, help children resolve the learnability problem or arrive at language-specific knowledge. On the other hand, linguistic models espousing an innate linguistic learning device have not satisfactorily specified how such a device would work and how it interfaces with the rich network of general cognitive mechanisms available to even very young children. Resolution of these problems constitutes the most challenging of current questions about language development.

## Summary of Normal Language Development

Overall, the outcomes of two decades of child-language research lead to the following picture of children's language. There is a remarkable similarity in the general acquisition sequence for language skills across language and cultures, although there is considerable individual variability in learning strategies and rate of acquisition. Children learn language as a means of talking about what they know so they can accomplish social goals important to them. Explicit language teaching from adults is not necessary. In fact, if adults try to structure and direct a child's language learning, the outcome may be interference with, instead of enhancement of, a child's language skill. Language emerges from a child's explorations of the world in a rich social setting. Although children's cognitive and social knowledge contribute to language mastery, they do not fully account for language development. Not all aspects of language have close parallels to general cognitive or social skills. The specifics of how children manage to combine their mental resources with the environmental input to master language continue to elude scholars, but much progress has been made in terms of the empirical validity of explanatory models.

## IMPAIRED OR DELAYED LANGUAGE DEVELOPMENT

Not all children develop language effortlessly. Instead, some youngsters struggle to achieve linguistic competence. Their difficulty is made more poignant in a society that places a high premium on an individual's ability to express himself or herself well. Traditional teaching methods are based on the assumption that a learner can process language readily and use verbal language as a means of conveying ideas.

From kindergarten through higher education to subsequent high-status roles such as those of professors and physicians, it is assumed that a learner or practitioner can understand and manipulate linguistic symbols.

If children cannot master the fundamentals of language during their preschool years, they are greatly at risk for educational achievement, particularly for reading skills. Furthermore, their limited verbal skills affect their social skills. It is difficult for a youngster to win an argument over a desired toy if he or she cannot negotiate verbally.

Language-learning difficulties can be secondary to another handicapping condition, such as a hearing loss, limited intellectual ability, or atypical social/affective functioning. Of all handicapped children served by speech-language pathologists, more than 40% have other primary handicaps (Dublinske, 1981). The remainder have communication problems as a primary handicap (i.e., without other significant handicaps). Overall, 5% of school-age children receive services for communication handicaps (Dublinske, 1981). These children include those whose problems are with production aspects of communication, such as fluency and voice disorders. It is estimated that approximately 3% of preschoolers lag significantly behind their peers in language development, even though their general sensory, cognitive, and emotional abilities are commensurate with their cohorts (Leske, 1981). These children are referred to by a variety of labels, including *language delayed, language impaired,* and *specific language disability.*

The existence of children whose only significant handicap is that of language development is an interesting challenge to current models of language acquisition. If language is such a robust human-skill domain, why are some children at such risk? What is known about these children is certainly less extensive than the data base for normally developing children. The safest conclusions are about what is not true of language-disabled children. First, by definition, they do not have general intellectual limitations, as indicated by performance within the normal range, or above, on nonverbal measures of intelligence. In other words, they are defined as demonstrating a discrepancy between linguistic and general cognitive ability. This discrepancy is often not recognized by lay persons and educators, presumably because they expect a close association of linguistic and intellectual abilities. The implied erroneous causal interpretation of slow language because of slow intellect can be particularly distressing to a youngster and his or her parents.

Second, language-disabled children are not necessarily from environments with insufficient or inappropriate input, although that can sometimes be the case. It is very difficult to ascribe causal effects to environmental input, in part because communication with a child with limited skills is different from that with a more interactive or responsive youngster, and therefore unusual input patterns can be a consequence instead of a cause of the delayed language. Furthermore, the effects of unjustly attributing guilt to parents are unproductive, at best.

If not general intellect or environmental input, what does account for the difficulties of some children in acquiring language? At present, there is no consensus as to etiology (cf. Johnston, 1988; Leonard, 1979). Among the current hypotheses are specific problems in mental representation or information processing that have close parallels to language but are not crucial for performance on nonlinguistic intelligence tests (Johnston, 1988; Nelson, Kamhi, & Apel, 1987). Another candidate is a problem with on-line linguistic processing, evident in the limited ability of language-delayed preschoolers to fast map new words (Rice, 1987; Rice, Buhr, & Nemeth, 1988).

## TEACHABILITY OF LANGUAGE

Although not usually necessary, in some cases language must be explicitly taught to children. For children who do not have them, language skills can enhance their social worlds, increase their learning capability, contribute significantly to their chances for academic success, and help ensure their eventual functioning as independent, self-actualizing adults. This teaching responsibility is distributed across teachers, speech/language pathologists, and parents.

In line with the three subdivisions of the first section of this article, the teachability of language depends upon the extent to which certain language skills are learnable, the characteristics of the individual learner, and the match between learner and teaching strategy. Principles of teachability are in the formative stages, and given the time demands inherent in evaluation of teaching methods, definitive conclusions will not be available immediately. With these caveats in mind, I have proposed a basic principle for each of the three components of teachability (Rice & Schiefelbusch, 1988, 1989):

1.  The key dimension of language to be targeted for training is the lexicon (word meanings), especially verbs, insofar as they are the key to grammar, according to current theoretical models. Therefore, formal syntax is a secondary training target.

2.  Children bring a wide variety of intellectual, perceptual, social, and motor competencies to language learning. Their teachability depends upon a synergistic balance of interacting skills and knowledge bases.

3. Teaching new language skills requires the use of converging strategies to enhance the aspects of the environment relevant to linguistic mapping in a manner that matches a learner's style of language learning with the targeted linguistic skill.

## CONCLUSIONS AND APPLICATIONS

Naive intuitions about children's language development greatly underestimate the complexities of the achievement, the significance of the accomplishment for related areas of development, and the child's strong but apparently effortless contribution to the acquisition process. As adults, our language facility is so intimately ingrained in our thinking and social functioning that it is difficult to imagine the perspective of the language-learning youngster. We routinely assume that children understand what is said to them and that children mean what they say. We bring our assumptions to our plans for caring for and educating young children. In our culture, verbal communication is the primary means of managing the behavior of children and gaining access to their minds. With this in mind, there are two major conclusions.

First, for normally developing preschoolers (including infants and toddlers), it is important to remember that one of the ways in which these children are qualitatively different from school-age children is that they have not mastered the fundamentals of language. Although much of English grammar is mastered by age five, and kindergarten children can readily follow simple verbal instructions displaced by time and space, preschool children are still working on these skills. Language development is a primary educational objective for preschoolers. The best way to encourage development of language is to provide many opportunities for a child to interact with objects and events and other children. Children's play is a primary source of language enrichment. Adult-directed teaching drills are not appropriate. In other words, most children do not need to be taught language, but they do need opportunities to develop language. The role of the adult in language facilitation is to follow the child's interests, paraphrase what the child says with simple elaborations, and interact in a conversational manner about objects and events on which the child's attention is focused. Also, children do not always need to respond in order to learn new language skills. They can benefit greatly by the opportunity to absorb the conversations of others. At the same time, they do need opportunities to practice expressing words and sentences when they are ready to do so. An easy way to allow for opportunities is to provide pauses in conversations with children; in other words, for adults to refrain from doing all the talking.

Second, some children do need to be taught. Furthermore, a deficiency in language skill should not automatically be equated with limited intelligence, sensory handicaps, poor parental skills, or impoverished environmental circumstances. Careful assessment of the child and the family by trained professionals will be required to identify causal factors. Language teaching requires specialized strategies designed to meet the needs of individual children. Given that these children have not been able to benefit from ordinary communicative situations, it is unlikely that they will profit from placement in a typical preschool classroom, without directed focusing on targeted language forms. Instead, an appropriate preschool is one designed to enhance language, in which the teacher input is adjusted to the children's comprehension levels, communication opportunities are socially engineered in the context of meaningful play activities, and specific linguistic skills are targeted as goals for individual children (cf. Fey 1986). Furthermore, special adjustments to the school curriculum, in which a specific focus on language is provided, are likely to be needed throughout the secondary level as a child makes the transition from oral to written language, from language to express what is known to the use of language as a mental tool for acquiring new knowledge.

Overall, the study of children's language acquisition provides insight into fundamental human mental abilities, contributes to formal models of linguistic knowledge, provides a challenge to accounts of how children learn and how adults can teach, and reminds us of the priority of the social/communicative nature of human existence.

## REFERENCES

Baker, C. L. (1979). Syntactic theory and the projection problem. *Linguistic Inquiry, 10,* 533–581.

Bates, E. (1979). *The emergence of symbols.* New York: Academic Press.

Bates, E., Bretherton, I., & Snyder, L. (1988). *From first words to grammar.* Cambridge, England: Cambridge University Press.

Belmont, J. M. (1989). Cognitive strategies and strategic learning. *American Psychologist, 44,* 142–148.

Berko Gleason, J. B. (1985). *The development of language.* Columbus, OH: Charles E. Merrill.

Bloom, L. (1970). *Language development: Form and function in emerging grammar.* Cambridge, MA: MIT Press.

Bowerman, M. (1973). *Early syntactic development: A cross-linguistic study with special reference to Finnish.* Cambridge, England: Cambridge University Press.

Bresnan, J. (Ed.). (1982). *The mental representation of grammatical relations.* Cambridge, MA: MIT Press.

Brown, R. (1973). *A first language: The early stages.* Cambridge, MA: Harvard University Press.

Carey, S. (1978). The child as word learner. In M. Halle, G. Miller, & J. Bresnan (Eds.). *Linguistic theory and psychological reality* (pp. 264–293). Cambridge, MA: The MIT Press.

Chomsky, N. (1957). *Syntactic structures.* The Hague, the Netherlands: Mouton Publishers.

Chomsky, N. (1965). *Aspects of the theory of syntax.* Cambridge, MA: MIT Press.

Chomsky, N. (1981). *Lectures on government and binding.* Dordrecht, Holland: Foris.

Dublinske, S. (1981). Action: School services. *Language, Speech, and Hearing Services in Schools, 12,* 192–200.

Ferguson, C. (1989). Individual differences in language learning. In M. L. Rice & R. L. Schiefelbusch (Eds.), *Teachability of language.* Baltimore: Brookes.

Fey, M. E. (1986). *Language intervention with young children.* San Diego: College Hill.

Fillmore, C. J. (1968). The case for case. In E. Bach & R. T. Harms (Eds.), *Universals in linguistic theory* (pp. 1–90). New York: Holt, Rinehart, & Winston.

Fletcher, P., & Garman, M. (Eds.) (1986). *Language acquisition: Studies in first language development.* London: Cambridge University Press.

Goodluck, H. (1986). Language acquisition and linguistic theory. In P. Fletcher & M. Garman (Eds.), *Language acquisition: Studies in first language development* (pp. 49–68). London: Cambridge University Press.

Gopnik, A., & Meltzoff, A. N. (1987). Language and thought in the young child: Early semantic developments and their relationships to object permanence, means-ends understanding, and categorization. In K. Nelson & A. Van Kleeck (Eds.), *Children's language* (Vol. 6, pp. 191–212). Hillsdale, NJ Erlbaum.

Heath, S. B. (1989). The learner as cultural member. In M. L. Rice & R. L. Schiefelbusch (Eds.), *Teachability of language.* Baltimore: Brookes.

Hymes, D. (1972). On communicative competence. In J. B. Pride & J. Holmes (Eds.), *Sociolinguistics* (pp. 269–285). Harmondsworth, Middlesex, England: Penguin.

Ingram, D. (in press). *First language acquisition: Method, description, and explanation.* London: Cambridge University Press.

Johnston, J. R. (1988). Specific language disorders in children. In N. Lass, L. McReynolds, J. Northern, & D. Yoder (Eds.), *Handbook of speech-language pathology and audiology* (pp. 697–727). Philadelphia: B. C. Decker.

Lakoff, G. (1987). *Women, fire, and dangerous things: What categories reveal about the mind.* Chicago: University of Chicago Press.

Leonard, L. B. (1979). Language impairment in children. *Merrill-Palmer Quarterly, 25*(3), 205–232.

Leske, M. C. (1981). Speech prevalence estimates of communicative disorders in the U.S. *ASHA, 23,* 229–237.

MacWhinney, B., & Snow, C. (1985). The child language data exchange system. *Journal of Child Language, 12,* 271–296.

Nelson, K. (1973). Structure and strategy in learning to talk. *Monographs of the Society for Research in Child Development, 38*(1–2, Serial No. 149).

Nelson, K. E. (1989). Strategies for first language teaching. In M. L. Rice & R. L. Schiefelbusch (Eds.), *Teachability of language.* Baltimore: Brookes.

Nelson, K. E., Kamhi, A. G., & Apel, K. (1987). Cognitive strengths and weaknesses in language-impaired children: One more look. *Journal of Speech and Hearing Disorders, 52,* 36–43.

Newmeyer, F. J. (1986). *Linguistic theory in America.* New York: Academic Press.

Pinker, S. (1989). Resolving a learnability paradox in the acquisition of the verb lexicon. In M. L. Rice & R. L. Schiefelbusch (Eds.), *Teachability of language.* Baltimore: Brookes.

Pye, C. (1986). Quiché Mayan speech to children. *Journal of Child Language, 13,* 85–100.

Rice, M. L. (1987, July). *Preschool children's fast mapping of words: Robust for most, fragile for some.* Paper presented at the International Congress for the Study of Child Language, Lund, Sweden.

Rice, M. L., Buhr, J., & Nemeth, M. (1988). *Fast mapping abilities of language-delayed preschoolers.* Unpublished manuscript.

Rice, M. L., & Kemper, S. (1984). *Child language and cognition: Contemporary issues.* Baltimore: University Park Press.

Rice, M. L., & Schiefelbusch, R. L. (1988, June). *Principles of language teachability.* Paper presented at the National Institute of Child Health and Human Development Conference on Biobehavioral Foundations of Language Development, Washington, DC.

Rice, M. L., & Schiefelbusch, R. L. (Eds.). (1989). *Teachability of language.* Baltimore: Brookes.

Rice, M. L., & Woodsmall, L. (1988). Lessons from television: Children's word learning when viewing. *Child Development, 59,* 420–429.

Slobin, D. I. (1985). *The cross-linguistic study of language acquisition* (Vols. 1 & 2). Hillsdale, NJ: Erlbaum.

Snow, C. E. (1984). Parent-child interaction and the development of communicative ability. In R. L. Schiefelbusch & J. Pickar (Eds.), *Communicative competence: Acquisition and intervention* (pp. 69–108). Baltimore: University Park Press.

Templin, M. C. (1957). *Certain language skills in children.* Minneapolis: University of Minnesota Press.

Wanner, E., & Gleitman, L. R. (Eds.). (1982). *Language acquisition: The state of the art.* London: Cambridge University Press.

Wexler, K., & Culicover, P. W. (1980). *Formal principles of language acquisition.* Cambridge, MA: MIT Press.

# On Inner Speech

## Lev Semenovich Vygotsky

### EDITOR'S INTRODUCTION

The social context of language, and of thinking itself, is at the heart of Lev Vygotsky's influential work. Vygotsky, a Russian educator-turned-psychologist, explored ways children use language to interact with their world. In the following excerpt from *Thought and Language,* Vygotsky lays out his underlying theory that even our private thought and language are originally shaped through the ways we learn to interact with others. An internalization of private, or "inner," speech was a key concept in his work, one that differed sharply from the theories of his contemporary, Jean Piaget. Both men see strong links between developing language and cognitive abilities, but their theories and analyses of data couldn't be more different and remain a source of debate among child development experts.

We must probe still deeper and explore the plane of inner speech lying beyond the semantic plane. We shall discuss here some of the data of the special investigation we have made of it. The relationship of thought and word cannot be understood in all its complexity without a clear understanding of the psychological nature of inner speech. Yet, of all the problems connected with thought and language, this is perhaps the most complicated, beset as it is with terminological and other misunderstandings.

The term *inner speech,* or *endophasy,* has been applied to various phenomena, and authors argue about different things that they call by the same name. Originally, inner speech seems to have been understood as verbal memory. An example would be the silent recital of a poem known by heart. In that case, inner speech differs from vocal speech only as the idea or image of an object differs from the real object. It was in this sense that inner speech was understood by the French authors who tried to find out how words were reproduced in memory—whether as auditory, visual, motor, or synthetic images. We shall see that word memory is indeed one of the constituent elements of inner speech but not all of it.

In a second interpretation, inner speech is seen as truncated external speech—as "speech minus sound" (Mueller) or "subvocal speech" (Watson). Bekhterev defined it as a speech reflex inhibited in its motor part. Such an explanation is by no means sufficient. Silent

*Source: Thought and Language* (pp. 130–138) by L. S. Vygotsky (translated and edited by E. Hanfman and G. Vakar), 1962, Cambridge, MA: M.I.T. Press. Copyright 1962 by Massachusetts Institute of Technology. Reprinted by permission of publisher.

"pronouncing" of words is not equivalent to the total process of inner speech.

The third definition is, on the contrary, too broad. To Goldstein (1927, 1932) the term covers everything that precedes the motor act of speaking, including Wundt's "motives of speech" and the indefinable, nonsensory, and nonmotor specific speech experience—i.e., the whole interior aspect of any speech activity. It is hard to accept the equation of inner speech with an inarticulate inner experience in which the separate identifiable structural planes are dissolved without trace. This central experience is common to all linguistic activity, and for this reason alone Goldstein's interpretation does not fit that specific, unique function that alone deserves the name of inner speech. Logically developed, Goldstein's view must lead to the thesis that inner speech is not speech at all but rather an intellectual and affective-volitional activity, since it includes the motives of speech and the thought that is expressed in words.

To get a true picture of inner speech, one must start from the assumption that it is a specific formation, with its own laws and complex relations to the other forms of speech activity. Before we can study its relation to thought, on the one hand, and to speech, on the other, we must determine its special characteristics and function.

Inner speech is speech for oneself; external speech is for others. It would indeed be surprising if such a basic difference in function did not affect the structure of the two kinds of speech. Absence of vocalization per se is only a consequence of the specific nature of inner speech, which is neither an antecedent of external speech nor its reproduction in memory but is, in a sense, the opposite of external speech. The latter is the turning of thought into words, is materialization and objectification. With inner speech, the process is reversed: Speech turns into inward thought. Consequently, their structures must differ.

The area of inner speech is one of the most difficult to investigate. It remained almost inaccessible to experiments until ways were found to apply the genetic method of experimentation. Piaget (1926) was the first to pay attention to the child's egocentric speech and to see its theoretical significance, but he remained blind to the most important trait of egocentric speech—its genetic connection with inner speech—and this warped his interpretation of its function and structure. We made that relationship the central problem of our study and thus were able to investigate the nature of inner speech with unusual completeness. A number of considerations and observations led us to conclude that egocentric speech is a stage of development preceding inner speech: Both fulfill intellectual functions, their structures are similar; egocentric speech disappears at school age, when inner speech begins to develop. From all this we infer that one changes into the other.

If this transformation does take place, then egocentric speech provides the key to the study of inner speech. One advantage of approaching inner speech through egocentric speech is its accessibility to experimentation and observation. It is still vocalized, audible speech, i.e., external in its mode of expression, but at the same time inner speech in function and structure. To study an internal process it is necessary to externalize it experimentally, by connecting it with some outer activity; only then is objective functional analysis possible. Egocentric speech is, in fact, a natural experiment of this type.

This method has another great advantage: Since egocentric speech can be studied at the time when some of its characteristics are waning and new ones forming, we are able to judge which traits are essential to inner speech and which are only temporary, and thus to determine the goal of this movement from egocentric to inner speech—i.e., the nature of inner speech.

Before we go on to the results obtained by this method, we shall briefly discuss the nature of egocentric speech, stressing the differences between our theory and Piaget's. Piaget contends that the child's egocentric speech is a direct expression of the egocentrism of his thought, which in turn is a compromise between the primary autism of his thinking and its gradual socialization. As the child grows older, autism recedes and socialization progresses, leading to the waning of egocentrism in his thinking and speech.

In Piaget's conception, the child in his egocentric speech does not adapt himself to the thinking of adults. His thought remains entirely egocentric; this makes his talk incomprehensible to others. Egocentric speech has no function in the child's realistic thinking or activity—it merely accompanies them. And since it is an expression of egocentric thought, it disappears together with the child's egocentrism. From its climax at the beginning of the child's development, egocentric speech drops to zero on the threshold of school age. Its history is one of involution rather than evolution. It has no future.

In our conception, egocentric speech is a phenomenon of the transition from interpsychic to intrapsychic functioning, i.e., from the social, collective activity of the child to his more individualized activity—a pattern of development common to all the higher psychological functions. Speech for oneself originates through differentiation from speech for others. Since the main course of the child's development is one of gradual individualization, this tendency is reflected in the function and structure of his speech.

Our experimental results indicate that the function of egocentric speech is similar to that of inner speech: It does not merely accompany the child's activity, it serves mental orientation, conscious understanding, it helps in overcoming difficulties; it is speech for oneself, intimately and usefully connected with the child's thinking. Its fate is very different from that described by Piaget. Egocentric speech develops along a rising, not a declining, curve; it goes through an evolution, not an involution. In the end, it becomes inner speech.

Our hypothesis has several advantages over Piaget's: It explains the function and development of egocentric speech and, in particular, its sudden increase when the child faces difficulties which demand consciousness and reflection—a fact uncovered by our experiments and which Piaget's theory cannot explain. But the greatest advantage of our theory is that it supplies a satisfying answer to a paradoxical situation described by Piaget himself. To Piaget, the quantitative drop in egocentric speech as the child grows older means the withering of that form of speech. If that were so, its structural peculiarities might also be expected to decline; it is hard to believe that the process would affect only its quantity, and not its inner structure. The child's thought becomes infinitely less egocentric between the ages of 3 and 7. If the characteristics of egocentric speech that make it incomprehensible to others are indeed rooted in egocentrism, they should become less apparent as that form of speech becomes less frequent; egocentric speech should approach social speech and become more and more intelligible. Yet what are the facts? Is the talk of a 3 year old harder to follow than that of a 7 year old? Our investigation established that the traits of egocentric speech which make for inscrutability are at their lowest point at 3 and at their peak at 7. They develop in a reverse direction to the frequency of egocentric speech. While the latter keeps falling and reaches zero at school age, the structural characteristics become more and more pronounced.

This throws a new light on the quantitative decrease in egocentric speech, which is the cornerstone of Piaget's thesis.

What does this decrease mean? The structural peculiarities of speech for oneself and its differentiation from external speech increase with age. What is it then that diminishes? Only one of its aspects: vocalization. Does this mean that egocentric speech as a whole is dying out? We believe that it does not, for how then could we explain the growth of the functional and structural traits of egocentric speech? On the other hand, their growth is perfectly compatible with the decrease of vocalization—indeed, clarifies its meaning. Its rapid dwindling and the equally rapid

growth of the other characteristics are contradictory in appearance only.

To explain this, let us start from an undeniable, experimentally established fact. The structural and functional qualities of egocentric speech become more marked as the child develops. At 3, the difference between egocentric and social speech equals zero; at 7, we have speech that in structure and function is totally unlike social speech. A differentiation of the two speech functions has taken place. This is a fact—and facts are notoriously hard to refute.

Once we accept this, everything else falls into place. If the developing structural and functional peculiarities of egocentric speech progressively isolate it from external speech, then its vocal aspect must fade away; and this is exactly what happens between 3 and 7 years. With the progressive isolation of speech for oneself, its vocalization becomes unnecessary and meaningless and, because of its growing structural peculiarities, also impossible. Speech for oneself cannot find expression in external speech. The more independent and autonomous egocentric speech becomes, the poorer it grows in its external manifestations. In the end it separates itself entirely from speech for others, ceases to be vocalized, and thus appears to die out.

But this is only an illusion. To interpret the sinking coefficient of egocentric speech as a sign that this kind of speech is dying out is like saying that the child stops counting when he ceases to use his fingers and starts adding in his head. In reality behind the symptoms of dissolution lies a progressive development, the birth of a new speech form.

The decreasing vocalization of egocentric speech denotes a developing abstraction from sound, the child's new faculty to "think words" instead of pronouncing them. This is the positive meaning of the sinking coefficient of egocentric speech. The downward curve indicates development toward inner speech.

We can see that all the known facts about the functional, structural, and genetic characteristics of egocentric speech point to one thing: It develops in the direction of inner speech. Its developmental history can be understood only as a gradual unfolding of the traits of inner speech.

We believe that this corroborates our hypothesis about the origin and nature of egocentric speech. To turn our hypothesis into a certainty, we must devise an experiment capable of showing which of the two interpretations is correct. What are the data for this critical experiment?

Let us restate the theories between which we must decide. Piaget believes that egocentric speech stems from the insufficient socialization of speech and that its only development is decrease and eventual death. Its culmination lies in the past. Inner speech is something new brought in from the outside along with socialization. We believe that egocentric speech stems from the insufficient individualization of primary social speech. Its culmination lies in the future. It develops into inner speech.

To obtain evidence for one or the other view, we must place the child alternately in experimental situations encouraging social speech and in situations discouraging it, and see how these changes affect egocentric speech. We consider this an *experimentum crucis* for the following reasons.

If the child's egocentric talk results from the egocentrism of his thinking and its insufficient socialization, then any weakening of the social elements in the experimental setup, any factor contributing to the child's isolation from the group, must lead to a sudden increase in egocentric speech. But if the latter results from an insufficient differentiation of speech for oneself from speech for others, then the same changes must cause it to decrease.

We took as the starting point of our experiment three of Piaget's own observations. (1) Egocentric speech occurs only in the presence of other children engaged in the same activity, and not when the child is alone, i.e., it is a collective monologue. (2) The child is under the illusion that his egocentric talk, directed to nobody, is understood by those who surround him. (3) Egocentric speech has the character of external speech: It is not inaudible or whispered. These are certainly not chance peculiarities. From the child's own point of view, egocentric speech is not yet separated from social speech. It occurs under the subjective and objective conditions of social speech and may be considered a correlate of the insufficient isolation of the child's individual consciousness from the social whole.

In our first series of experiments (Vygotsky, Luria, Leontiev and Levina, unpublished; Vygotsky and Luria, 1930), we tried to destroy the illusion of being understood. After measuring the child's coefficient of egocentric speech in a situation similar to that of Piaget's experiments, we put him into a new situation: either with deaf-mute children or with children speaking a foreign language. In all other respects the setup remained the same. The coefficient of egocentric speech dropped to zero in the majority of cases, and in the rest to one-eighth of the previous figure, on the average. This proves that the illusion of being understood is not a mere epiphenomenon of egocentric speech but is functionally connected with it. Our results must seem paradoxical from the point of view of Piaget's theory: The weaker the child's contact is with the group—the less the social situation forces him to adjust his thoughts to others and to use social speech—the more freely should the egocentrism of his thinking and speech manifest itself. But from the point of

view of our hypothesis, the meaning of these findings is clear: Egocentric speech, springing from the lack of differentiation of speech for oneself from speech for others, disappears when the feeling of being understood, essential for social speech, is absent.

In the second series of experiments, the variable factor was the possibility of collective monologue. Having measured the child's coefficient of egocentric speech in a situation permitting collective monologue, we put him into a situation excluding it—in a group of children who were strangers to him, or by himself at a separate table in a corner of the room; or he worked quite alone, even the experimenter leaving the room. The results of this series agreed with the first results. The exclusion of the group monologue caused a drop in the coefficient of egocentric speech, though not such a striking one as in the first case—seldom to zero and, on the average, to one-sixth of the original figure. The different methods of precluding collective monologue were not equally effective in reducing the coefficient of egocentric speech. The trend, however, was obvious in all the variations of the experiment. The exclusion of the collective factor, instead of giving full freedom to egocentric speech, depressed it. Our hypothesis was once more confirmed.

In the third series of experiments, the variable factor was the vocal quality of egocentric speech. Just outside the laboratory where the experiment was in progress, an orchestra played so loudly, or so much noise was made, that it drowned out not only the voices of others but the child's own; in a variant of the experiment, the child was expressly forbidden to talk loudly and allowed to talk only in whispers. Once again the coefficient of egocentric speech went down, the relation to the original figure being 5 : 1. Again the different methods were not equally effective, but the basic trend was invariably present.

The purpose of all three series of experiments was to eliminate those characteristics of egocentric speech that bring it close to social speech. We found that this always led to the dwindling of egocentric speech. It is logical, then, to assume that egocentric speech is a form developing out of social speech and not yet separated from it in its manifestation, although already distinct in function and structure.

The disagreement between us and Piaget on this point will be made quite clear by the following example: I am sitting at my desk talking to a person who is behind me and whom I cannot see; he leaves the room without my noticing it, and I continue to talk, under the illusion that he listens and understands. Outwardly, I am talking with myself and for myself, but psychologically my speech is social. From the point of view of Piaget's theory, the opposite happens in the case of the child: His egocentric talk is for and with himself; it only has the appearance of social speech, just as my speech gave the false impression of being egocentric. From our point of view, the whole situation is much more complicated than that: Subjectively, the child's egocentric speech already has its own peculiar function—to that extent, it is independent from social speech; yet its independence is not complete because it is not felt as inner speech and is not distinguished by the child from speech for others. Objectively, also, it is different from social speech but again not entirely, because it functions only within social situations. Both subjectively and objectively, egocentric speech represents a transition from speech for others to speech for oneself. It already has the function of inner speech but remains similar to social speech in its expression.

The investigation of egocentric speech has paved the way to the understanding of inner speech.

## REFERENCES

Bekhterev, V. *General Principles of Human Reflexology.* New York: International Publishers, 1932.

Goldstein, K. "Ueber Aphasie." Abh.aus.d.Schs. Arch.F. Neurol. U. Psychiat. Heft 6, 1927.

Goldstein, K. "Die Pathologischen Tatsachen in ihrer Bedeutung fuer das Problem der Sprache." Kongr. D. Ges. Psychology, 12, 1932.

Piaget, J. *La Representation de Monde Chez L'Enfant.* Paris, F. Alcan, 1926.

Watson, J. *Psychology from the Standpoint of a Behaviorist,* Philadelphia and London, G. B. Lippincott, 1919.

# The Language and
# Thought of the Child

## Jean Piaget

### EDITOR'S INTRODUCTION

The Swiss psychologist Jean Piaget is considered one of the giants of twentieth century child development research and theory. His work in the area of child-language research emphasizes the egocentrism of children's speech, a factor that is disputed by other researchers, even as early as Vygotsky in the 1930s. Despite these many critiques, his influence in the field of language acquisition and the development of cognitive processes has been enormous.

We have chosen a brief excerpt from his controversial study focusing on egocentrism in child language and thought. It was originally published in French in 1923.

## CONCLUSIONS

Having defined, so far as was possible, the various categories of the language used by our two children, it now remains for us to see whether it is not possible to establish certain numerical constants from the material before us. We wish to emphasize at the very outset the artificial character of such abstractions. The number of unclassifiable remarks, indeed, weighs heavily in the statistics. In any case, a perusal of the list of Lev's first 50 remarks, which we shall give as an example for those who wish to make use of our method, should give a fair idea of the degree of objectivity belonging to our classification. But these difficulties are immaterial. If among our results some are definitely more constant than others, then we shall feel justified in attributing to these a certain objective value.

## The Measure of Egocentrism

Among the data we have obtained there is one, incidentally of the greatest interest for the study of child logic, which seems to supply the necessary guarantee of objectivity: we mean the proportion of egocentric language to the sum of the child's spontaneous conversation. Egocentric language is, as we have seen, the group made up by the first three of the categories we have enumerated—*repetition, monologue,* and *collective monologue.* All three have this in common: that they consist of remarks that are not addressed to anyone, or not to anyone in particular, and that they evoke no reaction

*Source: The Language and Thought of the Child* (3rd ed., pp. 34–40) by J. Piaget, 1959, London: Routledge & Kegan Paul Ltd. Copyright 1959 by Routledge & Kegan. Reprinted by permission of publisher.

adapted to them on the part of anyone to whom they may chance to be addressed. Spontaneous language is therefore made up of the first seven categories, *i.e.,* of all except *answers.* It is therefore the sum total of all remarks, *minus* those which are made as an answer to a question asked by an adult or a child. We have eliminated this heading as being subject to chance circumstances; it is sufficient for a child to have come in contact with many adults or with some talkative companion, to undergo a marked change in the percentage of his answers. Answers given, not to definite questions (with interrogation mark) or commands, but in the course of the dialogue, *i.e.,* propositions answering to other propositions, have naturally been classed under the heading *information and dialogue,* so that there is nothing artificial about the omission of questions from the statistics which we shall give. The child's language *minus* his answers constitutes a complete whole in which intelligence is represented at every stage of its development.

The proportion of egocentric to other spontaneous forms of language is represented by the following fractions:

$$\frac{Eg.\ L}{Sp.L} = 0.47 \text{ for Lev}, \quad \frac{Eg.L}{Sp.L} = 0.43 \text{ for Pie.}$$

(The proportion of egocentric language to the sum total of the subject's speech, including answers, is 39 percent for Lev and 37 percent for Pie.) The similarity of result for Lev and Pie is a propitious sign, especially as what difference there is corresponds to a marked difference of temperament. (Lev is certainly more egocentric than Pie.) But the value of the result is vouched for in yet another way.

If we divide the 1400 remarks made by Lev during the month in which his talk was being studied into sections of 100 sentences, and seek to establish for each section the ratio

$$\frac{Eg.L.}{Sp.L.}$$

the fraction will be found to vary only from 0.40 to 0.57, which indicates only a small maximum deviation. On the contrary, the *mean variation, i.e.,* the average of the deviations between each value and the arithmetical average of these values, is only 0.04, which is really very little.

If Pie's 1500 remarks are submitted to the same treatment, the proportions will be found to vary between 0.31 and 0.59, with an average variation of 0.06. This greater variability is just what we should expect from what we know of Pie's character, which at first sight seems more practical, better adapted than Lev's, more inclined to col-

laboration (particularly with his bosom friend Ez). But Pie every now and then indulges in fantasies which isolate him for several hours, and during which he soliloquizes without ceasing.

. . . Moreover . . . these two coefficients do actually represent the average for children between the ages of 7 and 8. The same calculation based on some 1500 remarks in quite another classroom yielded the result of 0.45 (a. v. = 0.05).

This constancy in the proportion of egocentric language is the more remarkable in view of the fact that we have found nothing of the kind in connection with the other coefficients which we have sought to establish. We have, it is true, determined the proportion of socialized factual language *(information* and *questions)* to socialized nonfactual language *(criticism, commands,* and *requests).* But this proportion fluctuates from 0.72 to 2.23 with a mean variation 0.71 for Lev (as compared with 0.04 and 0.06 as the coefficients of egocentrism), and between 0.43 and 2.33 with a mean variation of 0.42 for Pie. Similarly, the relation of egocentric to socialized factual language yields no coefficient of any constancy.

Of all this calculation let us bear only this in mind, that our two subjects of 6½ have each an egocentric language which amounts to nearly half of their total spontaneous speech.

The following table summarizes the functions of the language used by both these children:

| | | Pie | Lev |
|---|---|---|---|
| **1.** | Repetition | 2 | 1 |
| **2.** | Monologue | 5 | 15 |
| **3.** | Collective Monologue | 30 | 23 |
| **4.** | Adapted Information | 14 | 13 |
| **5.** | Criticism | 7 | 3 |
| **6.** | Commands | 15 | 10 |
| **7.** | Requests | 13 | 17 |
| **8.** | Answers | 14 | 18 |
| | Egocentric Language | 37 | 39 |
| | Spontaneous Socialized Language | 49 | 43 |
| | Sum of Socialized Language | 63 | 61 |
| | Coefficient of Egocentrism | 0.43 | 0.47 |
| | | ∓ 0.06 | ∓0.04 |

We must once more emphasize the fact that in all these calculations the number of remarks made by children to adults is negligible. By omitting them we raise the coefficient of egocentrism to about 0.02, which is within the allowed limits of deviation. In the future, however, we shall have completely to eliminate such remarks from our calculations, even if it means making a separate class for them. We shall, moreover, observe this rule in the next chapter where the coefficient of egocentrism has been calculated solely on the basis of remarks made between children.

## Conclusion

What are the conclusions we can draw from these facts? It would seem that up to a certain age we may safely admit that children think and act more egocentrically than adults, that they share each other's intellectual life less than we do. True, when they are together they seem to talk to each other a great deal more than we do about what they are doing, but for the most part they are only talking to themselves. We, on the contrary, keep silent far longer about our action, but our talk is almost always socialized.

Such assertions may seem paradoxical. In observing children between the ages of 4 and 7 at work together in the classes of the *Maison des Petits,* one is certainly struck by silences, which are, we repeat, in no way imposed nor even suggested by the adults. One would expect, not indeed the formation of working groups, since children are slow to awake to social life, but a hubbub caused by all the children talking at once. This is not what happens. All the same, it is obvious that a child between the ages of 4 and 7, placed in the conditions of spontaneous work provided by the educational games of the *Maison des Petits,* breaks silence far oftener than does the adult at work, and seems at first sight to be continuously communicating his thoughts to those around him.

Egocentrism must not be confused with secrecy. Reflection in the child does not admit of privacy. Apart from thinking by images or autistic symbols which cannot be directly communicated, the child up to an age, as yet undetermined but probably somewhere about seven, is incapable of keeping to himself the thoughts which enter his mind. He says everything. He has no verbal continence. Does this mean that he socializes his thought more than we do? That is the whole question, and it is for us to see to whom the child really speaks. It may be to others. We think on the contrary that, as the preceding study shows, it is first and foremost to himself, and that speech, before it can be used to socialize thought, serves to accompany and reinforce individual activity. Let us try to examine more closely the difference between thought which is socialized but capable of secrecy, and infantile thought which is egocentric but incapable of secrecy.

The adult, even in his most personal and private occupation, even when he is engaged in any inquiry which is incomprehensible to his fellow beings, thinks socially, has continually in his mind's eye his collaborators or opponents, actual or eventual, at any rate members of his own profession to whom sooner or later he will announce the result of his labors. This mental picture pursues him throughout his task. The task itself is henceforth socialized at almost every stage of its development. Invention eludes this process, but the need for checking and demonstrating calls into being an inner speech addressed throughout to a hypothetical opponent, whom the imagination often pictures as one of flesh and blood. When, therefore, the adult is brought face to face with his fellow beings, what he announces to them is something already socially elaborated and therefore roughly adapted to his audience, *i.e.,* it is comprehensible. Indeed, the further a man has advanced in his own line of thought, the better able is he to see things from the point of view of others and to make himself understood by them.

The child, on the other hand, placed in the conditions which we have described, seems to talk far more than the adult. Almost everything he does is to the tune of remarks such as "I'm drawing a hat," "I'm doing it better than you," etc. Child thought, therefore, seems more social, less capable of sustained and solitary research. This is so only in appearance. The child has less verbal continence simply because he does not know what it is to keep a thing to himself. Although he talks almost incessantly to his neighbors, he rarely places himself at their point of view. He speaks to them for the most part as if he were alone, and as if he were thinking aloud. He speaks, therefore, in a language which disregards the precise shade of meaning in things and ignores the particular angle from which they are viewed, and which above all is always making assertions, even in argument, instead of justifying them. Nothing could be harder to understand than the notebooks which we have filled with the conversation of Pie and Lev. Without full commentaries, taken down at the same time as the children's remarks, they would be incomprehensible. Everything is indicated by allusion, by pronouns and demonstrative articles—"he, she, the, mine, him, etc."—which can mean anything in turn, regardless of the demands of clarity or even of intelligibility. In a word, the child hardly ever even asks himself whether he has been understood. For him, that goes without saying, for he does not think about others when he talks. He utters a "collective monologue." His language only begins to resemble that of adults when he is directly interested in making himself understood; when he gives orders or asks questions. To put it quite simply, we may say that the adult thinks socially, even when he is alone, and that the child under 7 thinks egocentrically, even in the society of others.

# Language and the Mind

## Noam Chomsky

### EDITOR'S INTRODUCTION

This article by Noam Chomsky represents some of the most accessible explanations of his complex theories, theories that have revolutionized the study of language development over the past 40 years. Chomsky disputed Piaget's base of empirical/biological evidence, instead working from highly technical structural models of language development. This essay highlights many of Chomsky's key contributions to the field, including his refutation of B. F. Skinner's behaviorist theories, the concept of "surface" and "deep" structures in language, and the definition of transformational grammar.

How does the mind work? To answer this question we must look at some of the work performed by the mind. One of its main functions is the acquisition of knowledge. The two major factors in acquisition of knowledge, perception and learning, have been the subject of study and speculation for centuries. It would not, I think, be misleading to characterize the major positions that have developed as outgrowths of classical rationalism and empiricism. The rationalist theories are marked by the importance they assign to *intrinsic* structures in mental operations—to central processes and organizing principles in perception, and to innate ideas and principles in learning. The empiricist approach, in contrast, has stressed the role of experience and control by environmental factors.

The classical empiricist view is that sensory images are transmitted to the brain as impressions. They remain as ideas that will be associated in various ways, depending on the fortuitous character of experience. In this view a language is merely a collection of words, phrases, and sentences, a habit system, acquired accidentally and extrinsically. In the

formulation of Williard Quine, knowledge of a language (and, in fact, knowledge in general) can be represented as "a fabric of sentences variously associated to one another and to nonverbal stimuli by the mechanism of conditioned response." Acquisition of knowledge is only a matter of the gradual construction of this fabric. When sensory experience is interpreted, the already established network may be activated in some fashion. In its essentials, this view has been predominant in modern behavioral science, and it has been accepted with little question by many philosophers as well.

The classical rationalist view is quite different. In this view the mind contains a system of "common notions" that enable it to interpret the scattered and incoherent data of sense in terms of objects and their relations, cause and effect, whole and part, symmetry, gestalt properties, functions, and so on. Sensation, providing only fleeting and

*Source:* "Language and the Mind" by N. Chomsky, 1968, *Psychology Today,* *I*(9), pp. 48–51, 66–68. Copyright 1968 by *Psychology Today.* Reprinted by permission of publisher.

meaningless images, is degenerate and particular. Knowledge, much of it beyond immediate awareness, is rich in structure, involves universals, and is highly organized. The innate general principles that underlie and organize this knowledge, according to Leibniz, "enter into our thoughts, of which they form the soul and the connection . . . although we do not at all think of them."

This "active" rationalist view of the acquisition of knowledge persisted through the romantic period in its essentials. With respect to language, it achieves its most illuminating expression in the profound investigations of Wilhelm von Humboldt. His theory of speech perception supposes a generative system of rules that underlies speech production as well as its interpretation. The system is generative in that it makes infinite use of finite means. He regards a language as a structure of forms and concepts based on a system of rules that determine their interrelations, arrangement, and organization. But these finite materials can be combined to make a never-ending product.

In the rationalist and romantic tradition of linguistic theory, the normal use of language is regarded as characteristically innovative. We construct sentences that are entirely new to us. There is no substantive notion of "analogy" or "generalization" that accounts for this creative aspect of language use. It is equally erroneous to describe language as a "habit structure" or as a network of associated responses. The innovative element in normal use of language quickly exceeds the bounds of such marginal principles as analogy or generalization (under any substantive interpretation of these notions). It is important to emphasize this fact because the insight has been lost under the impact of the behaviorist assumptions that have dominated speculation and research in the twentieth century.

In Humboldt's view, acquisition of language is largely a matter of maturation of an innate language capacity. The maturation is guided by internal factors, by an innate "form of language" that is sharpened, differentiated, and given its specific realization through experience. Language is thus a kind of latent structure in the human mind, developed and fixed by exposure to specific linguistic experience. Humboldt believes that all languages will be found to be very similar in their grammatical form, similar not on the surface but in their deeper inner structures. The innate organizing principles severely limit the class of possible languages, and these principles determine the properties of the language that is learned in the normal way.

The active and passive views of perception and learning have been elaborated with varying degrees of clarity since the seventeenth century. These views can be confronted with empirical evidence in a variety of ways. Some recent work in psychology and neurophysiology is highly suggestive in this regard. There is evidence for the existence of central processes in perception, specifically for control over the functioning of sensory neurons by the brain-stem reticular system. Behavioral counterparts of this central control have been under investigation for several years. Furthermore, there is evidence for innate organization of the perceptual system of a highly specific sort at every level of biological organization. Studies of the visual system of the frog, the discovery of specialized cells responding to angle and motion in the lower cortical centers of cats and rabbits, and the somewhat comparable investigations of the auditory system of frogs—all are relevant to the classical questions of intrinsic structure mentioned earlier. These studies suggest that there are highly organized, innately determined perceptual systems that are adapted closely to the animal's "life space" and that provide the basis for what we might call "acquisition of knowledge." Also relevant are certain behavioral studies of human infants, for example, those showing the preference for faces over other complex stimuli.

These and other studies make it reasonable to inquire into the possibility that complex intellectual structures are determined narrowly by innate mental organization. What is perceived may be determined by mental processes of considerable depth. As far as language learning is concerned, it seems to me that a rather convincing argument can be made for the view that certain principles intrinsic to the mind provide invariant structures that are a precondition for linguistic experience. In the course of this article I would like to sketch some of the ways such conclusions might be clarified and firmly established.

There are several ways linguistic evidence can be used to reveal properties of human perception and learning. In this section we consider one research strategy that might take us nearer to this goal.

Let us say that in interpreting a certain physical stimulus a person constructs a "percept." This percept represents some of his conclusions (in general, unconscious) about the stimulus. To the extent that we can characterize such percepts, we can go on to investigate the mechanisms that relate stimulus and percept. Imagine a model of perception that takes stimuli as inputs and arrives at percepts as "outputs." The model might contain a system of beliefs, strategies for interpreting stimuli, and other factors, such as the organization of memory. We would then have a perceptual model that might be represented graphically, as in Figure 1.

Consider next the system of beliefs that is a component of the perceptual model. How was this acquired? To study this problem, we must investigate a second model, which takes certain data as input and gives as "output" (again, internally represented) the system of beliefs operating in the perceptual model. This second model, a model of learning, would have its own intrinsic structure, as did the first. This structure might consist of conditions on the nature of the system of beliefs that can be acquired, of innate inductive strategies, and again, of other factors such as the organization of memory (see Figure 2).

Under further conditions, which are interesting but not relevant here, we can take these perceptual and learning models as theories of the acquisition of knowledge, rather than of belief. How then would the models apply to language? The input stimulus to the perceptual model is a speech signal, and the percept is a representation of the utterance that the hearer takes the signal to be and of the interpretation he assigns to it. We can think of the percept as the structural description of a linguistic expression which contains certain phonetic, semantic, and syntactic information. Most interesting is the syntactic information, which best can be discussed by examining a few typical cases.

The following three sentences seem to be the same syntactic structure.

1. I told John to leave
2. I expected John to leave
3. I persuaded John to leave

Each contains the subject *I*, and the predicate of each consists of a verb (*told, expected, persuaded*), a noun phrase (*John*), and an embedded predicate phrase (*to leave*). This similarity is only superficial, however—a similarity in what we may call the "surface structure" of the sentences, which differ in important ways when we consider them with somewhat greater care.

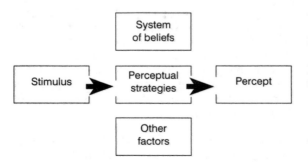

**Figure 1**
Each physical stimulus, after interpretation by the mental processes, will result in a percept.

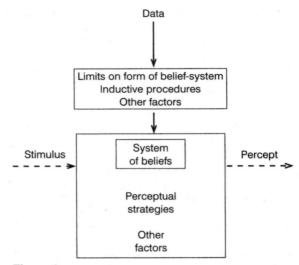

**Figure 2**
One's system of beliefs, a part of the perception model, is acquired from data as shown above.

The differences can be seen when the sentences are paraphrased or subjected to certain grammatical operations, such as the conversion from active to passive forms. For example, in normal conversation the sentence "I told John to leave" can be roughly paraphrased as:

**1a.** What I told John was to leave

But the other two sentences cannot be paraphrased as:

**2a.** *What I expected John was to leave
**3a.** *What I persuaded John was to leave

Sentence (2) can be paraphrased as:

**2b.** It was expected by me that John would leave

But the other two sentences cannot undergo a corresponding formal operation, yielding:

**1b.** *It was told by me that John would leave

or

**3b.** *It was persuaded by me that John would leave

Sentences (2) and (3) differ more subtly. In (3) *John* is the direct object of *persuade*, but in (2) *John* is not the direct object to *expect*. We can show this by using these verbs in slightly more complex sentences:

**4.**   I expected the doctor to examine John

**5.**   I persuaded the doctor to examine John

If we replace the embedded proposition *the doctor to examine John* with its passive form *John to be examined by the doctor,* the change to the passive does not, in itself, change the meaning. We can accept as paraphrases "I expected the doctor to examine John" and

**4.**   I expected John to be examined by the doctor

But we cannot accept as paraphrases "I persuaded the doctor to examine John" and

**5a.**   I persuaded John to be examined by the doctor

The parts of these sentences differ in their grammatical functions. In "I persuaded John to leave" *John* is both the object of *persuade* and the subject of *leave*. These facts must be represented in the percept since they are known, intuitively, to the hearer of the speech signal. No special training or instruction is necessary to enable the native speaker to understand these examples, to know which are "wrong" and which "right," although they may all be quite new to him. They are interpreted by the native speaker instantaneously and uniformly, in accordance with structural principles that are known tacitly, intuitively, and unconsciously.

These examples illustrate two significant points. First, the surface structure of a sentence, its organization into various phrases, may not reveal or immediately reflect its deep syntactic structure. The deep structure is not represented directly in the form of the speech signal; it is abstract. Second, the rules that determine deep and surface structure and their interrelation in particular cases must themselves be highly abstract. They are surely remote from consciousness, and in all likelihood they cannot be brought to consciousness.

A study of such examples, examples characteristic of all human languages that have been carefully studied, constitutes the first stage of the linguistic investigation outlined above, namely the study of the percept. The percept contains phonetic and semantic information related through the medium of syntactic structure. There are two aspects of this syntactic structure. It consists of a surface directly related to the phonetic form, and a deep structure that underlies the semantic interpretation. The deep structure is represented in the mind and rarely is indicated directly in the physical signal.

A language, then, involves a set of semantic-phonetic percepts, of sound-meaning correlations, the correlations being determined by the kind of intervening syntactic structure just illustrated. The English language correlates sound and meaning in one way, Japanese in another, and so on. But the general properties of percepts, their forms and mechanisms, are remarkably similar for all languages that have been carefully studied.

Returning to our models of perception and learning, we can now take up the problem of formulating the system of beliefs that is a central component in perceptual processes. In the case of language, the "system of beliefs" would now be called the "generative grammar," the system of rules that specifies the sound-meaning correlation and generates the class of structural descriptions (percepts) that constitute the language in question. The generative grammar, then, represents the speaker-hearer's knowledge of his language. We can use the term *grammar of a language* ambiguously, as referring not only to the speaker's internalized, subconscious knowledge but to the professional linguist's representation of this internalized and intuitive system of rules as well.

How is this generative grammar acquired? Or, using our learning model, what is the internal structure of the device that could develop a generative grammar?

We can think of every normal human's internalized grammar as, in effect, a theory of his language. This theory provides a sound-meaning correlation for an infinite number of sentences. It provides an infinite set of structural descriptions; each contains a surface structure that determines phonetic form and a deep structure that determines semantic content.

In formal terms, then, we can describe the child's acquisition of language as a kind of theory construction. The child discovers the theory of his language with only small amounts of data from that language. Not only does his "theory of the language" have an enormous predictive scope, but it also enables the child to reject a great deal of the very data on which the theory has been constructed. Normal speech consists, in large part, of fragments, false starts, blends, and other distortions of the underlying idealized forms. Nevertheless, as is evident from a study of the mature use of language, what the child learns is the underlying ideal theory. This is a remarkable fact. We must also bear in mind that the child constructs this ideal theory without explicit instruction, that he acquires this knowledge at a time when he is not capable of complex intellectual achievements in many other domains, and that this achievement is relatively independent of intelligence or the particular course of experience. These are facts that a theory of learning must face.

A scientist who approaches phenomena of this sort without prejudice or dogma would conclude that the acquired knowledge must be determined in a rather specific way by intrinsic properties of mental organization. He would then set himself the task of discovering the innate ideas and principles that make such acquisition of knowledge possible.

It is unimaginable that a highly specific, abstract, and tightly organized language comes by accident into the mind of every four-year-old child. If there were not an innate restriction on the form of grammar, then the child could employ innumerable theories to account for his linguistic experience, and no one system, or even small class of systems, would be found exclusively acceptable or even preferable. The child could not possibly acquire knowledge of a language. This restriction on the form of grammar is a precondition for linguistic experience, and it is surely the critical factor in determining the course and result of language learning. The child cannot know at birth which language he is going to learn. But he must "know" that its grammar must be of a predetermined form that excludes many imaginable languages.

The child's task is to select the appropriate hypothesis from this restricted class. Having selected it, he can confirm his choice with the evidence further available to him. But neither the evidence nor any process of induction (in any well-defined sense) could in themselves have led to this choice. Once the hypothesis is sufficiently well-confirmed, the child knows the language defined by this hypothesis; consequently, his knowledge extends vastly beyond his linguistic experience, and he can reject much of this experience as imperfect, as resulting from the interaction of many factors, only one of which is the ideal grammar that determines a sound-meaning connection for an infinite class of linguistic expressions. Along such lines as these one might outline a theory to explain the acquisition of language.

As has been pointed out, both the form and meaning of a sentence are determined by syntactic structures that are not represented directly in the signal and that are related to the signal only at a distance, through a long sequence of interpretive rules. This property of abstractness in grammatical structure is of primary importance, and it is on this property that our inferences about mental processes are based. Let us examine this abstractness a little more closely.

Not many years ago, the process of sentence interpretation might have been described approximately along the following lines. A speech signal is received and segmented into successive units (overlapping at the borders). These units are analyzed in terms of their invariant phonetic properties and assigned to "phonemes." The sequence of phonemes, so constructed, is then segmented into minimal grammatically functioning units (morphemes and words). These are again categorized. Successive operations of segmentation and classification will lead to what I have called "surface structure"—an analysis of a sentence into phrases, which can be represented as a proper bracketing of the sentence, with the bracketed units assigned to various categories, as in Figure 3. Each segment—phonetic, syntactic, or semantic—would be identified in terms of certain invariant properties. This would be an exhaustive analysis of the structure of a sentence.

With such a conception of language structure, it made good sense to look forward hopefully to certain engineering applications of linguistics—for example, to voice-operated typewriters capable of segmenting an expression into its successive phonetic units and identifying these, so that speech could be converted to some form of phonetic writing in a mechanical way; to mechanical analysis of sentence structure by fairly straightforward and well-understood computational techniques; and perhaps even beyond to such projects as machine translation. But these hopes have by now been largely abandoned with the realization that this conception of grammatical structure is inadequate at every level, semantic, phonetic, and syntactic. Most important, at the level of syntactic organization, the surface structure indicates semantically significant relations only in extremely simple cases. In general, the deeper aspects of syntactic organization are representable by labeled bracketing, but of a very different sort from that seen in surface structure.

There is evidence of various sorts, both from phonetics and from experimental psychology, that labeled bracketing is an adequate representation of surface structure. It would go beyond the bounds of this paper to survey the phonetic evidence.

Deep structures are related to surface structures by a sequence of certain formal operations, operations now generally called "grammatical transformations." At the levels of sound, meaning, and syntax, the significant structural features of sentences are highly abstract. For this reason they cannot be recovered by elementary data-processing techniques. This fact lies behind the search for central processes in speech perception and the search for intrinsic, innate structure as the basis for language learning.

How can we represent deep structure? To answer this question we must consider the grammatical transformations that link surface structure to the underlying deep structure that is not always apparent.

Consider, for example, the operations of passivization and interrogation. In the sentences (1) John was examined by the doctor, and (2) did the doctor examine John, both have a deep structure similar to paraphrase of Sentence 1,

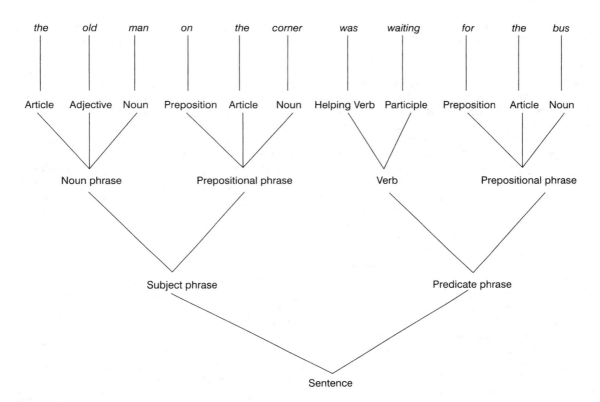

**Figure 3**
A type of sentence analysis now abandoned as inadequate at every level in this labeled
bracketing which analyzes the sentence by successive division into larger units with each
unit assigned to its own category.

(3) the doctor examined John. The same network of grammatical relations determines the semantic interpretation in each case. Thus two of the grammatical transformations of English must be the operations of passivization and interrogation that form such surface structures as Sentences (1) and (2) from a deeper structure which in its essentials also underlies Sentence (3). Since the transformations ultimately produce surface structures, they must produce labeled bracketings (see Figure 3). But notice that these operations can apply in sequence: we can form the passive question "was John examined by the doctor" by passivization followed by interrogation. Since the result of passivization is a labeled bracketing, it follows that the interrogative transformation operates on a labeled bracketing and forms a new labeled bracketing. Thus a transformation such as interrogation maps a labeled bracketing into a labeled bracketing.

By similar argument, we can show that all grammatical transformations are structure-dependent mappings of this sort and that the deep structures which underlie all sentences must themselves be labeled bracketings. Of course, the labeled bracketing that constitutes deep structure will in general be quite different from that representing the surface structure of a sentence. Our argument is somewhat oversimplified, but it is roughly correct. When made precise and fully accurate it strongly supports the view that deep structures, like surface structures, are formally to be taken as labeled bracketings, and that grammatical transformations are mappings of such structures onto other similar structures.

In speaking of mental processes we have returned to our original problem. We can now see why it is reasonable to maintain that the linguistic evidence supports an "active" theory of acquisition of knowledge. The study of sentences and of speech perception, it seems to me, leads to a perceptual theory of a classical rationalist sort. Representative of this school, among others, were the seventeenth-century Cambridge Platonists, who developed the idea that our perception is guided by notions that originate from the mind and that provide the framework for the interpretation of sensory stimuli. It is not sufficient to suggest that this framework is a store of "neural models" or "schemata" which are in some manner applied to perception (as is postulated in some current theories of perception). We must go well beyond this assumption and return to the view of Wilhelm von Humboldt, who attributed to the mind a system of rules that generates such models and schemata under the stimulation of the senses. The system of rules itself determines the content of the percept that is formed.

We can offer more than this vague and metaphoric account. A generative grammar and an associated theory of speech perception provide a concrete example of the rules that operate and of the mental objects that they construct and manipulate. Physiology cannot yet explain the physical mechanisms that affect these abstract functions. But neither physiology nor psychology provides evidence that calls this account into question or that suggests an alternative. As mentioned earlier, the most exciting current work in the physiology of perception shows that even the peripheral systems analyze stimuli into the complex properties of objects, and that central processes may significantly affect the information transmitted by the receptor organs.

The study of language, it seems to me, offers strong empirical evidence that empiricist theories of learning are quite inadequate. Serious efforts have been made in recent years to develop principles of induction, generalization, and data analysis that would account for knowledge of a language. These efforts have been a total failure. The methods and principles fail not for any superficial reason such as lack of time or data. They fail because they are intrinsically incapable of giving rise to the system of rules that underlies the normal use of language. What evidence is now available supports the view that all human languages share deep-seated properties of organization and structure. These properties—these linguistic universals—can be plausibly assumed to be an innate mental endowment rather than the result of learning. If this is true, then the study of language sheds light on certain long-standing issues in the theory of knowledge. Once again I see little reason to doubt that what is true of language is true of other forms of human knowledge as well.

There is one further question that might be raised at this point. How does the human mind come to have the innate properties that underlie acquisition of knowledge? Here linguistic evidence obviously provides no information at all. The process by which the human mind has achieved its present state of complexity and its particular form of innate organization are a complete mystery, as much of a mystery as the analogous questions that can be asked about the processes leading to the physical and mental organization of any other complex organism. It is perfectly safe to attribute this to evolution, so long as we bear in mind that there is no substance to this assertion—it amounts to nothing more than the belief that there is surely some naturalistic explanation for these phenomena.

There are, however, important aspects of the problem of language and mind that can be studied sensibly within the limitations of present understanding and technique. I think that, for the moment, the most productive investigations are those dealing with the nature of particular grammars and with the universal conditions met by all human languages. I have tried to suggest how one can move, in successive steps of increasing abstractness, from the study of percepts to the study of grammar and perceptual mechanisms, and from the study of grammar to the study of universal grammar and the mechanisms of learning.

In this area of convergence of linguistics, psychology, and philosophy, we can look forward to much exciting work in coming years.

# Encounter at Royaumont: The Debate Between Jean Piaget and Noam Chomsky

## Howard Gardner

**EDITOR'S INTRODUCTION**

Noam Chomsky's "nativist" position of language acquisition challenged Piaget's views that human linguistic capacities are part of intellectual development that is "constructed." In his writing and speaking, Chomsky began to comment quite critically on Piaget's works. At Piaget's urging, Jacques Monod, the president of the Center for the Study of Man, arranged a symposium entitled "On Language and Learning." In the following essay, Howard Gardner summarizes the arguments that were presented at the historic Piaget-Chomsky debate, highlighting the similarities and the key differences in these two influential leaders' work.

In October 1975 a confrontation of considerable importance to the temper of future intellectual discourse took place at a chateau in the Parisian suburb of Royaumont. The principal participants in this debate were Jean Piaget, the renowned Swiss psychologist and epistemologist, and Noam Chomsky, the noted American linguist and political activist. Their subject was no less than the nature of the human mind itself.

For a number of years, Piaget had hoped that such a meeting could be arranged. Sensitive to currents in contemporary social science, he had known about the threat to his position represented by the work of Chomsky and his collaborators. Chomsky had also been reading Piaget's works and had commented upon them critically. While less eager than Piaget for a personal encounter, he accepted the invitation proffered by the late Nobel laureate Jacques Monod, president of the Center for the Study of Man, to join together in a symposium dubbed (and later published as) "On Language and Learning."

The encounter at the Abbaye de Royaumont was historically important for several reasons. To begin with, Chomsky and Piaget were recognized leaders of two of the most influential (possibly the most influential) schools of contemporary cognitive studies. Taken seriously by all scientists in their respective fields of linguistics and developmental psychology, they had achieved international reputations that far transcended their areas of specialization. Accompanied by colleagues who were associated in varying degrees with their own programs of research, Piaget and Chomsky presented their ideas to an illustrious gathering of scholars: Nobel laureates in biology, leading figures in philosophy and mathematics, and several of the most prominent behavioral scientists in the world today. Those in attendance listened

*Source:* Chapter 2, pages 16–26 from *Art, Mind, and Brain: A Cognitive Approach to Creativity* by Howard Gardner. Copyright (c) by Howard Gardner. Reprinted by permission of BasicBooks, a division of HarperCollins Publishers, Inc.

critically to the arguments and joined vigorously in the ensuing discussion, seldom hesitating to make pronouncements and take sides. It was almost as if two of the great figures of the seventeenth century—Descartes and Locke, say—could have defied time and space to engage in discussion at a joint meeting of the Royal Society and the Académie Française.

The Royaumont meeting may well have had additional significance. Possibly for the first time figures at the forefront of such relatively "tender-minded" disciplines as psychology and linguistics succeeded in involving a broad and distinguished collection of "tough-minded" scholars in debates formulated by the behavioral scientists themselves—with scarcely a hint of condescension by the representatives of such firmly entrenched disciplines as biology and mathematics. Equally noteworthy, the protagonists represented the cognitive sciences—a field hardly known (and not even christened) two decades ago, and one far less familiar to both the general public and the scholarly community than many other pockets of the behavioral sciences.

The stakes in the exchange were also considerable, for the outcome of the Royaumont meeting might very well influence the future awarding of research funds; the interests of the brightest young scholars; and, indeed, the course of subsequent investigations of human cognition—arguably the most important line of inquiry in the social sciences today. Would the next generation of scholars be more attracted to pursuing the method of Piaget, observing children as they slowly construct knowledge of the physical world, or, inspired by Chomsky, would they find more challenge in formulating abstract characterizations of the presumably innate knowledge that a child has in such rule-governed domains as language, music, or mathematics? The Royaumont meeting brought together two men who not only represent different approaches but who were also dissimilar in background and style. On the one hand there was Noam Chomsky, the intense, urban intellectual, forty-six years old, employed for many years in the highly technical study of linguistics, and long engaged in political commentary and disputation about United States foreign policy. Chomsky had, with his devastating critiques, almost singlehandedly discredited two dominant schools of social science—behavioral psychology and traditional structural linguistics. And on the other hand there was Jean Piaget, thirty-two years Chomsky's senior, a European savant in the grand tradition, involved for half a century in widely known studies of the growth of children's thought. While equally proud, Piaget, a relatively non-political citizen of that most neutral of all countries, had always avoided drawing hard battle lines between himself and other investigators. Indeed, to use

one of his own terms, he had filled the role of "perpetual assimilator," eager to make contact with those of apparently opposing points of view and to assimilate their ideas to his own or, if necessary, accommodate his to theirs.

If the two men's styles and backgrounds were different, their ideas seemed, at least from a distance, remarkably akin. Both had vigorously opposed those who believed in a science built up of elements, those who mistrusted theoretical constructs, and those who felt that overt behavior was all that should be studied. Both were firmly in the rationalist tradition, worthy successors to René Descartes and Immanuel Kant. Believers in the organized human mind as an appropriate subject for study, Chomsky and Piaget were eager to discover universal principles of thought, convinced of the severe constraints built into human cognition, and relatively uninterested in social and cultural influences and in differences among individuals. Both believed in the importance of a biological perspective, but both were equally attracted to the formulation of logical models of the human mind.

Indeed, their deepest similarity lay in a belief (shared with Freud) that the important aspects of the mind lie beneath the surface. One could never solve the mysteries of thought by simply describing overt words or behaviors. One must, instead, search for the underlying structures of the mind: in Chomsky's view, the laws of universal grammar; in Piaget's, the mental operations of which the human intellect is capable.

Why, then, given this common enterprise (at least Piaget saw it that way), was there need for a debate? And why was there such a heated dispute at Royaumont about the proper future course for the sciences of the intellect? The answer is that there were important differences in the basic assumptions and methods by which the two men arrived at their respective models of human thought.

It is instructive that neither Piaget nor Chomsky was a psychologist by training, nor would either have answered readily to the label of cognitive scientist. Originally trained as a biologist, Piaget long stressed the continuity of the evolution of the species and the development of human intellect. As an adolescent he was intrigued by alterations in the shape of mollusks placed into lakes of differing climates and turbulences; he observed the same adaptiveness at work in the young infant gradually exploring the physical objects of the world. Moreover, Piaget realized that adaptation is never a simple reaction to the environment; rather, it is an active constructive process, in which problem-solving proceeds at first through the exercise of one's sensory systems and motor capacities, but eventually evolves to the height of cognition through logical operations "in the head."

All individuals pass through the same stages of intellectual development, Piaget proposed, not because we are "programmed" to do so but rather because, given the interaction of our inborn predispositions with the structure of the world in which we live, we are inevitably going to form certain hypotheses about the world, try them out, and then modify them in light of the feedback we receive. The image of thought that motivated Piaget was that of an active, exploring child systematically seeking solutions to a puzzle until he ultimately hits upon the right one, and then moves on to a yet more challenging puzzle. The "nativist" notion that all intellect is present at birth, waiting only to unfold, was anathema to Piaget, as was the rival empiricist view that all knowledge already exists in the world, just waiting to be etched into the blank infant mind.

And that was where the issue was joined with Noam Chomsky. A linguist from his earliest student days, ever committed to rigorous philosophical analysis and formal logical-mathematical methods, Chomsky's lifelong pursuit has been to understand the core of human language—the syntax that undergirds our verbal output. Chomsky views human language as marvelous and self-contained; he sees it, in fact, as a separate region of the mind. The phenomena that have intrigued Chomsky are the deep differences between superficially similar sentences: how we know instantly that "John is easy to please" functions differently from "John is eager to please"; how we recognize at once the underlying affinities between superficially different sentences, such as "The girl hit the boy," and "The boy was hit by the girl"; how we turn a statement effortlessly into a question or a question into a command.

But how did Chomsky move from these highly particularistic observations to a theory of mind? His route involved a demonstration that linguistic understanding requires mental work of a highly abstract sort. One must somehow be able to represent in one's mind the content of sentences at a level far removed from the surface properties of an utterance. Indeed, convinced early on of the inadequacy of previous attempts to explain language, Chomsky introduced into linguistics a set of wholly novel concerns. In fact he reformulated an agenda for scientific linguistics: to find a (and preferably *the*) set of grammatical rules that would generate syntactic descriptions of all of the permissible and none of the impermissible sentences in any given language. Such a grammar would constitute a valid description of the knowledge that a language user must employ when producing and understanding the sentences of his language.

Chomsky put forth a set of specific proposals concerning the formal nature of a grammatical system that could fulfill these goals. Because it is so difficult to determine how a child, exposed only to the surface structure of language, could ever "construct" these abstract representations, Chomsky arrived at a strong but highly controversial conclusion: knowledge of certain facets of language (and, by extension, of other intellectual "faculties") must be an inborn property of mind. Such knowledge requires, to be sure, a triggering environment (exposure to speech). But there is no need for active construction by the child or for more specific social or cultural input—the plan is all there. Nor are there separate stages of development based on changes in the child's mental capacities and on interaction with the environment: language unfolds in us in as natural a manner as the visual system or the circulatory system. The model lurking behind Chomsky's position, then, is that of a totally preprogrammed computer, one that needs merely to be plugged into the appropriate outlet.

And so we encounter the heart of the dispute between the two redoubtable thinkers. Whereas Piaget saw the child's efforts as engaging the full range of inventive powers as he stalks ahead from one stage to the next, Chomsky viewed the child as equipped with requisite knowledge from the beginning, only needing time to let that knowledge unfold.

At the conference both men made statements that were true to form in their examples, style of argument, and vision of science. Piaget characteristically focused on the arresting behavioral phenomena of children that he and his collaborators had discovered—the understanding of the permanence of objects, which does not occur until the end of infancy; the general capacity to symbolize, which is said to underlie both linguistic and pretend-play activities; the ability to appreciate the conservation of matter, which arises only during the early school years. Although Piaget criticized his old nemeses, the behaviorists and the nativists, for the most part he remained eager to convert others to his general picture of universal human development—a portrait attractive and convincing in its overall outlines but difficult to formulate in terms sufficiently precise for ready confirmation or disconfirmation.

Chomsky also offered a number of intriguing specific examples to support his point of view, but his overall approach was markedly different. Unlike Piaget's, his examples were not of dramatic behavioral phenomena; rather he pointed to abstract internal rules that seem necessary to account for certain regularities of linguistic output. For instance, he returned a number of times to the following illustration. When we transform the sentence "The man who is here is tall" into a question, we unfailingly produce the query "Is the man who is here tall?" rather than: "Is the man who here is tall?" Somehow we know that the relative phrase "the man who is here" must be treated as a single unit rather than broken up in the course of changing the order of the words.

Such rules are discovered by examining the features of correct linguistic utterances and of certain incorrect but "possible" syntactic constructions that seem never to appear. Once pointed out, such regularities are evident, and further experimentation to demonstrate their validity seems superfluous. Accordingly, Chomsky relied heavily on such examples to discount alternative rules and rival points of view. Disenchanted with accounts that had even a tinge of empiricism, he displayed little patience with the version of genetic-environmental contact that stands at the core of Piaget's interactionism. What impelled Chomsky's stance was a vivid image of what scientific practice should be like: metaphoric or impressionistic accounts must be avoided in favor of more precise statements phrased in a sufficiently formal manner to allow clear testing and decisive disconfirmation.

A number of other crucial differences emerged in the course of the debate. Perhaps the most dominant issue at Royaumont was one that took its original formulation from the pages of Shakespeare and has constituted a continuing source of contention between philosophers on opposite sides of the English Channel: whether (as Chomsky held) knowledge is largely inborn, part of the individual's birthright, a form of innate ideas existing in the realm of "nature"; whether (as traditional empiricists like Skinner have contended) knowledge is better conceived of as a product of living in an environment, a series of messages of "nurture" transmitted by other individuals and one's surrounding culture, which become etched onto a *tabula rasa;* or whether (as Piaget insisted) knowledge can be constructed only through interaction between certain inborn modes of processing available to the young child and the actual characteristics of physical objects and events. This issue of genetic versus cultural contributions to the mind was pointedly phrased by the convener of the conference, Jacques Monod: "In asking myself the vast question, 'What makes man man?' it is clear that it is partially his genome and partially his culture. But what are the genetic limits of culture? What is its genetic component?"

Whether by design or happenstance, considerable time was spent discussing Chomskian nativism versus Piagetian "interactionism," a conflict that at Royaumont centered particularly on questions pertaining to the origins of language. At issue was whether human linguistic capacities can in any interesting sense be considered a product of general "constructed" intellectual development (as Piaget contended), or whether they are a highly specialized part of human genetic inheritance, largely separate from other human faculties and more plausibly viewed as a kind of innate knowledge that has only to unfold (as Chomsky insisted).

To be sure, whether language is interestingly dependent on certain nonlinguistic capacities is crucial, and this question was discussed at a sophisticated level during the conference. Yet the specific debate between nativism and interactionism strikes many observers, including me, as unnecessary and sterile. Within the biological sciences many feel it is no longer fruitful to attempt to sort out hereditary from environmental influences, and within the behavioral sciences even those seduced by this question often have difficulty agreeing on just what counts as evidence in favor of one side or the other. That Chomsky and Piaget could draw such different conclusions from equally pertinent bodies of data about early cognitive and linguistic milestones and that they occasionally shifted positions on what might count as evidence for their positions indicates to me that the reason this issue was so extensively reworked was that the two spokesmen had strong views on it, rather than that either of them was likely to convince the other or skeptical "others."

Topics more susceptible to solution were also addressed at Royaumont. In particular, three related and recurring issues are worth citing, for they underline pivotal differences between the two protagonists and, unlike the nature/nurture miasma, may well be resolved in the coming years. A first argument centers on the Rousseauan dilemma of the relationships between child and adult thought: whereas Piaget and his followers believed in the utility of stages, with children as they become older attaining qualitatively different (and increasingly more powerful) modes of reasoning, Chomsky and his colleague Jerry Fodor argued strongly that such an account of stages of thought is logically indefensible. In fact, according to Fodor, it is in principle impossible to generate more powerful forms of thought from less powerful ones; essentially, all forms of reasoning that an individual will eventually be capable of are specified at birth and emerge via a maturational process during development.

A second discussion concerned the nature of the mental representations by which we conceive of our experiences, including the objects and persons of the world. In the Piagetian view, the ability to represent knowledge to oneself and to others is a constructive process that presupposes a lengthy series of actions upon the environment. Mental representation awaits the completion of sensorimotor development at age two; its emergence makes possible symbolic play, dreams, mental images, language—in fact the whole gamut of symbolic capacities. Chomsky and his colleagues, on the other hand, expressed doubts about the legitimacy of grouping together a family of representations, and of referring to a symbolic function that is supposed to emerge at a certain point in development. In their view, language as a symbol system should be radically dissociated from other symbolic forms.

The final issue, intimately related to the first two, involved the generality of thought and of thought processes. According to Piaget, thought is an extremely broad set of capacities: identical mental operations underlie one's encounters with a wide range of cognitive materials and topics (space, time, morality, causality), and the roots of later forms of thought (for example, reasoning in language) can be located in earlier forms (such as sensorimotor problem-solving by the one-year-old). From Chomsky's radically different point of view, language is divorced from other (and earlier) forms of thinking. Moreover, each intellectual faculty is *sui generis*—a separate domain of mentation, possibly located in a discrete region of the brain, exhibiting many of its own processes and maturing at its own rate. Indeed, Chomsky repeatedly invoked the striking, if somewhat bizarre, metaphor of the mind as a collection of organs, rather like the liver or the heart. We do not speak of the heart as learning to beat but rather as maturing according to its genetic timetable. So, too, we should conceive of language (and other "organs of the mind" such as those that account for the structure of mathematics or music) as mental entities that are programmed to unfold over time. Just as the physiologist dissects the heart in order to unravel its anatomy and its mechanisms, the linguist must perform analogous surgery on the human faculty of language.

The positions taken by the protagonists on these issues conveyed their general intellectual styles and substance, facets of their intellectual bequest that came across with increasing clarity and finality as the discussions progressed. Although both Piaget and Chomsky paid homage to models provided by biology and logic, they were fundamentally interested in quite different kinds of examples and explanations. Piaget was fascinated by the behaviors children emitted—and, more specifically, the errors they made—when solving the challenging puzzles he posed. He had developed an elaborate technical vocabulary, rooted in biology, to describe these phenomena—a rich description of the stages through which children pass in each of these realms of achievement. He also developed his own logical formalism to describe the affinities underlying structurally related behaviors and the differences that obtain across discrete mental stages. The phenomena he discerned offer a convincing series of snapshots of how development proceeds, but the specific terms he devised and the models he formulated have fared less well in the face of rigorous criticism. At most, Piaget's adventures into technical vocabulary and formal models offer a convenient way of synthesizing the enormous amount of data he accumulated. In the end, it is his overall *vision* of how capacities relate and of how knowledge in its varied forms develops that inspires workers in the field.

Though similar in certain respects, Chomsky's achievement is of a fundamentally different order. Rather than being struck by behavioral phenomena that he feels compelled to describe, Chomsky is driven by a powerful vision of how linguistic science should be pursued and by a belief in the way this analytic approach should be extended across the human sciences. In his view, the student of linguistics should construct models of human linguistic competence and thereby specify the "universals" of language. Stating the rules, steps, and principles with utmost (mathematical) precision becomes a prerequisite for work in this area. And so, even as Chomsky has high regard for models stated in such a way that they can be definitively tested, he dismisses more general and more allusive "positions," "schemas," and "strategies." Those domains of thought that are susceptible to study must be investigated in the way that a linguist studies language: the analyst must propose a formal system of rules that will either generate just the acceptable behaviors in that domain or will be shown in principle to fail (because, for example, they generate too many, too few, or the wrong behaviors), and he must strive to discover just those rules that the human mind actually follows.

Given those different approaches and philosophies of science, it is not surprising that, when the two scholars faced each other, there was serious and continuing disagreement. At the beginning of the discussion, each man paid homage to the other: Piaget noted "all the essential points in this about which I think I agree with Chomsky." And Chomsky acknowledged "Piaget's interesting remarks." As the discussion proceeded and became increasingly heated, the tone became distinctly less friendly. Piaget criticized the nativist position as "weak" and "useless," even as Chomsky described certain Piagetian assertions as "false," "inconceivable," and (in a mathematical sense) "trivial." Not surprisingly, neither of the scholars conceded that he might be wrong, even as each of their "seconds" rallied strongly to their positions. My reading of the interchanges suggests that most of the disinterested natural scientists were more swayed by Chomsky's presentation, but it is difficult to determine whether they were persuaded by Chomsky's rigor or were simply "turned off" by Piaget's old-fashioned, Lamarckian views on biological evolution. The social scientists in attendance at Royaumont seem to have been divided equally between the two camps.

It is too early to say which of these competing perspectives will carry the day in the burgeoning discipline of human cognition. While the issues at Royaumont are being widely discussed, the energies of future scholars have yet to be fully marshaled in either man's behalf. My own guess is that the kind of rigorous formal treatment espoused by the Chomsky circle will be increasingly embraced, but that it will be applied to the kinds of data, and addressed to the sorts of problems, that concerned Piaget and his colleagues. The academic journals of 1990 may well be filled with Chomsky-style grammars representing the child's knowledge at different stages of development. In other words, some kind of illuminating synthesis of the two men's theories may well be possible in the future.

In reading the transcript, I was struck by the grandeur of each perspective. No finer minds in our time have confronted the problem of the nature of thought: each exemplifies the power of his views both in formal presentations and informal exchanges.

At the same time, however, I was disturbed by a paradox. Piaget insisted throughout on the active exploratory nature of human intelligence; yet he offered a description of intellect that applies equivalently to all individuals and takes no account whatsoever of the heights of creative thought—the kind of inventiveness epitomized by his own work. For his part, Chomsky gave ample illustration of the creative genius of human language—the ways in which all of us are able to produce and understand sentences that have never before been uttered. Yet, at the same time, his assertion that we "know it all" in the beginning seems to leave remarkably little room for the flowering of genuinely new ideas—like those of Chomsky himself. As with many theorists, the works—and the lives—of the two men belie their own efforts to produce an overarching account of their field of inquiry.

In fact, to my mind the keynote for the conference at Royaumont was set by the biologist Guy Céllerier. After hearing the two presentations, Céllerier proposed a metaphor that he felt described the growth of intellect: he compared the development of the mind to climbing a hill. Extending that metaphor, we can assume that the broad steps of the journey are preordained but that the broad steps that one will actually take—the footholds gained, the heights one will ultimately reach, one's perspective at the end of the journey—cannot be anticipated.

Yet in their heroic effort to explain all of human thought, Piaget and Chomsky seem to have underestimated the extent to which such an exploration is open, impossible to predict, reducible neither to one's birthright nor to an inevitable sequence of stages. Perhaps the most apt metaphor for the colloquy on the regal mountain is the Sisyphean task—which each human is destined to repeat in his own turn and his own way—of striving to attain the summits of knowledge.

# Relevant Models
# of Language

## M. A. K. Halliday

### EDITOR'S INTRODUCTION

M. A. K. Halliday's contribution to language study is primarily in defining the functions of language. By concentrating on the meanings and purposes children ascribe to languages as they learn, Halliday developed a scheme for classifying different types of utterances. This article briefly presents Halliday's categories for the functions of language, categories that continue to inform many literacy programs in schools today.

The teacher of English who, when seeking an adequate definition of language to guide him in his work, meets with a cautious "well, it depends on how you look at it," is likely to share the natural impatience felt by anyone who finds himself unable to elicit "a straight answer to a straight question." But the very frequency of this complaint may suggest that, perhaps, questions are seldom as straight as they seem. The question "what is language?," in whatever guise it appears, is as diffuse and, at times, disingenuous as other formulations of its kind, for example "what is literature?" Such questions, which are wisely excluded from examinations, demand the privilege of a qualified and perhaps circuitous answer.

In a sense the only satisfactory response is "why do you want to know?," since unless we know what lies beneath the question we cannot hope to answer it in a way which will suit the questioner. Is he interested in language planning in multilingual communities? Or in aphasia and language disorders? Or in words and their histories? Or in dialects and those who speak them? Or in how one language differs from another? Or in the formal properties of language as a system? Or in the functions of language and the demands that we make on it? Or in language as an art medium? Or in the information and redundancy of writing systems? Each one of these and other such questions is a possible context for a definition of language. In each case language "is" something different.

The criterion is one of relevance; we want to understand, and to highlight, those facets of language which bear on the investigation or the task in hand.

It is not necessary to sacrifice a generation of children, or even one classroomful, in order to demonstrate that particular preconceptions of language are inadequate or irrelevant. In place of a negative and somewhat hit-and-miss approach, a more fruitful procedure is to seek to establish certain general, positive criteria of relevance. These will relate, ultimately, to the demands that we make of language in the course of our lives. We need therefore to have some idea of the nature of these demands, and we shall try to consider them here from the point of view of the child. We

*Source:* Abridged from "Relevant Models of Language" by M. A. K. Halliday, 1969, *Educational Review, 22,* 26–37. Copyright 1969 by Carfax. Reprinted by permission of publisher.

shall ask, in effect, about the child's image of language: what is the "model" of language that he internalizes as a result of his own experience? This will help us to decide what is relevant to the teacher, since the teacher's own view of language must at the very least encompass all that the child knows language to be.

The child knows what language is because he knows what language does. The determining elements in the young child's experience are the successful demands on language that he himself has made, the particular needs that have been satisfied by language for him. He has used language in many ways—for the satisfaction of material and intellectual needs, for the mediation of personal relationships, the expression of feelings, and so on. Language in all these uses has come within his own direct experience, and because of this he is subconsciously aware that language has many functions that affect him personally. Language is, for the child, a rich and adaptable instrument for the realization of his intentions; there is hardly any limit to what he can do with it.

As a result, the child's internal "model" of language is a highly complex one, and most adult notions of language fail to match up to it. The adult's ideas about language may be externalized and consciously formulated, but they are nearly always much too simple. In fact it may be more helpful, in this connection, to speak of the child's "models" of language, in the plural, in order to emphasize the many-sidedness of his linguistic experience. We shall try to identify the models of language with which the normal child is endowed by the time he comes to school at the age of 5, the assumption being that if the teacher's own "received" conception of language is in some ways less rich or less diversified it will be irrelevant to the educational task.

We tend to underestimate both the total extent and the functional diversity of the part played by language in the life of the child. His interaction with others, which begins at birth, is gradually given form by language, through the process whereby at a very early age language already begins to mediate in every aspect of his experience. It is not only as the child comes to act on and to learn about his environment that language comes in; it is there from the start in his achievement of intimacy and in the expression of his individuality. The rhythmic recitation of nursery rhymes and jingles is still language, as we can see from the fact that children's spells and chants differ from one language to another: English nonsense is quite distinct from French nonsense, because the one is English and the other French. All these contribute to the child's total picture of language "at work."

Through such experiences, the child builds up a very positive impression—one that cannot be verbalized, but is nonetheless real for that—of what language is and what it is for. Much of his difficulty with language in school arises because he is required to accept a stereotype of language that is contrary to the insights he has gained from his own experience. The traditional first "reading and writing" tasks are a case in point, since they fail to coincide with his own convictions about the nature and uses of language.

Perhaps the simplest of the child's models of language, and one of the first to be evolved, is what we may call the INSTRUMENTAL model. The child becomes aware that language is used as a means of getting things done. About a generation ago, zoologists were finding out about the highly developed mental powers of chimpanzees, and one of the observations described was of the animal that constructed a long stick out of three short ones and used it to dislodge a bunch of bananas from the roof of its cage. The human child, faced with the same problem, constructs a sentence. He says "I want a banana," and the effect is the more impressive because it does not depend on the immediate presence of the bananas. Language is brought in to serve the function of "I want," the satisfaction of material needs. Success in this use of language does not in any way depend on the production of well-formed adult sentences; a carefully contextualized yell may have substantially the same effect, and although this may not be language there is no very clear dividing line between, say, a noise made in a commanding tone and a full-dress imperative clause.

The old *See Spot run. Run, Spot, run!* type of first reader bore no relation whatsoever to this instrumental function of language. This by itself does not condemn it, since language has many other functions beside that of manipulating and controlling the environment. But it bore little apparent relation to any use of language, at least to any with which the young child is familiar. It is not recognizable as language in terms of the child's own intentions, of the meanings that he has reason to express and to understand. Children have a very broad concept of the meaningfulness of language, in addition to their immense tolerance of inexplicable tasks; but they are not accustomed to being faced with language which, in their own functional terms, has no meaning at all, and the old-style reader was not seen by them as language. It made no connection with language in use.

Language as an instrument of control has another side to it, since the child is well aware that language is also a means whereby others exercise control over him. Closely related to the instrumental model, therefore, is the REGULATORY model of language. This refers to the use of language to regulate the behavior of others. Bernstein (1970) and his colleagues have studied different types of regulatory behavior by parents in relation to the process of socialization of the child, and their work provides important clues concerning what the child may be expected to derive from this experience in constructing his own model of language. To adapt one of Bernstein's examples, the mother who finds that her small child has carried out of the supermarket, unnoticed by herself or by the cashier, some object that was not paid for, may exploit the power of language in various ways, each of which will leave a slightly different trace or afterimage of this role of language in the mind of the child. For example, she may say *you mustn't take things that don't belong to you* (control through conditional prohibition based on a categorization of objects in terms of a particular social institution, that of ownership), *that was very naughty* (control through categorization of behavior in terms of opposition approved/disapproved), *if you do that again I'll smack you* (control through threat of reprisal linked to repetition of behavior), *you'll make Mummy very unhappy if you do that* (control through emotional blackmail), *that's not allowed* (control through categorization of behavior as governed by rule), and so on. A single incident of this type by itself has little significance, but such general types of regulatory behavior, through repetition and reinforcement, determine the child's specific awareness of language as a means of behavioral control.

The child applies this awareness in his own attempts to control his peers and siblings, and this in turn provides the basis for an essential component in his range of linguistic skills, the language of rules and instructions. Whereas at first he can make only simple unstructured demands, he learns as time goes on to give ordered sequences of instructions, and then progresses to the further stage where he can convert sets of instructions into rules, including conditional rules, as in explaining the principles of a game. Thus his regulatory model of language continues to be elaborated, and his experience of the potentialities of language in this use further increases the value of the model.

Closely related to the regulatory function of language is its function in social interaction, and the third of the models that we may postulate as forming part of the child's image of language is the INTERACTIONAL model. This refers to the use of language in the interaction between the self and others. Even the closest of the child's personal relationships, that with his mother, is partly and, in time, largely mediated through language; his interaction with other people, adults and children, is very obviously maintained linguistically. (Those who come nearest to achieving a personal relationship that is not linguistically mediated, apparently, are twins.)

Aside, however, from his experience of language in the maintenance of permanent relationships, the neighborhood and the activities of the peer group provide the context for complex and rapidly changing interactional patterns which make extensive and subtle demands on the individual's linguistic resources. Language is used to define and consolidate the group, to include and to exclude, showing who is "one of us" and who is not, to impose status, and to contest status that is imposed, and humor, ridicule, deception, persuasion, all the forensic and theatrical arts of language are brought into play. Moreover, the young child, still primarily a learner, can do what very few adults can do in such situations: he can be internalizing language while listening and talking. He can be, effectively, both a participant and an observer at the same time, so that his own critical involvement in this complex interaction does not prevent him from profiting linguistically from it.

Again there is a natural link here with another use of language, from which the child derives what we may call the PERSONAL model. This refers to his awareness of language as a form of his own individuality. In the process whereby the child becomes aware of himself, and in particular in the higher stages of that process, the development of his personality, language plays an essential role. We are not talking here merely of "expressive" language—language used for the direct expression of feelings and attitudes—but also of the personal element in the interactional function of language, since the shaping of the self through interaction with others is very much a language-mediated process. The child is enabled to offer to someone else that which is unique to himself, to make public his own individuality, and this in turn reinforces and creates this individuality. With the normal child, his awareness of himself is closely bound up with speech: both with hearing himself speak, and with having at his disposal the range of behavioral options that constitute language. Within the concept of the self as an actor, having discretion, or freedom of choice, the "self as a speaker" is an important component.

Thus for the child, language is very much a part of himself, and the "personal" model is his intuitive awareness of this, and of the way in which his individuality is identified and realized through language. The other side of the coin, in this process, is the child's growing understanding of his environment, since the environment is, first of all, the "nonself," that which is separated out in the course of establishing where he himself begins and ends. So, the child has a HEURISTIC model of language, derived from his knowledge of how language has enabled him to explore his environment.

The heuristic model refers to language as a means of investigating reality, a way of learning about things. This scarcely needs comment, since every child makes it quite obvious that this is what language is for by his habit of constantly asking questions. When he is questioning, he is seeking not merely facts but explanations of facts, the generalizations about reality that language makes it possible to explore. Again, Bernstein has shown the importance of the question-and-answer routine in the total setting of parent-child communication and the significance of the latter, in turn, in relation to the child's success in formal education: his research has demonstrated a significant correlation between the mother's linguistic attention to the child and the teacher's assessment of the child's success in the first year of school.

The young child is very well aware of how to use language to learn, and may be quite conscious of this aspect of language before he reaches school; many children already control a metalanguage for the heuristic function of language, in that they know what a "question" is, what an "answer" is, what "knowing" and "understanding" mean, and they can talk about these things without difficulty. Mackay and Thompson (1968) have shown the importance of helping the child who is learning to read and write to build up a language for talking about language, and it is the heuristic function which provides one of the foundations for this, since the child can readily conceptualize and verbalize the basic categories of the heuristic model. To put this more concretely, the normal 5 year old either already uses words such as *question, answer* in their correct meanings or, if he does not, is capable of learning to do so.

The other foundation for the child's "language about language" is to be found in the imaginative function. This also relates the child to his environment, but in a rather different way. Here, the child is using language to create his own environment, not to learn about how things are but to make them as he feels inclined. From his ability to create, through language, a world of his own making he derives the IMAGINATIVE model of language, and this provides some further elements of the metalanguage, with words like *story, make up,* and *pretend.*

Language in its imaginative function is not necessarily "about" anything at all: the child's linguistically created environment does not have to be a make-believe copy of the world of experience, occupied by people and things and events. It may be a world of pure sound, made up of rhythmic sequences of rhyming and chiming syllables, or an edifice of words in which semantics has no part, like a house built of playing cards in which face values are irrelevant. Poems, rhymes, riddles, and much of the child's own linguistic play reinforce this model of language, and here too the meaning of what is said is not primarily a matter of content. In stories and dramatic games, the imaginative

function is, to a large extent, based on content, but the ability to express such content is still, for the child, only one of the interesting facets of language, one which for many purposes is no more than an optional extra.

So we come finally to the REPRESENTATIONAL model. Language is, in addition to all its other guises, a means of communicating about something, of expressing propositions. The child is aware that he can convey a message in language, a message which has specific reference to the processes, persons, objects, abstractions, qualities, states, and relations of the real world around him.

This is the only model of language that many adults have; and a very inadequate model it is, from the point of view of the child. There is no need to go so far as to suggest that the transmission of content is, for the child, the least important function of language; we have no way of evaluating the various functions relatively to one another. It is certainly not, however, one of the earliest to come into prominence, and it does not become a dominant function until a much later stage in the development toward maturity. Perhaps it never becomes in any real sense the dominant function, but it does, in later years, tend to become the dominant *model.* It is very easy for the adult, when he attempts to formulate his ideas about the nature of language, to be simply unaware of most of what language means to the child; this is not because he no longer uses language in the same variety of different functions (one or two may have atrophied, but not all), but because only one of these functions, in general, is the subject of conscious attention, so that the corresponding model is the only one to be externalized. But this presents what is, for the child, a quite unrealistic picture of language, since it accounts for only a small fragment of his total awareness of what language is about.

The representational model at least does not conflict with the child's experience. It relates to one significant part of it, rather a small part, at first, but nevertheless real. In this it contrasts sharply with another view of language which we have not mentioned because it plays no part in the child's experience at all, but which might be called the "ritual" model of language. This is the image of language internalized by those for whom language is a means of showing how well one was brought up; it downgrades language to the level of table manners. The ritual element in the use of language is probably derived from the interactional, since language in its ritual function also serves to define and delimit a social group, but it has none of the positive aspects of linguistic interaction, those which impinge on the child, and is thus very partial and one sided. The view of language as manners is a needless complication, in the present context, since this function of language has no counterpart in the child's experience.

Our conception of language, if it is to be adequate for meeting the needs of the child, will need to be exhaustive. It must incorporate all the child's own "models," to take account of the varied demands on language that he himself makes. The child's understanding of what language is is derived from his own experience of language in situations of use. It thus embodies all of the images we have described: the instrumental, the regulatory, the interactional, the personal, the heuristic, the imaginative, and the representational. Each of these is his interpretation of a function of language with which he is familiar.

Let us summarize the models in terms of the child's intentions, since different uses of language may be seen as realizing different intentions. In its instrumental function, language is used for the satisfaction of material needs; this is the "I want" function. The regulatory is the "do as I tell you" function, language in the control of behavior. The interactional function is that of getting along with others, the "me and him" function (including "me and my mummy"). The personal is related to this: it is the expression of identity, of the self, which develops largely *through* linguistic interaction; the "here I come" function, perhaps. The heuristic is the use of language to learn, to explore reality: the function of "tell me why." The imaginative is that of "let's pretend," whereby the reality is created, and what is being explored is the child's own mind, including language itself. The representational is the "I've got something to tell you" function, that of the communication of content.

What we have called "models" are the images that we have of language arising out of these functions. Language is "defined" for the child by its uses; it is something that serves this set of needs. These are not models of language acquisition; they are not procedures whereby the child learns his language, nor do they define the part played by different types of linguistic activity in the learning process. Hence no mention has been made of the chanting and repeating and rehearsing by which the child practices his language. The techniques of mastering language do not constitute a "use," nor do they enter into the making of the image of language; a child, at least, does not learn for the luxury of being a learner. For the child, all language is doing something: in other words, it has meaning. It has meaning in a very broad sense, including here a range of functions which the adult does not normally think of as meaningful, such as the personal and the interactional and probably most of those listed above—all except the last, in fact. But it is precisely in relation to the child's conception of language that it is most vital for us to redefine our notion of meaning, not restricting it to the narrow limits of representational meaning (that is, "content") but including within it all the functions that language has as purposive, nonrandom, contextualized activity.

We are still very ignorant of many aspects of the part language plays in our lives. But it is clear that language serves a wide range of human needs, and the richness and variety of its functions are reflected in the nature of language itself, in its organization as a system: within the grammatical structure of a language, certain areas are primarily associated with the heuristic and representational functions, others with the personal and interactional functions. Different bits of the system, as it were, do different jobs, and this in turn helps us to interpret and make more precise the notion of uses of language. What is common to every use of language is that it is meaningful, contextualized, and in the broadest sense social; this is brought home very clearly to the child, in the course of his day-to-day experience. The child is surrounded by language, but not in the form of grammars and dictionaries, or of randomly chosen words and sentences, or of undirected monologue. What he encounters is "text," or language in use: sequences of language articulated each within itself and with the situation in which it occurs. Such sequences are purposive—though very varied in purpose—and have an evident social significance. The child's awareness of language cannot be isolated from his awareness of language function, and this conceptual unity offers a useful vantage point from which language may be seen in a perspective that is educationally relevant.

## REFERENCES

Berstein, B. 1970. "A Critique of the Concept of 'Compensatory Education.'" In S. Williams (Ed.), *Language and Poverty: Perspectives on a Theme*. Madison, WI: University of Wisconsin Press.

Mackay, D., and Thompson, B. 1968. *The Initial Teaching of Reading and Writing*. Programme in Linguistics and English Teaching. Paper 3. London: Longmans' Linguistic Library.

# Ian Caught in Infancy

## Russell Martin

### EDITOR'S INTRODUCTION

Russell Martin's acclaimed book *Out of Silence: A Journey into Language* is a case study of one boy's struggle with autism and his parents' struggle to make sense of his needs. In this excerpt, Martin considers many of the theories of language development highlighted in the earlier articles. They come to life through the case of Ian, a boy who doesn't develop language in normal ways.

*Infancy,* a word we tend to associate only with the first few weeks and months of a child's life—life's brief beginning, a time, almost solely it seems, of suckling and untroubled sleep—comes to use from Anglo-French by way of Middle English, and it is most distantly rooted in the Latin word *infantia,* which means "without speech." Curiously, whether we are eight months or eighty years old—too young to have taken up words or old enough that stroke and disease insidiously have begun to take them from us—those of us who cannot speak are caught in the clutch of infancy. At ages two and three and then at four, the growing boy named Ian Drummond remained a troubled infant—absent speech, bereft of the kinds of language skills other children take command of in those years, Ian somehow lacking the cerebral apparatus with which this most *human* of his talents otherwise would have emerged.

Only three weeks following conception, the human embryo, three millimeters in length, has formed two paired structures at one end of its simple neural tube—bulging, symmetrical pieces of tissue that soon will become a brain. By the twelfth week of gestation, the brain's cerebrum and cerebellum have taken shape; at four months, the several forebrain structures are intact and the cerebrum has begun to form the lateral fissures that distinguish its temporal lobes; and at eight months, the fully developed brain is tightly packed inside the bony box of the cranium. By birth, an infant's head is almost half its body length; its brain weighs a quarter of its adult weight, and every one of its *billions* of neurons already is intact. Except for the intricate coating of long nerve fibers with insulating myelin and what in two years' time will be a doubling in its weight, the brain at birth is entirely ready to function, to begin to form the dazzling interconnections between its neurons that will allow it to engage with the world, to recognize, remember, and learn, someday even to speak.

Whether the phenomenon can be accounted for by the presence in the brain of a Chomskian language organ or whether it is simply the product of decidedly less mysterious natural selection, every human newborn with normal hearing quickly begins to focus on the sounds of speech. Tests performed in experimental settings have shown that six-month-olds can distinguish between "ah" and "ee"

---

sounds made by their mothers and that they likewise can discern the differences in those sounds when made by voices they have never heard. And just as infants spend the first six months of life listening to the sounds of speech, they devote the subsequent half year to trying them out for themselves. Babies begin to babble four to six months before their first word emerges, making speechlike sounds in a manner that is unmistakably playful, pleasurable; and intriguingly, they tend to begin to make the same sounds at roughly the same times and in the same sequences regardless of the language they have become accustomed to and are about to learn to speak—Arabic, English, or Chinese.

First words, the first fledgling elements of speech, are little more than labels, a means of identifying those people and objects the youngster considers most important—*cow, cookie, Mama, me*—the child's initial sense of self taking shape in the simple context of naming names. Then, subject-only utterances give way to subject and verb: an eager "me, me!" is soon supplanted by the more communicative "me juice," and not long later the phrase "give juice me" introduces a grammatical object well before a child gains command of the particularities of syntax and grammar. Finally, and now from a certified speaker—language alive in his or her brain—a sentence like "please give me some apple juice" emerges as if by some sleight of mind, a true linguistic accomplishment. And perhaps even more remarkably, toddlers at fourteen months and even tykes of four or five years are capable of learning two very different languages simultaneously, as effortlessly as one alone is acquired, and although their limits seldom are truly tested, they likely are capable of learning many more. Those first few years of a child's life appear, in point of fact, to be *for* learning language, for discovering ten thousand things through imitation and endless hours of play, for playing foremost with language.

Although Ian's first forms of autistic play were limited to his silent and solitary imitations of action in his movies, by the time he was three he did begin to entertain himself—to explore and exercise and even have a bit of irrefutable fun—in several other ways, normally alone but occasionally even in the company of others. He loved, for instance, to tug and push his mother, father, and sister Sarah into precise positions in their long, sunlit living room, where they could serve as sentient sorts of fence posts whom he could run beside; and it seemed sure that it would have become one of his favorite recreations—combining the joys of running, repetition, and a real if rather peculiar way of interacting with his family—had it not become quickly obvious to the other three that they simply could not allow themselves to become prisoners to that particular pastime,

stuck in place perhaps for hours as Ian brushed beside them, racing back and forth across the carpet.

But his other entertainments tended to be far easier to sanction—less disruptive of some semblance of regular family life, if often equally unusual: It was during the year he was three that Ian seemed to discover trees—the ponderosas, Douglas firs, and aspens that he lived among—and he would spend long stretches of time outdoors licking trees as if to determine what their taste could teach him, similarly pressing his cheeks against their trunks, craning his neck to peer into their upper branches, running past them in lieu of posts or people. And then he discovered water to similar delight, splashing in puddles and fearlessly jumping into shallow pools. Bathtime too became an occasion he eagerly sought out, several times a day if his parents would acquiesce—the tub's warm and soapy water a realm he comfortably could enter with his prized plastic figurines, Pooh and Tigger and ten others joining him for his nightly soak, an environment where you could watch him subtly unwind, physically and somehow even emotionally, where the water seemed to hug him or caress him, or at least to offer some support, where he was free simply to splash and kick and play. Ian also became an intrepid climber, as fearless clinging to the upper rungs of the ladder that led to a loft in his bedroom as he was in the water, regularly scrambling up the metal slide outside the house with what appeared to be a kind of cool disinterest, scrambling too to the tops of the granite knobs as big as barns that lay scattered across the rolling steppe.

In his isolation—his bedroom door often shut to shield out some noise, some simple commotion he couldn't stand—Ian would spend hours burrowed under blankets pulled from his bed and mounded on the floor, sleeping bags and clothes dumped from drawers offering similar subterranean pleasures, the boy becoming a mole. And on those days when it seemed safe to venture into the larger world of the living room, he would pull the cushions from the couch and try as well to bury himself beneath them, or angle them to the floor to turn them into a makeshift, spongy slide.

But for the longest time, Ian didn't play with vocal sounds in any way. Unlike other children, he didn't babble as if engaged in some splendid experiment, he didn't try to imitate words he heard. He seemed instead to be deaf, hearing nothing—neither his mother's patient and tender pledges nor the songs his father sang, neither his sister's carefully scripted fantasies nor his own continuing shrieks. He seemed as mute as those rocks and trees were, incapable of speaking polished words, incapable of their practice, unable to make himself understood, as other children could, with nascent sounds that sprang from his mouth.

Theoretical explanations of how normal children somehow utter their first words and then rapidly acquire language tend to be composed of opposing and contradictory perspectives. It isn't surprising, nor is it news, that one of them is championed—quite persuasively, for many people—by Noam Chomsky. Yet it is curious that many of Chomsky's ideas about the specific ways in which language comes to life in almost all children first emerged not in the context of his own primary writing but rather in his 1959 review of Harvard psychologist B. F. Skinner's 1957 book *Verbal Behavior,* a widely influential account of how language is acquired, then used throughout a lifetime.

Skinner's ideas dominated psychology back in that era, particularly his contention that all of human behavior is best explained by what he called operant conditioning. In the context of the theory that has become known as behaviorism, an "operant" is any action that achieves a specific outcome. If the outcome is favorable, the probability increases that the action will occur again, and the action is "reinforced"—positively reinforced if it produces some sort of pleasant or attractive outcome, negatively reinforced if the operant is followed by the end or removal of something painful or unpleasant. If, on the other hand, the outcome of an operant is unfavorable, the probability *decreases* that it will occur again, and rather than being reinforced, that operant is "punished."

In terms of the acquisition of language, Skinner theorized, all linguistic stimuli are external—morphemes, word, sentences—and an individual child develops the ability to respond to those stimuli via the principles of operant conditioning, the spoken word "juice" tending to result in the offering of juice, for instance, while "juice please" is even more likely to produce the desired result. But a specific operant can be generalized to apply to a variety of related behaviors as well, and can also be associated with a wide range of unrelated behaviors. "Cookie please" is readily "learned" by generalization, in other words, and "teddy bear please" is acquired with similar ease by means of association. In Skinner's view, a child learns to talk, just as he or she learns to walk, because talking tends to produce so many favorable outcomes.

But Chomsky was unpersuaded by a theory based entirely on response to external stimuli. Although he could imagine, for instance, that the rules of operant conditioning might comprehensively account for the way in which an infant shakes a rattle, then shakes it again repeatedly because he or she delights in the sounds it makes—or the way in which a child learns to walk because certain operants, certain physical actions, result in the positive reinforcement of

reaching a parent's outstretched arms—Chomsky simply dismissed Skinner's attempt to treat language analogously. Neither Skinner nor anyone else could make the case, he argued, that language acquisition was solely the product of external conditions, in part because its "stimuli" inherently were so difficult, if not impossible, to identify and quantify. And how could Skinner account for one of language's most elemental attributes, its creativity? If language was acquired solely from external sources, were the concepts of generalization and association enough to explain the ways in which children begin to link words they have never heard linked before?

In Chomsky's opposing view, language acquisition cannot be imagined to be set in motion by external forces, by stimuli that lead to specific linguistic responses. Instead, he proposed the existence of a "language organ" in every child that receives external input in the form of so-called primary linguistic data—parents' words, phrases, pauses, and inflections. The acquisition device then somehow cooks that data down into the stew of syntax—the linguistic rules and regulations that the parents' words adhere to—finally allowing the output of a grammatically acceptable version of the very language from which the original data have been drawn. What emerges is a facility with that language that is capable of enormous creativity, of course, because it is not mimicry, nor is it a specific operant response. Rather, it is language built on an innate apprehension of those rules and on a similar ability to employ them, on what Chomsky labeled a "universal grammar," which he has defined more recently as "a characterization of the genetically determined language faculty. One may think of this faculty as a 'language acquisition device,' an innate component of the human mind that yields a particular language through interaction with presented experience." The average six-year-old, in other words, becomes expert at speech production and comprehension because he or she is born with its rules already in hand, or, if you will, somewhere within the neural walls of that acquisition device.

Chomsky's assessment of the way in which children acquire language seems clearly wrongheaded to a linguist like Philip Lieberman, who remains far more charitable toward the ideas of Skinner and his fellow behaviorists than does Chomsky and who argues for the primacy of evolution, rather than syntax, when it comes to the question of language's rules and regulations. The fundamental flaw in the universal grammar theory, as far as Lieberman is concerned, is that it assumes that all humans are born with an identical "plan," a genetically coded set of interlocked principles, components, and conventions that allows a child to turn the aural data of spoken speech into creative language—a system in which every component plays a specific and crucial role, and in which every component therefore is always present in everyone who learns to talk. But that assumption, he argues, flies in the face of the formidable verity of genetic variation: No two individuals (save identical twins) are genetically alike, and those genes at the specific chromosomal locations that account for each particular aspect of who we are vary between us and our parents about ten percent of the time. It is an evolutionary certainty, Lieberman contends, that if a universal grammar were genetically transmitted, all its components could not always be present in every individual. If a genetically coded "language faculty" is absolutely necessary to acquire language, he writes in *Uniquely Human,*

> [t]hen it would follow that some children would lack one or more of the genetically coded components of the language faculty. Some "general principle" or some component of the "markedness system" would necessarily be absent in some children because it is genetically transmitted. This is the case for all genetically coded aspects of the morphology of human beings or any other living organisms. . . . A biologically plausible universal grammar cannot have rules and parameters that are so tightly interlocked that the absence of any single bit of putative innate knowledge makes it impossible for the child to acquire a particular language. In other words, we cannot claim that a single set of innate principles concerning language exists that is (a) absolutely necessary for the acquisition of language and (b) uniform for all human beings.

Yes, Lieberman acknowledges—anticipating the responses of Chomsky and fellow "nativists" who view language as genetically innate—all people do have lungs, hearts, brains, and it may be that all of us also possess universal grammars, but if so, and as is the case with those other organs, they necessarily would vary from person to person, and in some people, they necessarily would be faulty— faulty far more often than could be accounted for by children like Ian who do not learn to speak. Instead, suggests Lieberman, children learn how to speak simply because they know how to play.

Lieberman does not argue with the notion that the input of parents' (particularly mothers') spoken speech is a crucial and catalytic component of language acquisition; without it, the acquiring process could not get under way. But as far as he is concerned, "there is nothing very mysterious about syntax," particularly with regard to its supposed innate role in turning complex, sometimes contradictory, often garbled input into grammatical output. What happens instead, he posits rather more concretely, is that children begin to respond to the language sounds they hear simply by imitating them. Studies have shown that newborns at just a day or two of age are capable of imitating adult facial expressions, and by age six months children can imitate the sounds their mothers make; by nine months, they are able to imitate expressions, sounds, and activities they discerned the day before; by fourteen months, they can replay by imitation what they saw or heard a week ago. Are these children dutifully and determinedly going about the business of learning language as they do so? No, says Lieberman, they are *playing,* a highly evolved form of behavior that allows us to learn a multitude of things, languages among them, without having to knuckle down or even to sit still— learning by association, generalization, analogy, and the kinds of trial and error that are the nuts-and-bolts business of Skinner's behaviorism.

There is no argument among these linguistic partisans that children learning language are confronted with what would seem to be a daunting task. Although it takes them years of schooling to master geometry or algebra, they quickly come to grips—in the most casual of look-Ma-no-hands fashion—with a system of communication and representation that scientists cannot completely or even adequately describe. It isn't surprising therefore that one attractive explanation for children's cheery facility with language's complexity is that knowledge of its rules, or perhaps the rules themselves, are innate, somehow built into every baby. But that perspective digs too deeply and with far too blunt a shovel, Lieberman believes, when a much more plausible possibility can be observed readily in almost every household. Children learn language so effortlessly, he contends, because they inherently are so playful, so curious, because they can pay rapt attention without knowing they do so, and because their brains are utterly impelled to learn.

Children—and former children as well—daily employ a diverse and varied number of so-called cognitive strategies in order to learn, one of the most important and fundamental of which is known as "concept formation," or rule learning. And in the context of learning the rules of language, children make use of concept formation to acquire the foundations of syntactic structure; syntax isn't so complex that it must be innate, Lieberman says, but rather it is so simple that it's discernible just from listening.

All humans are adept at generalizing—forming categories, patterns, and rules from separate cases or incidents—

and children begin to generalize very early on. Their interest in naming objects, for instance, is part of an obsession with creating categories—all four-legged animals likely included in a category called "dog" at first, then soon divided into subcategories called "dog" and "horse" and "cat." Similarly, and surely unaware, children generalize from the language that they hear, noting—among many other things— that utterances tend to come in bursts separated by breaths, that key words receive intonational stress, that those words are made up of specific sounds, and that words, once recognized, tend to be grouped in repeated and dependable patterns. As children then begin to imitate what they hear, their first words, not surprisingly, tend to be those key words, words their parents have spoken a thousand times and each time have given a vocal stress. Later, as they begin to link words grammatically, their grammars simply reflect those orderings, those rule-governed arrangements that they have heard most often. If they hear "I goed to town" more often than "I went to town," then *I goed* becomes grammatical; if "I went to town" is commonplace and "Town went I to" is odd, then the latter is discarded. Rather than depending on an innate rule-dispensing system, they depend instead on their abilities to generalize from observation—learning by listening, and then by imitating those curious articulations that they most often hear.

In making this behavioral kind of case, however, Lieberman does not quarrel with the proposition that the acquisition of language involves specialized brain mechanisms or some set of highly evolved neural capabilities. The brain's adaptability and its task-specific prowess, in fact, have allowed us to achieve all manner of miracles in the millennia since we lumbered to our feet. But there simply is no need, he argues by analogy,

> to postulate a special-purpose innate fork-using mechanism to account for the way that children learn to use forks, or universal clothes or cars grammars to account for the way that people rush to outfit themselves in the latest style in clothes or cars. Imitation and a desire to "be like the others" clearly can account for most of the short-term changes in human culture, and perhaps for many of its major achievements.

Of all our human acquisitions and accomplishments, only language is utterly dependent on being acquired at an early age, during the "critical period," from twelve months of age to six or seven years, perhaps to the onset of puberty, during which time language proficiency must be won, if it ever will be. By the time we become adolescents our language-acquisition device seems somehow to have atrophied, or perhaps to have moved on to another neural occupation. Have the folds and creases of our cortices by then become so definitively formed that we cannot reshape them and effectively teach ourselves new tricks? Do we forget after only a short expanse of years how to pay wide-eyed attention and to play?

From the cows he first was fascinated by to the elephants and monkeys in his movies, from the squirrels and rabbits he encountered in the nearby forests to a wily character called Tigger he certainly seemed to cherish, Ian, like most children, took great interest in animals, particularly if they were at an imaginary or spatial remove from him. He would utterly ignore long-suffering Sheila, the collie who had come west with the family from Illinois, when she would wander into his room, and the cat Sarah lived for during that time surely seemed invisible to him. Yet books like *The Smiley Lion* and *Franny Bunny* at last began to intrigue him—*books!* to his parents' pure pleasure and excitement—Ian sitting still and seeming briefly comfortable beside them as they read, Ian sometimes pointing with the help of their wrist prompts to the colorful drawings of these creatures, sometimes even pointing to the words his parents read. He still loved to—still demanded to—make the daily drive to call on the cows, and despite his fears and anxieties about most exotic settings, he once responded with his own sort of enthusiasm to an experimental trip to the zoo. In subsequent visits to zoos both in Denver and in Colorado Springs, Ian would demonstrate—by means of those places where he chose to run ritually back and forth—the animals he liked best: snakes of all shapes and sizes, as well as the apes, who would stare inscrutably back at him.

They did then and still do intrigue me—these two choices he made without anyone's direction or influence. Wasn't it curious that a boy who was terribly afraid of so much that seemed innocuous was, nonetheless, drawn to those slithering reptiles that so many of the rest of us are innately fearful of? And what did he see in the faces of the gorillas, orangutans, and chimpanzees that made him tarry near their cages? Did their silence make them seem kindred to him? Did the cages themselves seem to be something he knew well by analogy?

Much experimentation has been done during the second half of the twentieth century in an effort to determine whether our close cousins the apes are capable of acquiring true language, and several impressive results indeed have been obtained—from the young gorilla named Koko in California who built a working vocabulary of four hundred signed words to the sardonically named Nim Chimpsky, a chimpanzee in New York city who once spontaneously produced a string of sixteen words in American Sign Language (ASL): *Give orange me give eat orange me eat orange give me eat orange give me you;* a lot of words for a rather simple request.

This series of separate studies began in the 1960s with a chimpanzee named Vicki who was trained literally to speak, but her vocabulary was limited to four words—*mama, papa, cup,* and *up*—each produced only with real effort and pronounced in a kind of whisper. Then early in the 1970s, a chimp named Sarah made news when she mastered rudimentary elements of a visual-symbol language, reaching a level at which she could begin to communicate creatively, generalizing from a phrase like *Randy give apple Sarah* to *Randy give banana Sarah,* a very subtle but nonetheless significant step. Subsequently, two chimps called Sherman and Austin, who were trained simultaneously to use a similar visual language called Yerkish, were sometimes observed using it to communicate privately with each other after class sessions had ended and trainers had gone away for the day.

But surely the star of these whiz chimps was Washoe, a chimpanzee who was brought at eleven months of age to live with Allen and Beatrix Gardner and their family in Nevada, each of whom had learned ASL prior to her arrival. In Washoe's presence, the Gardners communicated only in ASL, and soon she began to sign herself. By the time she was five, her vocabulary included at least 132 signs. Her exaggerated, expansive style of signing was similar to that of human children learning ASL, and she could employ the signing equivalent of intonation to give her words emphasis; but she seldom offered more than a two-word utterance, and she was far more repetitive than human children normally are, whether signing or speaking. Yet Washoe had become quite creative: After she had acquired the sign for *flower,* she began to use it in the context of a variety of smells, but as soon as she learned the actual sign for *smell,* her use of *flower* reverted solely to its proper usage. Impressively, a nightcap she had never seen before she called a *hat;* a Brazil nut seemed to her to be a *rock berry;* and the first time she saw a duck, she labeled it a *water bird.*

In the intervening years, no other pongid has significantly surpassed the achievements of Washoe and her fellow captives. The most precocious of them have been capable of reaching a language level roughly comparable to that of a two-and-a-half-year-old child, and they have learned—normally, and perhaps significantly, only with the aid of the rigorously controlled techniques of operant conditioning—how to use complex symbolic systems to communicate. Yet they have been unable to progress beyond those plateaus they reached, and that, as well as the virtual absence of a grasp of syntax, combine to make most researchers unwilling to call their communication "language." But if these chimps and gorillas aren't employing language, then what is this marvel of which they've become capable? If Nim Chimpsky isn't using language when he signs *Me sorry hug me,* what else can we possibly call it?

Derek Bickerton, the University of Hawaii linguist who, like Chomsky, views an inherent sense of syntax as key to language's emergence in our species as well as to its acquisition by each of us individually, posits intriguing answers to those questions in *Language and Species.* There are at least two allied but fundamentally distinct *types* of language, Bickerton contends—both having come to us evolutionarily in ways Philip Lieberman wouldn't argue with—what Bickerton calls "language" and "protolanguage," and the case he makes for them depends as much on rare examples of so-called wild children who have grown up in worlds without language as it does on eloquent and pioneering pongids like precocious Nim and Washoe.

It was in the autumn of 1970 that a tiny thirteen-year-old girl—just four feet six inches tall and weighing fifty-nine pounds—appeared with her cataract-blinded mother at a social services office in suburban Los Angeles, the two of them seeking help, seeking asylum from the father and husband who long had made their lives nightmarish beyond belief. Inside the father's autocratic and horrific household, the girl—who became known by the pseudonym "Genie"—had been harnessed naked to a potty chair since infancy, able to move only her fingers and hands, her feet and toes, the room where she was kept empty except for the potty chair and a wire-covered crib where she sometimes was placed at night, her only glimpse of the world two slivers of sky she could see above the curtains that covered the windows.

Genie was incontinent when she first was examined by doctors. She could not chew solid food, her vision was very poor, she could not stand erect or fully extend her limbs, and she virtually was mute. She understood the words *red, blue, green, brown, Mother, walk,* and *go;* she could utter only what sounded like "stop it" and "no more." Genie was admitted to Children's Hospital of Los Angeles for initial treatment of severe malnutrition, and as she slowly began to gain strength and then quickly to acquire new skills, she also became the subject of an enormous amount of curiosity on the part of social scientists from several disciplines. By the time a battery of tests determined that Genie was not retarded—although, as hospital psychologist James Kent put it, she was "the most profoundly damaged child I've ever seen . . . [her] life was a wasteland"—a number of researchers in linguistics had become fascinated by her, by what, in particular, she might now be able to acquire in the way of speech and language skills. Yet although Genie did make enormous progress, although she could say "I want Curtiss play piano," "Think about Mama love Genie," and could utter hundreds of similar simple phrases by 1977, seven years after her liberation, her language skills seemed stuck at that rather primitive level.

According to Susan Curtiss, the UCLA linguist who had worked most intensively with Genie during those years and whose doctoral dissertation had been published under the title *Genie: A Psycholinguistic Study of a Modern-Day "Wild Child,"* Genie quickly had developed an impressive vocabulary, but, in large part because she had aged beyond the critical acquiring period by the time she began to learn language,

> she never mastered the rules of grammar, never could use the little pieces—the word endings, for instance. She had a clear semantic ability but could not learn syntax. There was a tremendous unevenness, or scatter, in what she was able to do. . . . One of the interesting findings is that Genie's linguistic system did not develop all of a piece. So grammar could be seen as distinct from the non-grammatical aspects of language, and also from other mental faculties. . . . She demonstrated that after puberty one could not learn language simply by being exposed to it.

Yet as Russ Rymer would note in his *New Yorker* series based on Genie's story and the research she engendered, her linguistic development also posed a substantial theoretical conundrum:

> Though it appeared to affirm Chomsky, it could also be read as refuting him. If some parts of language were innate and others were provided by the environment, why would Genie's childhood hell have deprived her of only the innate parts? How could a child who lacked language because she had been shut away from her mother be proof that our mothers don't teach us language? Why should she be unable to gain precisely the syntax that Chomsky said she was born with? . . . [I]f syntax is "innate" why must it be "acquired" at all?

Derek Bickerton's sharply drawn distinction between language and protolanguage considers those questions by forging a linguistic—actually, a *proto*linguistic—link between adolescents and adults like Genie, who have been deprived of language, normal children who are acquiring their initial speech, and the speaking apes, connections that at first perhaps appear implausible. Bickerton is convinced that the kinds of language the three groups produce have much in common: they are comprised solely of lexical (vocabulary) items and they lack discernible grammatical structure—the same observation Susan Curtiss makes regarding Genie's speech—and Bickerton goes to some length in making his case for their commonality.

Yet if all are virtually the same sort of speech, why does only one of the three transform itself into fully flowered language? Bickerton's response is that no satisfactory or even passable explanation is possible so long as it depends on the assumption that mature language evolves or derives from its primitive counterpart, so long as language acquisition is seen as a single continuous process. But on the other hand, he writes,

> [i]f we assume that there exists some primitive type of language—some protolanguage, as we might call it, that is just as much a part of our biological endowment as language is, but that lacks most of the distinguishing formal properties of language—then all three . . . can be readily explained. Genie acquired protolanguage because protolanguage is more robust than language (having formed part of the hominid endowment for much longer) and it does not have a critical period. . . . Genie's acquisition ceased because the faculties of protolanguage and of language are disjoint, and acquisition of the one in no way entails acquisition of the other.

This is the core of Bickerton's contention: Hominids and pongids alike can pick up protolanguage, whether at thirteen months or thirteen years or thirty. And it is this rough and spotty kind of speech that is acquired through the application of normal cognitive processes to the input of experience, in much the same way that Philip Lieberman describes. Yet the other sort of language—the one almost all of us acquire when we are small as if by some strange metaphysical frolic, the one that depends on syntax for its clarity and nuance and a kind of fluid grace—clearly must be latched onto very early in our lives; and we alone among the primates, among *all* animals so far as we know now, are capable of achieving it. It is a curious thought to consider: It isn't our ability to communicate that makes us unique; neither is it our register of words that we can count into the many thousands. What sets us truly apart, it seems, is that while we are young—and somehow *only* then—we discover how wonderfully to weave those words.

But Rymer's queries still echo here: If Chomsky is correct in claiming that this stuff called syntax with which we create true language is genetically handed down to us, then why does it disappear? Or if, in contrast, Lieberman's outlook is the clearer one, then why is it that we can acquire words at any age, but grammar only in the years soon after we are infants?

# REFERENCES

Bickerton, D. 1990. *Language and Species.* Chicago: University of Chicago.

Lieberman, P. 1991. *Uniquely Human: The Evolution of Speech, Thought, and Selfless Behavior.* Cambridge, MA: Harvard University Press.

Skinner, B. F. 1957. *Verbal Behavior.* New York: Appleton-Century-Croft.

# Myths about Acquiring
# a Second Language

## Katharine Davies Samway and Denise McKeon

**EDITOR'S INTRODUCTION**

Katharine Samway and Denise McKeon provide a valuable service in this article by presenting the realities that counter common myths about second language acquisition. Building on the work of second language acquisition researchers like Virginia Collier and Jim Cummins, the authors clearly demonstrate the importance of current theory and research to classroom practice.

## Second Language Acquisition Myth #1: Learning a second language is an entirely different proposition from learning one's own native language.

## Reality: There are many parallels between learning a first and second language.

### Background/Overview

It may be comforting for educators to know that learning the linguistic structures and rules of a second language occurs in much the same way as it does for the first (Dulay, Burt & Krashen 1982; Lindfors 1989). In fact, if we think of language as a coin, we can think of first and second language learning as its two sides: essentially the same in composition, but with different designs and different features.

Whether first or second language learning, people learn language because they are in real situations communicating about important and interesting things. Furthermore, this communication is seen and perceived as something that is highly valued (Urzúa 1989). An initial look at the environments in which young children develop their lan-guage reveals a great deal of linguistic variety, yet virtually all children effortlessly and naturally learn their native tongues. Children's first language development before they come to school takes place largely through conversations that they hear and have with members of their families.

At one time, it was thought that children learned language by imitating their parents. More recent research suggests, however, that children learn language by actively constructing principles for the regularities that they hear in the speech of others, such as parents, brothers and sisters, and those they interact with on a regular basis (Brown 1973; Chomsky 1969). Evidence of these principles can be seen when children use forms such as *goed,* (as in, "My daddy goed to the store yesterday"), *foots,* and even *feets.* Such errors in children's speech provide us with clues that children are indeed constructing their own hypotheses of how the language functions, since they haven't heard these particular forms in the speech of adults (Wells 1986). As language develops, children become capable of dealing with greater degrees of complexity. They begin to recognize the inconsistencies of their own speech. They modify their hypotheses about the rules of language and gradually reorganize their language system so that their language approximates more complex adult forms—*goed* becomes *went*.

Learners who are acquiring a second language typically "try out" the language with equal creative fervor, making errors that are similar to the errors made by young monolingual speakers of the language. These errors are an integral part of the second language learning process, helping learners to refine and revise their understanding of how the second language works. Beginning learners of English as a second language (ESL), regardless of age, are as likely to say *goed* and *foots* as first language learners of English, suggesting that learners gradually organize the language they hear according to rules they construct in the new language. Gradually, as the learner's language system develops, these rules are refined to incorporate more and more of the language system.

Second language learners, like children who are acquiring their first language, often appear to understand language before being able to produce it (Dulay, Burt & Krashen 1982). In fact, many children who are acquiring a second language have been observed to exhibit a "silent period," saying nothing (or very little) in the new language being learned for periods ranging from several days to several months. For schools and teachers, these features of second language acquisition are often a source of confusion and concern about a child's learning abilities. It may be reassuring to know, therefore, that these silent periods are considered to be a natural part of second language acquisition, have no long-term detrimental effect on language learning overall, and may, in fact, be beneficial to the second language learning process, providing learners with time to hypothesize about the rules of the new language they are learning.

Although first and second language acquisition are similar processes in many ways, they are by no means identical. Second language learners are more sophisticated learners, in that they already have acquired some, if not most, of the components of one language. Second language learners are more cognitively mature than are first language learners (unless, of course, they are acquiring two languages from birth). See *Features of L2 Acquisition* on this page for features of L2 Acquisition.

## Scenario

*It is just before Thanksgiving, and the students in Raúl Castro's kindergarten class are preparing to make construction paper turkeys, complete with multicolored tails.*

*For the first time, Mr. Castro's class includes several students whose parents speak a language other than English at home. One of these students, Mee Lon, has Mr. Castro worried. She seems to understand what's going on in class and is a willing participant in activities such as the one going on today, but Mee Lon rarely, if ever, speaks. Mr. Castro decides to consult with Karen Kelly, Mee Lon's ESL teacher.*

*Raúl Castro: Karen, I just don't understand what's going on with Mee Lon. She's really got me wondering if I should refer her for Special Education testing. She never speaks in class, although she seems to be following along with what we're doing—much better than she did at the beginning of the year—and is fairly outgoing with her peers. But even with the other children, she almost never says anything.*

### Features of L2 Acquisition

- L1 and L2 acquisition are similar processes, *but*
  - L2 learners are more cognitively mature than L1 learners
- Language learning involves hypothesis construction and testing:
  - Errors are integral to language learning
- Understanding language usually precedes language production
  - A "silent period" is normal
- Younger learners do not necessarily have greater facility with languages:
  - Older learners generally confront more complex linguistic situations
  - Younger learners may pronounce the L2 with minimal accent, *but*
  - Older learners are often more efficient learners
- Mastering academic language may take L2 learners up to 7 years
- L2 acquisition and academic success are influenced by sociocultural factors, e.g.,
  - Personality
  - Cultural affiliation
  - Prior schooling
  - Teacher expectations

*Karen: I know. She's that way in ESL class, too. And you can imagine how frustrating it is for me when we do oral work—telling stories and playing games. But, you know I recently reread something about a phenomenon called "the silent period." It occurs sometimes when kids are learning another language. Even though they may be listening to and processing what's going on around them, they just don't speak—at least not in the beginning.*

*Raúl: But it's almost Thanksgiving! And Mee Lon has been in school since late August.*

*Karen: I know, but sometimes that's how long it takes. Sometimes, even longer. I asked our family outreach worker to check with Mee Lon's parents to see if she's that way at home. They said that when she's home playing with her brothers, she's a regular motor-mouth in Mandarin. I guess it must be pretty intimidating to be placed in a school where everything is happening in a language you don't understand—and plus, the fact that this is her first school experience must be contributing to her shyness.*

*Raúl: So what did your book say about dealing with this? Can I ever hope to hear a peep out of her? Won't this delay her development in English?*

*Karen: Actually, what I read suggested that this "silent period" won't hurt her development in any way. If you can find activities that she can participate in by drawing or pointing, that will help you know that she's understanding. Also, if you can get her to join in to games or songs where others are talking or singing at the same time, that might alleviate some of the pressure on her to give a "solo" performance. You know, the book said that some adults have been known to go through this "silent period," too. I plan to hang on, be patient, and give her a chance to work it out. Although I read that a silent period can last up to 6 months, I bet she'll be talking by Christmas. If she's this into the turkeys, imagine when we get to the reindeer!*

## Second Language Acquisition Myth #2: Younger children are more effective language learners than are older learners.

## Reality: While younger language learners may learn to pronounce a new language with little or no accent, older language learners are often more efficient learners.

### Background/Overview

Although it has long been thought that young children are more effective language learners, there is some evidence to suggest that this is not the case, except for a greater facility with pronunciation (Dulay, Burt & Krashen 1982). What leads people to imagine that young children are expert linguists is the fact that the types of linguistic tasks young children are expected to perform are generally simple face-to-face communicative activities that fit their developmental level. With increasing age, the language (including the written form of the language) that students must comprehend and use to match their developmental level rapidly outstrips their rudimentary command of the second language, thus creating a mismatch (if not a tremendous chasm) between conceptual and linguistic competence.

The mismatch between conceptual and linguistic competence is often seen most starkly in school settings. Older school-age learners require more sophisticated language skills, which help them maneuver through complex social situations and challenging academic situations. Language researchers and theoreticians have recently begun to explore the ways in which these more complex forms of language vary and, in turn, how that variation affects the ability of students to learn and use language in academic settings (Bialystok 1991; Collier 1987, 1989; Chamot and O'Malley 1985; Crandall 1987; Cummins 1981b; Mohan 1986). The context in which language is used and the conceptual content of communication are two possible sources of variation that have been explored.

Differences in the context in which language is used also help to account for some of the reasons why younger children may be seen as better language learners. The context of language use refers to the degree to which the environment is rich with meaningful clues that help the language learner decipher and interpret the language being used. Face-to-face conversations, for example, provide the opportunity to observe nonverbal cues such as facial expressions and gestures. Tone of voice convey meaning far beyond what mere words can express, as any child listening to a frustrate parent demand that toys be picked up *now* can attest.

Children learning to play a game not only have the verbal directions to rely on in helping them figure out the game, but also can actually watch others playing. Language used in environments that contain plentiful clues to meaning is described a context-embedded (Cummins 1981a, 1981b), and these environments are generally thought to be "easier" for learners to navigate. Context-embedded or contextualized language use is evident in some types of school activities, as well. In a science demonstration, for example, as the teacher explains the steps in performing an experiment, students can actually watch the actions, tying the language to something in "the here and now."

Decontextualized or context-reduced language use, on the other hand, occurs in environments that provide few meaningful clues to the learner. There is little in the immediate environment (other than the language itself) that will help learners derive meaning from the language being used, and it is thus seen as "harder" for second language learners. Oral language that is decontextualized can be exemplified by telephone conversations, when a listener no longer can rely on facial expressions or gestures to infer meaning. Reading (especially in books with no pictures) requires that the learner depend strictly on the message conveyed through the words on the page. Lectures (such as those often given in the upper elementary grades, middle school, and high school) that deal with topics such as the American Revolution or the greenhouse effect, provide little in the way of nonlinguistic clues to support meaning.

For children who are learning English as a second language, the implications of such language variation are significant. While children may be able to deduce meaning from context-embedded language, the process of understanding and mastering decontextualized language use is much more difficult. Since much of school language once one moves beyond the earliest grades tends to be decontextualized, children learning English as a second language in school often find themselves lost in a world of meaningless words.

## Second Language Acquisition Myth #3: Once second language learners are able to speak reasonably fluently, their problems are likely to be over in school.

### Reality: The ability to speak a second language (especially in conversational settings) does not guarantee that a student will be able to use the language effectively in academic settings.

### Background/Overview

Do you remember what it was like to take a foreign language? You struggled with pronunciation and vocabulary, the conjugation of verb forms eluded you, the fight to make nouns and verbs (not to mention articles) agree seemed futile, your reading slowed to a snail's pace of translating word by painful word, and as your frustration level grew, you probably wondered, "Is it *really* worth it?" Now imagine the burden of having to cope with content area instruction in a subject like geometry or earth science at the same time. This is the challenge that LEP students face in school every day.

The content of communication—that is, what the language is about or relates to—is another variation that determines whether language is "easy" or "hard." Variation in content can result in different levels of cognitive demand on learners. Language used to communicate about objects and concrete concepts tends to place less of a cognitive load on learners than does language about complex notions or abstract ideas. Language that expresses what one already knows and understands is less cognitively demanding than that which teaches a new concept or principle.

In addition, researchers are now beginning to suggest that specific content domains (such as math; science, and history) are associated with specific varieties of language (Dale & Cuevas 1987; Kessler & Quinn 1987; King et al. 1987). The use of distinctive words, structures, and communicative functions has been found to vary with the particular content area being taught (e.g., the word *cabinet,* learned in a general context, refers to a cupboard; *cabinet* takes on a very different meaning in a social studies context, when used to refer to a group of presidential advisors).

It has been shown that school language becomes more complex and less contextualized in successively higher grades (Collier 1989; Cummins & Swain 1986). Thus, the ability to learn content area material becomes increasingly dependent on interaction with and mastery of the language connected to such material. The ability to demonstrate what one has learned also increasingly requires extensive use of oral and written forms of language. The academic consequences of such increased language demands on students are readily apparent. Careful planning of instruction is needed in order to help LEP students develop the decontextualized language skills they will need to master the cognitively demanding content in the higher grades.

## Second Language Acquisition Myth #4: Learning academic English is equally challenging for all second language learners.

### Reality: The challenge of learning English for school varies tremendously from learner to learner and depends on many factors.

### Background/Overview

Discussions of language learning in an academic environment must also take into account students' previous exposure to content in their first language. Studies show that children who have had formal academic preparation in a given content area in their first language usually make greater progress initially in academic content in the second language (Collier 1989; Cummins 1981b). Unfortunately, some of the children entering U.S. schools today are students who lack even basic academic skills in the first language; many come from countries torn by war or civil unrest and have seldom, if ever, seen the inside of a classroom. Some may be illiterate in their first language or come from a language background that does not have a written form. It is clear that for such students, learning English in an academic setting will be a much more challenging task than for their counterparts who have received adequate schooling and who are literate and performing on grade level in their first language.

## Second Language Acquisition Myth #5: If we focus on teaching the English language, learning in all areas will occur faster.

## Reality: Language learning is a developmental process; while learning a language will not occur in the absence of exposure to the language, increased exposure to the language (particularly in academic settings) does not guarantee quicker learning.

### Background/Overview

For schools, the bottom line of all the research on second language acquisition is probably embodied in the question, "How long does it take?" The answer is, "It depends." This answer is often seen as an unsatisfactory one by policymakers, in particular, who may try to legislate English language acquisition. The passage of California's Proposition 227 (also known as the Unz amendment), requiring that students be schooled exclusively in English, is an unfortunate case in point.

The fact is that the rate of second language acquisition (particularly in academic settings) is really a function of several variables. The age of students at the time of initial exposure to the second language, previous schooling in the first language, and the type of instruction provided in the second language—all influence the rate of L2 acquisition. Collier's (1989) synthesis of research on academic achievement in a second language offers the following generalizations drawn from an exhaustive review of the literature:

1. When students are schooled in two languages, with solid cognitive academic instruction provided in both the first and second language, they usually take from 4 to 7 years to reach national norms on standardized tests in reading, social studies and science, whereas their performance may reach national norms in as little as two years in mathematics and language arts

(when the skills being tested include spelling, punctuation, and simple grammar points).

2. Immigrants arriving at ages 8 to 12, with at least 2 years of schooling in their first language, take 5 to 7 years to reach the level of average performance by native speakers of English on standardized tests in reading, social studies and science when they are schooled exclusively in English after arrival. Their performance may reach national norms in as little as 2 years in mathematics and language arts.

3. Young arrivals with no schooling in their first language may take as long as 7 to 10 years to reach the average level of performance of native English speakers on standardized tests in reading, social studies and science.

4. Adolescent arrivals with no previous exposure to the second language who are not provided with an opportunity to continue academic work in their first language do not have enough time left in high school to make up the lost years of academic instruction. This is true both for adolescents with a good academic background and for those whose schooling has been limited or interrupted.

5. Consistent, uninterrupted cognitive academic development in all subjects throughout students' schooling is more important than the number of hours of instruction in the second language for successful academic achievement in the second language.

The generalizations drawn by Collier (1989) point out the complex nature of second language acquisition in an academic environment. They also help to explain why some LEP students seem to perform better than others. The variety of factors that influence a student's ability to master challenging subject matter while acquiring another language (proficiency in the first language, ability to read and write in the first language, and previous schooling in the first language) also help to point out one inescapable fact that seems to have eluded many school districts: Just learning English will not guarantee a student's academic success.

The length of time that LEP students appear to need in order to master language for academic purposes accounts for some of the confusion experienced by teachers working with such learners. Many LEP children puzzle their teachers with displays of relatively proficient English in social settings such as the playground and the cafeteria, where contextualized language skills are sufficient. When these students move back into the classroom, however, their teachers are sometimes heard to say, "I think he knows more than he's letting on. I hear him using English on the playground, and yet when it's time to do social studies, his English suddenly disappears. Is he trying to fool me into thinking that he doesn't understand so that he can get out of work?" Probably not. In other words, in many cases, children who have achieved modest levels of contextualized English proficiency find themselves "mainstreamed" or exited from support programs that are needed to help them continue the process of acquiring the decontextualized language skills they need to cope with higher order concepts that are language dependent. The disparity between children's linguistic capabilities in social settings compared with their capabilities in academic settings often results in children being asked to handle a larger linguistic load than they are ready to carry, thus falling behind in the "regular" classes in which they've been placed.

## Second Language Acquisition Myth #6: Students from Asian countries are better English language learners and more academically successful than students from Spanish-speaking backgrounds.

**Reality: Students from all language and cultural backgrounds are equally capable of learning English as a second language; academic success cannot be attributed to language or cultural background, but rather to a variety of social, emotional, intellectual, and academic factors.**

### Background/Overview

No discussion of language minority and LEP children would be complete without some mention of the relationship of academic performance to cultural affiliation. Scholars have long documented cultural differences that exist between students' homes and the school (Guthrie 1985; Heath 1983, 1986; Ogbu 1992; Scarcella 1989), suggesting that there are discontinuities that exist for many groups who are not part of the "mainstream middle class." While such discontinuities may create hardships for all groups, some groups clearly seem to experience more difficulty in making the transition from home to school than do others. This is particularly true for language minority students. Many educators have observed that some language minority students seem to perform better in U.S. schools than do others, and they point to Asian "whiz-kids" who top out on the SATs and win science fairs.

Ogbu and Matute-Bianchi (1986) have examined variability in the school performance of different linguistic minority groups around the world. While the specific linguistic minority groups that do well in school vary from country to country, each country appears to achieve success in schooling some groups, while other groups languish. In addition, there appears to be evidence that variability in performance is affected by the country in which a particular group finds itself. Such a group may do well in one country, but poorly in another. One example of such variable performance is the case of Korean students, who have been shown to perform quite poorly in schools in Japan, while doing quite well in schools in the United States (DeVos & Lee 1981).

Researchers speculate that variability in the performance of linguistic minority students may be partly explained by examining the connection between education and other societal institutions and events affecting minorities (Cummins 1989; Matute-Bianchi 1986; Ogbu & Matute-Bianchi 1986; Ogbu 1992). In addition, they suggest that the social perceptions and experiences of particular minority groups can affect the outcome of their children's schooling. Immigrant minorities and "caste-like" or indigenous minorities are two of the categories of minority groups that have been described (Ogbu & Matute-Bianchi 1986; Ogbu 1992; Ovando & Collier 1985). Let us say at the outset that it is important not to stereotype the behavior of any individual according to the categories, since within each category there is a wide range of adaptations to life in a given culture, and the designation of a particular group may change over time or in a particular context. The categories do help, however, to build a framework in which minority achievement can be better understood.

Immigrant minorities include groups that have moved more or less voluntarily to their new country for political, social, or economic reasons. Examples of such minorities in the United States are the Koreans (mentioned earlier), Japanese Americans, Cuban Americans, and Chinese Americans. Immigrants in the immigrant minority category tend not to evaluate their success in the new country by comparing themselves with elite members of the host society; their frame of reference is still in the country from which they emigrated. They compare themselves either with their peers in the "old country" or with peers in the immigrant community.

Education is an important investment for such immigrant groups because it is perceived as the key to advancement, particularly for their children. Immigrant children are taught to accept schools' rules for behavior and achievement; they learn to switch back and forth between two cultural frames of reference—that of the home and that of the school. Their ability to make these adjustments without feeling that they are losing their own culture enhances their ability to perform effectively in school.

Caste-like or indigenous minorities are minorities that have become incorporated into a society more or less permanently and involuntarily (through such processes as conquest, colonization, and slavery), then relegated to a menial status within the larger group (Ogbu & Matute-Bianchi 1986). For example, Koreans (mentioned earlier) who were originally sent to Japan as colonial subjects in forced labor, perform poorly in school there and function as a caste-like minority in that setting. Mexican Americans, Native Americans, and Puerto Ricans may be examples of such minority groups in the United States.

Caste-like minorities tend to believe that they cannot advance into the mainstream of society through individual efforts in school or by adopting the cultural beliefs and practices of the dominant group. As Ovando and Collier (1985, 270) point out, "There is a tendency in the United States for mainstream whites to perceive indigenous minorities as being non-American, even if they have been here for generations." The belief that they cannot make it leads these minorities to adopt survival strategies to cope with the conditions in which they find themselves and to make them distinct from the dominant group. Such strategies may eventually become cultural practices and beliefs in their own right, requiring their own norms, attitudes, and skills. These strategies might be incompatible with what is required for school success, and, thus, caste-like minorities may tend to experience the conflict of two opposing cultural frames of reference—one appropriate for the dominant group and one appropriate for minorities.

Caste-like minorities are reluctant to shift between the two frames because they perceive the frame of the dominant group as clearly inappropriate for them. Since schooling tends to be bound up with the ideals and practices of the majority group, it also tends to be seen as something that is less than appropriate for members of the minority group. Members of the minority community who try to behave like members of the majority community (i.e., learning English, striving for academic success and school credentials) may be ostracized by their peers. The dilemma for such minority students is that they must choose between two competing cultural frames: one that promotes school success and one that does not, but is considered appropriate for a good member of the minority group (Ogbu & Matute-Bianchi 1986; Ogbu 1992; Trueba 1984).

Schweers & Velez (1992) vividly illustrate these points as they describe the conflict that Puerto Ricans face when learning English on the island. In 1902, following the Spanish-American War, when Puerto Rico became an unincorporated territory of the United States, English was declared an offical language of equal status to Spanish. Shortly thereafter, English was imposed on the public school system, not only as a required subject, but also as the preferred language of instruction. Although the policy has changed dramatically since then (in 1992, Spanish was declared the sole official language of government on the island), English still enjoys great prestige among Puerto Ricans, who have held U.S. citizenship since 1917. English represents real political power, the language of the most powerful and influential country in the world, and to most Puerto Ricans is the *sine qua non* for professional advancement and economic security. Schweers and Velez (1992) point out, however, that there has been persistent resistance to the spread and use of English on the island of Puerto Rico throughout the course of this century, citing a 1992 poll that showed that although 83% of respondents favored official status for both English and Spanish on the island, only 20% of the population was reported to be functionally bilingual. As Schweers and Velez (1992, 14) explain, "Many Puerto Ricans resist learning English precisely because of the beliefs and advantages that support its presence on the island."

While the relationship between culture and schooling is one that is extremely complex, one fact again becomes starkly apparent: Although learning English is essential for success in school for all linguistic minority students, the acquisition of English alone in no way guarantees that every linguistic minority student will succeed academically. The question of school achievement is not solely a linguistic one; the cultural messages received by children from both the school and the larger society may influence their feelings about school as well as their feelings about themselves in relation to school. The way in which children view themselves is connected to the way schools (and the larger community) view them.

# What's Going On?

## John Russell Rickford and Russell John Rickford

### EDITOR'S INTRODUCTION

John Rickford, an internationally recognized scholar on African-American Vernacular English, teamed up with his son Russell, a journalist to write a fascinating history of the use of Black English in literature, the arts, religion, and everyday conversation in their book, *Spoken Soul*. In this excerpt, they explore America's relationship with Black English, including the furor around the use of Ebonics as a springboard to teaching Standard English.

> *For what shall it profit a man, if he shall gain the whole world and lose his own soul?*
>
> —Mark 8:36

> *SOUL [sōl] 1. The animating and vital principle in humans . . . 5. The central or integral part; the vital core . . . 9. A sense of ethnic pride among Black people and especially African Americans, expressed in areas such as language, social customs, religion and music.*
>
> —*The American Heritage Dictionary of the English Language*
> (4th edition, 2000)

"Spoken Soul" was the name that Claude Brown, author of *Manchild in the Promised Land,* coined for black talk. In a 1968 interview he waxed eloquent in its praise, declaring that the informal speech or vernacular of many African Americans "possesses a pronounced lyrical quality which is frequently incompatible to any music other than that ceaselessly and relentlessly driving rhythm that flows from poignantly spent lives." A decade later, James Baldwin, legendary author of *The Fire Next Time,* described black English as "this passion, this skill . . . this incredible music."

Now, at the beginning of the twenty-first century, the Spoken Soul these writers exalted is battered by controversy, its very existence called into question. Though belittled and denied, however, it lives on authentically. In homes, schools, and churches, on streets, stages, and the airwaves, you can hear soul spoken every day. Most African Americans—including millions who, like Brown and Baldwin,

*Source:* From *Spoken Soul: The Story of Black English.* John Russell Rickford and Russell John Rickford. Copyright 2000 by John Wiley and Sons, Inc. Reprinted by permission of publisher.

are fluent speakers of Standard English—still invoke Spoken Soul as we have for hundreds of years, to laugh or cry, to preach and praise, to shuck and jive, to sing, to rap, to shout, to style, to express our individual personas and our ethnic identities (" 'spress yo'self!" as James Brown put it), to confide in and commiserate with friends, to chastise, to cuss, to act, to act the fool, to get by and get over, to pass secrets, to make jokes, to mock and mimic, to tell stories, to reflect and philosophize, to create authentic characters and voices in novels, poems, and plays, to survive in the streets, to relax at home and recreate in playgrounds, to render our deepest emotions and embody our vital core.

The fact is that most African Americans *do* talk differently from whites and Americans of other ethnic groups, or at least most of us can when we want to. And the fact is that most Americans, black and white, know this to be true.

In this book, we will explore the vibrancy and vitality of Spoken Soul as an expressive instrument in American literature, religion, entertainment, and everyday life. We will detail the features and history of Spoken Soul. We will then return to the Ebonics firestorm that flared up at century's end, considering its spark (the Oakland, California, School District's resolutions and their educational significance), its fuel (media coverage), and its embers (Ebonics "humor"). In the final chapter we will reflect on the vernacular's role in American life and society, and seek the truth about the dizzying love-hate relationship with black talk that is as old and new as the nation itself. Who needs this information and insight? We all do, because Spoken Soul is an inescapable vessel of American history, literature, society, and popular culture. Regardless of its status, we need to come to terms with this beloved and beleaguered language.

In coming to terms with Spoken Soul, what it is and why it matters, the first thing to know is how high it ranks in the esteem of its maestros. Echoing the sentiments of Claude Brown and James Baldwin, Nobel Prize-winning author Toni Morrison insisted in 1981 that one distinctive ingredient of her fiction was

> the language, only the language. . . . It is the thing that black people love so much—the saying of words, holding them on the tongue, experimenting with them, playing with them. It's a love, a passion. Its function is like a preacher's: to make you stand up out of your seat, make you lose yourself and hear yourself. The worst of all possible things that could happen would be to lose that language. There are certain things I cannot say without recourse to my language. It's terrible to think that a child with five different present tenses comes to school

to be faced with books that are less than his own language. And then to be told things about his language, which is him, that are sometimes permanently damaging. He may never know the etymology of Africanisms in his language, not even know that "hip" is a real word or that "the dozens" meant something. This is a really cruel fallout of racism. I know the standard English. I want to use it to help restore the other language, the lingua franca.

June Jordan, celebrated essayist and poet, in 1985 identified "three qualities of Black English—the presence of life, voice and clarity—that testify to a distinctive Black value system." Jordan, then a professor at Stony Brook College, chided her students for their uneasiness about the colloquial language in Alice Walker's novel *The Color Purple,* and went on to teach them about the art of the vernacular.

The second thing to bear in mind is that between the 1960s and 1990s, a dramatic shift occurred. By the end of the 1990s, we could find scarcely a spokesman or spokeswoman for the race who had anything flattering to say about Spoken Soul. In response to the Oakland school board's December 18, 1996, resolution to recognize "Ebonics" as the primary language of African American students in that California district, poet Maya Angelou told the *Wichita Eagle* that she was "incensed" and found the idea "very threatening." NAACP president Kweisi Mfume denounced the measure as "a cruel joke," and although he later adopted a friendlier stance, the Reverend Jesse Jackson on national television initially called it "an unacceptable surrender, borderlining on disgrace." Jackson found himself curiously aligned with Ward Connerly, the black University of California regent whose ultimately successful efforts to end affirmative action on University of California campuses and in the state as a whole Jackson had vigorously opposed. Connerly called the Oakland proposal "tragic," and went on to argue, "These are not kids who came from Africa last year. . . . These are kids that have had every opportunity to acclimate themselves to American society, and they have gotten themselves into this trap of speaking this language—this slang, really, that people can't understand. Now we're going to legitimize it."

Other African Americans from different ends of the ideological spectrum fell into step. Black conservative academic and author Shelby Steele characterized the Oakland proposal as just another "gimmick" to enhance black self-esteem, while black liberal academic and author Henry Louis Gates Jr., chairman of Afro-American Studies at Harvard, dismissed it as "obviously stupid and ridiculous."

Former Black Panther Eldridge Cleaver agreed, as did entertainer Bill Cosby.

The virtual consensus blurred political lines among white pundits as well. Conservative talk-show host Rush Limbaugh assailed the Ebonics resolution, while leading Republican William Bennett, former U.S. secretary of education, described it as "multiculturalism gone haywire." Leading liberal Mario Cuomo, former governor of New York, called it a "bad mistake," and Secretary of Education Richard Riley, a member of President Clinton's Democratic cabinet, declared that Ebonics programs would not be eligible for federal bilingual education dollars, maintaining that "elevating black English to the status of a language is not the way to raise standards of achievement in our schools and for our students." At the state level, anti-Ebonics legislation was introduced both by Republicans, such as Representative Mark Ogles of Florida, and by Democrats, such as Georgia state senator Ralph Abernathy III.

Millions of other people across the United States and around the world rushed in to express their vociferous condemnation of Ebonics and the proposal to take it into account in schools. ("Ebonics" in fact quickly became a stand-in for the language variety and for Oakland's proposal, so the recurrent question "What do you think about Ebonics?" elicited reactions to both topics.) Animated conversations sprang up in homes and workplaces and at holiday gatherings, as well as on television and radio programs, in letters to the editor, and on electronic bulletin boards that were deluged after the Oakland decision. According to *Newsweek,* "An America Online poll about Ebonics drew more responses than the one asking people whether O. J. Simpson was guilty."

The vast majority of those America Online responses were not just negative. They were caustic. Ebonics was vilified as "disgusting black street slang," "incorrect and substandard," "nothing more than ignorance," "lazy English," "bastardized English," "the language of illiteracy," and "this utmost ridiculous made-up language." And Oakland's resolution, almost always misunderstood as a proposal to teach Ebonics instead of as a plan to use Ebonics as a springboard to Standard English, elicited superlatives of disdain, disbelief, and derision:

"Idiocy of the highest form." (December 21, 1996)

"Man, 'ubonics will take me far back to de jungo!" (December 21, 1996)

"I think it be da dumbest thing I'd eber heard be." (December 23, 1996)

These comments, dripping with scorn, are far removed from the tributes that Brown, Baldwin, Morrison, and Jordan had paid to the African American vernacular in earlier decades. Why the about-face? What had happened to transform Spoken Soul from an object of praise to an object of ridicule?

For one thing, the focus was different. The Ebonics controversy of the 1990s was about the use of the vernacular in school, while the earlier commentaries were more about the expressiveness of the vernacular itself in literature and informal settings.

Moreover, the general misconception that the Oakland school board intended to teach and accept Ebonics rather than English in the classroom—perhaps assisted by the resolution's vague wording and the media's voracious coverage—made matters worse. Most of the fuming and fulminating about Ebonics stemmed from the mistaken belief that it was to replace Standard English as a medium of instruction and a target for success.

This misunderstanding was not new, nor was it unique to the United States. The 1979 ruling by Michigan Supreme Court justice Charles Joiner that the negative attitudes of Ann Arbor teachers toward the home language of their black students represented a barrier to the students' academic success was similarly misinterpreted as a plan "to teach ghetto children in 'black English'" (in the words of columnist Carl Rowan). And from the 1950s on, proposals by Caribbean linguists to take students' Creole English into account to improve the teaching of Standard English (in Jamaica, Trinidad, and Guyana) have been similarly misinterpreted and condemned as attempts to "settle" for Creole instead of English.

But the backlash against Ebonics in the 1990s was certainly fueled by new elements, and by considerations unique to the contemporary United States. There is more concern today about what we have in common as Americans, including English. Some who thrashed Ebonics in Internet forums voiced this concern:

There seems to be a movement with the cultural diversity, bilingualism, and quota-oriented affirmative action campaigns to balkanize the country and build walls between people and dissolve the concept of being an American. This Ebonics . . . will . . . keep a segment of the black community in ghetto mode. (December 20, 1996)

As in this case, critiques of Ebonics were often couched in larger objections to bilingual education, affirmative action, and any measure that seemed to offer special "advantages" to ethnic minorities and women—despite the centuries of disadvantage these groups have endured. A month before Oakland passed its Ebonics resolution, Californians endorsed Proposition 209, outlawing affirmative action in education and employment, and in June 1998, they approved Proposition 227, prohibiting most forms of bilingual education. Many states passed English-only legislation in the 1980s and 1990s, and lawmakers continue to lobby for similar legislation at the federal level.

The 1990s also saw internal divisions within the African American population—by socioeconomic class, generation, and gender—grow more pronounced than they had been in the 1960s. This accounts for some of the stinging criticism of Ebonics that originated "within the race." While the 1960s featured "*The* March on Washington," a united protest by African Americans and others against racial and economic inequality, blacks in the 1990s participated in separate "Million Man" and "Million Woman" marches, and competing "Million Youth" marches. While the proportion of African Americans earning more than $100,000 (in 1989 dollars) tripled between 1969 and 1989 (from 0.3 percent to about 1 percent of all African American households), the proportion earning below $15,000 remained the same (about 43 percent of all African American households), and the mean income actually dropped in the interim (from $9,300 to $8,520). When we consider that Ebonics pronunciation and grammar are used most frequently by poor and working-class African Americans, and that it was primarily the comments of middle- and upper-middle class African Americans heard over the airwaves and read on the Internet in 1996 and 1997, their disdain is not surprising.

What's more, the distance between the younger hip-hop generation and older African American generations—marked by the politics of dress, music, and slang—has in various ways also grown more stark in the 1990s. Some middle-aged and elderly black folk have increasingly come to view baggy-jeans-and-boot-wearing, freestylin' youth as hoodlums who are squandering the gains of the civil rights movement. Not entirely coincidentally, most of the publicly aired comments on Ebonics came from black baby boomers (now in their forties and fifties) or older African Americans. When discussing the slang of hip-hop youth—which they (mis)identified with Ebonics—they often bristled with indignation. So did others, of other races, who vented their prejudices quite openly.

While today's debate is charged with new elements, the question of the role of the vernacular in African American life and literature has been a source of debate among African Americans for more than a century. When Paul Laurence Dunbar was establishing his reputation as a dialect poet in the late 1800s, James Weldon Johnson, who wrote the lyrics to "Lift Every Voice and Sing" (long hailed as "The Negro National Anthem"), chose to render the seven African American sermons of *God's Trombones* in standard English because he felt that the dialect of "old-time" preachers might pigeonhole the book. During the Harlem Renaissance of the 1920s, a similar debate raged among the black intelligentsia, with Langston Hughes endorsing and exemplifying the use of vernacular, and Alain Locke and others suggesting that African Americans ought to put the quaintness of the idiom behind them and offer the world a more "refined" view of their culture. These enduring attitudes reflect the. attraction-repulsion dynamic, the oscillation between black and white (or mainstream) poles that W. E. B. Du Bois defined a century ago as "double-consciousness."

This century marks a watershed for the vernacular. One purpose of this book is to help rescue Spoken Soul from the negativity and ignorance in which it became mired during the Ebonics debate, and to correct the many misconceptions people have about black talk. Another is to offer a fresh way to think and talk about Spoken Soul that does justice to its persistence and potency.

Like virtually everyone else, we acknowledge that African Americans must master Standard English, corporate English, mainstream English, the language of wider communication, or whatever you want to call the variety of English needed for school, formal occasions, and success in the business world. But we also believe that Ebonics, African American Vernacular English, Black English, Spoken Soul, or whatever you want to call the informal variety spoken by many black people, plays an essential, valuable role in our lives and in the life of the larger society to which we all belong.

The reasons for the persistence and vitality of Spoken Soul are manifold: it marks black identity; it is the symbol of a culture and a life-style that have had and continue to have a profound impact on American popular life; it retains the associations of warmth and closeness for the many blacks who first learn it from their mothers and fathers and other family members; it expresses camaraderie and solidarity among friends; it establishes rapport among blacks; and it serves as a creative and expressive instrument in the present and as a vibrant link with this nation's past.

If we lost all of that in the heady pursuit of Standard English and the world of opportunities it offers, we would indeed have lost our soul. We are not convinced that African Americans want to abandon "down-home" speech in order to become one-dimensional speakers. Nor—to judge from the ubiquity of the distinctive linguistic style of African American music, literature, and popular culture—do whites and other people in this country and around the world want to see it abandoned either, quiet as that viewpoint is kept. Certainly it is not necessary to abandon Spoken Soul to master Standard English, any more than it is necessary to abandon English to learn French, or to deprecate jazz to appreciate classical music.

Moreover, suggesting, as some do, that we abandon Spoken Soul and cleave only to Standard English is like proposing that that we play only the white keys of a piano. The fact is that for many of our most beautiful melodies, we need both the white keys and the black, in the same way that, in the Chinese dualistic philosophy, the *yin* is as essential to the whole as the *yang*. Bear in mind that language is an inescapable element in almost everyone's daily life, and an integral element of human identity. If for that and no other reason, we would all do well to heed the still-evolving truth of the black language experience. That truth promises to help us confront one of the most critical questions of our day: Can one succeed in the wider world of economic and social power without surrendering one's distinctive identity? We hope to transform the conventional wisdom.

# A Lot of Talk About Nothing

## Shirley Brice Heath

### EDITOR'S INTRODUCTION

Shirley Brice Heath's work builds upon the studies of researchers like Labov, emphasizing the logic governing language styles of different social, economic, and cultural groups. But her work was also groundbreaking in the ways she clearly articulated how schools are biased toward certain language patterns, ignoring the language strengths of students who aren't from mainstream cultures. This article presents findings from her landmark study *Ways with Words*. In the interview that follows, she talks further about the influence of this work on teachers and her own later studies of language and culture.

Inside a third-grade classroom described by the principal as a class of "low achievers," several pairs of children are working over tape recorders in dialogues with each other. One small group of children is dressed in costumes performing "Curious George" scenes for a few kindergartners who are visiting. Yet another group is preparing illustrations for a story told by one of their classmates and now being heard on tape as they talk about why their drawings illustrate the words they hear. A lot of talk about nothing? Why are these children who presumably lack basic skills in language arts not spending their time with obvious instruction from the teacher in reading, writing and listening?

These are students in the classroom of a teacher-researcher who has adapted information about the oral and written language experiences of these children at home into a new language arts curriculum for school. She has developed for her children a program in which they spend as much of the day as possible talking—to each other and the teacher, and to fifth- and sixth-graders who come into the class one-half hour each day to read to small groups. This teacher has 30 children and no aides; she enlisted the help of fifth- and sixth-grade teachers who were willing to have some of their students write stories for the younger children and read to them several days of each week. The kindergarten teacher helps out by sending a few of her children for the third-graders to read to each week.

Talk in the classroom is about personal experiences, stories, expository textbook materials and, perhaps most important, about their own and others' talk. Their teacher gives no reading or writing task which is not surrounded by talk about the content knowledge behind the task and the kinds of language skills—oral and written—needed to tackle the task.

Since the beginning of the year, the teacher has asked visitors from the community into her class to talk about their

---

*Source:* "A Lot of Talk About Nothing" by S. B. Heath, 1983, *Language Arts, 60* (8), pp. 39–48. Copyright 1983 by the National Council of Teachers of English. Reprinted with permission.

ways of talking and to explain what they read and write at home and at work. The children have come to think of themselves as language "detectives," listening and learning to describe the talk of others. Grocery clerks have to use many politeness terms, and the questions they ask most often of customers require only a yes or no answer. On the other hand, guides at the local nature museum talk in "long paragraphs," describing what is around them and usually asking questions only at the end of one of their descriptions. The children have also learned to analyze their talk at home, beginning early in the year with a simple record of the types of questions they hear asked at home, and moving later in the year to interviews with their parents about the kinds of talking, reading and writing they do at their jobs.

The teacher in this classroom comments on her own talk and the language of textbooks, of older students, and of the third-graders themselves during each day. "Show and tell" time, usually reserved for only first-graders, occurs each day in this class, under the supervision of a committee of students who decide each week whether those who participate in this special time of the day will: (1) narrate about an experience they or someone else has had, (2) describe an event or object without including themselves or another animate being, or (3) read from their diary or journal for a particular day. The children use terms such as *narrative, exposition,* and *diary* or *journal* with ease by the end of the year. Increasingly during the year, the children use "show and tell" time to talk, not about their own direct experiences, but about content areas of their classroom. Also by the end of the year, the children are using this special time of the day for presenting skits about a social studies or science unit. They have found that the fifth- and sixth-graders can offer assistance on these topics, and planning such a presentation guarantees the attention of the upper classmen. By the end of the year, most of these children score above grade level on reading tests, and they are able to write stories, as well as paragraphs of exposition on content areas with which they feel comfortable in their knowledge. This is clearly no longer a class of "low achievers."

## TEACHERS AS RESEARCHERS

All of these ideas sound like pedagogical practices that many good teachers bring intuitively to their instruction. What was different about the motivations of this third-grade teacher for approaching language arts in these ways? The teacher described here was one of a group of teacher-researchers who cooperated with me for several years during the 1970s. I worked as an ethnographer, a daily participant and observer in homes and communities similar to those of the children in their classrooms, studying the ways in which the children learned to use oral and written language. As I studied the children at home, the teachers focused on their own language uses at home and in the classroom. We brought our knowledge together for comparison and as the baseline data from which to consider new methods and approaches in language arts.

We do not need educational research to tell us that different types of attention spans, parental support systems, and peer pressures can create vast differences among children in the same classroom, school, or community. But what of more subtle features of background differences, such as the amount and kind of talk addressed by adults to children and solicited from children? How can teachers and researchers work together to learn more about children's language experiences at home? And what can this knowledge mean for classroom practice?

For nearly a decade, living and working in three communities located within a few miles of each other in the southeastern part of the United States, I collected information on ways in which the children of these communities learned to use language: (1) Roadville is a white working-class community, (2) Trackton is a black working-class community in which many of the older members have only recently left work as sharecroppers on nearby farms, (3) the townspeople, black and white residents of a cluster of mainstream, school-oriented neighborhoods, are school teachers, local business owners, and executives of the textile mills.

Children from the three groups respond differently to school experiences. Roadville children are successful in the first years of the primary grades. Most Trackton children are not successful during this period, and only a few begin in the higher primary grades to move with adequate success through their classes. Most of the mainstream children of the townspeople, black and white, are successful in school and obtain a high school diploma with plans to go on to higher education. Children from backgrounds similar to those of these three groups make up the majority of the students in many regions of the southeastern United States. They bring to their classrooms different patterns of learning and using oral and written language, and their patterns of academic achievement vary greatly.

Intuitively, most teachers are aware of the different language background experiences children bring to school, but few means exist for providing teachers with information about these differences and their implications for classroom practice. Recent development of the notion of "teacher-as-researcher" has begun to help bridge the long-standing gap between researcher and teacher. This approach pairs the roles of teacher and researcher in a cooperative search for answers to questions raised by the teacher about what is happening in the classroom and why. Answering *why* questions more often than not calls for knowledge about the background experiences of both children and teachers. Thus, researcher working with teacher can help bridge yet another gap—that between the classroom and the homes of students.

Throughout most of the decade of the 1970s, I worked in the Piedmont Carolinas with teachers in several districts as research partners. Together, we addressed the questions teachers raised during the sometimes tumultuous early years of desegregation and ensuing shifts of curricular and testing policies. These teachers accepted the fact that language was fundamental to academic achievement, and their primary concerns related to how they could help children learn to use oral and written language in ways that would bring successful classroom experiences. They asked hard questions of language research. Why were some children seemingly unable to answer straightforward questions? Why were some students able to give elaborate directions and tell fantastic stories on the playground, but unable to respond to assignments calling for similar responses about lesson materials? Why did some children who had achieved adequate success in their first two or three years of school begin to fail in the upper primary grades?

In the 1960s, social scientists had described the language habits of groups of youngsters who were consistently failing to achieve academic excellence. The teachers with whom I worked were familiar with these studies, which had been carried out primarily in black urban areas. Most accepted the fact that children who spoke a nonstandard variety of English had learned a rule-governed language system and, moreover, that these students reflected learned patterns of "logic," considerable facility in handling complicated forms of oral discourse, and adeptness in shifting styles. But knowing this information about language learned at home did not answer the kinds of questions noted above about classroom performance. Neither did it provide for development of improved classroom materials and practices.

## ETHNOGRAPHY OF COMMUNICATION

Late in the 1970s, as some language researchers tried to describe the contexts in which children of different cultures learned to use language, they turned to ethnographic methods. Participating and observing over many months and

even years in the daily lives of the group being studied, these researchers, who were often anthropologists, focused on oral and written language uses. My work in Roadville, Trackton, and among the townspeople centered on the children of these groups as they learned the ways of acting, believing and valuing around them in their homes and communities. Following the suggestions of anthropologist Dell Hymes, who first proposed in 1964 that ethnographers focus on communication, I lived and worked within these three groups to describe where, when, to whom, how, and with what results children were socialized as talkers, readers and writers. The three communities—located only a few miles apart—had radically different ways of using language and of seeing themselves in communication with their children.

Roadville parents believe they have to teach their children to talk, and they begin their task by talking with infants, responding to their initial sounds as words. They respond with full sentences, varying their tone of voice and emphasis, and affectionately urging infants to turn their heads in the direction of the speaker. As they talk to their infants and young children, they label items in the environment, and as children begin to talk, adults ask many teaching questions: "Where's your nose?" "Can you find Daddy's shoes?" Adults fictionalize their youngsters in talk about them: "He's a little cowboy; see those boots? See that cowboy strut?" Parents read to their children and ask them to name items in books, answer questions about the book's contents and, as they get older, to sit quietly listening to stories read to them. Parents buy coloring and follow-the-number books for their children and tutor them in staying within the lines and coloring items appropriately. All of these habits relate to school practices, and they are transferred to the early years of reading and writing in school. Yet, by the fourth grade many of these children seem to find the talking, reading and writing tasks in school foreign, and their academic achievement begins to decline.

In nearby Trackton, adults immerse their children in an ongoing stream of talk from extended family members and a wide circle of friends and neighbors. Children become the responsibility of all members of the community, and from birth they are kept in the center of most adult activities, including eating, sleeping, or playing. Adults talk about infants and young children, and as they do so, they fictionalize them and often exaggerate their behaviors and physical features. They nickname children and play teasing games with them. They ask young children for specific information which is not known to adults: "Where'd that come from?" "You want what?" By the time they are toddlers, these children begin to tell stories, recounting events or describing objects they have seen. Adults stop and listen to their stories occasionally, but such stories are most often addressed to other children who challenge, extend, tease, or build from the youngster's tales. By about 2, children begin to enter ongoing conversations by actively attracting adults' attention with some physical gesture and then making a request, registering a complaint, or reporting an event. Very quickly, these children are accepted as communicating members of the group, and adults respond directly to them as conversational partners.

Most of these children first go to school with enthusiasm, but by the end of the first half of the first grade, many are coming home with reports that their teacher scolds them for talking too much and working too little. By the third grade, many Trackton children have established a record of failures which often they do not break in the rest of their school careers.

After hearing from me how children of these communities learned to use language, some of their teachers agreed to work with me to study either their own uses of language with their preschoolers at home or those of their mainstream friends. They found that when talking to very young infants, they asked questions, simplified their sentences, used special words and changed their tone of voice. Moreover, since most of these mainstream mothers did not work outside the home while their children were very young, they spent long hours each day alone with their pre-schoolers as their primary conversational partners. They arranged many outings, usually with other mothers through voluntary associations, such as their church groups or local social memberships.

These teachers' findings about mainstreamers' uses of language with their pre-schoolers indicated that they and the Roadville parents had many language socialization habits in common. Parents in both communities talked to their children and focused their youngsters' attention at an early age on labels, pictures in books, and educational toys. Both groups played with their children and participated in planned outings and family recreation with them. Yet mainstream children and Roadville children fared very differently in their progress through the middle primary grades.

A close look at the home habits of these two groups indicated that a major difference lay in the amount of running narrative or ongoing commentary in which mainstream parents immersed their young children. As these youngsters pass their first birthday, mothers and other adults who are part of their daily network begin to provide a running commentary on events and items surrounding the child. In these commentaries, adults tell the child what is happening: "Mummy's going to get her purse, and then we're going to take a ride. Mummy's got to go to the post office." As soon as the child begins to talk, adults solicit these kinds of running commentaries: they ask children what they are doing with their toys, what they did when they were at someone else's house, and what they had to eat on a trip to the grocery store. These requests for running descriptions and cumulative accounts of past actions provide children in these families with endless hours of practice of all the sentence-level features necessary to produce successful narratives or recounts of experiences.

In using their own experiences as data, children begin their developmental progression of story conventions and narrative structures which they will be asked to replay in school from the first day of school through their college courses. They learn either to use an existing animate being or to create a fantastic one as the central actor in their stories; they take these actors through events in which they may meet obstacles on their way to a goal. The scripts of the stories that the children have heard read to them and the narratives that have surrounded them and storied their own and others' experiences are replayed with different actors and slightly different settings. Gradually, children learn to open and close stories, to give them a setting and movement of time, and occasionally, even to sum up the meaning of the story in a moralistic pronouncement ("He shouldn't have gone without his mother"). Some children move from linking a collection of events related to one another only by their immediacy of experience for the child to tying a story together by incorporating a central point, a constant goal or direction, and a point of view which may not be that of the child as experiencer and narrator.

When children are very young toddlers, parents talk of and ask children about events of the here-and-now: the immediate tasks of eating, getting dressed, and playing with a particular toy or person. Of older toddlers, adults increasingly ask questions about events that occurred in the past—tasks, settings, and events that the child is expected to recount from memory. These recountings are, however, then interpreted by adults or older siblings in a future frame: "Do you want to go again?" "Do you think Billy's mother will be able to fix the broken car?" Questioners ask children to express their views about future events and to link past occurrences with what will come in the future.

In many ways, all of this is "talk about nothing," and adults and older siblings in these mainstream households model and elicit these kinds of narratives without being highly conscious of their having a didactic purpose or a heavily positive transfer value to school activities. Yet when teacher-researchers examined closely the instructional situations of the classrooms into which these children usually go, they found that, from first-grade reading circles to upper-primary social studies group work, the major activity is producing some sort of commentary on events or objects. In the early primary years, teachers usually request commentary in the form of labels or names of attributes of items or events ("What did the boy in our story find on his walk?"). Later, the requests are for descriptive commentary ("Who are some community helpers? What kinds of jobs do they do for us?"). Gradually the requests are mixed and students have to learn when it is appropriate to respond with labels or features (brief names or attributes of events or objects), fantastic stories, straightforward descriptions, or interpretations in which they comment on the outcome of events, the relative merits of objects, or the internal states of characters.

## A CLOSER LOOK

On the surface, these summaries of the early language socialization of the children from these three communities support a commonly held idea about links between language at home and at school: the more parents talk to their children, the more likely children are to succeed in school. Yet the details of the differences and similarities across these three communities suggest that this correlation is too simple. Trackton children hear and take part in far more talk around them than the children of either Roadville or the townspeople. Yet, for them, more talk does not have a positive transfer value to the current, primary-level practices of the school. Roadville children have less talk addressed to them than the townspeople's children. Yet, from an early age, they are helped to focus on labels and features of items and events. They are given books and they are read to by parents who buy educational toys for their children and spend many hours playing with their toddlers. As the children grow older, these parents involve their children in handicrafts, home building projects, and family recreational activities such as camping and fishing. Both Trackton and Roadville parents have strong faith in schooling as a positive value for their children, and they believe success in school will help their children get jobs better than those they have held as adults. Yet, neither Roadville nor Trackton children manage to achieve the same patterns of sustained academic success children of townspeople achieve with relatively little apparent effort. Why?

A primary difference seems to be the amount of "talk about nothing" with which the townspeople surround their children and into which they socialize their young. Through their running narratives, which begin almost at the birth of the child, they seemingly focus the attention of their young

on objects and events while they point out verbally the labels and features of those that the child should perceive and later talk about. It is as though, in the drama of life, these parents freeze scenes and parts of scenes repeatedly throughout each day. Within the frame of a single scene, they focus the child's attention, sort out labels to name, and give the child ordered turns for sharing talk about these labels and the properties of the objects or events to which they refer; adult and child thus jointly narrate descriptions of scenes. Through this consistent focus, adults pull out some of the stimuli in the array surrounding the child and make these stand still for cooperative examination and narration between parent and child. Later occurrences of the same event or object are identified by adults who call the child's attention to similarities and differences. Thus, townspeople's children are not left on their own to see these relations between two events or to explore ways of integrating something in a new context to its old context. These children learn to attend to items both in real life and in books, both in and out of their usual locations, as they practice throughout their pre-school years running narratives with adults.

In much of their talk, mainstream adults ask: "What do you call that?" "Do you remember how to say the name of that?" Thus, children are alerted to attend to the particulars to talk about talk: names, ways of retelling information, and ways of linking what one has told with something that has gone before. Thus, mainstreamers' children hear a lot of talk about talk and are forced to focus on not only the features and names of the world around them, but also on their ways of communicating about that world. From the earliest days of their infancy, these habits are modeled repeatedly for them, and as soon as they learn to talk, they are called upon to practice similar verbal habits. Day in and day out during their pre-school years, they hear and practice the kinds of talk in which they will display successful learning in school.

The teacher in the third-grade classroom described at the beginning of this essay recognized that her students needed intense and frequent occasions to learn and practice those language uses they had not acquired at home. She therefore created a classroom that focused on talk—all kinds of talk. The children labeled, learned to name the features of everyday items and events, told stories, described their own and others' experiences, and narrated skits, puppet shows, and slide exhibits.

Many classrooms include such activities for portions of the day or week; others provide some of these activities for some children. A critical difference in the case given here, however, and one driven by a perspective gained from being part of a research team, was the amount of talk about talk in this classroom. School-age children are capable of—and can be quite proficient at—stepping back from and commenting upon their own and others' activities, *if* the necessary skills are modeled and explicated. In this classroom, and in others which drew from ethnographic data on the home life of their students, teachers and visitors to the classroom called attention to the ways they used language: how they asked questions, showed politeness, got what they wanted, settled arguments, and told funny stories. With early and intensive classroom opportunities to surround learning with many different kinds of talk and much talk about talk, children from homes and communities whose uses of language do not match those of the school *can* achieve academic success. A frequently heard comment, "Talk is cheap," is, in these days of bankrupt school districts and economic cutbacks, perhaps worth a closer examination—for more reasons than one.

# Crawling on the Bones of What We Know: An Interview with Shirley Brice Heath

## Brenda Miller Power

In talking with Shirley Brice Heath, you realize that Heath accomplishes more in a day than most of us manage in a week. A faculty member at Stanford University since 1980, Heath's study *Ways with Words: Language, Life and Work in Communities and Classrooms* is recognized as one of the most important language research projects of all time. A 10-year qualitative longitudinal study of differences in language among lower-income whites, middle-income blacks and whites, and lower-income blacks in the Piedmont range, *Ways with Words* (Cambridge University Press, 1983) demolished some long-held axioms about language norms. The study was awarded the David Russell Research Award from the National Council of Teachers of English in 1984. Heath has received many other awards and accolades for her research, including the prestigious MacArthur Fellowship in 1984.

On the day we chatted, it was 8 p.m. Heath's time. Heath had just finished emotional goodbyes with her freshman English students after the last class of the quarter. Earlier in the day, she had read through all the applications for an English department position on her faculty. Heath had also found time that day to send out some ethics guidelines for youth reporting to hundreds of newspaper editors across the country. Loose ends from her just-completed research trip to a rare-book library in Boston were tied up, and plans for a conference and museum display in England she is coordinating were developed. What you realize in talking to Heath is that she not only uses the full 24 hours in her workday, she has more fun in the process than most of us manage in a month of Sundays!

What this interview also reveals is Heath's heartfelt commitment to teaching. While most researchers of her stature have long since given up most of the daily practice of teaching, Heath finds herself in the classroom 4 days a week, working with the youngest students on the Stanford campus. After more than 30 years in the field, Heath still provides fresh insights into all of the possibilities for language research in schools and communities. And she sees these possibilities through a teacher's eyes.

*Brenda Power: Can you tell me what led you into language research?*

*Shirley Brice Heath:* I think what got me most interested in language was both the gentle gift and curse of where and how I grew up. My parents weren't around very much, so I lived with foster families and a grandmother in a mostly black area for much of my early life. I grew up around children who were speaking varieties of English, so I grew up speaking these varieties. I think southern African-American vernacular was my first dialect. My grandmother would also shift across these dialects. So, I had an intrinsic interest in language, but no education whatsoever. I grew up in southwestern Virginia in a corner of the tobacco growing area of the state. The nearest town was about 60 miles away. There wasn't anyone around with a sophistication about language; people just knew how to communicate.

Then I began teaching when I was in college. The natural thing for me to do was to begin to teach about aspects of language. So that's what I began doing, teaching English as a second language to so-called "mentally retarded" kids in California. They weren't mentally retarded, they were Spanish-speaking! I have continued these interests in English as a second language and dialect work all my life.

*BP: I was just rereading the first section of* Ways with Words *where you talk about your research process. It was interesting thinking of you as a beginning language researcher. I couldn't help but connect your work with the process of teachers doing language research in their classrooms. It seems so natural the way you merged your life with your research interests.*

*SH:* It's been quite curious to me that no one ever looks at *Ways with Words* as an illustration of teacher research. From my point of view, those teachers that I learned from were some of the best researchers I ever worked with. They're not seen as teacher researchers in the way we typically use that term today. I think that for me, as it was for many women before the present generation, a lot of learning to teach was learning by intuition. We were always working in new situations, and those were the situations that for the most part didn't come up in the textbook cases. We had learned our Thorndike, and we learned our William S. Gray, and all the things you could teach in textbook cases. But a lot of what you did in the classroom was based on intuition. As we know now, many women went into teaching because they were highly creative, highly professional, and highly committed to getting something new for themselves, as well as doing something for their students.

This is a very delicate balance that I believe in many cases we've lost these days. Teachers always need to get something for themselves out of teaching. We spend a lot of time talking about what teachers could be doing and should be doing for their students. I suspect if you talked to most of us over 40, we would say we got into teaching because it was a way of learning. It was a way of pushing ourselves. I grew up in a three-room school, where I was always teaching someone else or learning on my own while waiting to be taught by the teacher. That was what started me in this interest of watching how people learn and teaching others to learn about the most effective ways of getting them to learn. Teacher research is an important concept now, but teacher research comes out of a spirit that many of us had carried on for many years. Any time you're teaching, you have to be getting an awful lot in terms of what you're learning about learning.

*BP: The delicate balance is between your own learning and what it is you're doing for others?*

*SH:* Right. That is still true now for me. I never teach the same course twice. It may have the same title. But I tell students, "if you talk to someone who has taken this course before, it will not be the same course they took." I cannot teach the same class twice—I would become so bored. That doesn't mean I won't teach some of the same strategies or principles, but I have to teach it through a different medium. You can never step into the same river twice. I have to be coming to new knowledge or new ways all the time. I hope it's a way of getting students to think that there is this incredible adventure or romance (or whatever you want to call it that doesn't trivialize it) out there in learning. There is so much to learn. Every little venture into that path is just that—an adventure. Part of the adventure is finding our learning self.

*BP: Let's switch gears just a bit. In terms of finding your learning self, in* Ways with Words *we get these glimpses of you with your daughter going to baby-sit, or standing at an ironing board. When or how did you start turning the tape recorder on? How did you get into the process of detailed analysis of language?*

*SH:* I've always been interested in the grains of sand. I'm not so interested in the dunes on the beach. Once I can understand the grains, I can lift my head and see the dunes. I was always listening and watching for the grains of sand. I was looking at the way a head was held when some laughter came around the table. I was always observing the responses to a joke by males or females. That enabled me to have something of a photographic memory of scenes.

In terms of tape recorders, I was determined not to bring things in that weren't indigenous to the community and tape recorders were not as common as they are now. Once I could write things down, because I had paid such attention to the grains, I could recreate a scene almost nod by nod. That happens to be a talent that has stuck with me all my life. I can walk into a situation, and if I'm in my observing mode (which I usually am), I can recreate that incident or situation almost down to the minute detail within a few hours after the event.

*BP: Maybe we're missing the boat by emphasizing tape recording in language research so much. You seem to be talking about the teacher or researcher as the instrument, and developing yourself as the instrument. It's a whole lot more involved than turning on the tape recorder and doing some transcribing. It's about living in the moment—that moment-to-moment awareness of those nuances.*

*SH:* Absolutely. It's one thing I try so hard to do in training my students. I try to get them to think of themselves always as the research instrument. Your questionnaire, your survey, your interview or think-aloud protocol are nothing more than additional instruments. Certainly now I use tape recordings because they help. They allow you to retrieve the data in ways that other people can look at it as well. But *you* are the key instrument, and you must keep that instrument on all the time.

For myself, this is what's most important in long-term anthropological work. It is both a great advantage and a great disadvantage. Once you get habituated to close observation, it's very difficult to cut it off. You're on at the dinner table, you're on at the family holiday party. It's not a particularly healthy state in which to handle human relations!

*BP: I've experienced that inability to turn it off myself at times.*

*SH:* My friends say to me that I'm always living on the edge. I'm always putting myself in these new positions where I have to pick up every new cue in order to survive.

*BP: One of the challenges that will face readers of this book is the many ways language can be analyzed. If someone is just beginning, what advice do you have for them?*

*SH:* I think the first advice I have is to listen generically. Then you need to ask yourself, what are you hearing as the major kinds of differences? Are you hearing differences between the playground and classroom? Where would you demarcate time and space and language differences? I think time and space are neutral. If I said, "How would you demarcate the cultural differences in your classroom?" all kinds of things come roaring into the air. I have people look at spatial and time differences, and then begin to tease apart other differences. What language do children use when they are creating the rules for a game on the playground, as opposed to monitoring a game? These are the patterns we need to observe and then track how these vary with surrounding situations. Cultural or ethnic differences are always situated.

I often talk with my students in my freshman classes about how I talk to them. I talk early in the term more formally than I do the last month of class. By the last four weeks of class, I know them so well that I am teasing them. I know them by nicknames, I'm giving them my own nickname. I ask them to notice the changes in language, and then think about why my language has changed. What is the knowledge base? What are my presuppositions that cause these changes? The first few weeks of class, students think I'm the meanest woman on campus. But by the end, they see I'm a firm but warm person. I ask about how much sleep they got the night before, I give them teasing directions about how to get to my house for dinner.

*BP: My language pattern with students is similar. It's an issue of student power for me. I think it does give students more power early in the semester if the boundaries are firm and fair. I've been embarrassed more than once early in the term when a student calls as they're being wheeled into the emergency room, or from a funeral home, to explain an absence. They know how strict I am about attendance and checking in. But those clear boundaries are critical for all of us. They know the rules, and there is safety in that.*

*SH:* That's exactly the way I feel about it. I say, "I would love to have you stay if you want to work within the rules. Make no mistake—these are my rules. But they are rules for your safety, because you always know where you stand."

In the recent work I've done with inner-city kids, it's clear that they yearn for people who will give them strict guidelines. They want to know where they stand. I was with a high school teacher last week in Boston who was grading her end-of-term papers. She read from one of them to me. It was from a high school senior who was doing drugs and staying out all night and running around with her boyfriend. The student used this wonderful expression, "I'm constantly daring my parents to show me they care." What a wonderful expression! I *dare* you to care. I think a lot of times we're afraid to show we care by setting down very strict rules. I want students to observe and feel those safety nets.

*BP: I think this does circle back to teachers' language. Teachers wonder what their role is in a whole language classroom or writer's workshop, when they read so much about students being in control. Teachers read that children should set the curriculum, and the teacher is just an equal participant. I think to believe this you'd have to ignore the social structures in your classroom. There is never complete equality among students. The language patterns are important—between peers and with the teacher. If you do want to understand issues of control, you have to look closely at your language and that of your students.*

*SH:* That's so true. I will also often say to students, "Reflect on how your own language has changed." As you know from *Ways with Words,* I learned that from Mrs. Gardiner who would have her second graders talk about the way their language changed. These kids were also noticing the way the principal talked on the intercom differed from the way he talked to them when he said hello in the hall.

I had a student in my freshman English class this term who used this incredibly convoluted language. His high school teacher had taught him that when in doubt, use the word with the greatest number of syllables. Of course, when he came into my class, I said, when in doubt, use the quickest and fastest Anglo-Saxon word you can find. And *don't ever* write "utilize" in my class! "Use" will do fine, thank you. By the end of the term, he said, "I know I'm changing some of my habits finally, but they die hard. I was so attuned to that SAT mentality. I thought if I had the vocabulary, I had to use it." I told him, "Most of us can read those words, but we don't *speak* them. We don't create sentences just to put five-syllable words in them." He reflected on how he changed, how it was changing his language in other classes. That's the point—to crawl on the bones of what you know, instead of flying above it.

One of the things we do is have "grandma" talks in class. After my freshmen have done their research studies, I have them talk about the research in class as if they were explaining it to their grandmother. I tell them, "If you haven't done work that you can talk about in words that others can understand, you haven't done anything that's good for you." I want my students to leave class knowing how to have a good, intelligent conversation.

*BP: What are you working on now?*

*SH:* I'm working on several different things, which is my usual bent. I've been doing research into 16th century manuscripts from Bolivia and Peru, working on the history of the Aymara in the highlands of Latin America. Though I'm giving up my Latin American work, I haven't given up my interest in social history.

What I'm working on now is the manuscript library of a woman who was a vicar's wife in Lincolnshire, England in the early 18th century. She created the only manuscript library for children that we now have in existence. It's over 400 different pieces in over 20 sets of reading materials for young children. She had three children of her own. I have worked with the manuscripts in rare book libraries over five years. I'm preparing for an opening to a conference that will be held in Cambridge, England in April on her work. It's called "Scrapbooks and Chapbooks: Visions of Domestic Literacy In the 18th Century." I've also been looking at all the ladies' magazines and novels published at this time to figure out what this mother might have been reading, what might have influenced her in creating this marvelous set of materials for her children. I've arranged an exhibition that I'll be setting up and artistically designing for the Fitzwilliam Museum in Cambridge, England. That's going to be great fun. It's called "Hand-Made Readings."

I'm also continuing to do the work on the lives of inner-city youth. That work is with Milbrey McLaughlin in youth organizations. We have just this year finished the first year of our work with youth in rural and midsized towns. We're looking at issues related to causes of violence and how kids spend their time. Knowing that kids spend 78% of their time *not* in classrooms, how do they spend their discretionary time? What are they doing? What's available for kids? How are they using oral and written language and other symbol systems in that space of time?

As always, I have practical things going, too. I have just come back from a meeting with the American Society for Newspaper Editors. The issue of representation of youth in American newspapers was what I talked about. I'm trying to get them to establish a code of ethics and principles of operation with respect to the presentation of youth. I just today arranged for a report on young people's reading of newspapers to be reproduced for all the members of the society. I hope I can influence some people to think more positively about young people and the ways we represent them.

*BP: It's interesting to me in terms of youths that you've talked a lot about teaching freshmen. I think academics reading this interview might be surprised that you're not working solely with graduate students. With your research agenda, they might even be surprised that you're still teaching.*

*SH:* People are always very surprised. In fact, I'm working with a number of research networks across the country where it suddenly hit me like a great dash of cold water between the eyes that most other members of these teams were teaching only graduate students, or they weren't teaching at all.

I'm usually teaching four days a week. I've had a conversation with people about this over the last few months. An anthropologist can't spend a lot of her time going to class meetings because you have to be in field sites. You can't simply pull up your database on the computer. Your database exists in the boys' and girls' clubs in a city that's 1,500 miles away. I've had to rethink the frenetic pace of my life, particularly as this manuscript work is coming to a head with the conference and a book.

One of the things that is amusing to me is that people are surprised at how rarely I teach graduate students. I don't teach graduate courses more than once a year. Most of my classes are undergraduate, and my favorite classes are with first-quarter freshmen. I *love* getting them early, because I can really exert some influence over them at that point. I can make them think seriously about what their intellectual life might be like at Stanford. Everyone else is telling them to take advantage of all there is to do at Stanford and in the Bay Area. I'm saying that this is the only time you'll have four years of an intellectual life. Live it to the fullest. I'm not saying don't have any fun, but an intellectual life can be fun as well.

*BP: What would you call yourself—teacher, researcher, ethnographer?*

*SH:* When I'm asked by strangers, the first thing I say is that I'm an anthropologist. And then I say that I'm an anthropologist who studies the way that people use language and culture in all sorts of settings, from the hillsides of New Guinea to freshmen English courses in America.

Secondly, I see myself as a social historian. These two are encased in the notion that I'm ever the teacher-researcher. I don't know how to be one without the other.

*BP: It only makes sense that you'd like to work with first-year students. From an anthropological perspective, they are the most interesting culture on campus.*

*SH:* Exactly. They bring so much that they haven't sorted out. They have to sort it out at the same time that they are living in a totally new culture. A lot of my students come to me after the first few weeks and ask for help with something they are having a hard time figuring out. You can see quite literally how they are working their way through this new culture.

I am first and foremost an anthropologist. Studying the uses of language and culture in all sorts of different settings includes dealing with the reading of literature, the learning of reading, the reading of children's literature, why people read certain kinds of literature, why is the reading of children's literature in the western world so different than it is in other cultures. . . . When you say that you're an anthropologist and the province of your study is language and culture, you realize you're either incredibly arrogant, or naive, or both. There isn't much that's left out of that province. As my friend Milbrey says, living life with these kinds of questions means a life with no seams.

*BP: One of the things that impresses me is that you really have broken all the rules. You were doing ethnography when few people were, especially within the place you were living. You don't have a clear, systematic profile to your research. Your research is all over the place. This is not the way you're supposed to build a professional life, according to. . . .*

*SH:* According to all the rules. What's interesting is that I'm on a search committee in our English department here, and I read all the candidate files today. It's clear that the top four or five candidates are very much all over the map already. Whatever they've done, they've done well. But they are not confined to a narrow set of questions. They also borrowed from many different disciplines. It's no accident that those folks rose to the top of the pile for us. This is what interdisciplinary means—you're able to bring to your region of interest a multitude of interests, and you can apply them in a very disciplined and theory-based way. It's something that it took me a long time to learn. I look at these new young candidates. I think, "Oh my gosh, you're so young! How did you learn to do that so quickly?" It is extremely impressive when young people can pull it off so well. I feel I'm continually learning how to do it better.

In my case, it had nothing to do with thinking that this was the way to do it, or that I was smart or theoretically advanced. It had to do with what is characteristic of the way I've run my life. I've never been able to figure out what I am going to be when I grow up. That meant that I found it necessary to explore lots and lots of things. Someone once said to me, "If I asked you for a recipe for apple pie, you'd take me all the way back to the story of Adam and Eve. You never know where to stop." It's irritating for people, but it has to do with my sense that I'm not sure I know something well enough yet. I have to go off into this other little branch or that new direction.

That was certainly the case in my first work in the 1960s on the history of Mexican language policy. I started with the arrival of Cortez. But then I said, "Gee. How come he had this woman at the border when he arrived on the shores of Mexico who could already speak Spanish? Hmm. This is very strange." So then I had to search back to her origins, to find out that she had been taken captive and had been in Cuba with earlier Conquistadors.

That's an example of how I get captivated by a question. It's those questions that keep teaching exciting. Those are the same kinds of questions you ask about every student in your class. "What is it about her that enables her to reach around these questions in this way? What is it about him that enables him to see only these dimensions, or to prefer this style of writing? How can I challenge him to move out into more conversational styles?" You're constantly pushing the boundaries.

*BP: It's almost a passion for the ordinary. It's being engaged where you are right now, linked to what you talked about earlier in looking for the nuances, following back to the earliest threads.*

*SH:* The passion for the ordinary is the passion for the grains of sand. Seeing in every grain of sand how it is that that grain goes to make up certain kinds of dunes, that respond in certain ways to the wild oats or to the wind, or give you a certain feel between the toes. It is definitely trying to get that understanding.

I talk to my freshmen students about it, in terms of this adventure story I'm working on about this 18th century woman. I try to imagine what it must have been like to sit around the hearth of her home in 1737. How much of Jane Austen's *Emma* is there? How much can I recreate? It means I've gotten back into the ballads of the time. I'm researching the nursery furniture. Given her level of income, what kind of furniture would she have been likely to have? I actually found the house that she and her husband built in the 1750s. It is a sense of trying to recreate it all.

A friend reading *Ways with Words* asked me, "Shirley, *why* did you have to tell us that the doily around the lamp was starched? What *difference* does it make?" I said, "Oh, it makes all the difference in the world! Don't you understand? It's an indication of the way the Roadville people lined and circled everything." That circle around the doily and the stiffness in it is emblematic of the furniture lined against the walls, of the kinds of stories they told of domestic labor by women. It's not that you expect consistency in a culture, but there are certain consistencies in the ways that these people used space to provide boundaries and to get a sense of place.

*BP: That starched doily is the grain that can tell more than a dozen language transcripts.*

*SH:* Especially when you see that and compare it with the way the middle-class people line up their furniture and trim their hedges and leave their tables bare with no starched doilies. I can still close my eyes and see the color of those shears, and when they first got electric shears. I can still see them on Saturday mornings with those shears and those crazy long extension cords. It's those grains, all piled together, that begin to give you a sense of the dunes.

*BP: One last thing I wanted to ask. Every time I read your work or hear you speak it's something that's almost totally different than what I've heard before from you. Do you ever get bored with people asking you about* Ways with Words, *because you have such a diverse agenda?*

*SH:* I don't get bored. I sometimes wish that people wouldn't stay with what they regard as the classics. I'm delighted that people like *Ways with Words,* and I'm delighted they've learned from it. But we need to move on beyond that. There are so many new interesting questions now. Not that they are more interesting than some of the questions raised there at that time. In a sense, I'm very gratified and honored, but I'm saddened that there isn't more opportunity, particularly for graduate students, to read more widely, to seek more widely, to expand their grasp of a whole range of things beyond what's already recognized.

# PART II

# Talk in Schools

# Do Teachers Communicate with Their Students As If They Were Dogs?

## Lowell Madden

### EDITOR'S INTRODUCTION

Lowell Madden challenges teachers to think about the way they use language with students. In this humorous and challenging essay, he compares the talk of many teachers with the language people use to train their pets. He ends with recommendations for how "teacher talk" might change to support students without promoting dependence.

## PROLOGUE

Ambi, my three-month-old Golden Retriever puppy, and I strolled through a community park early one summer morning. As she walked beside me, I began to put her through the standard obedience-training procedures. "Heel, sit, stay, come, down!" were the commands to which she was learning to respond. Her rewards for following my orders were commendations from me, "Good doggy! What a nice puppy! You did such a good job!" She was my puppy, and I wanted her to behave in ways which pleased me. Ambi was trained to walk beside me, sit when I stopped, and lie down and stay when I lowered my hand. This was all accomplished by using the language of praise. Through the use of positive, verbal reinforcers, I shaped her behavior to meet my expectations. Through the language of praise I was dedicated not only to the goal of turning her into a well-trained pet but also to helping her become a happy and well-adjusted dog.

## DO TEACHERS TREAT THEIR STUDENTS LIKE DOGS?

As Ambi's behavior continued to be shaped during our many walks, it gradually became apparent to me that well-meaning teachers, including myself, try to affect the behavior of human students in like manner. By also using the language of praise with such statements as "You did a great job!" or "You are an excellent student!" the desired behavior of students is "engineered." Although the use of the language of praise is well intentioned, it is also judgmental and manipulative. Teachers also tend to use the language of praise to affect their students' self-perceptions. Beane and

Lipka (1984) state that self-perception has two dimensions. One is self-concept which is defined as the way a person views himself or herself; the other is self-esteem which is the degree to which one values or is satisfied with the self-concept.

Although developing positive self-perceptions in students is a commendable objective and although Purkey (1970) relates that there is a positive relationship between how students feel about themselves and academic achievement, the use of the language of praise to accomplish this goal may put students in the same learning circumstance as trainers place dogs. When their behavior pleases their teachers, they are rewarded with statements of praise and they view themselves as having worth; if they displease them, their worth becomes questionable. Their feelings about themselves become contingent on teachers' judgments of their performances. They become dependent on these judgments rather than on their own feelings of satisfaction of personal growth and contribution. Unfortunately these students become adults who continuously look for approval from significant others in their lives.

## WHAT HAPPENS WHEN STUDENTS TRY TO PLEASE TEACHERS?

It probably is safe to say that most students want to please their teachers. However, in their attempts to please they distribute themselves across a "teacher pleasing continuum." Those who are unable to meet their teachers' expectations tend to gravitate toward one side of the continuum and ultimately decide to give up trying. They become discouraged and tend to act out their disappointment by misbehaving. According to Walton and Powers (1978), the misbehavior of students can be described as attempts to gain the goals of attention, power, revenge, or to exhibit inadequacy. The following self-messages illustrate what is happening within students who elect misbehavior to reach such goals:

| | |
|---|---|
| **Attention** | I'm not outstanding, but at least I will not be overlooked if I can obtain special attention, fuss, or service. |
| **Power** | I may not be a winner, but at least I can show people that they cannot defeat me, or stop me from doing what I want, or make me do what they want. |
| **Revenge** | People do not care for me, but at least I can do things to strike back when I am hurt. |
| **Inadequacy** | I will not be able to measure up, but at least if I do nothing people may let me alone. (p. 6) |

On the other hand, those who are quite capable of meeting teacher expectations gather toward the opposite side of the continuum. These students are the ones who receive positive reinforcers for jobs well done. They perform so well that in time they tend to become trapped by rewards and see their worth as contingent on teacher-pleasing performance.

Of the two situations described, perhaps students who avidly please may experience more difficulty gaining control of their lives than those who withdraw and find validation in other ways. Although very capable students are able to function at high levels of performance, their abilities to achieve may far exceed their ability to manage emotionally the pressures and consequences of their own successes. They may find themselves laden with well-deserved awards, but the price they pay may be emotional upheaval and the lost control of managing their academic progress as well as their own lives. Their worth remains contingent on teachers' opinions or judgments.

Teachers tend to use beginning sentence patterns such as the following to impact their student's behaviors:

> My expectations for you are . . .
> You should . . .
> You shouldn't . . .
> I'm proud of you for . . .
> You please me by . . .
> I'm disappointed in you for . . .

Although these messages are intended to be positive insertions into the lives of their students and are very effective in managing behavior they, in effect, may keep students from taking control of their own progress and development. This condition has potential for the long-range effect of keeping students from becoming independent and self-reliant adults.

It is obvious that canine pets can never be independent and are merely loved property of their owners, but students are not possessions. They are unique individuals who have the right to self-determination and the joy of personal worth and dignity based on the undisputed value of their personhood.

## UPON WHAT SHOULD SELF-PERCEPTION BE BASED?

It certainly is prudent to manage dogs in such a way that they are well-disciplined and adjusted, but should there be a difference between the way they are controlled and the way in which students are educated? Even though there is a positive relationship between academic achievement and self-perception, shouldn't teachers be careful in the type of communication that they use in elevating students' feelings of worth? Should students' feelings of self be based on pleasing teachers or should their feelings about self be based on the unrefutable fact that they have unquestionable value, because they exist? To state it in another way, should students' self-perceptions be based on their performance or their personhood? The poster which depicts the young boy saying, "I know I'm somebody, because God don't make no junk!" exemplifies the difference. He does not need to behave at a desirable level of performance to be worthy, because he is already good enough, as is, because he exists.

Marquees of flower shops often give prices for frequently purchased flowers, such as "roses one dollar each" and "carnations three for a dollar." It may be simple advertising, but it also asserts that some flowers are worth more than others. Perhaps this situation is analogous to what sometimes happens in classrooms. Through the use of reward systems, such as the language of praise, students receive the message that some of them are valued more than others due to their performance level. Being considered number one in academic achievement makes them more valuable than being rated as number twenty-five. Rarely are students made to feel valuable for being just plain and ordinary and certainly not for below-average achievement in anything. Students certainly do not have equal talents, but all students have equal worth. The way that teachers communicate with them may affect their understanding of that truth. If students are praised for their performance, they may erroneously infer that their worth is based on behavior or achievement. This misunderstanding may greatly impact their self-perceptions.

## WHY SHOULD STUDENTS DEVELOP GOOD SELF-PERCEPTION?

What is the bottom line for helping students attain healthy self-perceptions? Should they be aided to grow up thinking that the major purpose in their lives is themselves? If students continue to receive messages of praise, they risk growing up with a personal orientation of "I and Me, I and Me, I and Me." Should students develop positive self-perceptions only to enhance themselves? Or should students with good self-perceptions make substantial contributions for the welfare of others? Which is a more important outcome?

What can be done to develop their "We and Us" orientations? Perhaps teachers might wish to change the way in which they communicate with students. Rather than use the language of praise, they might wish to consider employing the *language of encouragement*. What is the difference? According to Dinkmeyer and Losoncy (1980) the language of praise is judgmental and usually tells students how great they are or how great their works are. Praise is based on achievement; it communicates to students that they will be valued if they please their teachers. Although it holds great potential for bringing out adult-pleasing behavior, it also may cause students to be anxious, dependent, and very competitive.

Dreikurs and Cassel (1972) state that the language of encouragement recognizes the growth and contributions that students make and promotes within them self-reliance, self-direction, and cooperation. The use of the language of encouragement implies that students are good enough as they are, rather than as teachers wish them to be. This does not mean that students may not wish to please their teachers, because they may truly wish to do so because they admire and respect them. It does mean that their feelings of self-worth should not be based on their successful attempts to please. Rather, their feelings of self-worth should be based on the fact that they exist.

Through the language of encouragement students' specific actions are recognized and are appreciated for the growth or contributions that are made. Comments such as "Thank you! That was very helpful! You are obviously learning a lot about . . . !" are examples of the language of encouragement. Ginott (1972) states that encouragement consists of two parts: What is said to the students and what the students say to themselves. He offers the following example:

Marcia helped the teacher rearrange the books in the class library. The teacher avoided personal praise (You did a good job. You are a hard worker. You are a good librarian.) Instead she described what Marcia accomplished. The books are all in order now. It'll be easy for the children to find any book they want. It was a difficult job. But you did it. Thank you. (pp. 126–127)

The teacher's words of recognition allowed Marcia to make her own inference. "My teacher likes the job I did. I am a good worker." Statements of praise can be changed to statements of encouragement by recognizing the contribution or growth of the behaviors of students and refraining from making judgments about the students as a result of their behavior. For instance, the following praise judgments have been changed to encouragement declarations: "You are an excellent student" to "You really enjoy learning. Your skills are growing. All of your hard work is paying off."; "You are terrific for helping me" to "Thank you for helping me. It will make our work go much easier."; and "You wrote the best essay in the class" to "It is obvious that you are working hard on your writing techniques."

Through the use of encouragement students can develop good feelings about self without becoming dependent upon teachers' judgments. They may learn that making a contribution for the welfare of those around them is appreciated and they develop a "We and Us" spirit of cooperation. They can learn to gain control of their own lives without becoming super competitive and self-centered.

All of us as teachers have a choice to make regarding how we will educate our students. We can control them through the use of behavioral engineering as dogs are trained and consequently make them dependent upon us, or we can nurture and encourage them to become who they can be. Ultimately the bottom line is found through the thoughtful answers to the questions, what is the purpose of education and what should students become?

## EPILOGUE

Two years after the initial walk in the park, Ambi died of epilepsy. Although her life span was brief, perhaps it was a fruitful one, because it led to this manuscript. Thank you, Ambi. Your contribution is highly valued. Perhaps we as teachers, because of you, will learn a new way to communicate with our students and in so doing avoid treating them like dogs!

## REFERENCES

Beane, J., & Lipka, R. (1984). *Self-concept, self-esteem and the curriculum.* Boston: Allyn and Bacon.

Dinkmeyer, D., & Losoncy, L. (1980). *The encouragement book.* Englewood Cliffs: Prentice-Hall.

Dreikurs, R., & Cassel, P. (1972). *Discipline without tears.* New York: Hawthorne.

Ginott, H. (1972). *Teacher and child.* New York: Macmillan.

Purkey, W. (1970). *Self-concept and school achievement.* Englewood Cliffs: Prentice-Hall.

Walton, F. & Powers, R. (1978). *Winning children over.* Chicago: Practical Psychology Associates.

# Teacher Research Extension: "You Talk Too Much"

**Andie Cunningham**
**K-8 Physical Movement Teacher**

In a special issue of *Teacher Research Journal* (Fall 1995), several teacher researchers wrote that the best research questions often seem to be framed around what's really bugging them. For me, it was those sleepless nights in January that finally prodded me into action. My notes from an enlightening day of conferences caused me to spend many nights tossing and turning, listening to the rain, and trying to figure out what to do about my students' opinions.

During individual sixth-grade conferences in January, many students answered my question about what I could do to make this class work better by informing me that I talked too much. Did I really talk too much? Was that problem universal throughout all of the grades? Was there something more I should be focusing on with my language? What would make so many of the students during individual conferences say that one way to make the class better was for me to talk less? Why was it that only the sixth-grade classes said that? My well-intentioned, protecting brain said, "No way. It's just them," but my quieter, more calm side said, "What are they really saying?"

I decided to tape record three 45-minute classes from the sixth grade and calculate the amount of time spent talking by me and my students. I discovered it wasn't the *amount* of my talk so much as the number of times I *interrupted* my students' learning. Though my students actually spoke 66% of the time, I couldn't believe it when I realized how frequently I interrupted their work time. I could hear my voice on the tape occasionally calling out to students, redirecting their focus, or giving them tips to encourage creations or successful work. On the first day, I interrupted each of the work station activities seven times, moving them to the next station. As a result, I changed the second day of the assignment and let them work without interruptions for 18 minutes. By the end of class, all of the students knew where they wanted to design their project, and they were ready to customize their work.

The beauty of taping worked for me in a variety of ways. Besides helping me address the nagging question that had been keeping me tossing and turning at night, new questions were raised for me. While taking the same amount of time as my after-school anecdotal notes, taping allowed me to pay attention to things I had previously missed: male voices were speaking loudest during class meetings, female voices sang quietly only during the activities. I also realized there were some voices that didn't seem to be speaking at all.

More specific questions now loom: Have I been speaking for the absent female voices? What platforms must be present for the girls to risk speaking out to the whole class? What will their voices sound like when they do speak up? Taping helped me uncover a deeper layer to my classroom dynamics. Now, as I search for ways to find out who my students really are, I can look beyond the silent cooperation of the girls and the "you talk too much" comments of the boys.

# Telling Stories

## Tom Newkirk and Patricia McLure

**EDITOR'S INTRODUCTION**

In *Listening In: Children Talk about Books (and Other Things),* the authors examine the kinds of talk that occur during the small literature discussion groups in McLure's first- and second-grade classroom. This excerpt, "Telling Stories," shows how these groups are a powerful tool for teachers and students in understanding student culture.

Near the end of *The Catcher in the Rye* (Salinger, 1951), Holden Caulfield reflects on an oral expression class he took at one of the several prep schools he had attended. In the class, students were coached to yell "Digression!" at any speaker who strayed from his topic. The "digression business" got on Holden's nerves because he liked it when someone digressed, it was "more *in*teresting and all." He recalls a boy in the class who didn't stick to the point.

> There was this one boy, Richard Kinsella. He didn't stick to the point too much, and they were always yelling "Digression!" at him. . . . He made this speech about this farm his father bought in Vermont. They kept yelling "Digression" at him the whole time he was making it, and the teacher, Mr. Vinson, gave him an *F* on it because he hadn't told what kind of animals and vegetables and stuff grew on the farm and all. What he did was, Richard Kinsella, he'd *start* telling you all about that stuff—then all of a sudden he'd start telling you about this letter his mother got from his uncle, and how his uncle got polio and all when he was forty-two years old, and how he wouldn't let anyone come to see him in the hospital because he didn't want anyone

to see him with a brace on. It didn't have much to do with the farm—I admit it—but it was *nice*. (Salinger, 1951, 183–84)

Holden, unlike his former teacher, Mr. Vinson, views talk as organic, evolving, unpredictable. For him, it has the power to illuminate experience when it deviates from a preset agenda. He insists on the openness of talk, and, despite the urging of a battery of advisors that he reduce his life to a plan, he is unwilling to eliminate the role of chance in his life.

> A lot of people, especially this one psychoanalyst guy they have here, keeps asking me if I'm going to apply myself when I go back to school next September. It's a stupid question, in my opinion. I mean how do you know what you're going to do till you *do* it? The answer is, you don't. I *think* I am, but how do I know? I swear it's a stupid question. (213)

---

*Source: Listening In: Children Talk about Books (and Other Things)* (pp. 80–94) by T. Newkirk and P. McLure, 1992, Portsmouth, NH: Heinemann.

Vinson's class is a parody of normal classroom talk, but it doesn't miss the reality by much. Courtney Cazden (1988) argues that teacherly expectations for relevance and conciseness are often dramatically at odds with the storytelling patterns of students. She offers the following example in which a teacher seeks to narrow and focus a child's account of an outing. In her own way, the teacher is yelling "Digression!"

*Nancy:* I went to Old Ironsides at the ocean. [*Led by a series of teacher questions, Nancy explains that Old Ironsides is a boat and that it's old. The teacher offers the real name, the* Constitution. *Then Nancy tries to shift her story.*]
*Nancy:* We also spent our dollars and we went to another big shop.
*T:* Mm. 'N what did you learn about Old Ironsides? [*Led by teacher questions, Nancy supplies more information about the furnishings inside and the costumes of the guides, and then tries to shift focus again.*]
*Nancy:* And I had a hamburger, french fries, lettuce, and a—
*T:* OK. All right, what's—Arthur's been waiting and then Paula, OK? (16)

In a way, we can sympathize with the teacher's reluctance to allow the story to move to Nancy's lunch (and the rest of her outing). Arthur and Paula are waiting. But Cazden warns that "while there may be situational reasons for pressing children to speak relevantly and to the point, there are developmental and cultural reasons why it may be difficult for children to meet such expectations" (193).

Underlying this reluctance to allow stories and conversations to evolve is a concept of topicality or task-centeredness. Few distinctions in education are as uncritically invoked as those of on-task/off-task behavior or on-topic/off-topic talk. Most of the research I have read treats these binary distinctions As significant and self-evident. And if we think of the turn-of-the-century factory as the model for the classroom, it is easy to see why. Workers in these factories were typically involved in acting upon raw material in a preset way; they were not allowed to make decisions. Talk among themselves was considered a distraction, so breaks were instituted to segregate socializing from on-task work.

In reading, the student is the worker, the text the raw material, and understanding of the text is the uniform product the teachers (bosses) want manufactured. The primary action of the worker, aside from actually reading the text, is to answer questions about the text posed by the teacher or the collateral materials created by the reading system.

Answering a question about the text is "on topic"; telling a story related to the text is "off topic." If a child tells a story, he or she is no longer working on the raw material of text to manufacture comprehension. The child has strayed from the assembly line.

According to this mechanical view of classroom talk, each text sets clear and firm boundaries for discussion—just as Richard Kinsella's topic, the farm, set boundaries for him. Yet one of the features of conversation is the shifting of topics: each turn shifts the topic to some degree; each speaker bridges to something new. Few social skills are as important as the capacity to handle what Irving Goffman has called "the etiquette of reach" (1976, 291). We admire the speaker who listens carefully and moves the discussion gracefully forward; we are put off by those who abandon topics that are still warm and cause the talk to lurch unpredictably. And I believe that we resist situations in which we cannot digress at all; we find it unpleasant to talk to people who must immediately get down to business, who resist any deviation, who always talk as if they are double-parked.

Goffman's term "etiquette of reach" is useful for looking at the storytelling that goes on in Pat McLure's first- and second-grade classroom. The word "etiquette" suggests that "topicality," being on topic, is socially defined instead of being a self-evident function of the texts under discussion. If we consider six- and seven-year-olds to constitute a culture, as I have argued, it becomes clear that the etiquettes of their social group may be quite different from those of adults (and even adult conversations, when they work, are less rigidly on topic than so-called discussions led by a teacher).

I became aware of these conventions several years ago when I was recording class discussions for a chapter in *More than Stories* (1989). It was chick season, and Joshua shared his three-page information book on chicks.

The eggs have to be turned twenty-two times and the last three days you do not turn them.
You must keep the incubator moist.
We put letters on one side, numbers on the other.

Imagine the questions you would ask regarding this text: Why do you keep the incubator moist? Why do you put letters on the side? The discussion turned out to be on copying machines. Pat asked how Joshua got the information on chicks.

*Joshua:* Well, we went to the library and we asked the librarian how we could get a copy of this paper and she said the copy machine and my mother said, "How does it work?" and somebody said, "I'll do it," and then they came over and they put the book like this [*demonstrates in pantomime*]. This was a heavy book. It had the picture like this and you put it like this and it goes "shhhhhhhh" and then it spits out.

Aaron asked how long it took to learn the information, and Joshua answered, "One night." Then we were back to the copying machine.

*Aaron:* Did you mean when the copy machine spit out the paper did it go "vroo, vroo?"
*Joshua:* It just went "shhhhhh." The lady said it would spit out at you, but it didn't.

There were a couple of comments about Joshua's illustrations—and then back to copying machines.

*Carin:* Once when I went with Mrs. ___ we had to use the copy machine and she laid the book flat on the thing, whatever you call it. . . .
*Joshua:* They buckle it in, the book in. And it goes "shhh-hhh" and then it comes out.
*Carin:* We just used Mrs. ___'s and we just put it flat down and then it just went "rrrrrr" like that and then she had to get it off and put another page on it until it was done.

As the discussion continued, several other students told their copying stories, each adding a new element, a new piece to the puzzle. John told about putting a cover over the book. Jimmy described a copier from his old school that was smaller and slower than the one Joshua used. Ginger told about working the copier at her dad's office and feeling the warmth of the copy as it came out.

In general, the members of Pat's class treated the text being shared, whether by a student or by a professional author, as a first long turn in a conversation. But a turn does not permanently fix in place the topic (or even the general theme) to be discussed. In the share group on Joshua's book on chicks, the ostensible topic of chicks was dropped once he told the more interesting narrative about using the copy machine. It was that narrative that set the theme for the discussion. According to the "etiquette of reach," this shift from chicks to copying machines was perfectly acceptable.

If the published text is treated as a turn in a conversation, it is no longer the inescapable focus of attention. It does not set fixed boundaries (patrolled by the teacher). Instead, it becomes one story among many. Ezra Jack Keats (1974) has his *Snowy Day,* and, as I watch the snow pile up on the

frozen Oyster River, so do I. Keats takes his turn, and I take mine. His story evokes mine, enables me to see mine. The initiating text may become a focus for talk or, as in the case of Joshua's chick story, it may give way to a different kind of narrative, which in turn sets off a chain of stories. Ultimately, the stories go on forever. Ellen Blackburn Karelitz, who has described how this chain of narratives works in her own classroom, quotes one of her students, Brian: "You know, Mrs. Blackburn, when you said that numbers never end. Well, I just noticed something. Stories never end either" (1985, 13).

## THE ETIQUETTE OF REACH

According to Goffman, the etiquette of reach defines the kinds of bridges we can properly construct when taking a conversational turn. The speaker can "respond to something smaller or larger than the [previous] speaker's statement, or to one aspect of it, or even to the non-linguistic elements of the situation" (1976, 291). In the case of Joshua's sharing session, members of the class were not constrained to respond to the text being shared; they could pick up on a piece of contextual information—using the copying machine—and then, as a group, make that the central topic. This freedom to shift subjects, to take an element from a previous turn and bridge to a new topic, was the defining characteristic of their etiquette of reach. Sometimes the shifts were so abrupt that Pat and I were left in the dust—along with some of the second graders who played by more conventional rules. In cases like these, Pat would not try to rein them in; she would ask, "How is that connected? How did we get here?"

The purest example of this freedom to shift topics came in a discussion of *The Night Before Christmas,* which Jennifer, a first grader, shared. The experience of listening to this discussion was a little like holding on to a runaway toboggan. Up to this point, the group had talked about three Christmas shows, summarizing the plots; they had noted the double-page illustrations in Jennifer's book; and Pat had complimented Jennifer on her fluent reading. Then the toboggan took off. As you read it, try to follow the bridges that participants make to new topics. The ride begins with Jennifer remembering other Christmas stories.

*Jennifer:* And that reminds me I got one that's about a reindeer.
*Pat:* Oh, another Christmas story.
*Jennifer:* And I got Christmas carols and my sister got Christmas carols too. Kristy got *Santa's Runaway Elves* and Christmas stories.

*Pat:* Um, you got lots of books.

*Sandy:* Well, I got *The Bear That Slept Through Christmas*—

*Michelle:* Me too.

*Sandy:* —and I got a pop-up book and a tape.

*Jennifer:* That reminds me. Last year I got Tic-Tacs. I don't remember what else I got but I know I got some potatoes and oranges. I didn't eat my oranges at all. It was all sort of plastic. So it wasn't—

*Sandy:* What color Tic-Tacs did you get? Orange?

*Jennifer:* Light green.

*Sandy:* Light green? I like the orange.

*Jennifer:* So do I. I like the colored. Once my sister went to the emergency room to get stitches. My mom was working and we had to call my mom. Our neighbor is a nurse so she really needed to get stitches. She got seven stitches, two on top and five on bottom.

*Michelle:* I had four stitches all on my forehead.

*Sandy:* I've never had stitches.

*Corrine:* I've had stitches.

*Michelle:* They don't hurt at all. [*Overlapping talk about whether they hurt.*]

*Pat [to Jennifer]:* What made you remember that right now?

*Jennifer:* When she had green stitches.

*Pat:* Oh, she had green stitches and the green reminded you of Tic-Tacs.

*Corrine:* I had white stitches.

*Michelle:* When I first had my stitches it didn't hurt at all on my forehead.

*Sandy:* When you said stitches it reminded me of the day when . . . I think it was a wedding . . . and we went too and my aunts and my cousin and he was playing with the cat's toy and they had a glass table up there and it fell on the floor and he was on the couch on his knees and tried picking it up but he fell down and hit the glass and he had fifteen stitches.

*Jennifer:* That reminds me . . . that reminds me, my cousin's friend got a hundred stitches.

*Corrine:* Sandy reminds me of when I was a flower girl—

*Sandy:* I was too.

*Corrine:* My cousin, he was the person that carries the rings and he was looking over the balcony and he was at the hotel and he was looking over the balcony—and he didn't have the ring.

*Pat [laughs]:* You mean he lost the ring?

*Corrine:* But my aunt, she had one.

The conversation goes on for a couple more turns and concludes with Sandy saying to Pat, "Boy, that was a lot of talking." It surely was. Even Pat, with her considerable tolerance for digression, admitted that the discussion went "far afield" and wondered in the margins of the transcript whether she shouldn't have stepped in earlier. In four minutes, the conversation had shifted from *The Night Before Christmas* to Christmas books to Tic-Tacs to stitches to weddings.

Yet if we view the participants in this group as members of a six- and seven-year-old culture that has its own conversational rules, it is not as easy to dismiss such talks as off-topic and educationally insignificant. For one thing, members of the group easily found their way into the discussion, even Corrine, who was consistently reticent at other times. This ease of participation was created by the minimal bridge requirement. To take a turn, according to this requirement, a speaker must simply connect with any element in the previous turn, as when the greenness of Tic-Tacs led to a story featuring green stitches. The child may announce the connection with "that reminds me" but does not have to make the connection explicit.

This simple bridge requirement is less constraining than is the etiquette of other, more adult types of talk. One more stringent type of connection is the story-type bridge that we saw in the discussion of the copying machine. According to that constraint, a turn must connect to major thematic elements of the previous turn. For example, if someone tells a lost tooth story, the following speakers will also tell lost tooth stories (or stories that keep to major themes of that story type, such as pain, loss, or fear) until the topic becomes cold, at which point it is time for a more substantial shift.

An even more stringent rule might be called the text-based bridge. It is based on the presupposition that one text has priority in the discussion and that no bridge can take the speaker away from commentary on the text that has been given priority. Many conventional book discussions (and the report of Richard Kinsella) are expected to work within this more stringent set of constraints. Therapeutic and counseling discussions similarly focus on the principal narrative of the person seeking help.

From the standpoint of the six- and seven-year-old culture, however, the less stringent bridges seem the most congenial and allow for a wider range of participation. To exclude these less stringent bridges is to turn a deaf ear (literally) to this culture.

## STORIES AND COMMUNITY

Theories of reading comprehension have acknowledged the value of personal narratives, particularly *before* students read a text. By exploring and telling their prior knowledge, by activating frames of experience, readers put in place lenses that will help them comprehend a story. Rather than passively processing a story, they actively use this prior knowledge to anticipate what will happen. The storytelling, according to this view, is subordinate to the act of comprehension, an oral means to a literate end.

In many of the book discussions in Pat's class, the priorities were reversed. The text activated schemas, suggested story types that enabled the children to tell their own stories. This is not to say there was no traditional comprehension work (for example, in the summaries). But it does mean that telling stories was not viewed simply as a means to comprehension. Pat does not continually nag students to get back to the text because the stories themselves are central to the way these groups work—just as they are central to all communities.

Collectively, the stories told by the group members celebrated life in rural New Hampshire. A great many concerned animals, wild and domesticated. Abby was the class expert on cats and had a seemingly inexhaustible set of stories about them. In one session, Jennifer asked Abby how her sister had named her cat. Abby responded:

I don't know. Because her first name was Tiger Eyes because when her eyes closed up they looked like tiger eyes. And then she said, "Mom, I wish I could name her Jessica Fisher just like me" [laughs]. And my mom goes, "Go ahead, if you want to." And then she changed her name to Jessica Tiger Eyes Fisher. Probably by next year her name will be a different name.

Billy, as we have seen, loved tooth stories, but he also told dog stories.

Once I saw this dog going past our house and then I saw three people running right after it. And then just when I opened the door to get out the dog came in our house and we had to get it out of the house. And then it went and people asked, "Did you see a dog coming into your house?" and we said, "Yes, it's over there." And they had to run all the way around and finally they caught it.

There was also a type of "gross" story that the boys told. The electricity scene in *Two Bad Ants* (Van Allsburg, 1988) reminded Martin of a dream.

Last night I had a dream about this lady. She picked up the phone and then electricity started coming out and into her ear and she went "Ahhhhh." And the phone was being sucked into her ear and she kept on screaming and her body got all wrinkled and she fell down dead.

More typically, the gross stories involved the mutilation of insects like spiders:

*Rob:* My brother thinks that daddy longlegs have long legs so they take off and put them to make a web [*calls on Martin*].
*Martin:* That reminds me when we went to Scott's party, remember the part when we took the daddy longlegs spider and he picked off the legs and he saw the legs still moving.
*Rob:* Yeah.
*Martin:* That was neat.

Or flies:

*Jake:* Have you ever seen a black fly stick out his tongue?
*Pat [laughs]:* I don't think I've seen one.
*Jake:* That's what [the space creatures] look like. I've seen one. Really. They have this pink thing goes [*pantomimes it sticking out from his head*]. Because one day we were eating fish. We were camping and my dad caught some fish and we were eating it and all these flies came over and we had this fire and we started burning them up, all the flies. We would trap them and then sssssss [*sound of flies sizzling*].

While the mutilation stories were told only by boys, both sexes shared accounts of dealing with raccoons and skunks.

*Susan:* I think we had a raccoon in our house because our trash can was tipped over and there were four holes inside the trash can.
*Sandy:* That reminds me at my grandmother's house, one night. They're watching TV and then they heard a big bang out in the front and they went and they saw this mother raccoon and a baby raccoon. They knocked over the rubbish and they ran off.
*Vicky:* In "The Great Outdoors at Night" these raccoons get in a trash can and so in the morning the father has to clean up all the trash and the mother gets to cook.
*Tommy:* Just like a cat does.
*Sandy:* That reminds me once at my young Dad's friend's, well, a raccoon kept getting into the trash so he had to put these rocks on and one night they took a picture of a raccoon in someone else's chimney.

Each participant in the discussion added a new element to the general raccoon narrative (just as in the copier discussion). In Susan's, there was evidence of the raccoons' presence (teeth marks); in Sandy's first story, the raccoons are discovered, and the rubbish overturned; in Vicky's, the raccoons make a major mess; and, in Sandy's second story, the raccoon is photographed.

Many of these digressions during talk about animals could be justified fairly easily because they extended the children's knowledge of the natural world—reading time turned into science time. But the TV/video-game culture was also a major part of these children's experience, and it, too, made its way into the talk about books. For example, in the discussions of the *Stupids* books that I have quoted, the talk moved to TV shows and video games. The picture of the dog, Kitty, driving the car reminded Rob of a scene in "America's Funniest Home Videos."

*Don:* [pretending to be Kitty driving the car]: RRRRRRRRRR. There goes one door. RRRRRRRR. Konk. [*He makes an explosion sound to indicate a crash.*]
*Jed:* There goes everything.
*Rob:* On "The World's Funniest Home Videos" there was this person—
*Jed:* Oh, yeah.
*Rob:* He was in a car. There was only the front of it. But the back was broken off so there was only front wheels so he was like this [*demonstrates*] and driving the car.
*Jed:* Yeah, he was like this. The guy said, "Hey, Mom, do you like my new car?" And he was driving with the back off. And it worked good.

At another point in the discussion, the boys in the group made a fairly extensive inventory of video games. The picture of King Stupid the Fourteenth reminded Jed of the video game *King Friday the Thirteenth,* and they were off:

*Jed:* Have you ever played *King Friday the Thirteenth?*
*Rob:* King Friday the Thirteenth. Yeah.
*Jed:* It is fun.
*Rob:* Mm-hm.
*Scott:* How do you do it?
*Jed:* I don't know.
*Don:* It is a Nintendo game?
*Jed:* Yeah.
*Scott:* What do you do with it?
*Jed:* I don't know.

Don is reminded of the movie *Friday the Thirteenth.*

*Don:* I do not want to look at the cover of the movie *Friday the Thirteenth* one bit.

*Pat [laughing]:* No, I don't like it either.
*Don:* It's like URRRRRRRRR and it's like this gigantic thing bigger than the universe coming up and smashing the whole world into two thousand pieces.

Then the conversation goes back to how to play *King Friday the Thirteenth* and on to the games that Rob has rented—*Mario, Batman, Sesame Street,* and *Jeopardy.* Jed asks Rob how to play *Sesame Street,* and Rob starts a fairly complicated description of "Ernie's Magic Skates."

As I was transcribing this section of the tape, I inserted a question: "I would bet many teachers would try to get back to the book at this point. Why do you let them go on?" Pat's answer, I feel, was one of the most revealing comments she made concerning these groups.

I'm not sure—I see this as a very interesting social situation for these boys. I feel almost like I'm eavesdropping on some "free play." It's like they're not really aware that we're there.

In reading and thinking about her answer, I realized that I was still thinking in binary terms—wondering when she would get back on task. But Pat does not view talk in on/off terms. She is interested in what children say and saw this talk about Nintendo games as important for the social functioning of this group. She didn't split the talk into social and academic, on task (what counts) and off task (what diverts). Her position is closer to one taken by Anne Dyson:

Talk about academic tasks is often contrasted with social talk: individuals achieve because of the time they spend "on task." My observations suggest that the "academic" and the "social" are not so simply—or so profitably— separated. The social laughing, teasing, correcting, and chatting that accompany children's academic work are byproducts of the need to link with others and be recognized by them. But they can also be catalysts for intellectual growth. (1987, 417)

The share groups that failed were the ones that lacked social interaction and energy; they stuck to questions and answers (usually formulaic) about the book. They seemed to lack digressionary possibility. They never moved.

When Pat invites the children in her class to share their culture in reading groups, she subtly influences which parts of the culture they bring in. As I reread the video-game discussion, I was surprised to see that it really wasn't that long, not nearly as long as some lost-tooth discussions. I suspect that it seemed long because it was not the type of story—not the type of digression—that usually occurred. More typically, the stories featured animals, brothers and sisters, other books, topics that did not center on secondhand video experiences and on acquisitions.

A colleague of mine, Brenda Miller Power, who had spent considerable time in Pat's class once made the distinction between holiday time (measured by special days when children receive candy and presents) and seasonal time (ordered by natural growth and change). When Pat brings the brood hens into class, for example, she is announcing a preference for natural time. In this classroom, it is turning eggs, counting days, and then watching chicks hatch that mark the coming of spring. Likewise, stories of lost teeth and of younger brothers and sisters enable these students to measure their own growth.

Literature has the power to evoke these stories. It offers a way into memory. It opens up our own experiences and enables us to talk about them. Sometimes, when I see children tied to preset questions about a text, I imagine tiny lilliputian creatures dwarfed by the giant book that they are crawling over. The book is dominant and imposing; those attending to it are antlike to the point of insignificance. A more companionable image is of the author seated at a table—or better, with others around a campfire—ready to take the first turn in a conversation, to begin a chain of stories that cannot be predicted ahead of time. It's a position, I believe, that many authors would like to take.

## REFERENCES

Cazden, C. (1988). *Classroom discourse.* Portsmouth, NH: Heinemann.

Dyson, A. H. (1987). "Individual differences in beginning composing: An orchestral vision of learning to write." *Written Communication 4,* 411–442.

Goffman, I. (1976). "Replies and responses." *Language in Society 5* (December). pp. 257–313.

Karelitz, E. B. (1985). "Common ground: Developing relationships between reading and writing." *Language Arts 61* (April). pp. 10–17.

Keats, E. J. (1974). *The snowy day.* New York: Viking Press.

Newkirk, T. (1989). *More than stories: The range of children's writing.* Portsmouth, NH: Heinemann.

Salinger, J. D. (1951). *Catcher in the rye.* Boston, MA: Little, Brown.

Van Allsberg, C. (1988). *Two bad ants.* Boston, MA: Houghton Mifflin.

# A Love of Words

## Ralph Fletcher

**EDITOR'S INTRODUCTION**

Ralph Fletcher is a writer who has spent many years working with children in public schools. His book, *What a Writer Needs,* draws on his own experience as a writer and teacher to look at the essential support writers of any age need. In this excerpt, Fletcher looks at how his love of language emerged, and how schools can foster a similar love.

> *Language permits us to see. Without the word, we are all blind.*
>
> Carlos Fuentes, *The Old Gringo,* 1985

STRANGE OCCURRENCES. In November I took a group of kids to the Bronx Zoo. We reached the buffaloes and stopped to admire the immense bulk, the shaggy shredding coats.

"Buffaloes!" a little boy said, and I felt a stab of pure emotion, sharp, bittersweet.

"C'mon, let's go," another kid said. But I couldn't move. Buffaloes. The word reverberated oddly inside my head. I was dazed, rooted to the spot. I was actually on the brink of tears. Yet I couldn't quite bring it to the surface, that deep memory fragment. I shook it off and all but forgot it. But on the way home from the zoo the kids started singing "Home on the Range," and when they got to the part "where the buffaloes roam" there it was again—pungent emotion, pure and sad and sweet, surging up inside me.

Months passed. One day I was hanging up JoAnn's white bathrobe and just like that the memory came flooding back. Dad's bathrobe. When I was little, for some reason (the shaggy bulk?) we always called Dad's bathrobe his "buffalo." He traveled a lot during those years, selling books all over New England. The first thing he did when he came home on Friday night was to don slippers and that big white terrycloth bathrobe. We would snuggle hard against that buffalo while he read stories to us before bed.

Some nights during the week while Dad was away we would start pestering my mother. Couldn't we take Dad's buffalo out of his closet? Just for a little while? If she agreed, we'd race upstairs to the closet in his bedroom. The buffalo always hung on a particular hook; we would jostle each other to be first to pull it down. The buffalo got dragged downstairs to the living room where we would wrap it around us while we watched tv. It was so big that two or even three kids could nestle within its white bulk. Beyond its warmth and softness, the most wonderful thing about the robe was how it had soaked up Dad's essence, his *smell.* We would sit there, wrapped in the warmth and comforting

*Source: What a Writer Needs* (pp. 31–41) by R. Fletcher. Reprinted by permission of Ralph Fletcher: WHAT A WRITER NEEDS (Heinemann, A division of Reed Elsevier Inc., Portsmouth, NH, 1993).

scent of the father we missed so much. I discovered that if I closed my eyes it was nearly possible to believe that he really was there himself, holding us in his strong arms.

Today the word *buffalo* sounds to me like power commingled with regret: the mighty beasts that were all but wiped out as white America moved west. But also a deeper and more personal regret tangled up with missing my father.

Artists develop a love for the feel of their tools, the smell and texture of clay, wood, or paint. My brother Jim has imported ebony all the way from Nigeria for some of his most memorable sculptures. The lithographer Tanya Grosman searched the world to find paper of astonishing beauty and rarity to lure artists such as Jasper Johns, Larry Rivers, Buckminster Fuller, and Robert Rauschenburg to her Universal Limited Art Editions studio in West Islip, New York.

Writers are no different. Writers love words. And while some writers get excited over a particular pen or a more powerful word processing program, words remain the most important tool the writer has to work with.

"If you want to write and you're not in love with your language, you shouldn't be writing," Jane Yolen says bluntly. "Words are the writer's tools."

"When I write," Cynthia Rylant says, "my mind's not filled with visual imagery. It's filled with language. Words. I seek words, I chase after them. When I write I'm trying to put the most beautiful words in the world down on paper."

Not all writers work like Rylant; some writers do begin with images, others with emotion. Either way the writer must use words to communicate the story/image/emotion. Writers obsess over words, their origins, their sounds. Writers have pet words, favorite and worst words, words imbued with other associations and personal meanings. In *One Writer's Beginnings,* Eudora Welty (1984) describes the sensual awareness she developed of particular words such as moon: "The word 'moon' comes into my mouth as though fed to me out of a silver spoon. Held in my mouth the moon became a word. It had the roundness of a Concord grape Grandpa took off his vine and gave me to suck out of its skin and swallow whole, in Ohio."

Writers love their language, but the language they love may not be a conventional tongue. Mark Twain's many books captured the colorful vernacular of the Mississippi region. Eloise Greenfield is one of many African-American writers to use Black English for her sparkling book of poems, *Honey, I Love* (1978). And Darrell H. Y. Lum, a Hawaiian writer, uses a rich and musical pidgin English in a short story like "The Moiliili Bag Man" (1992). The language used by a writer may be powerful or lyrically beautiful even while it does not conform to conventional grammar.

The writer's fascination with words has roots in the child's natural play with language. In late May of 1989, my friend Jenifer Hall took a trip up north with her daughter, Emma. Jenifer explained that they were going to see Ralph and JoAnn get married in Ludlow, Vermont. Emma, who was about twenty months old at the time, fell instantly in love with that word: Ludlow. For two solid hours she sang and chanted and played with its sounds: "Lud-low, lud-low . . . lud-lud-lud and low-low-low . . . LUD-low LUD-low, LUD-low-low-low-low . . . luddy-luddy-luddy-lud . . . luddy-luddy-luddy-low . . ."

"Read like a wolf eats," Gary Paulsen says to young readers, and as a boy I did that. I was a ravenous reader, and it didn't take long to figure out that each new word brought you into a whole new room, with new views and distinct intellectual furniture. The Boy Scout Oath's lofty aims ("trustworthy, loyal, helpful, friendly, courteous, kind, obedient, cheerful, thrifty, brave, clean, and reverent") were counterbalanced by less pure descriptors such as *voluptuous,* and *callipygean*—exotic and barely understood words I first encountered in books, words that took on sultry new nuances as I moved into adolescence.

One sweltering summer day, while my young father struggled to mow the lawn with a hand mower, I was sitting with my best friend on the porch. He confided to me the worst swear in the world. Only nine years old, I watched from a safe distance my father mop sweat off his forehead while my friend whispered the muggy monosyllabic word, softly, so my father would not hear. It seemed monstrous that such a word could co-exist juxtaposed (another of my favorite words) against the image of my saintly, toiling father. Swears amazed me. "Duck" was perfectly all right, but if your mother heard you rhyme that word with another word only two letters after the "D" you could get your mouth washed out with soap.

Another amazing thing: Words could mean different things at different times. The spoken word "see" might also mean "sea"—or even the letter "C." Many words contained delightful shades of ambiguity. When I was five I loved to play with homonyms: "bear" and "bare," "red" and "read." This early language play would later blossom in a poem like "Waves" (from *Water Planet*):

Waves on the ocean,
Ripples on the sand,
My father calling me
With a wave of his hand.
The wavy grain of wood,
The wave in my hair,
Waves of fiery autumn leaves

Tumbling through the air.
A wave of sadness
When I think of the way
My best friend Vinnie
Moved far far away.

I grew up in Brant Rock, Massachusetts, where there was a fabulous candy store: Buds. Once a week, if we were lucky, my mother would walk us down to Buds, where the bins and counters were crammed with chocolate cigarettes and bubblegum cigars, red wax lips and black wax mustaches, dots and red hots, jaw-breakers and ju-ju beads . . . Many of the candies were priced two or even three for a penny; if you shopped wisely you could end up with a whole bag of sweets for a nickel or a dime.

At that time *bamboozled* and *flabbergasted* were my favorite words. I loved the feel of those words in my mouth, and still cannot conjure them up except in terms of taste. *Bamboozled* has a fizzly Sweet Tart taste that begins in a rush of sweetness but always ends with a tingly, tickly feeling at the top of the mouth. *Flabbergasted,* on the other hand, tastes and sounds as nutty as a Heath Bar.

I kept a mental list of my favorite words, some of which I loved for the odd pictures they made in my mind, others merely for their exotic sounds: *babushka, cockatoo, pumpernickel,* and *periwinkle.* Later I would keep actual lists of words and trade them with similarly inclined friends. (We were not necessarily the most popular kids in the school.) Each word carried its own peculiar kind of melody. While words like *umber, mellow, sonorous,* and *quiescent* sounded smoothing, words like *obstreperous, truculent, vituperative,* and *obdurate* seemed to jut their very chins out at the world.

The Fletcher family was a den of rabid Boston Bruin hockey fans. Back then the Bruins had a few future Hall of Fame players, like Phil Esposito and Bobby Orr. Otherwise, the team consisted primarily of players who hustled, checked hard, and enjoyed fighting, or appeared to, at least. The Bruins were forever getting into brawls. I was an avid reader of the *Boston Globe* sports section, and it was great fun trying to envision the sports writers thumbing through their thesauruses in search of new words for these nightly altercations. My siblings and I roared over the words they came up with: *imbroglio, fisticuffs, slugfest, donnybrook,* and (my favorite) *brouhaha.*

In high school, while other kids admired teachers with the best looks, biggest muscles, or fastest cars, I admired those teachers with the most remarkable vocabularies. Mr. Thompson and Mr. Plumer were able to take words like *perspicacious, numinous,* or even *contemporaneous* and weave

them seamlessly into their lectures. I would copy down the words and race home to look them up.

Fancy words like *perspicacious* were one thing. But sometimes, I discovered two ordinary words placed next to each other could wake up and create an effect that went far beyond the capabilities of either one. This is exactly what led to my deciding to title my first book *Walking Trees* (1991), taken from a conversation I had with a first-grade girl. Put together, these two words try to pull each other in opposite directions. The phrase *walking trees* embodies a concept almost impossible to put in words: paradox, when two opposing ideas can both be true at the same time.

In the early 1960s, my siblings and I roamed through the thick pine woods around our house in Marshfield, Massachusetts. My brother Jim was a born naturalist, with vacuum eyes that sucked up incredible treasures during his long solitary treks through the woods. Every single day he would bring home some unusual insect, snake, or turtle he had found.

One day, after a bad windstorm, Jim and I were walking through a swampy part of the woods. A tree had fallen in the storm; a shallow pool had formed in the crater left by the huge mass of uplifted roots. At the edge of the water we saw something lurch into the water, a kind of lizard we had never seen before. We got just the briefest glimpse of red before the creature disappeared.

"Didya see that?"

"It looked some kind of newt," I said. "A salamander."

"That was no salamander," Jim said. "Didn't you see the red on its gills?"

Jim went home and proceeded to pull out several volumes of the World Book Encyclopedia. For two hours he sat poring through volumes A (amphibians), L (lizard), and R (reptiles).

"I found it," he said, showing me a picture. "A mud puppy. That's definitely it. We saw a mud puppy. They're common around here, found in the swamps, rivers, and lakes of northeastern America. Their external gills are bright red."

Mud puppy! I fell in love with the odd name, the internal rhyme, the funny image it forced into my head. The name clicked. By the end of that week all the kids in the neighborhood were calling the swampy area near that uprooted tree Mud Puppy Place.

Journal entry, January 30, 1991. JoAnn is studying for the GREs. Three hundred core words for the vocabulary section. Stacks of vocabulary cards in the bathroom. Big, cocky, multisyllabic words. Abstemious, convivial, concatenation. These words strut around the house, loud and arrogant.

Worse, they have actually shouldered their way into our spoken sentences.

"Don't you think the war is *reprehensible?*"

"Don't *prevaricate*. The point is that when it comes to contributions, some of our allies certainly haven't been very *munificent*."

These words are obnoxious, but we cater to them. At least for now, we need them far more than they need us.

Words are the writer's primal tools. But anyone who tries to write English—child or adult—immediately gets caught in a kind of linguistic stranglehold that makes it difficult to use those tools. Our English language contains about 490,000 words, along with another 300,000 technical terms. No one, of course, not even the great writers, can utilize so much richness. It has been said that Shakespeare had a working vocabulary of around 33,000 words. In 1945, the average American student between the ages of six and fourteen had a written vocabulary of 25,000 words. Today, that vocabulary has shrunk to about 10,000 words.

The mass media has helped to further tighten this noose. Popular print media draw from a small group of words; television, of course, draws from the smallest word pool of all. The implications for this stranglehold go far beyond the dangers of falling SAT scores.

It seems to me that the first step toward breaking this linguistic stranglehold is for teachers to model our own curiosity with words. Recently I decided to bring a bag of words into the schools where I work as a writing consultant. I wanted to let kids know how crucial words are to me as a writer. But how to proceed? I was surer about what I *didn't* want to do. I knew I didn't want to turn it into a vocabulary lesson, carefully disguised instruction on roots or suffixes, or an exercise in using the dictionary.

I walked into a fifth-grade classroom and began by writing some of my favorite words on the blackboard. Some were funny sounding words: *persnickety, oxymoron,* and *troglodyte* (which the students especially liked for its usefulness in insulting people). I had chosen several small words for their sheer potency: *triage, quisling, quietus.*

Kids started scrambling for the dictionaries. It turned out, however, that the school-use dictionaries in the classroom didn't house most of the words I had brought in with me. I sent a student down to the library. A few minutes later he returned, grunting under the weight of Webster's monstrous 2,347-page 320,000-word *New Universal Unabridged Dictionary*. We were in business.

*Mnemonic. Touchstone. Onomatopoeia.* The kids were delighted to learn that *fontanel* is the word for the soft spot at the top of a baby's head. Next, I scribbled on the board several truly bizarre words:

*jirble*—a craving for unnatural food, such as dust
*geniophobia*—fear of chins
*xenoglossy*—understanding a language one has never learned

"Probably the longest word in the English language is *pneumonoultramicroscopicsilicovolcanoconiosis,*" I told the students. "Forty-five letters. It's a kind of lung disease miners can get."

The kids howled, impressed that I knew what it meant and could actually pronounce it. They asked me to say it several more times, and insisted I write it on the board.

"How about you?" I asked. "Do you have any favorite words?"

"I've always liked *plummet,*" one boy said. "I like the way it sounds."

"I like *tintinnabulation,*" one girl said, pronouncing the word perfectly. "It means the ringing of the bells."

I wrote down their words: *déjà vu, exposé, deciduous.*

"I like the word *mistress,*" one very tall girl said. "I mean, I don't like what it means but I like how it sounds." She paused and looked at me with narrowed eyes. "What *does* it mean?"

I glanced at the fifth-grade teacher. The teacher answered quickly, casually, as if she had been expecting the question.

"Mistress is one of those words with more than one meaning," she explained. "Mistress can be a proper title for a woman. And it can also be the word for a woman who goes out with a married man."

"Oh," the girl said.

Jane Yolen (1973) describes three different vocabularies: a reading vocabulary, a writing vocabulary, and a speaking vocabulary. "There are some words that are wonderful but they're reading words only, or writing words—not speaking words," Yolen says. "And those of us who are writers also have a secret vocabulary."

My secret vocabulary includes words I often save for a long time, several years, until I can actually use them in a piece of writing. I hoarded *postprandial* (an adjective meaning "after dinner," as in "postprandial coffee") for no less than five years and was thrilled to actually be able to use the word in my first book. Another secret word of mine is *gegenschein*—a faint, glowing spot in the sky exactly opposite the position of the sun; also called "counterglow." I have kept this word for a long, long time; I'm not at all sure I shall ever find a legitimate place to use it in a sentence. Still, it's good to have such a word around in case the need arises.

A rich vocabulary allows a writer to get a richness of thought onto the paper. However, the writer's real pleasure comes not from using an exotic word but from using the *right* word in a sentence. Not long ago, while writing an article, I labored over this sentence: "Many school districts are finding it difficult to ___ a whole-language approach with existing reading programs, which rely heavily on basals."

I could not think of the missing word. But I knew it was out there—the single word that would make the sentence click, make its meaning snap into instant focus. It had something to do with paradox, with linking two things that don't quite go together. *Juxtapose* was close, but it wasn't the right word. I kept plugging other, less precise words into the sentence and rereading to see how it sounded. Link? No. Equate? No. Compare? Bridge? Nope. Finally, I gave up and moved to another part of the article.

That night, in bed, I suddenly opened my eyes. Sat bolt upright.

"RECONCILE!" I said to JoAnn.

"Huh?"

"Reconcile!" I grinned at her. "The word I've been looking for. 'School districts are finding it difficult to *reconcile* a whole-language approach with existing reading programs, which rely heavily on basals.' Eureka!"

As teachers, we can share with students the pleasure in finding the precise word to communicate a nuance of thought. We can encourage students to play naturally with language. And we can celebrate their language breakthroughs wherever and whenever they occur. After reading *Charlotte's Web* (White, 1952), Donna, a third grader, told her teacher: "I think I want to use the word *perish* in my story instead of *die*."

Is *perish* a better word than *die?* Not necessarily. Not always. Often a simple word is better than the fancy word. But in this case Donna took a big risk: She moved a word from her reading vocabulary to her writing vocabulary, a word she had never before used in a piece of writing. That's what I mean by a language breakthrough.

In the Bronx, Denton, a first grader, wrote the story shown in Figure 1.

I hoard yet one more vocabulary. This one has less to do with exotic words than with words saturated in strong memories. Words and phrases like *buffalo* and *mud puppy* contain potent medicine; their music conjures up an entire era of my life. I think of them as "trapdoor" words. For some words, the conventional meaning hides a secret trapdoor that leads down to an unexpected or previously forgotten layer of memory underneath. The mere mention of such a word is enough to bring it all back in a flood.

Take the word *sheriff.* This serious word has been altered forever by the association I have with Valerie Sheriff, a girl on whom I had a hopeless crush (the perfect word!) during eleventh and twelfth grades. She was stunning, and she was in the classes with all the smartest kids, which only intensified the awe in which I held her. Today I cannot watch a western with outlaws and sheriffs without immediately thinking of Valerie Sheriff, her straight blond hair and flawless features, the cool California air about her, the impossibly long legs beneath her cheerleader miniskirt, the energetic splits she did on the sidelines during football games that always left me feeling weak.

Or take *elegant.* My grandmother, Annie Collins, came from Arlington, Massachusetts, each year to spend Christmas with our family in New York. At our Christmas Eve dinner, Grandma Annie, Aunt Mary, my parents, and all seven or eight or nine kids would be sitting around the big table with the best plates and silverware, the food heaped high, a glass of red wine for the grownups, even a thimbleful for the kids. After the food was served, and grace said, everyone paused. We kids had to wait, drooling over our drumsticks, mouths watering over mounds of butternut squash with molten craters of butter on top. It was traditional that before the rest of us could dig in, Grandma Annie had to be the first one to take a mouthful of turkey.

"Oh, Jean, this is *elegant,*" she would say. That set everything into motion. Now Mom could blush her thanks, everyone else could laugh, and we could all start eating. But we knew. Young as we were, we understood some of the significance of that word spoken here in New York by our Bostonian grandmother, a word that seemed to rhyme with "delicate," a word that carried its nostalgic ring of old Boston, maybe more civilized times, legends of Ted Williams and Jack Kennedy, the times she marched on the Boston Commons as a suffragette, and the night she danced with "Honey" Fitz at an office party in Filene's Bargain Basement, where she worked.

Grandma Annie died in 1979, at the age of ninety-two. Today, in my family, the word "elegant" still gets spoken around the holidays, and always with a great deal of reverence.

## REFERENCES

Fletcher, R. (1991). *Walking trees*. Portsmouth, NH: Heinemann.

Fuentes, C. (1985). *The old gringo*. New York: Farrer Straus Giroux.

Greenfield, E. (1978). *Honey, I love and other love poems*. New York: Crowell.

Lum, D. (1992). "The Moiliili Bagman" in Watanabe, S. (Ed.), *Talking to the dead and other stories*. New York: Doubleday.

Welty, E. (1984). *One writer's beginnings*. Cambridge, MA: Harvard University Press.

White, E. B. (1952). *Charlotte's web*. New York: Harper and Row.

Yolen, J. (1973). *Writing books for children*. Boston, MA: The Writer, Inc.

my beloveed loves me becuse I love her one day Seh kiss me I wassak

**Figure 1**

    Where had Denton come upon *beloved,* an old-fashioned word that intermingles love, respect, and a kind of religious reverence? I told Denton: "It's a wonderful piece of writing. That word *beloved* makes it even more special to read."

# Ways to Look at the Functions of Children's Language

**Gay Su Pinnell**

## EDITOR'S INTRODUCTION

Gay Su Pinnell is a national leader in Reading Recovery. In her work, she is a strong voice for teachers developing skills as close observers of students. In this article, she applies Halliday's categories for the functions of language to the talk of students in one classroom. Her work is a fine example of how language theories can inform and extend the work of teachers researchers.

Six year old Andrew has just been to a concert given by a harpist at his school. He is now drawing a harp and talking to himself: "Harperoo. Harperoo. Harperdy dart, harperdy dart, parperdy dart, arp arp, arpity, dart, dart, arpity dart, arpity, dart, arpity, dart, dart, arp, arp, parpity, dart. . . . OK, this was a fine assembly . . . but I can tell you something. That harp was about six feet tall! And if you don't believe me, ask the woman that was playing it. Whew! Boy!"

"New, new, new" declares a catalog designed to persuade teachers to purchase the latest materials to help children develop skills in language. Some of the catchy titles include "growth in grammar," "phonics in context," "word attack and comprehension," "spelling for beginners." These materials may indeed help youngsters look at various forms of language and perhaps to perform well on worksheets and tests designed to measure the lessons the materials teach. But most are usually based on assumptions about what children do not know about language while ignoring their competence—what they do know. Such materials fail to recognize and respond to the natural and enthusiastic

language play we observe in Andrew's example above. And they are not "new." Most important, they are inconsistent with language research of the past decade which urges us to focus less on the form of language and more on its social function and meaning.

This article will concentrate, therefore, on what teachers can learn about children's language—their ability to communicate and to engage in conversation—through observation and on ways to extend their language for a range of uses in real life situations.

## DEVELOPING A FUNCTIONAL VIEW OF LANGUAGE

A functional view of language means focusing on how people use language in their everyday lives to communicate, to present themselves, to find out about things, to give information, to negotiate and interact. What is important about

*Source:* "Ways to Look at the Functions of Children's Language" by G. S. Pinnell, 1985. In *Observing the Language Learner* (pp. 57–72), A. Jaggar and M. T. Smith-Burke, Eds., Newark, DE: International Reading Association.

language is what we can do with it—how it functions in a world of people. What we can *do* with language is worth assessing and teaching.

Children live in a rich social world of language. They hear language, reorganize it and use it to express their own meanings. As they interact with others, they gradually learn how to share their meanings and, as they do so, construct a set of beliefs and expectations about language. They learn that language can be used to meet their needs, to learn and to communicate with others. The more they use language the more they learn about the forms of language—the words and patterns—that will help them to accomplish their purposes. When we think about children learning language, we can apply the simple principle: form follows function.

As Harold and Connie Rosen (1973) have pointed out, "language is for living with," and we might add, "learning with" (p. 21). Research for at least the past decade supports the idea that function and meaning are the most important, and probably the most neglected, concerns of parents, researchers, teachers, and others who must make decisions about the assessment and development of young children's language (Cazden, John, & Hymes, 1972).

A productive way to monitor language development—and one which will also help teachers to evaluate their own effectiveness in fostering language use—is to observe children in a systematic way to determine the range of language functions used in the classroom. There are several established systems for observing and categorizing functions of language. These systems are useful for assessment and also for devising strategies to extend children's use of language for a variety of social purposes.

One simple and useful category system has already been developed by M.A.K. Halliday (1973, 1975), who maintains that the linguistic system is a "range of possible meanings, together with the means whereby these meanings are realized or expressed" (1975, p. 8). He identifies seven categories for functions of language and stresses the importance of children experiencing the whole range in their homes, communities, and schools. The categories based on Halliday's frame-work are listed below. The definitions were formulated by Pinnell for use in a study (1975) of language in the classroom.

## Function Categories

**Instrumental Language.**  Instrumental language is what we use to get what we want, to satisfy needs or desires. At the early stages it may be to satisfy simple needs or wants; at later stages of sophistication, it may take the form of polite requests or persuasion. Appropriate and effective use of instrumental language in conversation, on the telephone, and in writing is important for the skillful language user. Little intervention is needed to elicit instrumental language. Children use it all the time. As they grow more independent, instrumental language should, in fact, decrease and become more complex, taking on forms of persuasion and argument.

**Regulatory Language.**  The regulatory function means using language to control the behavior of others, or getting them to do what we want them to do. Regulatory language may include giving orders or at more subtle levels, manipulating and controlling others. This kind of language is often used in competitive game situations in which there is a rule-governed "right" answer. Positive regulatory language is one of the "life skills" that every parent, shop owner, foreman, or administrator must know. The student who leads a committee or serves on Student Council will practice regulatory language every day.

**Interactional Language.**  Interactional language is used to establish and define social relationships. It may include negotiation, encouragement, expressions of friendships, and the kind of "maintenance" language all of us use in group situations. The "setting, joking and small talk" adults do before a meeting begins is also an example. Because those who are effective in building informal relationships are likely to succeed, children need to develop a comfortable awareness of their ability to use language to establish relationships with other people, to work cooperatively with them, and to enjoy their companionship.

**Personal Language.**  Personal language is used to express individuality and personality. Strong feelings and opinions are part of personal language. Personal language is often neglected in classrooms and thought inappropriate. Yet, it is through personal language that children relate their own lives to the subject matter being taught, establish their own identities, build self esteem and confidence.

**Imaginative Language.**  Imaginative language is used to create a world of one's own, to express fantasy through dramatic play, drama, poetry or stories. This use of language flourishes in the kindergarten with its house corner, big blocks and toys. Unless it is fostered, it will rapidly disappear in later years. Its importance cannot be underestimated, especially when we consider how difficult some teachers find it to get students to write with imagination. Poetry, stories, drama—all are the result of active use of the imaginative function.

**Heuristic Language.**    Heuristic language is used to explore the environment, to investigate, to acquire knowledge and understanding. Heuristic language is for investigation, for wondering, for figuring things out. It is the language of inquiry and is one of the most important functions.

**Informative Language.**    Informative language is used to communicate information, to report facts or conclusions from facts. It is the language of school. Teachers most frequently use it themselves and require it of children, but informative language is not only recall of facts. Helping children synthesize material and draw inferences and conclusions is also important.

In this article, Halliday's framework will be used to look at children's use of language. But it is not the only system. Tough (1977), Smith (1977), Wood (1977) and others provide different frameworks for looking at the functions of language. Teachers can easily develop their own by thinking about all the ways they use language; these are the functions the child must eventually develop.

Whatever the system, sensitive observation, using a simple category system for language functions, can help a teacher determine children's competence in using language that relates to real life situations. Teachers need ways of assessing language that will help them to monitor the child's growing ability to use language skillfully in the social milieu. Test scores may be part of the assessment, but teachers' judgments of language ability are still the most trusted and reliable assessment. Studies (Black, 1979; Tough, 1977) show that observing and recording children's language behavior is a viable way to look at what they *can* do, thus giving an effective starting point for instruction.

The important thing is that teachers need to think carefully about the social interaction going on in the classroom, perhaps asking themselves questions such as:

1.  Does each child use language for a variety of purposes? How is the function of language linked with what the child is doing and who he/she is talking to?

2.  What range of language functions do we hear in the classroom? What situations promote different uses for language?

3.  How can I extend children's use of language as I work with them?

In order to answer these questions teachers must pay attention to the context in which language is used, in this case, the school and the classroom.

Children learn how to use language within a social context and as they do so, they learn the needed forms of expression. The language context, the environment, and the climate of the classroom and school are important factors that influence how children will use language. Context includes the other people in the situation, the expectations and background knowledge of speakers and listeners alike, as well as the physical surroundings in which the language takes place. As Clark and Clark (1977) have pointed out, the "function of language is intimately bound up with the speakers' and listeners' mental activities during communication, in particular with the speakers' intentions, the ideas speakers want to convey and the listeners' current knowledge" (p. 25).

## WHAT CAN WE LEARN FROM WATCHING AND LISTENING?

As the following examples will demonstrate, a great deal can be learned by careful watching and listening. In the example below, Anne and Amy, two first graders, are painting clay ash trays they have made.

*Anne:* Yeah, 'cause my mom really does need a ash tray. She only got three or four ash trays and she smokes a lot. And we always have to clean the ash trays out for. . . . I use the, uh, stuff that you dust the tables with but in the ashtrays and they turn out real clean. Don't you, Amy?

*Amy:* Mm, hm.

*Anne:* You're my sister but you had to get adopted by somebody cause mommy didn't like you. You were mean! (She giggles.)

*Amy:* She liked me, but she didn't wanta have that much children and . . .

*Anne:* Why? 'Cause she already got five kids now. 'Member, she gave away sister, and brother. We had two brothers until she had to give you and then two. We did have eight kids. Wasn't it? Yea, it was eight kids. (Pause) 'Cause five plus three equal eight.

*Amy:* I'm done with the inside now. Where's that pretty blue?

*Monica:* I know.

*Amy:* Here's that pretty blue on there. See the pretty blue on there, Sue Anne?

*Anne:* Yeah. (Laughs) Gosh, your ash tray is little. How come you just put it on a straw?

*Amy:* I'm gonna put some string around it.

*Anne:* It has tape underneath. I just made a big one because my mom smokes a lot. You know mommy's been smokin' more than she usually does since you've been gone. And she has to sleep with me at night. She thinks I'm you. 'Cause she likes to sleep with you. 'Member, she always did? But you never did wanta clean. I always did.

What do we know about Amy and Anne now that we have listened to them? Using Halliday's categories as a guide, we can identify many skillful uses of language in the girls' conversation. They can readily switch from interactional language (talking about work arrangements, etc.) to regulatory language (giving orders) to imaginative language (playing a role, such as "sisters"). When they switch to imaginative language, there is no verbal signal such as "let's pretend." They simply follow each others' cues. There is a system of subtle signals between the girls which helps them to make these switches smoothly and maintain their conversation. We also notice that they report and utilize knowledge gained from other situations; for example, "five plus three equal eight." They certainly weave some personal language, opinions, sharing of feelings and thoughts, etc., into the conversation. They seem relaxed and comfortable with each other. The work continues productively. Each girl is accomplishing her task while engaged in purposeful talk. The clay/painting situation was a fruitful context for developing both work skills and language skills.

A little later on in the same scene, Anne is still painting her ash tray; Monica is painting at the easel; Amy has been wondering what to do.

*Anne:* Why don't you paint your ash tray? It might be dry. Mine was dry and now I'm gonna paint it.

*Amy:* Ok, ok, ok.

*Anne:* I said, "Why DON'T you." I didn't say "PAINT your ash tray," Amy. I just said "Why DON'T you paint your ash tray."

*Amy:* (inaudible)

*Anne:* Well, how come you have to say it when you go "ok"? (She imitates Amy's earlier intonation.)

*Monica:* I'm going to make mine green!

*Anne:* I'm doin'. . . on the outside of mine I'm doin' it dark green but I ain't painting the bottom, girl, 'cause when you set it on a piece of paper to let the paint dry then it, the paint'll get stuck on that and then the paper'll come up with your ash tray and you won't get to take it home. You'll have to spend all your time takin' off that paper. That's why I won't put the, uh, I got to set this thing down. I can't paint with it like that.

What more do we know? Further observation of Anne and Amy shows that Anne can use language to describe, to report prior knowledge, and to project into the future. We also notice Anne and Amy are capable of using language to talk *about* language. Anne, in fact, makes a very fine distinction between an order, "Paint your ashtray," and a suggestion, "Why don't you paint your ashtray?" They are examining language and its meaning as they talk with each other.

During a more formal classroom activity, two first graders, Matt and Brett, are talking as they complete an assigned task, writing numerals. Their talk is casual, but they are using language to describe the work they are doing.

*Matt:* Ten hundred! That's far isn't it? Ten hundred's far isn't it?

*Brett:* Nine hundred's farther than ten hundred.

*Matt:* No, it's not.

*Brett:* Yes, it is.

*Matt:* Ten hundred is.

*Matt:* Oh, I messed up! (He has made a mistake on the paper.) How do you make a ten like, oh, I know how to make a ten.

*Brett:* You make a one, then you make a zero.

We might be tempted to direct a "shhh . . ." to the boys above. Yet, looking at it another way, the conversation is actually adding to the learning experience. They are learning to write numerals and learning to talk about math at the same time. Brett and Matt are helping each other understand complicated ideas through language. They are wondering aloud, asking questions and instructing each other. In Halliday's terms, they are using informative, interactive, heuristic, and personal language in a complex interaction while concentrating on the task at hand.

While the teacher's intervention is necessary to expand children's language, peer language is a rich social context in which to try out new language uses and receive feedback. Although teachers often think they must be everywhere doing everything and providing all the instruction, observation of children reassures us that children do encourage, instruct, and help each other effectively. And, in so doing, they develop communicative competence in using language. . . .

The above samples were of conversations between young children in the first year of school, but it is equally important to be aware of and foster a range of language functions with older children. The following group of Canadian fifth graders discussed a problem of national interest.

*Graham:* If Quebec separates from Canada, the Maritime Provinces will probably go to the United States. The

Grand Banks fishing area is important and the U.S. could use it.

*Doug:* I kinda do hope they separate, 'cept in one way—the Maritimes would be poor! But, I would be glad in another way because they cause so much trouble.

*Jeremy:* Doug, I don't think they cause all that many problems. They just want to speak their own language there. . . .

*Graham:* Doug, you have to remember that the French came over and did a lot of exploring as well as the English so it just wasn't the English people who have a right to Canada!

*Jeremy:* (nodding) I think the Canadians are being selfish to want just one language. There is no reason why we can't speak many languages and live together.

*Bob:* Yeah, we should be able to speak many languages but the French only want to speak French, Jeremy. They have to be willing to give a little, too!

*Doug:* Bob's right, they don't have the right to cause so much trouble! Even the labels on the cans have to be written in French. That's why we can't get half the stuff from the states!

*Caroline:* I think we should have only one main language. The labels cost a lot for the rest of us.

*Martine:* I would say the same as Caroline.[1]

The children in this example had had much experience in using language in a variety of ways and were accustomed to participating in discussion groups. Here they are using informative and personal language to deal with complex ideas, to make inferences, and to argue skillfully. The students were expressing opinions and backing them up with information. It is in genuine argument that one must muster his or her best command of language in order to be persuasive enough to get the point across. Youngsters need many opportunities to try themselves out in arguments and discussions with peers, older students, and even with adults—teachers, principals, and others in the community. The demands of group interaction are seldom assessed in classroom situations; yet, they are critical language skills and deserve careful attention.

In a study of first graders, Pinnell (1975) found that at least two elements are usually present when children are actively engaged in using language functionally: 1) students are encountering real problems to which they want to find the solutions, and 2) two or more students are working and talking together about the problems. The interactions in the examples above took place in classrooms with these characteristics. The activities were interesting and challenging so that children had something to talk about, a chance to guess, argue, make predictions and check them out, and a chance to use their imaginations. Rather than seeing talk as distracting, their teachers saw it as valuable. They structured activities and the environment to take maximum advantage of the way children learn. That is, they gave children a great many opportunities to talk. The key is a teacher who is aware of the importance of fostering a wide range of language use and who is a good observer.

## OBSERVING LANGUAGE USE

By observing language use in the classroom, we can make two kinds of assessment:

1. We can assess an individual child's competence by looking at the extent to which he/she uses the various functions of language and how effectively.

2. We can assess the language environment by determining which functions occur and where, and which are being neglected.

For the first kind of assessment, the teacher should observe the same child in several different settings in the classroom and in formal and informal activities in other areas of the school. Observations may be brief (three to five minutes), but they should be recorded and reported periodically so that progress can be noted. For the second kind of assessment, a teacher may observe the entire class or small groups in different areas of the classroom or at different times of the day. The teacher can also combine data from observations of individual students to form a group composite. For both kinds of assessment, simple forms and checklists connected to the teachers' own goals and classroom activities could be used.

Since Halliday's categories are relatively easy to use, a teacher might start with them. Become familiar with the categories and then observe students in several different settings. A simple approach would be to make a list of the seven functions, or use a form like the one in Figure 1, and jot down examples of each type of language. Statements may seem to fulfill several functions at once. That is not surprising since language is complex and the categories are not discrete. What we are looking for is a profile that describes the variety of functions used. While it seems impossible to note all the language that is taking place, teachers will be surprised how much they can record in a short time. And, observations over a period of time provide a good picture of students' language.

---

[1]Example from Mary Louise Skinner, Deep Cove Elementary School, Sidney, British Columbia.

Name: _____
          (individual, small group, large group observed)

Time: _____
          (time of day)

Setting: _____
          (physical setting and what happened prior to observation)

Activity: _____
          (activity, including topic/subject area)

| LAUNGUAGE FUNCTION | EXAMPLES |
| --- | --- |
| Instrumental | |
| Regulatory | |
| Interactional | |
| Personal | |
| Imaginative | |
| Heuristic | |
| Informative | |

Note: Check each time a language function is heard and/or record examples.

**Figure 1**
Functions of language observation form.

This simple system provides a guide for observing language in the classroom and for monitoring student progress. It also provides a framework for teachers—individuals, teams or the whole staff—to use in designing instructional activities that encourage students to use language for a variety of purposes. By examining observational records, the teacher can determine which functions are being used and which are not and plan accordingly. For example, if no personal language is noted over several observations of a child, the teacher may want to make some time for an informal one-to-one conversation or for a home visit to establish a more productive relationship with the child. If little or no heuristic language is used by the children, the teacher might need to introduce materials or plan problem situations that stimulate curiosity and question asking. If most of the talk in the classroom falls into only a few categories, the teacher may want to reexamine the whole environment and reor-ganize learning activities so that the use of a greater variety of functions is encouraged.

Listed below are a few instructional strategies for each language function. Teachers can add others to the list. Try them and observe the results.

## Instructional Strategies to Promote Language Functions

*Instrumental Language*—The teacher can:

1. Be accessible and responsive to children's requests, but teach independence by having children state their requests effectively.

2. Encourage the use of instrumental language with other children, helping them to expand their own language through providing help and direction to peers.

3. Analyze advertising, propaganda, etc., to help children become aware of how language can be used by people to get what they want.

*Regulatory Language*—The teacher can:

1. Create situations that let children be "in charge" of small and large groups.
2. Find instances in which regulatory language is used inappropriately to teach appropriate regulatory language or the alternative, instrumental language.
3. Attempt to use less regulatory language as a teacher.

*Interactional Language*—The teacher can:

1. Create situations that require children to share work areas or materials and talk about how they are to do it.
2. Find ways of having small group (especially pairs or trios) discussions in a variety of subject areas. Through these discussions, students not only learn the subject matter more thoroughly, they practice communication.
3. Let students work together to plan field trips, social events, and classroom and school projects.
4. Whenever possible, mix children of different ages, sexes, races in work groups or discussion groups.
5. Have informal social times and, as a teacher, engage in some talk that is not "all business."

*Personal Language*—The teacher can:

1. Use personal language to give permission to children to share personal thoughts and opinions.
2. Be willing to listen and talk personally during transition times; for example, when children are coming in in the morning. Converse with children while on cafeteria or playground duty.
3. Provide some comfortable, attractive areas in the classroom where students can talk quietly.
4. Encourage parents and family members to visit and participate in classrooms.
5. Read stories or books that prompt a very personal response from students.

*Imaginative Language*—The teacher can:

1. Create situations that naturally elicit spontaneous dramatic play; for example, house corner, dress up, blocks for younger children, and drama and roleplaying for older children.
2. Read stories and books which feed the imagination and which are a stimulus for art, drama, and discussion.
3. Provide time for children to talk in groups and/or with partners before they begin their writing or imaginative topics.
4. Encourage "play" with language—the sounds of words and the images they convey.

*Heuristic Language*—The teacher can:

1. Structure classroom experiences so that interest and curiosity are aroused.
2. Create real problems for children to solve.
3. Put children in pairs or work groups for problem-solving activities.
4. Use heuristic language to stimulate such language in children. Saying "I wonder why" often promotes children to do the same. (This should, however, not be contrived; it should be an honest problem.)
5. Try projects which require study on the part of the entire class, including the teacher. Find some questions that no one knows the answer to.

*Informative Language*—The teacher can:

1. Plan activities which require children to observe carefully and objectively and then to summarize and draw conclusions from their observations (field trips are a good opportunity).
2. Require children to keep records of events over periods of time and then to look back at their records and draw conclusions; for example, keeping records on classroom pets.
3. Use questioning techniques to elicit more complex forms of information giving.
4. Instead of having tedious classroom reports, have children give their reports to small groups and encourage feedback and discussion of those reports.

Once teachers have increased their sensitivity to the range of language functions used in their classrooms and in the school, several things happen:

1. They have good information on children that can be used to support and defend instructional strategies to develop language.

2. They can talk more specifically and persuasively to parents and others about each child.

3. They are more aware of language functions so they can informally and constantly perform assessment without using the checklists and only occasionally making records.

4. They can more effectively plan educational experiences.

## GETTING STARTED: SUGGESTIONS FOR TWO FACULTY MEETINGS

Studying language development in your own classroom is often difficult. Observing, recording, and teaching at the same time can be tricky. And sometimes questions come up—how to categorize a particular statement, how to interpret a puzzling remark, how to help a certain child use regulatory language more effectively. It is much more exciting and much easier when there are others to hear your ideas and to make suggestions. The following guide could be used by a school staff or student teachers to get started in assessing and fostering the uses of language.

### Meeting #1

1. Ask the group to "brainstorm" all of the uses of language they can think of. (In brainstorming, every idea is accepted and written down on the chalkboard or chart paper so everyone can see). You will come up with a long list, including joking, gossip, lecturing, giving directions, etc.

2. With their own list before them, have the group examine the categories established by Halliday. Provide an introduction to the idea of functions of language.

3. In small groups or as a whole group, ask participants to generate examples from their own experiences for each of Halliday's categories. For each example, try to specify elements of context: where the language occurred, the topic, who was speaking, who the speaker was addressing, what the people were doing at the time.

4. The group should then develop a plan for observing in the school. They can observe classrooms—their own or each others'—and someone should observe on grounds, in the library, in the cafeteria, and in the hallways. They should specify times of day so that a variety of observations can be collected.

5. Each person leaves the meeting committed to observing for a designated period or periods of time during the next week and recording examples, with full contextual information, on the observation form.

### Meeting #2

1. Staff members work in small groups or (if there are not too many) in the large group. They share and compile their observations from the previous week. They note the range of language observed and try to relate context to kinds of language. They come up with some summary statements about the language environment.

2. Using a checklist of the functions of language, the group discusses and generates a list of strategies for extending children's language.

3. Each group selects one or two language functions that they particularly want to observe for and foster during the next week. For each function they make a list of strategies to try. They specify the action plan they will follow.

4. Each person leaves the meeting committed to an action plan for extending children's language. They are to report on their success at the next meeting.

Meetings need not be as formally structured as the ones described above. The central goal is for school staff members to explore children's language together and to help each other become more aware. The greater a teacher's sensitivity to language, the less formal assessment tools will be needed.

## REFERENCES

Black, J. "There's more to language than meets the ear: Implications for evaluation," *Language Arts, 56* (May 1979), 526–533.

Cazden, C. B., John, V. P., & Hymes, D. (Eds.). (1972). *Functions of language in the classroom.* New York: Teachers College Press.

Clark, H., & Clark, E. (1977). *Psychology and language: An introduction to psycholinguistics.* New York: Harcourt Brace Jovanovich.

Halliday, M. A. K. (1973). "The functional basis of language," in B. Bernstein (Ed.), *Class, codes, and control, Volume 2. Applied studies toward a sociology of language.* London and Boston: Routledge & Kegan Paul.

Halliday, M. A. K. (1975). *Learning how to mean: Explorations in the development of language.* London: Edward Arnold Ltd.

# Teacher Research Extension: An Unexpected Lesson In Language

**Michelle Schardt**
**Bilingual Kindergarten Teacher**

Ruben, a bilingual child whose mother immigrated from Guatemala before he was born, has spent his six years of life in Portland, Oregon surrounded by speakers of English, Spanish, and Conjovál. His mother's native tongue is Conjovál (an indigenous language from Mexico and Guatemala), but she speaks to him in Spanish because she believes it to be the more useful language. She works long hours, and Ruben is left with neighbors who work different shifts and sleep most of the time they are with him.

Sadly, Ruben does not get a lot of verbal interaction in his home language. His mother is not formally educated, nor do they have any books in the house. Ruben has a negative attitude toward Spanish, which puts a strain on his relationship with his mother and their family friends. He constantly tells his mother to "speak English" and refuses to go into stores with her because of his shame. This limits Ruben's language development since he has cut off his main language-enhancing relationship. These issues make Ruben's language development very interesting to me, especially since Ruben's attitude toward himself as a communicator is common among many other English learners in this country.

As a teacher trained in bilingual education without a bilingual program in my district, I have found myself teaching English as a Second Language (ESL) and native language (Spanish) literacy this year. The school in which I work is in the inner city of Portland, Oregon, and has an interesting mix of recent immigrants from various parts of the world. It enrolls children from both lower income and middle class families. I work with children from kindergartnen to fifth grade with a wide range of needs. More than ever I have been paying close attention to the language my students use, whether it is English or Spanish. At first glance, many of the English as a Second Language students seem to be struggling with language or even at a loss for words. Further study of one of my students, Ruben, proved that this assumption was inaccurate.

I teach Ruben every day during an English as a Second Language reading group as well as a Spanish native-language literacy session in a pull-out program. His Spanish is much more developed than his English, but he does not appear to be particularly fluent with either language. When he is with Spanish-speaking peers or me, he opts to use Spanish, but he uses both of his languages in the same way. He is frugal with his words and sees language mainly as a way to give brief information, to meet his physical needs, and ask basic questions. He clearly does not enjoy language as an expressive or literary function but sees it as a tool. When we sing songs, perform poems, or do finger plays in English or Spanish group, Ruben always sits on the outskirts of the group playing with his fingers or looking the other way. If, however, I ask questions requiring oral responses, he will raise his hand if he knows the answer. If he has a question he will ask me or another student for the answer. He can clearly and concisely request a drink of water or a trip to the bathroom.

These behaviors initially led me to believe that Ruben was not completely understanding what was going on, and I wanted to understand what was happening with him linguistically that might explain why he didn't participate. I decided to do some taping sessions with Ruben so that I could get some solid data to analyze. During the transcribing process, I was amazed at how much he really does know. Many bilingual children experience confusion and frustration in their early years. I'm sure that as Ruben gains confidence in both languages he will reach a comfort level where he can participate in more literary, expressive ways. Right now he is using his language differently.

## FEETS

During our tape recording session, Ruben used some rubber stamps with paper and talked spontaneously about what he was doing. He gave information about the stamps he put on the paper, and I asked him some basic questions.

Ruben: I turn it upside down!

Michelle: Now what is it?

*R:* A feet!

*M:* Whose feet?

*R:* This person.

*M:* The farmer?

*R:* Mm Hm (affirmation). I'm doing another one!

*M:* Do we say two feet or two feets?

*R:* Two feets.

At this point I was curious about his stage of language development instead of how he used language. I was interested in verb-noun agreement, plural formation, and other dull stuff that might be missing from Ruben's speech. When I asked Ruben about the correct usage of feet, he responded by generalizing the rule of making plurals. So, I thought, he does know the rule, but he doesn't know the exceptions like feet. Later on when we were talking in a different situation, I noticed that he used feet correctly several times. This is interesting since it shows that Ruben knows how to use the word when he isn't thinking about language. He knows what sounds right but when asked a question directly about the usage, he applied a rule. This also illustrates perfectly how erroneous standardized tests can be since language is taken out of context.

## HALLIDAY'S MODEL

During the second part of the transcription, Ruben told me a story from a picture book:

*Ruben:* There's an old house.

*Michelle:* Now what's happening?

*R:* Him's in the house.

*M:* What does he see?

*R:* Some plates [really bowls]. A big plate and a big plate and a small plate.

*M:* What will he do next?

*R:* He will eat it up!

*M:* Then what?

*R:* Him eating it and him's sitting down at the table. Him's in that chair and him broke the chair. And him broke everything!

*M:* Now what?

*R:* Go sleep in the big, big bedroom. Here. And the small one.

*M:* What's he doing?

*R:* Him . . . him jumping around and him . . . doing the pillow . . . him messed up the . . . him hiding in the bed.

My first impulse was to look through the transcript and see what I should teach Ruben based on his language usage: new vocabulary words, verb tenses, etc. However, after reading Halliday (1969) and looking at his categories of functions of language, I thought I'd look to see for what purposes Ruben actually used language during the session. Halliday breaks language into seven different categories based on the goal for which it is used. Here is a brief summary explaining the seven language functions Halliday outlined:

- *Regulatory* language is used to regulate the behavior of others. This can be giving instructions, correcting a behavior, or simply telling someone what to do.
- *Instrumental* language servers to get things done. "I want" is a common way for instrumental language to begin. This type of communication is used when someone else is needed in order for the speaker to reach a certain goal.
- Some language is used to make public the speaker's individual personality. Language that a child creates to show someone that he or she is unique, and then reinforces his or her individuality is called *personal* language.
- *Heuristic* is a sort of "tell me why" way of using language to investigate and explore ones environment. Questions and oral observations relating to a child's environment would be heuristic language.
- A fairly sophisicated use of language is a type called *representational*. With representational language, children emerge as information-givers or propositioners using

processes and relationships to express themselves. This function of language emerges around two years of age and involves a lot of "I have something to tell you" type communication.

- *Imaginative* language is used for describing events, people, etc. from fantasy. This sort of expression also involves playing with rhythmic sounds such as in poetry or music. Pretending and make-believe fall under the category of imaginative language.
- *Interactional* language serves the purpose of establishing a relationship between the speaker and the recipients. This language serves to include or exclude people from the speaker's perceived group.

When we look at how many ways language is used, it is easy to see the sophistication required to communicate at all.

Ruben's language was predictive and informative. He used the picture cues to guess what would happen. Thus he described what *would* happen during some parts and what *was* happening during others. When asked at one point what he thought would happen next, he replied "He will eat it up." When asked what was happening in a certain picture, he told me, "Hims in the house." He could also use some words to describe objects in the environment: "old house," "big plate," and "little bed." In these instances, Ruben was using language to make sense of the environment in the book. This method of investigating reality would fall under the heuristic function in Halliday's model. In addition to the way Ruben used the language, we can see he knew the verb forms to use for each situation: "he will" and "hims" (he is). He also knew the *-ing* form of the verbs and used them in the appropriate context and tense. After examining Ruben's language, I had come a long way in appreciating what he could do linguistically.

Much of Ruben's language was also interactional. The whole activity consisted of his relating a story to me. He used several tactics to relate to me what his interpretations were. Several times he told me, "See!" to make sure I understood where his predictions or information came from. Sometimes his "See!" was to show me that his prediction was accurate. These instances went beyond him just giving me some information about the book; he was making sure that we had a relationship while he was telling me the story.

## REVELATIONS

The transcribing process taught me a lot about Ruben's language. I hear him talk every day, but I hadn't really paid close attention to the details. I saw that I could have been using a wider variety of language myself since most of my questions and cues were very prediction or information oriented. I barely gave him a choice of how to answer me. Most of my inquiries were, "What will happen next?" or "What does he see?" How boring! Instead I should have focused on a variety of ways to elicit more varied responses. For example, I should have tried to extract some empathetic language by asking, "How would you feel if you were there and why?" If my students are limited in the ways they produce language, I can elicit different responses by the language I use. Instead of trying to "fix" the student, I can rethink what I am doing.

ESL students are faced with the challenge of learning how to speak English as well as becoming literate in this very complex language that is replete with exception after exception. If we really take a close look at these students we can see how much they actually do know about language and its various functions and uses.

## REFERENCE

Halliday, M. A. K. (1969). Relevant models of language. *Educational Review, 22,* 26–37.

# What Should Teachers Do? Ebonics and Culturally Responsive Instruction

## Lisa Delpit

### EDITOR'S INTRODUCTION

Lisa Delpit, a leading scholar on teaching and learning language in settings of cultural diversity, argues that it is a teacher's job to provide access to Standard English, while at the same time sufficiently understanding a child's home language and celebrating its beauty. Her research documents that constant correction seldom has the desired effect. She urges teachers instead to recognize the linguistic form a student brings to school and make the actual study of language diversity a part of the curriculum for all students.

The "Ebonics Debate" has created much more heat than light for most of the country. For teachers trying to determine what implications there might be for classroom practice, enlightenment has been a completely non-existent commodity. I have been asked often enough recently, "What do you think about Ebonics? Are you for it or against it?" My answer must be neither. I can be neither for Ebonics or against Ebonics any more than I can be for or against air. It exists. It is the language spoken by many of our African-American children. It is the language they heard as their mothers nursed them and changed their diapers and played peek-a-boo with them. It is the language through which they first encountered love, nurturance and joy.

On the other hand, most teachers of those African-American children who have been least well-served by educational systems believe that their students' life chances will be further hampered if they do not learn Standard English. In the stratified society in which we live, they are absolutely correct. While having access to the politically mandated language form will not, by any means, guarantee economic success (witness the growing numbers of unemployed African Americans holding doctorates), not having access will almost certainly guarantee failure.

So what must teachers do? Should they spend their time relentlessly "correcting" their Ebonics-speaking children's language so that it might conform to what we have learned to refer to as Standard English? Despite good intentions, constant correction seldom has the desired effect. Such correction increases cognitive monitoring of speech, thereby making talking difficult. To illustrate, I have frequently taught a relatively simple new "dialect" to classes of pre-service teachers. In this dialect, the phonetic element "iz" is added after the first consonant or consonant cluster in each syllable of a word. (*Maybe* becomes miz-ay-biz-ee and *apple,* iz-ap-piz-le.) After a bit of drill and practice, the students are asked to tell a partner in "iz" language why they decided to become teachers. Most only haltingly attempt a few words before lapsing into either silence or into Standard English. During a follow-up discussion, all students

*Source:* "What Should Teachers Do?" by Lisa D. Delpit, 1997, *Rethinking Schools, 12* (1), pp. 6–7. Reprinted with the author's permission.

invariably speak of the impossibility of attempting to apply rules while trying to formulate and express a thought. Forcing speakers to monitor their language typically produces silence.

Correction may also affect students' attitudes toward their teachers. In a recent research project, middle-school, inner-city students were interviewed about their attitudes toward their teachers and school. One young woman complained bitterly, "Mrs. ___ always be interrupting to make you 'talk correct' and stuff. She be butting into your conversations when you not even talking to her! She need to mind her own business." Clearly this student will be unlikely to either follow the teacher's directives or to want to imitate her speech style.

## GROUP IDENTITY

Issues of group identity may also affect students' oral production of a different dialect. Researcher Sharon Nelson-Barber, in a study of phonologic aspects of Pima Indian language, found that, in grades 1–3, the children's English most approximated the standard dialect of their teachers. But surprisingly, by fourth grade, when one might assume growing competence in standard forms, their language moved significantly toward the local dialect. These fourth graders had the *competence* to express themselves in a more standard form, but chose, consciously or unconsciously, to use the language of those in their local environments. The researcher believes that, by ages 8–9, these children became aware of their group membership and its importance to their well-being, and this realization was reflected in their language. They may also have become increasingly aware of the schools's negative attitude toward their community and found it necessary—through choice of linguistic form—to decide with which camp to identify.

What should teachers do about helping students acquire an additional oral form? First, they should recognize that the linguistic form a student brings to school is intimately connected with loved ones, community, and personal identity. To suggest that this form is "wrong" or, even worse, ignorant, is to suggest that something is wrong with the student and his or her family. To denigrate your language is, then, in African-American terms, to "talk about your mama." Anyone who knows anything about African-American culture knows the consequences of that speech act!

On the other hand, it is equally important to understand that students who do not have access to the politically popular dialect form in this country, are less likely to succeed economically than their peers who do. How can both realities be embraced in classroom instruction?

It is possible and desirable to make the actual study of language diversity a part of the curriculum for all students. For younger children, discussions about the differences in the ways television characters from different cultural groups speak can provide a starting point. A collection of the many children's books written in the dialects of various cultural groups can also provide a wonderful basis for learning about linguistic diversity, as can audio taped stories narrated by individuals from different cultures, including taping books read by members of the children's home communities. Mrs. Pat, a teacher chronicled by Stanford University researcher Shirley Brice Heath, had her students become language "detectives," interviewing a variety of individuals and listening to the radio and television to discover the differences and similarities in the ways people talked. Children can learn that there are many ways of saying the same thing, and that certain contexts suggest particular kinds of linguistic performances.

Some teachers have groups of students create bilingual dictionaries of their own language form and Standard English. Both the students and the teacher become engaged in identifying terms and deciding upon the best translations. This can be done as generational dictionaries, too, given the proliferation of "youth culture" terms growing out of the Ebonics-influenced tendency for the continual regeneration of vocabulary. Contrastive grammatical structures can be studied similarly, but, of course, as the Oakland policy suggests, teachers must be aware of the grammatical structure of Ebonics before they can launch into this complex study.

Other teachers have had students become involved with standard forms through various kinds of role-play. For example, memorizing parts for drama productions will allow students to practice and "get the feel" of speaking standard English while not under the threat of correction. A master teacher of African-American children in Oakland, Carrie Secret, uses this technique and extends it so that students video their practice performances and self-critique them as to the appropriate use of standard English. (But I must add that Carrie's use of drama and oration goes much beyond acquiring Standard English. She inspires pride and community connections which are truly wondrous to behold.) The use of self-critique of recorded forms may prove even more useful than I initially realized. California State University-Hayward professor Etta Hollins has reported that just by leaving a tape recorder on during an informal class period and playing it back with no comment, students began to code-switch—moving between Standard English and Ebonics—more effectively. It appears that they may have not realized which language form they were using until they heard themselves speak on tape.

Young students can create puppet shows or role-play cartoon characters—many "superheroes" speak almost hypercorrect standard English! Playing a role eliminates the possibility of implying that the **child's** language is inadequate and suggests, instead, that different language forms are appropriate in different contexts. Some other teachers in New York City have had their students produce a news show every day for the rest of the school. The students take on the personae of famous newscasters, keeping in character as they develop and read their news reports. Discussions ensue about whether Tom Brokaw would have said it that way, again taking the focus off the child's speech.

Although most educators think of Black Language as primarily differing in grammar and syntax, there are other differences in oral language of which teachers should be aware in a multicultural context, particularly in discourse style and language use. Harvard University researcher Sarah Michaels and other researchers identified differences in children's narratives at "sharing time." They found that there was a tendency among young white children to tell "topic-centered" narratives—stories focused on one event— and a tendency among Black youngsters, especially girls, to tell "episodic" narratives—stories that include shifting scenes and are typically longer. While these differences are interesting in themselves, what is of greater significance is adults' responses to the differences. C. B. Cazden reports on a subsequent project in which a white adult was taped reading the oral narratives of black and white first graders, with all syntax dialectal markers removed. Adults were asked to listen to the stories and comment about the children's likelihood of success in school. The researchers were surprised by the differential responses given by Blacks and white adults.

## VARYING REACTIONS

In responding to the retelling of a Black child's story, the white adults were uniformly negative, making such comments as "terrible story, incoherent" and "[n]ot a story at all in the sense of describing something that happened." Asked to judge this child's academic competence, all of the white adults rated her below the children who told "topic-centered" stories. Most of these adults also predicted difficulties for this child's future school career, such as, "This child might have trouble reading," that she exhibited "language problems that affect school achievement," and that "family problems" or "emotional problems" might hamper her academic progress.

The black adults had very different reactions. They found this child's story "well formed, easy to understand, and interesting, with lots of detail and description." Even though all five of these adults mentioned the "shifts" and "associations" or "nonlinear" quality of the story, they did not find these features distracting. Three of the black adults selected the story as the best of the five they had heard, and all but one judged the child as exceptionally bright, highly verbal, and successful in school.

This is not a story about racism, but one about cultural familiarity. However, when differences in narrative style produce differences in interpretation of competence, the pedagogical implications are evident. If children who produce stories based in differing discourse styles are expected to have trouble reading, and viewed as having language, family, or emotional problems, as was the case with the informants quoted by Cazden, they are unlikely to be viewed as ready for the same challenging instruction awarded students whose language patterns more closely parallel the teacher's.

Most teachers are particularly concerned about how speaking Ebonics might affect learning to read. There is little evidence that speaking another mutually intelligible language form, per se, negatively affects one's ability to learn to read. For commonsensical proof, one need only reflect on nonstandard English-speaking Africans who, though enslaved, not only taught themselves to read English, but did so under threat of severe punishment or death. But children who speak Ebonics do have a more difficult time becoming proficient readers. Why? In part, appropriate instructional methodologies are frequently not adopted. There is ample evidence that children who do not come to school with knowledge about letters, sounds, and symbols need to experience some explicit instruction in these areas in order to become independent readers. Another explanation is that, where teachers' assessments of competence are influenced by the language children speak, teachers may develop low expectations for certain students and subsequently teach them less. A third explanation rests in teachers' confusing the teaching of reading with the teaching of a new language form.

Reading researcher Patricia Cunningham found that teachers across the United States were more likely to correct reading miscues that were "dialect" related ("Here go a table" for "Here is a table") than those that were "nondialect" related ("Here is a dog" for "There is a dog"). Seventy-eight percent of the former types of miscues were corrected, compared with only 27% of the latter. He concludes that the teachers were acting out of ignorance, not realizing that "here go" and "here is" represent the same meaning in some Black children's language.

In my observations of many classrooms, however, I have come to conclude that even when teachers recognize the similarity of meaning, they are likely to correct Ebonics-related miscues. Consider a typical example:

*Text:* Yesterday I washed my brother's clothes.
*Student's Rendition:* Yesterday I wash my bruvver close.

The subsequent exchange between student and teacher sounds something like this:

*T:* Wait, let's go back. What's that word again? {Points at *washed.*}
*S:* Wash.
*T:* No. Look at it again. What letters do you see at the end? You see "e-d." Do you remember what we say when we see those letters on the end of the word?
*S:* "ed"
*T:* OK, but in this case we say washed. Can you say that?
*S:* *Washed.*
*T:* Good. Now read it again.
*S:* Yesterday I wash*ed* my bruvver . . .
*T:* Wait a minute, what's that word again? {Points to *brother.*}
*S:* Bruvver.
*T:* No. Look at these letters in the middle. {Points to *brother.*} Remember to read what you see. Do you remember how we say that sound? Put your tongue between your teeth and say /th/ . . .

The lesson continues in such a fashion, the teacher proceeding to correct the student's Ebonics-influenced pronunciations and grammar while ignoring that fact that the student had to have comprehended the sentence in order to translate it into her own language. Such instruction occurs daily and blocks reading development in a number of ways. First, because children become better readers by having the opportunity to read, the overcorrection exhibited in this lesson means that this child will be less likely to become a fluent reader than other children that are not interrupted so consistently. Second, a complete focus on code and pronunciation blocks children's understanding that reading is essentially a meaning-making process. This child, who understands the text, is led to believe that she is doing something wrong. She is encouraged to think of reading not as something you do to get a message, but something you pronounce. Third, constant corrections by the teacher are likely to cause this student and others like her to resist reading and to resent the teacher.

Language researcher Robert Berdan reports that, after observing the kind of teaching routine described above in a number of settings, he incorporated the teacher behaviors into a reading instruction exercise that he used with students in a college class. He put together sundry rules from a number of American social and regional dialects to create what he called the "language of Atlantis." Students were then called upon to read aloud in this dialect they did not know. When they made errors he interrupted them, using some of the same statements/comments he had heard elementary school teachers routinely make to their students. He concludes:

The results were rather shocking. By the time these Ph.D Candidates in English or linguistics had read 10–20 words, I could make them sound totally illiterate. . . . The first thing that goes is sentence intonation: they sound like they are reading a list from the telephone book. Comment on their pronunciation a bit more, and they begin to subvocalize, rehearsing pronunciations for themselves before they dare to say them out loud. They begin to guess at pronunciations. . . . They switch letters around for no reason. They stumble; they repeat. In short, when I attack them for their failure to conform to my demands for Atlantis English pronunciations, they sound very much like the worst of the second graders in any of the classrooms I have observed.

They also begin to fidget. They wad up their papers, bite their fingernails, whisper, and some finally refuse to continue. They do all the things that children do while they are busily failing to learn to read.

The moral of this story is not to confuse learning a new language form with reading comprehension. To do so will only confuse the child, leading her away from those intuitive understandings about language that will promote reading development, and toward a school career of resistance and a lifetime of avoiding reading.

Unlike unplanned oral language or public reading, writing lends itself to editing. While conversational talk is spontaneous and must be responsive to an immediate context, writing is a mediated process which may be written and rewritten any number of times before being introduced to public scrutiny. Consequently, writing is more amenable to rule application—one may first write freely to get one's thoughts down, and then edit to hone the message and apply specific spelling, syntactical, or punctuation rules. My college students who had such difficulty talking in the "iz" dialect, found writing it, with the rules displayed before them, a relatively easy task.

To conclude, the teacher's job is to provide access to the national "standard" as well as to understand the language the children speak sufficiently to celebrate its beauty. The verbal adroitness, the cogent and quick wit, the brilliant use of metaphor, the facility in rhythm and rhyme, evident in the language of Jesse Jackson, Whoopi Goldberg, Toni Morrison, Henry Louis Gates, Tupac Shakur, and Maya Angelou, as well as in that of many inner-city Black students, may all be drawn upon to facilitate school learning. The teacher must know how to effectively teach reading and writing to students whose culture and language differ from that of the school, and must understand how and why students decide to add another language form to their repertoire. All we can do is provide students with access to additional language forms. Inevitably, each speaker will make his or her own decision about what to say in any context.

But I must end with a caveat that we keep in mind a simple truth: Despite our necessary efforts to provide access to standard English, such access will not make any of our students more intelligent. It will not teach them math or science or geography—or, for that matter, compassion, courage, or responsibility. Let us not become so overly concerned with the language **form** that we ignore academic and moral **content.** Access to the standard language may be necessary, but it is definitely **not** sufficient to produce intelligent, competent caretakers of the future.

## Focus on Research
# Talking the Talk and Walking the Walk: Researching Oral Language in the Classroom

**Karen Gallas, Mary Antón-Oldenburg,
Cynthia Ballenger, Cindy Beseler, Steve Griffin,
Roxanne Pappenheimer, and James Swaim**

### EDITOR'S INTRODUCTION

This piece brings together two powerful movements in research on children's language learning: teacher research and the recognition of multiple discourses in the classroom. Karen Gallas and her teacher-research colleagues have been meeting as a research group for a number of years now, supporting each other with various pieces of the research process and collaborating on the most effective ways to capture and learn from children's talk in schools. In this essay, members of the teacher research group collaborated on a reflection on the ways in which attending to and reflecting upon the multiple oral discourses of children in school can inform our understandings of learning and language development.

"Salutations!" said the voice.
Wilbur jumped to his feet. "Salu-what?" he cried.
"Salutations!" repeated the voice.
"What are they, and where are you?" screamed Wilbur.
"Please, please tell me where you are. And what are salutations?"

—E. B. White (1952. p. 35)

**Field Notes: 9:30 a.m.:** The students are straggling in; the level of confusion seems abnormally high. School has been delayed 1 hour due to snow. The vans transporting students with special needs are running late. . . . There is talk of another impending storm. As I answer the phone, E. M., a special education administrator, comes through the door and attempts to scurry invisibly across the classroom to a meeting in the next room. Penelope notices E. M. It is unusual for Penelope to move so quickly within the classroom. E. M. pauses

*Source: "Focus on Research* Talking the Talk and Walking the Walk: Researching Oral Language in the Classroom" by Karen Gallas, Mary Antón-Oldenburg, Cynthia Ballenger, Cindy Beseler, Steve Griffin, Roxanne Pappenheimer, and James Swaim, Language Arts, *73* (8) pp. 608–617. Copyright 1996 by the National Council of Teachers of English. Reprinted with permission.

and Penelope greets her: "Ellen, I'll tell my mom that you say 'hello'." E. M. smiles and says, "Thanks, Penelope." Penelope straightens her usually rounded shoulders and casts a radiant, triumphant smile in my direction. She turns around and ambles away with a confident gait.

Greetings, salutations, negotiations, instructions, questions, explanations, discussions, small talk, science talk, book talk, discussing writing, talking about a painting, reading a poem, telling of a story—these and many other kinds of talk form the domain of oral language in the classroom. Penelope orchestrates an unusual greeting. Juan, in a limbo of developing English and developing Spanish, labors to understand the meaning of a lunch count. Francesca demands to know where she's going to go when she dies. Around them some children negotiate recess plans as they work in their morning journals, while a few others are being queried about their understanding of yesterday's math lesson. Within a 5-minute window of time, the classroom offers the close observer a wave of talk that moves across private and public spaces, encompassing worlds of meanings.

It is within this context that classroom teachers work. And for those teachers who look closely at oral language, the world of talk rapidly breaks loose from its boundaries and becomes at once a point of fascination and confusion. This article examines some of the points of fascination and confusion that close study of classroom talk raises. It is written from the perspective of a group of teacher-researchers who use talk as a way to study issues of language and literacy. Just as Wilbur seeks an answer to his question—"Where are you?"—as teacher-researchers we seek to establish the context of all forms of classroom talk. We want to know the child in each encounter and to understand the meanings the child brings to the encounter. We need to examine closely our own intentions as teachers and uncover assumptions about language that our understandings embody.

Penelope, the focus of the opening field notes, is newly arrived from a Caribbean island, and she is a symphony of textures and colors that rarely match: Sneakers worn with nylons, and pants carefully ironed the night before but put on backwards. Outside the classroom she is animated and imaginative. Inside, however, she often loses her vibrancy and luster. At times her passive stance, blank stares, and silences are barriers difficult to hurdle. Given her usual classroom demeanor, it is interesting that in this brief encounter, she solicited a greeting from E. M., a school administrator.

In this case Penelope clearly had a verbal mission, placing herself in the middle of her "web," and securing that place through a greeting that was deeply situated within her own oral tradition. All told, quite a lot to accomplish by uttering one simple sentence that took only seconds.

Yet, Penelope's actions uncover many questions: What happens when students use language in their own way in the classroom? What happens if a child's intentions are not interrupted or corrected? When is it best practice for a teacher *not* to correct children's use of language? These are the kinds of questions that proliferate as teachers observe and examine oral language in all its forms. Often what is revealed is confusing and complex, even in what should be the simplest of actions: How to say hello. Penelope's triumph was that she alone created a complete social act by becoming the primary author of a greeting. Our triumph as teacher-researchers was that we did not interfere.

## THE SCHOOL AS A SITE OF DISCOURSES IN CONTACT

Talk is an inherently social act. In classrooms, however, teachers generally corral language use by defining when children talk, what they are supposed to talk about, and for how long. We also have implicit rules governing how talk can be used across classroom activities, requiring students to crack the code, as it were, and develop a language kit of discourses to suit the needs of different contexts. But the school is a site of many discourses in contact, including both those discourses that come from students' cultural backgrounds—their out-of-school ways of talking, reasoning, and valuing—and the many specialized discourses that are a part of academic domains. Math, science, social studies, art, gym, music, book studies, and writing workshop all stand as distinct discourses that children must master. But discourses, by definition, are complexly situated, socially, culturally, and historically. They crucially involve a set of values and viewpoints in terms of which one speaks, acts, and thinks (Bakhtin, 1981; Gee, 1990). And they are populated by multiple intentions, some of which are embodied by teaching goals, and others that are steeped in the social agendas of children. Appropriating a discourse involves taking a stance within the values and viewpoints that constitute it.

## WAYS OF TALKING

Sociolinguistic research has increased our understanding of the similarities and differences that individual children have in their ways of talking and making sense (Cazden, 1988; Heath, 1983). There has also been an increased understanding of the differing ways an individual child, or group of children, speaks in school based on the genre, content area, specific task, purpose, audience, and so forth (Barnes, Britton, & Torbe, 1990; Cazden, 1988; Dyson, 1993; Gallas, 1994, 1995; Michaels, 1982, 1985; Wells, 1986). As a result of such research, we now realize that all children have multiple ways of talking that can be used with differing success for a variety of literacy events. From the classroom teacher's perspective, talk has been transformed from something that we needed to control to teach well to an event that we must now orchestrate for a variety of purposes.

However, a commitment to the importance of talk as a central part of classroom discourse is accompanied by a need to investigate how children actually use talk in many different contexts—some of them academic, some social. We believe that talk must be explored from many perspectives: as an instructional device, as an assessment tool, as a path toward the understanding and mastery of new ideas, and as a point of contact between different social and cultural worlds. And, precisely because it is a social act, we attempt to examine talk in both orchestrated and unorchestrated forms.

## APPROPRIATING NEW DISCOURSES

(The word in a language) is half someone else's. It becomes "one's own" only when the speaker populates it with his own intention, his own accent, when he appropriates the word, adapting it to his own semantic and expressive intentions. Prior to this moment of appropriation, the word . . . exists in other people's mouths, in other people's contexts, serving other people's intentions: it is from there that one must take the word, and make it one's own. (Bakhtin, 1981, pp. 293–294)

In school, all children need to appropriate new forms of language as they become exposed to new school-based activities, spoken and written genres, and academic content areas. A child's success with acquiring each of these different ways of talking is affected by many things including the child's home culture and oral tradition, his or her experience with school ways of talking, as well as access to opportunities to practice those ways of talking. It is clear that school talk itself represents a distinct oral tradition, one orchestrated by primarily white, middle class teachers. As such, success in school talk is going to be more generally accessible to

children from middle class backgrounds for whom the talk in school will be familiar and congruent with their experiences outside of school.

For those children whose home-based ways of talking are not similar to school-based ways of talking, or for whom the rules of language are not clear, moving into the multiple discourses that schools present will be more difficult. These children, however, also have powerful ways of talking and thinking that, although not easily translated into traditional curricular models, must be incorporated into their educational experience to ensure that they experience success in school. Yet, even as we recognize and appreciate the different ways of making sense that children bring to school, providing a bridge between home-based ways of talking and school-based ways is a daunting task.

In classrooms where communicative competence is stressed and language instruction is consciously brought to the foreground, we have found that the rules imposed on language use must be constantly examined. As we consider what kinds of student talk are more or less useful than others, we also self-consciously try to uncover and question the assumptions that support our approaches to the teaching and learning of oral language. What happens when the language strategies a student chooses don't match our intentions and the rules of official language use are violated, however subtly? A brief examination of two different classroom discourses reveals the kinds of systems students must negotiate to meet different expectations for oral language.

Monday mornings in a high-school special needs class were set aside for hot chocolate and structured conversation practice, as students shared "What I did on my weekend" stories. Aspects of good conversations were explicitly highlighted: Take turns back and forth; look at the speaker; show interest as a listener; ask questions; talk about something in common; expand on main ideas; match facial expressions to words; be specific; and have a beginning and ending. Monday-Talk was instructional in nature. The purpose of it was to make conversational features explicit, and the focus was on how the students talked rather than on what they were saying.

Contrastingly, the same students were involved in Friday-Talk, a different discourse space that emerged in their volunteer placement at a general hospital. Their talk in that instance occurred without the teacher's functional intervention for practice, and most of the Friday-Talk appeared to the teacher-researcher to be "crazy," nonfunctional in a school context, and inappropriate for most social settings. For example, one Friday, 3 students—Bill, Douglas, and Arthur—were talking about a *Star Trek* episode in which a person was partially paralyzed. Bill then told a story of how John, one of his mother's college professors, was paralyzed from the neck down due to a racquetball accident. The 3 boys kept asking each other, "How did he do it?" They decided that John must have hit his head against the wall and twisted his neck. As they talked, they involved their whole bodies in the discussion, at times getting up to replay a racquetball shot while describing it. They animatedly debated the question uninterrupted for fifteen minutes, and then unanimously decided that John must have been hitting a backhand at the time of his accident. In these discussions it was sometimes hard for the teacher to understand Friday-Talk, but it was clear that it was an important kind of peer conversation that there would not have been space for in the classroom (Beseler, 1994). Both Monday-Talk and Friday-Talk were acceptable within their respective forums, and both yielded different but very valuable language and learning experiences.

## EXPLORING DIFFERENT LANGUAGE GENRES

For teachers, there is sometimes an irresistible urge to anchor children's oral language experiences in functional, goal-oriented, instructional activities. There has also been a recent push advocating increased explicitness by teachers in presenting the rules of school discourse (Delpit, 1986, 1988). We believe, however, that explicitness alone cannot bridge the gap between home and school ways of talking; there is a need for functional, *child-orchestrated* language practice within socially meaningful settings. As Dyson (1993) has pointed out, members of a classroom community will sometimes create a "folk genre," a language form that has real communicative importance for children.

For example, in a second-grade classroom, David, an African American boy, personally restructured sharing time into a storytelling genre in which the other members of the class acted out the story as he told it (Griffin, 1993). After taking the sharing chair, David would announce his intention by stating, "I need people." Eventually other members of the class also began to tell their own versions of these "I Need People" stories. David was able to tell wonderful stories, showing a narrative talent that needed to be encouraged and nurtured. However, David's teacher also observed that he had not yet mastered a more mainstream approach to storytelling in which there was a logical sequence of events and all the details tied together. By creat-

ing and participating in this performance style of storytelling, David practiced and extended his personal style of storytelling, while also being an actor in the more linear stories told by his classmates. Eventually he was able to show mastery of both types of storytelling. In this case, explicitness would not have been as successful as a point of language intervention for David, as was this type of immersion and extensive functional use of language within the social context of a group of children creating a new language genre. Moreover, "I Need People" stories emerged because the classroom teacher was working from the perspective of a teacher-researcher. That perspective allowed him to let his questions about how to honor children's intentions as communicators rise to the surface of his practice.

## EXPLICIT PRACTICE IN DISCUSSION

Of course there is a need for explicit instruction in the rules of how to talk in specific classroom literacy events. For example, a group of second-grade children who were reluctant to participate in whole class science discussions were provided the opportunity to have the same discussions in a small group (Griffin & Ross, 1990). They were taught the specific ways that the more successful second graders used language in these discussions and were then shown videotapes of their own small group discussions to self-critique their participation. After a few weeks of this separate science discussion time, the children rejoined the rest of their classmates and became much more successful participants in the whole group discussions. Here, the teacher orchestrated practice of explicit talk protocols to help children gain mastery of a particular kind of talk.

These examples represent two kinds of interventions, each based on a systematic research practice by a teacher-researcher. Enabling children to bring their oral language traditions into the heart of classroom life and then finding ways to build and extend those traditions require highly contextualized and systematic study by teachers of the speech events in their classrooms. In other words, teaching and planning for oral language experiences must also include study of the talk that results from those experiences.

## TALK ACROSS DISCIPLINES

Although it is becoming more common for teachers to recognize the strength of children's oral traditions and the importance of helping children develop multiple discourses, it is still difficult to understand how children's personal talk styles can contribute to their mastery of different subject matter. Yet, many children can extend their understanding of math, science, and social studies when classroom subjects are structured to build on their strengths as communicators. For example, most school science discussions are expected to include expository talk, listing of definitions, and straightforward, linear explanations. But children from diverse oral traditions that do not emphasize these ways of talking are often at a disadvantage and appear to be deficient in their abilities to be scientific.

Numerous studies have shown that the ways of knowing and talking that are valued most in current instructional practice in science (and other domains) differ from those of low-income and linguistic minority communities (e.g., Au & Jordan, 1981; Boggs, 1985; Heath, 1983; Philips, 1982; Scollon & Scollon, 1981). The question remains as to what is an effective response by teachers to these issues in the classroom. Many argue that if the socioculturally situated speech forms that these students bring to school with them are not honored, then they receive the message that the ways in which they make sense of the world are not important and not to be brought to bear on school learning (Cazden, 1988; Gallas, 1995; Gee, 1990; Lemke, 1990; Phillips, 1982; Warren, Rosebery, & Conant, 1994; Wertsch, 1991). And yet, others argue, when students' everyday views and practices are honored in the classroom, the students may remain where they are, comfortable in a non-academic discourse, and unlikely to explore a subject as a different way of thinking and acting (Delpit, 1986, 1988; Gee, 1994). In light of these dichotomies, it becomes imperative to explore these issues through complex and grounded accounts of teaching and learning.

## SCIENCE TALK

What happens when personal narratives are introduced into science discussion? Consider, for example, a discussion among sixth and seventh graders on what mold needs in order to grow. The students identified the bathroom as a place where mold could often be found. Their teacher, Mr. Hypolite, then asked them if mold grew in the living room, and the students for the most part said no because there was no water there. Jimmy then entered with this story. (This transcript has been translated from Haitian Creole, and dysfluencies have been taken out.)

*Jimmy:* Mr. Hypolite, at my house, in the living room, under the window, we always put food under the window. When my dad made oatmeal, a little bit of oatmeal fell out. When he put it hot under the window, it got out, into the window. One day, one day, I turned up there. When I looked, I saw, I saw a little green thing in the screen under the window and I took it out, I took a knife, I took it out, I cleaned it.

*Mr. H.:* Where did the thing come from? Where did it come from?

*Jimmy:* From food. Because I saw that the food was there a real long time and then it came.

*Caroline:* You see why room, um, why living rooms can't make mold?

*Students:* Yeah, the living room, really.

*Rachel:* Mr. Hypolite, Jimmy said that it's food that makes mold. Well, if I eat some food, will I have mold inside me?

*Students:* (laughing) No.

Jimmy has multiple purposes for this story. He begins it presumably to counter the developing consensus that mold does not grow in the living room. But at the end of his story, where you would expect to hear his main point, he chooses to make clear his membership in the community of clean children; he tells us he immediately cleaned up the mold. In the crucial final part, it seems to be a social need that dictates what he says, and he does not make any explicit connection to the preceding science question.

Jimmy's teacher and his peers set out to show him what else they saw in his story. First, his teacher asks where the mold came from. By answering that the mold came from food, Jimmy makes explicit one meaning for his story, one that he had not articulated directly. Then Caroline enters the discussion. She seems to be saying that this story goes to show that you have to clean the living room. She is connecting Jimmy's story to the preceding conversation about cleaning the bathrooms. Caroline had rarely spoken in previous science discussions; it seems that her knowledge of domestic routine is what gives her a point of entry into this discussion. Rachel next responds to the crux of this argument by restating Jimmy's claim—that food can make mold—and then, by invoking the logical consequence, that she must have mold inside her since she eats food; she challenges his argument. The children laugh, but the responses Jimmy receives provide him with a new version of his narrative, one in which different aspects are explicitly foregrounded.

Upon careful consideration, Jimmy's story and the other children's responses can be understood first as stories about the self, that is, the child's stature as part of a proper home. But they are also stories that contained evidence and scientific claims about mold (Ballenger, in press). Discourses are in contact in this sort of situation; they are bumping up against each other, and the conversations are multi-voiced and multi-purposed. Identifying the points of contact, however, and uncovering their purposes is crucial to understanding how these students are making meaning within the discipline.

Yet, little is known about how technical terms like "mold" come to be meaningful for children, meaningful not as stipulated taxonomies, but as a purposeful way to structure knowledge and experience. Consider, for example, science talk in one classroom where students had been keeping ant farms and researching their own questions about ants. For these students an initial organizing principle was in what ways ants and humans were alike. Some students thought ants did not have blood; others believed they did. Their teacher, Mr. H., asked the class who had seen blood inside an ant. Charley said he had, and Mr. H. asked him to tell them when he saw the blood. Charley answered, "There can be blood but it's not the same color . . ." Although he claimed he had seen ant blood, Charley did not tell the story of seeing the blood. He responded to his teacher's request for a story by making a claim: Not all blood is the same color. In making this claim, Charley took "blood" out of a common sense taxonomy, and looked at it in relation to its place in various organisms. His was a synthesizing approach to his teacher's question and stood in contrast to his classmates' more narrative approach to the talk. In essence, Charley wanted his argument to stand without him, not to depend on his personal experience and his story.

Charley and Jimmy demonstrate how children, through dialogue and the sharing of perspectives, can experience many socially, culturally, and historically constituted ways of knowing and understanding a discipline. Their understandings were built within classroom communities where the students' home culture and oral tradition were highly valued. Thus, discussion and inquiry were oriented toward uncovering the students' understandings, rather than the teacher's understandings. When we provide more opportunities for children to use discussion to identify their own understandings and answer their own questions, we will also have more opportunities to investigate the dynamics of discourse appropriation and to debate the advantages and disadvantages of fostering multi-voiced talk within each discipline.

## TALK ABOUT TEXT

A word is dead
When it is said.
Some say.
I say it just

Begins to live
That day. (p. 258)

*—Emily Dickinson*
*Reprinted with permission of*
*Little, Brown & Company*

Most teachers and researchers concerned with the issues of oral language would agree with Dickinson's poem and recognize in it the living quality of words in the classroom. When teachers and children meet to discuss different kinds of texts—literature, pictures, stories, poems, a solution to a math problem—they present multiple, divergent voices that sometimes compete, but are always involved in an ongoing struggle for meaning and growth (Bakhtin, 1981, 1984). Their words bring texts to life in ways neither the authors nor the discussants could have predicted.

Teachers of the writing process, especially, have acknowledged the importance of social interaction as they encourage children to use talk to encounter the texts they have written. Many of those teachers have turned to classroom ethnography as a way of preserving and understanding the talk that lives in a culture such as writing workshop. Writing process advocates, Calkins (1983) and Atwell (1987) in particular, have used ethnography to depict the individual writer grappling successfully with issues of process, composing, and revising, of audience and writer. Yet these accounts, while rich in detail, have often taken on a romantic "too good to be true" flavor for the practitioner. Only recently have ethnographers like Dyson (1993) and Lensmire (1994) provided stories that describe writing workshop as it really is: a place where children use talk and texts for powerful social purposes like performance, connection, respect, and negotiation.

### The Role of Intention

These kinds of descriptions, however, also highlight the role of intention in negotiating understandings of texts. Linguistic interactions among children play along a continuum of positive and negative outcomes, and have a variety of effects on writers, some of which teachers cannot mediate. For example, the following 2 stories about life in a third-grade writing workshop each describe a certain kind of linguistic interaction and its impact on the writer, and raise questions about how social dynamics influence learning. These stories demonstrate the extremes that talk and texts can take as emerging writers try to establish a place for themselves in the social world of writing workshop.

Deb and Lee presented a picturebook they had written for kindergartners about the adventures of a girl named

Judy who befriends the sun. The sun, who is named Jimmy, can talk to Judy but cannot move from his position in the sky. The two characters decide that the only game they can play is hide-and-seek. Following is an excerpt from the class share:

*Mark:* Aren't there too little words on each page? Are there 5 on each page?
*Lee:* It's a rough draft, and we want to draw pictures underneath it because we are doing it for kindergartners.

The next questioner asks how Jimmy and Judy could actually talk to each other. At this point the conversation takes on a life of its own as the children begin debating the story's scientific appropriateness.

*David:* How could the sun see her down on the Earth and like the sun is as high as anything?
*Lee:* It's a fantasy, David.
*Stuart:* David, David, if you see, your sight never ends. You will see forever unless something blocks it.
*Susan:* The higher you are, the more you can see.
*Stuart:* Let's say you are here, and there's a hill down like that and you're over here. You can't see. Your sight never ends. It goes on forever.
*Susan:* But the higher you are the more you can see because you can see over things.
*Deb:* Well, you guys, it's not all the way up in the sky. It's low down.

Perhaps if the authors had read this story to a kindergarten class as originally intended, the audience might have behaved differently and responded more empathetically to the playful personification and issue of friendship in the story. That kind of talk or mode of response would have affirmed the authors' intentions and focused on content, rather than on scientific appropriateness. Instead, in a vivid example of talk being shaped by its own momentum, a vocal minority either consciously or unconsciously shunned the stated intentions of the authors and chose instead to engage in science talk. Their response focused on what the text ought to have been, rather than what it really was. Because classmates did not respond to the real substance of the story, the writers came away from this interaction feeling diminished, marginalized, and excluded. It had affected not only their writing but their social status in the class.

A second story provides a contrasting outcome. Pamela, arguably the best writer in the class, had been working on *The Man Who Was Late for Dinner* for three months. It told the story of Bob Pomerance who was invited to a friend's house for dinner. On the appointed night, Bob overslept, and then rushed to his friend's house only to encounter a strange world of stores, each owned by an actual member of the class, including the teachers. Each store offered a product that was appropriate to its particular owner. In her third sharing session, Pamela read her story and then invited questions:

*Joe:* What is the last store going to be?
*Pam:* I don't know. I haven't made it up, Jacob?
*Jacob:* I have an idea what it can be. . . . It could be like Tutu's Tutu Store. Yo-yo's Yo-Yo store.
*Darlene:* I like being in your story, and the part when . . . Bob, he sees all the store signs. I like that part.
*Pam:* Thank you.
*Jacob:* I think, like, the woman should say, when he finally gets there, "WELL, WHAT TOOK YOU SO LONG!" and that will be the end.
*Pam:* Yeah, he'll get there and knock on the door and she'll say, "Well, Bob, what took you so long?"

Early in this share, Darlene set an interesting tone by telling Pamela that she "liked being in her story." Her response clearly affirmed at least one of Pamela's intentions for writing the piece, and that was to include all members of the class. At this point the response mode of the class changed dramatically. Instead of being outside the story and responding like a listening audience, classmates actually got inside Pamela's story and responded to it as writers. Unlike Deb and Lee, Pamela had connected with her audience; children were thinking and listening to her story like world creators (Bruner, 1990), not like readers concerned with information and clarity. In these stories, talk and text were used in opposite ways: in the first to undermine the intentions of the text, in the second to assume a collaborative tone.

These examples took place in the official sphere of class share, as do most descriptions of children's talk about texts, but, as Dyson (1993) has demonstrated, children's work in the "unofficial" world powerfully influences official classroom encounters. As teachers and children consider, through talk and discussion, a variety of classroom texts across the curriculum, the unofficial world of children has a pervasive effect on their actions in the official world. Thus, questions are raised about the interactions of social agendas with curricular agendas. What influence does talk have on texts when children work together or alone on a text? Does that talk, and the intentions that it embodies, then move into and influence the development of official classroom discourse? How can the teacher-researcher or the ethnographer use talk as a way to track children's movement between the official and unofficial worlds of the classroom?

## UNOFFICIAL TALK IN THE CLASSROOM

Classrooms are a cacophony of sound: chairs sliding, pencils scratching, small animals calling, a heater thumping as it turns on and off. Voices call out, share a joke, laugh, answer a question, tell a story. The voice of authority admonishes, "Talk in indoor voices" and "Please stop talking and get to work." Teachers, by definition, are not part of the unofficial conversations that go on throughout the school day. However, we need to know how and when the unofficial talk of the classroom supports the official classroom purpose in traditional and nontraditional ways. Children's spontaneous talk has the potential to reveal how children come to know the culture of "doing school," and also how they use the unofficial worlds of the classroom to explore concepts that they are learning in the official world (Antón-Oldenburg, 1994). The two conversations that follow illustrate how spontaneous peer talk in the unofficial realm link children to the agendas of the official realm.

In the first conversation, 4 kindergarten children were drawing and writing in their morning journals. Their exchange includes talk that is on task and talk that most teachers would find distracting to others. Each type of talk, in fact, is used to make sense of the tasks expected in the journaling process.

*Amy:* Yeah, we're gonna push the sides so like. 'Cause my Dad, know what he does?
*Susan:* What?
*Amy:* He always puts the Christmas lights on me to hold 'em up.
*Nate:* Ahhhwwahh (laughing).
*Amy:* And when he lights them up on me, I go like, "OWWW, they're burning me!"
*Issac:* Why does he put Christmas lights on you?
*Amy:* Because he has to hold them, so he doesn't drop them.
*Issac:* And what does he say?
*Amy:* He says, "Just be quiet!" That's what he says. And then my Mom comes running out and says, "John, please turn off the lights." I have to go out in the night to help Dad.
*Isaac:* To burn you, too.
*Amy:* Yeah, and he burns both of us 'cause we have so many lights on us. And he burns both of us.

Using this talk, Amy shares the story she is writing and elaborates upon it in response to almost teacher-like prompts from her friends.

In a separate conversation on the same day, the same 4 children explored another aspect of their school world. First to admonish, then to teach, and finally to tease, 2 of the 4 children attempted to teach the others the social and school significance of the middle finger. A teacher walking by, simply by her presence, ended the conversation.

*Isaac:* It's an unidentified flying . . . (waving his hands around).
*Amy:* Don't point your middle finger at anybody.
*Isaac:* I know. No, that's, no, this isn't your middle finger.
*Susan:* Your tallest finger is your middle.
*Amy:* Don't do that; don't show it!
*Susan:* I'll tell you which is your middle finger.
*Amy:* No, NO! Don't do it, Susan. Don't do it!
*Nate:* This is your middle finger.
*Issac:* Ahkkkkk, look what Nate is doing!
*Amy:* Don't! Put that down this MINUTE!
*Isaac:* We got you to put it down.
*Nate:* Yeah, I got 2 middle fingers.
*Amy:* Don't . . . don't.

The teacher walked by, asked a question, and the conversation stopped. As soon as she left, it continued:

*Isaac:* You were going to say "M."
*Nate:* The M-word. What's that M-m-m-middle finger.
*Amy:* [serious voice] If the teacher saw that, she'd be really angry.
*Isaac:* That's how it works. Let's try and be done soon and just leave him and tell on him.
*Amy:* Okay.
*Nate:* Why?
*Amy:* 'Cause you're saying a swear.
*Nate:* I am not!
*Isaac:* Yeah, that's what it is, a swear.

As these children so aptly demonstrate, unofficial talk in classrooms has both social and epistemological underpinnings. Yet, when talk moves into the control of children, it inevitably moves into murky epistemological territory, making it difficult to ascertain what, if anything, is being learned, by whom, and to what purpose. Because children's unofficial talk is situated so completely in social moments, it often appears to us to be surreptitious, under cover, and of a lower order of discourse. As Bakhtin pointed out, though, the unfolding of the ordinary events of daily life, of prosaics, has much to offer us by way of understanding a language, a culture, a social milieu (Morson & Emerson, 1990). Thus, the unofficial world becomes for us as teacher-researchers a point of study and description, so that our understanding of what constitutes rich oral language in the classroom expands to include all experiences that embody the social, expressive, and intellectual intentions of children.

## CONCLUSION

Talk is recursive, that is, each communicative encounter rebounds and reverberates into other talk spaces. As such, oral language in classrooms is not orchestrated solely by teachers into a coherent whole, but rather grows out of many different communicative encounters, and deeply influences every aspect of learning and teaching. As we, like Wilbur, struggle to understand and make plain the complexities of language, both to ourselves and to our students, children like Penelope, David, Deb, Lee, Jimmy, and Charley grow as communicators and learners. Research on the permutations of talk, its development across contexts and disciplines, and the points of contact between home and school discourses can be a powerful agenda, both for inquiry and for improvement of practice. We believe teachers are uniquely situated to carry out this kind of study.

## REFERENCES

Antón-Oldenburg, M. (1994, March). *Spontaneous story talk among kindergarten journal writers: Interwoven stories and collaborative themes*. Paper presented at the National Council of Teachers of English Spring Convention, Portland, OR.

Atwell, N. (1987). *In the middle: Writing, reading, and learning with adolescents*. Portsmouth, NH: Boyonton/Cook.

Au, K., & Jordan, K. (1981). Teaching reading to Hawaiian children: Finding a culturally appropriate solution. In H. Trueba, G. P. Guthrie, & K. H. Au (Eds.), *Culture and the bilingual classroom* (pp. 139–152). Rowley, MA: Newbury House.

Bakhtin, M. (1981). *The dialogic imagination* (C. Emerson, Ed.; C. Emerson, & M. Holquist, Trans.). Austin: The University of Texas Press.

Bakhtin, M. (1984). *Problems of Dostoevsky's poetics*. (C. Emerson, Ed. & Trans.). Minneapolis, MN: University of Minnesota Press.

Ballenger, C. (in press). Social identities, moral narratives, scientific argumentation: Science talk in a bilingual classroom. *Language in Education*.

Barnes, D., Britton, J., & Torbe, M. (1990). *Language, the learner, and the school*. Portsmouth, NH: Heinemann.

Beseler, C. (1994, April). *Out of bounds: Talk among learners with special needs*. Paper presented at the Annual Conference of the American Educational Research Association, New Orleans, LA.

Boggs, S. (1985). *Speaking, relating and learning: A study of Hawaiian children at home and at school*. Norwood, NJ: Ablex.

Bruner, J. (1990). *Acts of meaning*. Cambridge, MA: Harvard University Press.

Calkins, L. J. (1983). *Lessons from a child: On the teaching and learning of writing*. Portsmouth, NH: Heinemann.

Cazden, C. (1988). *Classroom discourse*. Portsmouth, NH: Heinemann.

Delpit, L. (1986). Skills and other dilemmas of a progressive black educator. *Harvard Educational Review, 56,* 379–385.

Delpit, L. (1988). The silenced dialogue: Power and pedagogy in educating other people's children. *Harvard Educational Review, 58,* 280–298.

Dickinson, E. (1961). *Final Harvest: Emily Dickinson's Poems* (p. 258). Boston, MA: Little, Brown & Company.

Dyson, A. H. (1993). *Social worlds of children learning to write*. New York: Teachers College Press.

Gallas, K. (1994). *The languages of learning: How children talk write, dance, draw and sing their understanding of the world*. New York: Teachers College Press.

Gallas, K. (1995). *Talking their way into science: Hearing children's questions and theories, responding with curricula*. New York: Teachers College Press.

Gee, J. P. (1990). *Social linguistics and literacies: Ideology in discourses*. London: The Falmer Press.

Gee, J. P. (1994, April). *"Science talk": How do you start to do what you don't know how to do*. Paper presented at the Annual Meeting of the American Educational Research Association, New Orleans, LA.

Griffin, S. (1993). "I need people": Storytelling in a second grade classroom. In *Children's voices, teachers' stories: Papers from the Brookline Teacher Research Seminar*. Literacies Institute Technical Report No. 11, Newton, MA: Education Development Center.

Griffin, S., & Ross, S. (1990). *Talking science in large and small groups*. Paper presented at Literacies Institute Workshop on Language and Culture in the Classroom, Newton, MA.

Heath, S. B. (1983). *Ways with words: Language, life, and work in communities and classrooms*. New York: Cambridge University Press.

Lemke, J. (1990). *Talking science: Language, learning, and values*. Norwood, NJ: Ablex.

Lensmire, T. J. (1994). *When children write*. New York: Teachers College Press.

Michaels, S. (1982)."Sharing time": Children's narrative styles and differential access to literacy. *Language in Society, 10,* 423–442.

Michaels, S. (1985). Hearing the connections in children's oral and written discourse. *Journal of Education, 167,* 36–56.

Morson, G. S., & Emerson, C. (1990). *Mikhail Bakhtin: Creation of a prosaics*. Stanford, CA: Stanford University Press.

Philips, S. (1982). *The invisible culture: Communication in classroom and community on the Warm Springs Reservation.* New York: Longman.

Scollon, R., & Scollon, S. (1981). *Narrative, literacy and face in interethnic communication.* Norwood, NJ: Ablex.

Warren, B., Rosebery, A. S., & Conant, F. R. (1994). Discourse and social practice: Learning science in bilingual classrooms. In D. Spencer (Ed.), *Adult biliteracy in the United States* (pp. 191–210). Washington, DC: Center for Applied Linguistics.

Wells, G. (1986). *The meaning makers.* Portsmouth, NH: Heinemann.

Wertsch, J. V. (1991). *Voices of the mind.* Cambridge: Harvard University Press.

White, E. B. (1952). *Charlotte's Web.* New York: Scholastic.

# The Research Mind is Really the Teaching Mind at Its Best: An Interview with Karen Gallas

**Susan Harris MacKay**

*The noise was almost deafening. Children were only loosely connected with any particular seat. It was the end of the first month of school, and my kindergartners and first graders were waiting for me to tell them to quiet down so we could have lunch. They knew the routine. Find a seat. Stop talking. Choose a song. Sing. Then up to wash their hands and get lunch. Five minutes had passed and we were stuck at step two. I walked around to each of the four tables and asked them to help each other settle down. It didn't work. And ten minutes had passed.*

*Every year a day like this would come. I'd begin to wonder: Why are they waiting for me? Why is it my responsibility to get them to settle down? They know we can't eat until we're quiet. Why don't they do it themselves? And every year on this day that it began to bother me the most, I'd wait. Five, maybe ten minutes. But then, always this tension in my stomach would lead to a breakdown of my will. What if they* never *get quiet? What if they talk through the whole afternoon? What if things get really out of control? What if somebody comes in and sees that I've got no control of the class? What* then?!

*So I would take control and get them quiet and I'd keep wondering why five, six, and seven year olds were so incapable of connecting their individual behavior to the big picture. It was with fascination and frustration that I would watch child after child look up from his or her table and yell, "Hey! You need to be quiet!" and go right back to chattering with the the person next to him. How was I going to convince them that everything they did as individuals affected our work as a group? I was searching for a method.*

*But this year, I sat down in a chair, and encouraged my intern to do the same. We stepped aside and behaved as members of the community needed to behave—we were* quiet. *Not quite fifteen minutes into the lunch period, the lights went off. Silence. Everyone looked toward the light switch and a tiny voice said, "Would everyone please be quiet so we can eat?" The smallest child in the class reached on tiptoes to turn the light back on, trotted back to his seat, and we were ready to move on.*

*Karen Gallas and her most recent book,* Sometimes I Can Be Anything: Power, Gender, and Identity in a Primary Classroom *(1998), gave me the courage to wait. She gave the children in my classroom the opportunity to take responsibility for their lives in the classroom. Karen doesn't research and write about her work with children to dazzle us with methodology. Her teaching voice, in fact, is conspicuously absent as she writes about the dailiness of her classroom and, in so doing, has the effect of speaking directly to what feels like "a collective teaching unconscious." She writes:*

> *Observations that describe points of rupture in the life of the classroom, points of confusion, missteps, and even chaos give us access to the points when teacher intention as it is embodied in a method encounters the prosaic world of children and daily life . . . [E]ach new human encounter must be freshly, and mutually constructed in the moment. (p. 17)*

*An over-reliance on methodology, she writes, "simplifies the process of human communication, making it static and dead." Her work has given me permission not to react at the children with a particular methodology based on my own sense of what is right or expected or happened before, but as a genuine member of a community working with endless possibilities. As a teacher researcher, I am more a scribe seeking patterns, than an interpreter offering explanations. The patterns in one community life help uncover patterns in another, and the real, complex work we do as teachers—helping children to make sense of their own lives—is more deeply understood. Real participation forces us to ask ourselves continually, as Karen does at the end of our interview, "Why are we in this?"*

*I don't know how lunch time will turn out for the rest of the year, or next year, or the next. But I do know that at least this group of five, six, and seven year olds is capable of taking responsibility for themselves—given the opportunity. The following day, it only took about five minutes to settle down. Five different children decided to see what power they could enforce by turning off the lights. But this problem was solved when the last one turned them off and announced, "Stop turning on and off the lights, you guys. It's getting really annoying." She turned them on, and that was the end of that.*

*Susan MacKay: How did you decide to become a teacher?*

*Karen Gallas:* It's a classic story of the sixties, I think. It might be a classic story of our own time. I was an undergraduate anthropology major, had never thought of teaching, and actually had very little experience with children. Then I got out of school, and a job fell through that I had gotten through the Journal of Anthropology. By that time, it was the late sixties and there were no jobs. It was a very bad market, similar to what it's been for many kids coming out now. So, I struggled to think what I could do. I actually started to apply for teaching jobs, but I could not get any of them because I wasn't credentialed. I began looking around at graduate programs and I found a description of one at Lesley College (in Cambridge, Massachusetts) in Open Education, written by Cynthia Coles, a brilliant woman. The write-up was so unusual; it was based on philosophical premises and I was hooked on the first page. I went into the program, and that was it! I found that I just loved the notion of rethinking education—especially my own. So that's how I got into it.

*SM: That's very similar to what happened to me, actually. It's interesting that you were an anthropology major. I wonder if that has had an impact on your teacher research?*

*KG:* Well, now that I'm down the line a little bit, I see very clearly that it has. And it's really influenced the kind of work that I do. I find it interesting to look back on the choices that you make early in life. You know, you think you're doing them on instinct, and somehow or other, they seem to circle back and then begin to make sense in the larger picture. Those early interests come back.

*SM: How long did you teach, do you think, before you began to see yourself as a teacher-researcher?*

*KG:* Oh, a very long time.

*SM: But do you think it was part of your teaching earlier on?*

*KG:* Yes, I see what you mean. I'd have to say the characteristics were there early.

*SM: What would you say those characteristics are?*

*KG:* Well, it's the start of the year, and I'm beginning to get ready to start teaching again, and I've always had the trouble that I can't plan my year. I can't hardly even plan the first day.

*SM: Right!*

*KG:* I find that happens because I don't know anything—about anything! That's an attitude that has become more formalized in my research. I can't really proceed with my teaching until I know the kids, their interests, the environment, the school. It wasn't formalized, certainly, for quite a while. I didn't know about the field because it's fairly new. I was very influenced by teacher writers in the sixties. People like Sylvia Ashton-Warner, Elwyn Richardson, and Herb Kohl may have created a viewpoint.

But, in answer to your question, I went back to get my doctorate in 1979, and that didn't really train me to do classroom research. Because at the time I thought I was on my way out of the classroom. That was what you were supposed to do when you got a doctorate. And so I did that, and I taught in university for a while, and then I *had* to go back to the classroom because I missed it so badly. And once I got back in, I stumbled upon this notion of teacher research through the Brookline Teacher Research Seminar. That was completely novel to me to think about applying my research practice to the classroom.

*SM: What is The Brookline Teacher Research Seminar?*

*KG:* Right now, it's a group of about 10 individuals, teachers mostly from Brookline, Massachusetts, but also a few teachers from other systems. Then we have a few people who are really sociolinguists who join us and have been involved since the beginning, and we always have a facilitator who is a teacher run the seminar. So, we are mostly classroom teachers, anywhere from K-high school, special ed., all kinds of teachers. Right now, the group is very stable. The members have been together for several years.

*SM: Do you think that most of the other teachers there are as comfortable as you are with not having the answers?*

*KG:* Yes, that's actually something that has come very strongly out of the seminar. And it's developed over time that if we didn't know what was going on, then that was something we could figure out: we should pursue it even though we might not know the question we were asking. You know, it was that tension. I believe it's a learning tension that certainly has been talked about for a long time.

*SM: In your book* Sometimes I Can Be Anything *you say that even once a teacher does figure out what his or her questions are, they're so obscured by their contextuality. . . .*

*KG:* Right.

*SM: . . . When I'm thinking about what my own questions are, I feel the same way. Especially at first, I can never frame my question quite right because I never know exactly where it's coming from. It's just something I notice and it bothers me. I'd like to hear your perspective on how this helps and why it's important.*

*KG:* Well, there's a couple of levels to that. One is, it immediately improves your teaching because you begin to look much more closely, and see more things in your classroom. So on that very basic level, we could say that teacher research obviously improves the process of teaching and learning in the classroom.

But on another level, the noodling around that is part of it where we don't really know why we're doing that or where we're going with it, is the early stage. . . . It's beginning to relate it to other things you've seen in other contexts. I always feel that the things I start to get bothered by I probably was bothered by earlier in my history, but I had not had the capability to even bring that tension to the surface. Because I was too busy doing other things, learning other things. I think once you begin to document the problem that's bothering you, you start to remember other occasions when this same thing had been taking place. So, you start to get a bigger picture of it. And if you study it long enough, it then begins to fit into the context of actual questions—important questions about education. I think one problem teachers have, is that it's very hard to write the question in a way that the research establishment thinks is appropriate. We don't ask them in the same way. But that doesn't mean that they are any less important.

*SM: What do you hope that people who read your books will get from them?*

*KG:* I hope that they will recognize themselves in them, and say, "Oh, my gosh, I have seen this," or "I have felt this way." I like people to see and begin to value the parts of teaching that are not the kinds that are written about concisely in books. I like them to recognize the things that are important that they do, that you can't quite describe to other people.

*SM: How do you make research part of your teaching?*

*KG:* I've really gotten so it's not separate. I think that's happened partly through the writing process, in that I write constantly. I don't mean I write formal things constantly, but whenever I think of something, if there's a piece of paper handy and I feel like this is a thought I should not lose, that's the first thing. I think it's that I have become more aware of my inner conversation. Teachers are aware of decision-making without being actually *conscious* of that inner decision-making conversation. It's usually quiet. I've gotten very aware of that inner comnversation and I'm constantly writing down things that I see and think as the day goes on. Sometimes they'll be on napkins, you know? And I try to keep a lot of notebooks around my classroom, which I'll write in.

I've also started to do the same thing with watching kids. I can't always have the tape recorder on, although I try to have it around a lot, but my fieldnotes have become tremendously important. So if I see children doing something, I'll write it wherever I have a place to write it. Really fast, and sometimes it's almost illegible.

*SM: The writing has helped make you conscious of important things?*

*KG:* Yes, I think that happens over time, too, as you collect data, you start to really know the data that you have to have. The funny thing is, that the documentation and the data collection that goes on in our classrooms can become a part of the teaching process. Kids really start to look to you to do that. I started out very narrowly looking at science talk: a very small, little part of my week. That was in the beginning, and it was focused and that was something I could really tape record and take notes on. So, I structured it specifically so that I could be watching. But later on, the tape recorder just became part of the classroom furniture, and taking notes is something that I do constantly. The kids will say to me, why don't you write that down?

*SM: Oh, yes—I know!*

*KG:* So you say, "OK, OK."

*They laugh.*

*KG:* And the other thing that has helped me is that I feel that the research mind is really the teaching mind at its best. It's a stance that helps you focus on whatever is coming at you. So, the research and the teaching are not separate at this point.

*SM: And yet when you went to write your most recent book, you took a year off.*

*KG:* Yes, that's true. When you get to the formal writing, you've got all this data, and you've got to have time to sit and look at it systematically.

*SM: Did you do that with your other books also?*

*KG:* No, I did not. But this time, I knew better. After the first two I had so exhausted myself that I had to take a year off. During that year I realized time off was critical, and it's obviously not realistic in the way teaching is structured now, to be able to take time off.

*SM: So . . . what are your thoughts on that?*

*KG:* Well, I have a lot of thoughts, which no one ever likes, or takes me up on. One is that teacher researchers should be part of the university structure, and that university professors should be part of the classroom teaching structure, so that you have this rotating door, this opening and closing door in which people go in and out of the classroom. You go in for a couple of years, come out, ready to write and teach. Conversely, I think there are some structures that could be developed so that teacher research is seen as a different sort of endeavor and the school week may allow a teacher to have a day out of the classroom, specifically to work on writing.

*SM: When you were at work on your latest book, can you explain how you went about collecting data? I know you had fieldnotes, but you also talked about specific relationships, or specific patterns that you were really investigating. I was curious about how you kept all that organized.*

*KG:* You know, it started out separately at first. I had a lot of little notebooks that I was writing in.

*SM: Yes I remember you talking about your Sharing Time Notebook and your "other times" notebooks.*

*KG:* Yes, all those notebooks! All of a sudden as I looked more at the power and the gender, I realized it was everywhere. It didn't matter what subject or whether it was something like sharing time. It was just everywhere, and I had gone through a transformation where that became the question I was working on. I needed to understand how power and gender worked. So, eventually all those little notebooks moved into one notebook. I just gave up on those separate categories, though when I went back to write about it, I started going back through my notes in some other areas, because I could look at them again and see where the ideas had come from. I also keep a large journal right in the middle of my classroom. It's really fat and it has pockets and in there I usually would keep artifacts, all kinds of papers and stuff the kids do, and very brief notes. That notebook was separate from my other stuff. It was very eclectic and it would cover every subject.

*SM: It's really interesting, thinking about how to set up teacher research space within the whole environment of the classroom. You also do a lot of audiotaping. How often would you say you actually transcribe things?*

*KG:* That's a very good question. I usually do one science talk a week—one side of a tape. And then I generally listen to them and transcribe sections. I've gotten much better at doing sections rather than entire tapes. Now I tape every day and listen to the tapes, but I don't transcribe everything.

   I still have old tapes I was listening to this summer that I took two years ago! I would listen to them for one specific thing, and I transcribed parts of them. I've gotten much more selective about transcribing, partly because its hard to do, and there's usually not money to do it. But also, I found I know the parts on the tape I need to take out and examine.

*SM: So, then you have all this data. What kind of process do you go through to pull it apart again and reorganize it, and think about it?*

*KG:* Usually the seminar helps with that. Different weeks, different seminar members will bring in a tape, or in some cases I might bring in art, or someone might bring in written texts. And we basically take chunks of our data, bring them to the seminar and then the members reflect on what it is we're thinking about and we try to help each other. It becomes clearer then what's going on on the tape. The seminar is very critical to that process. That's a place where you can think out loud. And because people have been together for a while, they know what you're talking about. They know your history as a thinker and know where you are and going with it. That's the way I usually start to sort things out, even though there's much more data than I can bring in. But it gets me on a track.

   Even when you're not presenting data, in the process of going to the Seminar you still are thinking about your own question or inquiry, and it's all very much melded together. You might be thinking about someone else's work, but really at the same time, you're thinking about your own work.

   But when it comes down to having all this data and trying to figure out how to write about it, I have a very elaborate Post-it system. I go through and code for themes or questions or things that I know I have isolated and seen as continuous over time. And I'll post those with cute little colors and I'll write my way through those. The same with the transcripts. I'll go and code them in different ways. But it's not as neat and tidy and formalized as people are taught in graduate school! It's much more random. Coding can be quite elaborate, but I don't do elaborate coding.

*SM: Can you describe a problem that you've faced and how you've dealt with it?*

*KG:* There are problems that come up in relation to the way that I have found myself evolving. When I create forums for kids to talk to each other, I really try my best not to intrude in those forums. And that's been something I've been grappling with for a long time. How to stay out.

*SM:* Oh, I was really wondering about that as I read your book. I was often struck by how absent you are in the interactions that you write about.

*KG:* That's been an ongoing struggle ever since my first work. When kids start to talk to each other, things come up that before, I would have censored. And the first time it happened, I didn't know what to do. But it's actually fortunate that I didn't know what to do! The kids took it right over, and they handled it much better than I ever could have. And it made such a tremendous difference in the life of the classroom. That was my first lesson on just staying out of it. But it's risky—you worry about it. We're always worrying about kids being hurt.

*SM: I was intrigued by the "fake stories" you write about: the stories the children create— often on the spot—for sharing time. They include each other as characters, sometimes in very compromising roles and situations. They were harsh sometimes!*

*KG:* Very harsh, yes. Often when I want to intervene, though, it's based on **my** stuff, my fears, my thoughts, being vulnerable. Every time I think that it's gone over the edge and I think "I have to stop this," the kids show the most presence of mind and the most grace. They teach me how to be graceful and respectful and supportive. Very subtly, in ways as a teacher I would just bungle through. They are more respectful and careful of everybody. But not protective.

　　That was always an immediate issue for me—knowing when to stay out. I've had people say to me, "How could you let children say that to each other? You've probably wounded them for life." And my response is that when I would talk to children afterwards, it was clear that they were not wounded.

*SM: But at the same time, you talk about the teacher researcher's role to intervene. When do you find yourself putting your own self into it?*

*KG:* I see myself as part of the audience, as part of the community—I'm there, too—I get to say what I think. And I usually find that when I am having a visceral response as an audience member, that's when my response is most effective. Instead of saying, "Don't do that here. It's wrong," I'd rather say, "That makes me so uncomfortable and I don't like it because it scares me," or whatever. That's the way I see my responses as authentic response, rather than "let's quash the response." So, yes, I do intervene in that way now, but I've found through my latest work that I have to do it as a full member, not as the member with the shove who's going to push it. Children have taught me to do that, I want to say. Especially little girls have shown me that that is a perfectly acceptable thing to do. The children see that as an appropriate response when you are truly honest about things.

*SM: It's amazing. I think that's why I like working with the youngest kids, because they have the power to teach me so much. They haven't learned yet that they are supposed to just let things go by them and pretend that everything's fine. Have you dealt with a specific ethical problem in your research?*

*KG:* Well, there's always issues when I write about children who are doing things that we might say are "yucky" or could be hurtful to other kids. There is always the issue, "How do I write about these children?"—children who I don't want to present as bad people, because they aren't bad people. The ethical issue for me there is accurately presenting them from a number of dimensions. Their behavior should be seen within the context of their whole way of acting in the world, rather than just isolating this one thing and saying "Look at what this child did here!" And assign it "X, Y or Z." So, when I'm writing about unpleasant things, I feel it is my obligation to find ways to present children as part of a larger picture.

It's akin to when researchers go into classrooms and observe teachers and they isolate the teacher's behavior from the full context of what they do every day and hold it up sometimes as wrong ways to teach. And I just feel that that's completely unethical. They take the instance they've observed and use it to serve a point. So, my issue is that I don't want to use kids to prove a point. I don't want to take their work out of context. I'd rather have the point come from the complete situation. Especially with my "bad boy" work. You can imagine the parents who had those little boys. They know who I'm writing about and I always wonder if this is going to come back at me. But what I tried to do was to create a broader picture of both the child and the behavior. So they could see their child in all his glory as well as his . . . struggle. So far, those parents know their children and they've appreciated those descriptions.

*SM: It comes clearly across that though these kids are tough—they also were really important in the class in a lot of positive ways. They moved things forward—they set a tone in some instances.*

*I also teach kids for two years—both kindergarten and first grade—and it felt good for me to read that you believe that having those kids for two years was helpful for them. I identified with that so clearly. I had one very bad boy in my class for the past two years. And he was a different guy by the end. And I can't put my finger on anything that I did. I think it was the ability to learn to trust, and it was wonderful to read that in your book too. I hear people gripe so often, "how can you keep the kids for two years?"*

*KG:* Oh, but it's the most wonderful opportunity for everybody!

*SM: Hard to convince some people . . .*

*KG:* I know. They don't quite know it until they see the two years pass.

*SM: If someone was going to give you money to support your research, how would you use it?*

*KG:* Well—how much money? A lot of money?

*They laugh.*

*KG:* That's a very interesting question. Obviously, the first thing we need is transcribers. Some people say, oh no, you must transcribe all your own tapes, but I'm like, "I don't think so!" I want someone to transcribe it and then I'll do the work after that. Transcribing is the first thing. But that's not large enough. I think this recycles back to an earlier question. If someone gives you a decent amount of money, it might be possible for someone doing this kind of work to be freed from the classroom for a day. So, the money might go toward a teaching partner of some sort.

I've always wanted to have remote mikes for every child in my class. 'Cause I know I want to hear their playground talk, and when they're inside working among themselves the small conversations that they have are so rich and I can't get them all. I would love to have a study where you have a remote mike on everybody and then have someone who transcribes all those texts! That's a lot of money!

*SM: Yes, and it's a lot of data also!*

*KG:* Yes, really a lot of data also . . . *They laugh.* You know, you could put it all on a data base, and it would be so rich.

Those would be the two things.

I also hear from people who are doing science talks at different grades levels all across the country. It would be really nice to have a project with all those people so they could begin to bring the data that they are collecting in settings with all different kinds of kids and be able to get together and really look at the notion of how kids talk about science. That's not something I would normally do in my own situation, but something I see now as an interesting project.

*SM: You mention the playground, and I wonder how you collect data out there. I have the hardest time because I don't think the kids act the way they normally do when I'm there.*

*KG:* I usually take strolls around. They see me roaming around the playground and every now and then I'll stop and I'll look thoughtful. It's like the classroom—they get used to seeing me there and they know I hang out. Usually they continue with their games. Sometimes I step back and just watch the physical behavior. I find that extraordinarily interesting because I can see so much stuff when I take the language out, in terms of how kids position themselves and so forth. It tells me a lot about their interactions in the classroom. It's just bigger. But that's where a remote mike, you see, would really help.

*SM: Exactly! They laugh. I really want my interns to see themselves as teacher-researchers right from the beginning and I want them to see me working as a teacher researcher. But I wonder what you tell them to help them see that as part of the process? Or can you?*

*KG:* Yes, it should be part of their practice from the beginning. I usually present it from the point of view that it's a way to document practice. When they are making decisions about teaching, they are not facing it just from intuition—they are working with data. We need data within which to assess what children are doing and to know where to go. And we need to be concrete. I usually start them out with the fieldnotes. So I introduce them to the point of view that you're always taking notes on what's happening in the class. Then we can go back and look at them and see what's happening, and design programs for learning.

*SM: A lot of the concern comes from people who are beginning their first year of teaching. They ask, "How can I possibly do this and do my first year of teaching?"*

*KG:* Well, that's a very good question.

*SM: Maybe it's just not trying to be too formal about it?*

*KG:* I think so. I have known teachers who did not want to do teacher research who I have worked and they say, "What the heck are you doing with that tape recorder on?" And I explain that I tape classroom talk, and they say "Gee, I'm going to go do that!" They don't do it with the intention that they are going to go and become teacher researchers, they do it with the intention of finding out what is going on. All that entails is putting the tape recorder on. and then listening to the tape afterwards. It's a way of really being able to view practice that we don't normally have. So, even that step of audiotaping and listening—that's a huge step.

And the step that I think is the most important one is writing down things that you see. That kind of data is data you can use with parents. When you have notes about their children and you want to give concrete examples of what a child does in the classroom and how that relates to what you're trying to explain to parents, that's really pretty useful stuff. You have notes and dates, written there, right in front of you. 'Here's what happened on this day.' So, in terms of documentation, I know many teachers are now being trained to do more.

*SM: I also hear a lot of concern, certainly with my intern last year: "Assessment! How do I do assessment! Why haven't you yet shown me how to do assessment?" This is what teacher research is!*

*KG:* It's all there! It's completely about assessment.

*SM: A few minutes ago, you mentioned Herbert Kohl, and Sylvia Ashton-Warner . . . who else has influenced you, do you think?*

*KG:* Elwyn Richardson. Do you know his book? It's out of print now. That's a tragedy—it's hard to find by many libraries have it. His book is *In the Early World.* It's from New Zealand also. And it's a really beautiful book—he would never characterize himself a teacher-researcher, but he was documenting the classroom and inquiring with children, and he had a multi-arts approach. He was way ahead of his time. Still is, I think in the way he conceptualized it. And I reread that book periodically. I reread *Teacher* often because there's so much in it. And right now—there are a lot of good books coming out, I think, by teachers. I just read *A Teacher's Sketchbook Journal.* Karen Ernst is doing some really interesting work. And I'm also heavily influenced by Ann Haas Dyson. She's not a teacher researcher, but she does similar work, in the sense that she's in there really looking. Obviously, Shirley Brice Heath is critical. And, Douglas Barnes *From Communication to Curriculum.* He started out as a teacher and a lot of his work grows from that process. So, I reread him a lot. And I'm a real Bahktin fan, as you probably know. Mikhail Bahktin, who was actually a literary critic, but has been used a lot in the field of language study. I think his work is amazing, although he wasn't a teacher. I love his insights into the meaning of cultures and how language is negotiated.

*SM: What about for fun?*

*KG:* I like to read a lot of historical novels and a lot of natural science. And I'm a gardener, so I read a lot of gardening books. I grow things!

*SM: Like kids. (they laugh) I'm really interested in what you're looking forward to with your kindergartners.*

*KG:* In terms of looking at this kindergarten class, I'm going to continue looking at identity. Not only how kids present themselves publicly, when they get in the group, but how they want you to see them before you even begin teaching them. I see them positioning themselves even before they know me as a teacher. They almost set themselves up so I can see them doing certain things that they obviously think are important that I should know. I can't describe how it is, but here's an example: the other day I saw this little boy who's going to be in my class, and he doesn't know me very well, but he knew I was in my office. So what he did was he positioned himself just outside the building door, so I could see him with a book, sitting on the ground very studiously turning the pages, not looking at me, you know, but I knew he knew I could see him because he had moved right to that spot. It's very interesting, the notion of what kids orchestrate to position themselves in the world so that you'll know who they are! They want to be seen as they are. I think they understand that when you know them, it's easier to really know their story.

*SM: You write about the plays your class wrote and performs at the end of the school year. Will you try that with your kindergartners?*

*KG:* I've never done it with kids that little, but it would probably be hysterical!

*SM: I think so!*

*KG:* I've only done it with first and second graders, and toward the end of the year. Kindergartners have all this performance and drama time in the context of kindergarten, at least when I do kindergarten they do. It will be interesting to see what they come up with—whether they want to turn them into full-fledged dramatic events.

*SM: Those plays seemed so incredibly sophisticated to me, and I wondered if they were an outgrowth of all the storytelling that they had done from the sharing chair?*

*KG:* Good question! Also, that sharing time format I have never done with kindergarten, and I have had people say to me, "Well, you really can't do that with kindergarteners—their stories just don't make any sense." But Vivian Paley would say, that's not necessarily true! I'm pretty firm that they can do this. But, going back to your question, when the first class did playmaking, I had not done sharing time in the way it later developed. We had had a very open sharing time, but "fake stories" were not a part of it. It was the year after that those really developed more formally, and story was emphasized. But the first one that ever developed, the kids wanted to do it, and I said, we can do a play but it's not going to be one that's written down anywhere. We have to make it up. And the format that I gave them was: we have to make it up, and everybody has to be in it. Those were the rules.

*SM: That's just brilliant.*

*KG:* You can't have one person writing it, I told them. And they seemed to take to it so naturally. That class had been doing science talks, of course, and so maybe that's what children need—a background with the opportunity to understand how you construct language together.

*SM: Can you explain how the science talks work?*

*KG:* Science talks are times when we as a class sit down to think about questions children raise about the world. We call them science talks, but sometimes they're about psychology or social science; it varies. And so, generally, early in the year when I introduce it, they need for me to do a lot of modeling of how you might discuss something when you're not sure of the answer, because that's the kinds of question we deal with. I usually do a lot of modeling early on, although I've had some classes where I haven't had to do that. There's been a child or two who've just known how to do the science talks. And then gradually, as it goes on, I try to be quiet. And so the children eventually take over the process and really develop a way to talk together. They can get quite good at listening to each other building a series of theories.

*SM: And you intend to do that with your kindergartners?*

*KG:* Yes. I do and I have been very encouraged this year. I met a lot of kindergarten teachers in Vermont who were starting to try it and they really were doing much more than people think is possible.

*SM: That's sort of my pet peeve—people telling me what kindergartners* **can't** *do. It happens a lot.*

*KG:* Well, these teachers obviously didn't believe that. Some of them I have to say were those doing the Reggio Emilia approach, and they felt science talks were extremely compatible with that approach, so they were developing science talks more. And since then, I've heard about other kindergarten teachers who are right on to it.

*SM: I've always struggled with sharing time because I don't want it to become a forum of "Look at my new toy." And so I struggle with how to define the boundaries. Do you define what you can and can't share? Or do you find that kids, once they start telling stories, stop bringing those things?*

*KG:* Well, some classes continue in and out of it. But what I do, is if they are really stuck in showing **things,** I then declare a moratorium on that. I intervene and say, "Well, now, here's what we have to do for a while." And I always start it off first, so you can see how it is, and then I wait, and they start to try it. Some classes are a little hesitant to move beyond the concrete "look at what I brought."

*SM: When the fake stories came up, they generated themselves the first year, and in later years did you suggest them? Or just wait?*

*KG:* No, although, the fourth grade class that I taught last, I didn't suggest anything to them, and they had a time each day when they sat and talked 'cause I felt it was so important. I told them "You can use this as a time to share what you've done, or talk about things you've seen or tell us a story, or . . ." And that's as far as I went. Then they started to make up these stories. The same thing!

*SM: That's amazing!*

*KG:* I also worked with a fifth-grade teacher who heard about sharing time stories and brought the idea to her class of story telling. She didn't tell them how the story telling should go, but said, "You know, we could tell some stories, if anybody wants to." And sure enough a couple of kids popped up and were fabulous at it, and they just made them up. And so, I do usually suggest it as a format, and I do show them how they can work and I'm not a great storyteller. I can make something up, but it's not superb, ever! But they usually go right for it. And the other thing they always do is tell class stories and they always include everyone in the class. I just think that's remarkable. They see that that's the perfect story.

Nobody tells them that.

*SM: Do you have any advice for readers of this reader?*

*KG:* The thing I have been thinking about lately is really elaborating on what the research process is for teachers—how it is different from other research as a discipline—and why. I think it's so important that the teacher's position be presented as one that accurately portrays the complexity of classroom life. I'm always interested in teachers who explore all the contradictions in their work. Because we really need to see them.

I also think that the notion of writing about research presents many problems for teachers because writing is time consuming, but I think it's culturally important—we need that reporting. But my concern is that teachers' writing still doesn't have access—there are a few journals that actively seek teacher work, but there aren't many. There are a lot of people writing out there, adding great duress to their lives—and families—and they need more forums. And not just forums other teachers—they need to be read by everybody. I'm going around talking to people in the research community who are more in the academy, and they say, 'Well what can we do to help?' and I say, 'Well, you could read teachers' work. That would be a beginning, and you could find ways to help publish their work—and have your colleagues read and discuss the work.' Because the notion of what is written and how it's written also needs to be looked at. Teachers have a whole different voice. Its not because it's a voice that only teachers recognize. It's useful. I'm worried about the practice of teacher research being just too onerous and not enough ways for teachers to stay with it because it's so tiring. We need to hear how people have made this do-able. I'm just always interested, too, in learning about how people's questions evolve in relation to their history as teachers.

*SM: I always wonder about the process someone used in deciding to be a teacher. It think it can be very telling.*

*KG:* People need to be very conscious of their relationship to teaching. Throughout their careers, asking themselves, "Why am I in it?"

# Teacher Research Extension: Focusing on Student Talk

**Sherry Young**
**Third-Grade Teacher**

The main focus of my research has been on student talk. I am interested in learning how boys and girls use language differently. I also want to know how these differences play role in students' ability to express their ideas and opinions. My goal has been to find new strategies to help all students find their voice by learning more about the ways they interact in whole group and small group situations.

I designed an interview on talk which I administered individually to all my students (See Figure 1 for the questions and a summary of the results). I enjoyed the personal contact with the students and appreciated the seriousness and honesty with which their answers were given. It was interesting how differently students interpreted the same question. At other times I noticed how their answers sounded like what they thought their teacher wanted to hear. I heard my voice in their replies.

In two of the interview questions, students indicated strongly they had heard teacher directions about how to participate in classroom talk. One of these questions was, "What do you do when you want to share something?" Two thirds of the students said, "Raise your hand." I had a hunch this might happen so I asked a follow-up question calling for another way to share. Girls had fewer strategies for what they would do, while boys had several ways to get their ideas heard. Two of the nine girls had no response at all.

The second question with responses that sounded like my voice was "How do you know when someone is listening to you?" This time, 16 students, or more than two thirds of the class, said, "When the person is looking at you." This is a strategy I have taught them to use to check for their audience to be ready.

Another set of questions asked about their feelings about speaking or participating in class discussions. Over three quarters of the students said that they feel good about participating in class discussions. Many students said they "liked it" or they "wanted to," but others hinged their participation on being part of the group. For example, one student said, "It's important. It's part of the community. I feel like I'm part of something important." One girl said, "I feel happy because I can help people." Several boys said participating was an important part of learning. One boy said, "It helps me out. Helps me learn!" Another boy said, "If you don't participate you might not learn something you are suppose to."

Grade 3

Talk Interview

Name: S. Young                                          Date:   March 97

1) When you are at school and you want to share something you've learned what do you do? Why?

   Raise hand 5 14              Ask teacher 4              Other 4
        5G      9B                    2G      2B              2G    2B

2) What is another way you share what you know?




3) During a class discussion, how do you feel about participating?

        Good   17                Depends   5                No    0
        7B      10B                  2G      3B

4) How do you feel if someone disagrees with what you say?

        O.K.  9            Bad  6            Mad  2            Other  5
        5G    4B            2G    3B            2B              2G    3B

5) What would a teacher do to help a person share their ideas?




6) When you talk to your classmates, do you prefer a small group, talking to a partner, or a whole class discussion? Why?

        Small  5            Partner  8            Whole  6            Other  3
        3G    2B              4G    4B              1G    5B            2B   1G

7) Do you prefer a group of all boys, (or all girls), or a mixed group of boys and girls?

        Boy                Girls                Mixed 17            Other 1
         2                   2                    6G                11B

8) How do you know when someone is listening to you?

        Looking at you  16                          Other  6
        7 G              9B                          2G        4B

9) What would you like to do better as a speaker?

10) Do you think you are a good speaker?

        Yes  12            No  4            Sometimes  6
        5G    7B            1 G    3 B        3 G    3 B

        Classmates  9        Grownups  6        Either  7
        4 G    5 B            2 G    4 B          3 G    4 B

**Figure 1**
Summary of Interview Results

Students view talk as an important part of our class, and most of them seem to have positive feelings about it. Over half of the students consider themselves good speakers.

Another section of the interview questions dealt with student preferences concerning the groups in which they work. One third of the students like working with a partner because it is easier to talk, or they trust their partner will be respectful. Seven of the nine girls prefer working with partners or in small groups. Only one girl liked the whole group learning better, while five of the boys preferred this grouping.

When I asked if they preferred working in a group of the same gender or a mixed group, students were overwhelming in their support for mixed groups. Only two girls and two boys thought they might like to work in groups of the same gender. Students thought it wouldn't be fair to leave out the other gender: "They would want to be part of the group." Many students thought that the mix of the boys and the girls brought more ideas to the group. "Different kinds of people, different ideas!" "Boys know stuff girls don't! Girls know stuff boys don't!"

Another question I asked concerning groups was whether they preferred talking to their classmates or grownups. I asked this question because in an earlier interview about students' home journals, some students had indicated that they didn't like talking about a book to their parents. During the talk interview, I had the feeling students strongly preferred to talk with their classmates rather than grownups, but the final tallies did not show this. Only nine students said they preferred talking to their classmates, while six students said they prefer talking to adults. Seven students said they liked to talk to either classmates or grownups. Students thought parents or teachers could help the most when they had a problem.

While I was interviewing my students about talk, I began a new class procedure to observe our classroom talk. During our daily morning meeting time, I appointed a student observer. The observer's job was to take notes about what he or she saw and heard during this time. I also used Post-its to record comments or observations I had during this time. Before we left the group, our observations were shared with the rest of the class.

Another way I used this role was to have students run small groups while I observed. In this role I did not participate as a talker, only as a watcher. On two occasions I was able to be an observer while another adult led the group in lessons on art and a discussion of paintings. I was able to contrast the work of the small group with that of the whole group situation. I recorded whether boys or girls did the talking, in addition to as much of the conversation as possible.

# Examining Teacher Talk: Revealing Hidden Boundaries for Curricular Change

## Deborah Rowe

### EDITOR'S INTRODUCTION

Using the lens of a teacher-researcher, Deborah Rowe considers how analyzing patterns of classroom talk provides teachers with an important opportunity to consciously consider the ways their talk works to define the nature of literacy events, students' roles, and the literacy strategies children come to use and value.

The most things change the more they stay the same. Teaching is a profession that is about change. As teachers, we are not successful if things are standing still. We work hard to nurture changes in our students' abilities as readers and writers. In the process, we are constantly making changes in our curriculum and in ourselves. As a teacher of young children, kidwatching (Goodman, 1985) has been one of the strongest motivators for change in my curriculum. Early in my professional training I learned to believe in the power of children as learners, and to "follow the child's lead." For me this has meant paying attention to anomalies—the times when children do and say things that surprise me. It is in these moments that I often get ideas about the ways in which my curriculum needs to change. I rearrange space, provide different kinds of materials, reallocate time, and provide new curricular invitations.

Recently, I have learned some surprising things about my own teaching that make me question whether such changes go deep enough. These insights have occurred as a result of my participation as a teacher researcher on a project aimed at creating rich, school-based reading and writing experiences for a group of two-year-olds (Rowe, 1994, in press). As part of this project, the classroom teachers and I video-

taped literacy events at the book and writing centers in order to track the children's responses to the literacy curriculum. Because I often read and wrote with the children, my interactions were captured on videotape, as well. In order to understand how the children learned literacy in the context of our classroom, I found it necessary to look closely not only at the children's behaviors, but also at my own role in reading and writing events. This required me to move from the safe and comfortable role of observing children, to the sometimes uncomfortable position of watching my own teaching. While this analysis confirmed much about my interactions with children that was known and familiar to me, it also uncovered much that had previously been implicit. In this article I share my personal insights about the role of talk—especially teacher talk—in creating unseen boundaries that limit curricular change. I also share the new kinds of reflections that are now helping me to examine the previously murky edges of my professional practice.

*Source:* "Examining Teacher Talk: Revealing Hidden Boundaries for Curricular Change." by Deborah Wells Rowe, 1988, *Language Arts 75* (2), pp. 103–107. Copyright 1998 by the National Council of Teachers of English. Reprinted with permission.

## "FOLLOWING THE CHILDREN'S LEAD": ATTEMPTING CURRICULAR CHANGE

In order to enrich the school-based literacy experiences for the two-year-olds who attended Walker School, I and my colleagues, Ginger Wells, Michelle Raybin, and Fran Rogers, planned a few basic changes in the literacy curriculum and then used kidwatching to guide us in translating our theory into practice. One important change was the introduction of *text sets* (Short, Harste, & Burke, 1996)— groups of books related by topic, language pattern, genre, author/illustrator and so on. A second change was to more frequently station one of the teachers in the classroom book center to read informally with the children. Over the course of the school year, kidwatching revealed a number of surprises that suggested better ways of supporting children as readers. For example, we observed almost immediately that children wanted sets of books related to their own personal interests in addition to (and sometimes instead of) books related to the teachers' themes. This led us to consult with parents to discover children's interests outside of school, and eventually to create text sets related to the children's interests. We also observed that the children continued to request favorite books over periods of time that were much longer than the one or two weeks usually devoted to thematic units. This observation led us to make text sets continuously available to children on open shelving—even when the teachers' curricular theme changed.

Perhaps the most surprising outcome of kidwatching, however, was our observation of the children's connections between book reading and play. At the beginning of the school year, we had envisioned the book center as a comfortable place to read books. We did not initially include play or play props in our planning for this area. Nevertheless, from the outset, children spontaneously made several kinds of connections between book reading and play. These included shifting from talking about books to book-related dramatic play during reading events, and searching for book-related toys to hold as we read. (See Rowe, in press, for a full description of the children's book-to-play connections.)

It was some time, however, before our kidwatching efforts helped us recognize these patterns in children's responses to books. Since many book-related play episodes involved only brief shifts of stance from book discussion to play and back again, and because we were so focused on the book discussions, we initially overlooked these playful responses. However, one evening as I was reviewing the day's videotapes, I recognized, with some discomfort, that I had been covertly pushing toys out of the book center as soon as children put them down or turned their attention elsewhere. When I shared this observation with our research/teaching team, we agreed that our curriculum had largely supported book-to-play connections only by default, and had even discouraged them in some ways. After some focused observation of the children's use of dramatic play and play props in the book center, we made the decision to follow the children's lead by adding book-related toys and props to our text sets. We introduced and displayed these *text and toy sets,* not only in the book center, but also in other areas of the classroom such as the block center and dramatic play area. Through kidwatching, we recognized the need to support children's use of toys and play as a mode of responding to books, and their use of books as a means of expanding their play.

At the close of the year of research and teaching, I felt particularly good about the ways in which kidwatching had allowed us to support book-to-play connections through changes in our use of space and materials. By the end of the school year, we had observed many dramatic play events where children used book language and themes as part of their playscripts. We had also recorded many reading events where children incorporated toys and play. I believed that we had expanded the alternatives during informal book reading events to support children's ways of linking books to play.

### Surprises from Teacher-Watching

What I found most interesting when I later began to look more closely at video tapes of informal book reading events was the way I used talk to incorporate toys and play into the book center after our curricular decision to support book-to-play links. Example 1 is typical of the ways that play became part of book reading events when I was the adult reader.

I am sitting on the floor in the book center with Christopher, Richard, and Julia. Displayed there are a variety of books including a text and toy set related to the theme of wild animals. Books include various genres such as information books and stories. Toys include wild animal puppets and small realistic wild animal models.

Christopher hands me a large information book. "Read this book," he says.

"OK. . . . " I reply, "It's called *Animal Encyclopedia* (Attmore, 1989) and it has pictures of real animals in it." I open the book to a page near the middle of the book and hold it so it faces Christopher and Richard. I point toward some toy animals lying on the floor near us. "We could probably find pages that tell about some of those animals."

Searching through the pile of animals, Christopher asks, "Where's that monkey one?"

"The gorilla one?" I ask. "I don't know. Richard, have you seen the gorilla laying around?"

No response from Richard.

I turn to the last pages in the book. "Let's look in the index and see if it tells anything about gorillas." Flipping through them, I continue with disappointment. "Well, no index. That's not good. Well, let's look up mammals." As the children look on, I turn to the entries about mammals. "Here's a page about monkeys. There! Look here: Gorillas!" I gesture toward the bag of animal toys. "This is like that black gorilla. Christopher! Is that his arm sticking out underneath the *Barn Dance* book?"

Christopher brings the toy gorilla to me, but continues to hold it.

I begin to read the entry about gorillas.

Christopher interrupts with excitement. He thumps the picture of the gorilla with his finger. "Here!"

"It says he walks on all fours. Let's . . . I think they kind of put their legs down like this." I arrange the toy gorilla's arms so they touch the ground as in the picture. "I think he walks along like that."

In this event, and in many others after we added toys and props to the book center, I led the book discussion in a way that focused attention on the use of books as resources for learning about the the real world objects represented by the toys. What I found particularly surprising was the similarity between the talk in this event and the analytic book talk I had encouraged in events prior to our decision to support book-to-play connections. Though, at the time this event occurred, I saw myself as following the children's lead in connecting books and play, a closer look at videotapes suggested that I had sanctioned only some aspects of the children's play, and for the most part had redefined it in ways that were in line with my previous notions about book reading events. Where before I had supported children in talking about connections between books and their life experiences, I now encouraged children to compare and contrast book information with features of the newly introduced toys.

Overall, my talk during book reading served to define children as critical readers and thinkers. As Heath (1991) suggests, critical thinkers learn to stand back and look at events and to compare their own experiences to information provided by books and other sources. The children's talk, however, indicated that they defined themselves not only as critical readers, but also as players and imaginative storytellers. Children often used play as a means of responding

to books, or creating a lived-through experience of some aspects of a book's text or illustrations. For example, during our reading of an information book about work machines, Christopher rode over on a toy bulldozer to listen, and soon the following exchange ensued.

*Christopher:* [*to imaginary character on other end of the phone*] "Hey . . ." His talk trails off into an unintelligible mumble into the phone.

*Christopher:* [*to participants in the book center*] "I'm calling one of the workmen."

*Rowe:* "You're calling one of the workmen?"

*Christopher:* [*into the phone*] "Hello?"

I return my attention to the book and begin reading aloud. Richard joins Christopher in his dramatic play.

*Rowe:* [*interrupting Christopher and Richard's play*] "Anyone know what this one is?" [*Points to picture of scraper in the book.*]

As this episode demonstrates, book-related dramatic play was an avenue of response left only partially open by my talk. Though I did not explicitly exclude the dramatic play introduced by Christopher in the example presented above, I did nothing to encourage it. Instead, I attempted to return the children's attention to the book. My talk sent the implicit message that dramatic play was an inappropriate response to the book. Children sometimes dealt with the limits I placed on their book responses by moving to other areas of the room where their actions were more acceptable. For example, it was not uncommon for children who received implicitly negative responses to dramatic play to leave the book center and continue their play elsewhere with another teacher or child. In reflecting on this situation, I've been grateful that the organization of this classroom allowed them this kind of flexibility. Not all classes do. However, I also recognize that it is likely that the rather narrow boundaries I set for book reading events also limited the comprehension and response strategies children were able to experience and learn.

My point in highlighting the surprising similarities in my talk at the book center before and after we made the curricular decision to support play as part of book reading events is to reveal the gap between the examined and unexamined aspects of my professional practice. While I had initially believed my new focus on the play-literacy connection changed book reading events in major ways, my unexamined ways of talking about books worked against change—and against allowing children to explore books in their own ways. In fact, my habitual ways of reading with children did not exactly match my examined beliefs. For example, at a theoretical level I believed that analysis was only one of many important kinds of response to books. The lived-through experience children created for themselves as they linked books to dramatic play was something I valued as well. Though children continued to experience this type of dramatic play when they were with peers, I now see many of my interactions at the book center as discouraging rather than supporting this type of response.

Having said this, I do not want to minimize or overlook the important impact the addition of toys had on our analytic book discussions. I continue to value the kinds of reading that took place at the book center. However, I am now keenly aware that my actions and talk limited the range of book responses in unintended ways. My usual patterns of book talk privileged my agenda over the alternate ones introduced by the children, and worked against the curricular changes I attempted to introduce.

## THE PROFESSIONAL POSSIBILITIES OF TEACHER-WATCHING

After closely examining my talk at the book center, I am highly aware of the power of teacher talk for setting boundaries for literate behavior, even in student-centered classrooms. It is talk that fills the gap between curricular plans and curricular experiences. Talk makes events come to life. It is through everyday talk that children learn their roles as students, the nature of school literacy, and what kinds of literacy strategies they should use in the classroom. Talk is also the most transparent and habitual part of a teacher's professional activity. As Barnes (1986) has pointed out, much of this information is signaled to students covertly by the way we ask questions and respond to students, rather than by any overt effort on our part to explain to them their roles as readers or to teach them the literacy strategies they need to participate successfully in school. We are much more likely to consciously consider how the arrangement of space or materials may facilitate reading and writing experiences than to consider (or plan for) the ways in which our own talk shapes these events. In short, our professional roles and beliefs are made real through the micro-patterns of our everyday talk in the classroom. And it is these habitual ways of talking with students of which we are most likely to be unaware—both because we have not always recognized the need for this kind of professional self-reflection and because of the difficulty of examining something that in the normal course of events fails to create a telltale trail. Despite the difficulties and discomfort of watching ourselves, my experience suggests that examining our own patterns of talk may provide us with an important opportunity to consciously consider the subtle ways our talk works to define the nature of literacy events, the roles of students, and the literacy strategies they come to use and value.

For me, teacher-watching has become a powerful tool which supports my work with students across the age span from the preschool to my university classes. In general, I audio- or videotape a classroom event that I'm concerned about—either because I want to change it or because I want to understand how to recreate a similar learning environment in other areas of my curriculum. I then watch or listen to the tape several times, taking note of such issues as what kinds of talk are initiated by students, and what reactions are provided by me and other students. I consider how my talk serves to define student roles, and what implicit messages students may be learning about my views of literacy or the purposes of classroom events.

Examining my talk has provided me with new insights concerning my own implicit values and beliefs about literacy learning and instruction. In some cases, it has also challenged me to change my interactive style so that it is more in line with my professional beliefs. At times, I have found this to be particularly difficult. Sometimes my patterns of talk seem to be so deeply ingrained that I find myself unable to make the changes I intend. This difficulty of changing my ways of teaching has led me to a set of professional questions for which I continue to seek better answers: How can I learn to talk differently with students? What other changes in the classroom environment are necessary to support changes in my talk and that of my students?

To date, my answers to these questions are quite tentative. I expect that language is difficult to change, not only because it is habitual and hard to examine, but also because it is inextricably linked to other aspects of classroom events. As Halliday (1974) has suggested, language is learned in context and its use is linked to social situations in powerful ways. I often find that unless I change other features of classroom events (e.g., the nature of the activity, roles and relationships of students and teacher, and the chosen communication channels), both I and my students have great difficulty changing existing patterns of talk. After all, I'm not the only one who has developed expectations for classroom events. Students, too, play their parts according to the scripts they have learned to associate with school. Sometimes it is student talk that pulls me away from new teaching roles and pushes me to respond in more familiar ways.

Thus, I find myself on the horns of a professional dilemma. I recognize the influence of talk—especially teacher talk—on students' definitions of literacy, themselves, and classroom events. At the same time, I realize that talk is not only a manifestation of participants' beliefs and relationships but also the medium through which these relationships and meanings are constructed. Attempting to change patterns of talk without also changing other features of classrooms seems difficult, if not impossible. Professional change is not as simple as following recommendations to talk differently with students—to ask higher level questions or to provide more wait time before responding. While such suggestions are often aimed at important goals, they fail to take into account the complex patterns of talk into which these practices must be inserted. For me, analysis of classroom talk provides an important window on my teaching and the learning of my students. By examining my own classroom talk, I have become consciously aware of the tendency of teacher talk to reshape innovative practices so that they fall within the boundaries of familiar classroom activities. My experiences suggest that connecting kid-watching with teacher-watching can help to reveal hidden limits on curricular change. Awareness of the features of classroom talk has the potential for helping teachers avoid the trap of unintentionally subverting plans for change by encasing new curriculum and beliefs in old patterns of talk.

# REFERENCES

Attmore, S. (1989). *Animal encyclopedia.* New York: Checkerboard Press.

Barnes, D. (1986). Language in the secondary classroom. In D. Barnes, J. Britton, & M. Torbe (Eds.), *Language, the learner, and the school* (3rd. ed., pp. 11–87). New York: Penguin.

Goodman, Y. (1985). Kidwatching: Observing children in the classroom. In A. Jaggar & M. T. Smith-Burke (Eds.), *Observing the language learner* (pp. 9–18). Urbana, IL & Newark, DE: National Council of Teachers of English & International Reading Association.

Halliday, M. A. K. (1974). *Language and social man.* London: Longman.

Heath, S. B. (1991). The sense of being literate: Historical and cross-cultural features. In R. Barr, M. Kamil, P. Mosenthal, & P. D. Pearson (Eds.), *Handbook of reading research.* (Vol. II, pp. 3–25). New York: Longman.

Rowe, D. W. (in press). The literate potentials of book-related, dramatic play. *Reading Research Quarterly.*

Rowe, D. W. (1994). Learning about literacy and the world: Two-year-old's and teachers' enactment of a thematic inquiry curriculum. In D. Leu & C. Kinzer (Eds.), *Forty-third yearbook of the National Reading Conference* (pp. 217–229). Chicago: National Reading Conference.

Short, K., Harste, J., & Burke, C. (1996). *Creating classrooms for authors and inquirers* (2nd. ed.). Portsmouth, NH: Heinemann.

# Inquiry Purpose
# in the Classroom

## Judith Wells Lindfors

### EDITOR'S INTRODUCTION

Lindfors argues eloquently for the power of authentic inquiry events in the classroom.
She considers several factors that make it difficult to provide genuine inquiry events in
the classroom—and shows ways that teachers can overcome them, making demonstration
and engagement central.

Children's and teachers' inquiry acts inside the classroom are, like those outside, communication acts. They are conversational turns that *turn* toward the partner(s) for help in going beyond present understanding. Like all language acts, each inquiry utterance provides whatever the speaker deems sufficient for the partner(s) to respond to (completion), and each is nonneutral, resonating with mood and tone and feeling (expressiveness)—curiosity perhaps or puzzlement, reflectiveness or tentativeness. It is a stance, an "accent," that is familiar to all of us, for we not only hear our students' inquiry voices; we also hear our own. We are inquirers too, which matters a great deal if our intention in the classroom is to support children's emergent inquiry. In the classroom, as outside, demonstration and engagement are central.

This chapter focuses on authentic inquiry events in classrooms: first, by contrasting examples of authentic and inauthentic inquiry events; next, by examining one authentic classroom example closely; and finally, by considering factors that make it more difficult to provide authentic inquiry events in classrooms than one might expect.

## RECOGNIZING AUTHENTIC INQUIRY

We begin with our own ability to hear the sounds that inquiry makes. Of course! How can we possibly support children's continuing development of something we cannot hear? Yet recognizing inquiry acts is not so easy as one might think. If it were, then the many earlier educational psychology research studies (mentioned previously) would not have missed it, for example, those studies in which researchers counted children's interrogative forms, mistakenly thinking that they were counting children's inquiry acts, though in fact the children were not trying to understand anything at all. Researchers are not the only ones to have problems identifying what is and what is not inquiry in the voices of children. My third-grade teacher, Mrs. McKenzie, had this problem too.

She would begin each social studies unit the same way: "We're going to be studying Eskimos [or Indians or

*Source:* "Inquiry Purpose in the Classroom" by J. W. Lindfors, 1999. In *Children's Inquiry: Using Language to Make Sense of the World.* New York: Teachers College Press.

**161**

Mexicans or whomever]. Let's think of all the questions we have about Eskimos. You tell me the questions and I'll write them on the board." This may sound reasonable enough, possibly even like a way to invite children to inquire. But it wasn't. There was absolutely nothing that I and my eight-year old suburban Philadelphia classmates wanted to know about Eskimos. But did this stop us? Not at all. Hands would fly up, Mrs. McKenzie would call on individual hand wavers, and the board would fill up with what I now recognize to be an extraordinary list of noninquiries:

What do Eskimos eat for breakfast?
What do Eskimos do for recreation?
What are Eskimos' hobbies?

Over time there came to be a sanctioned set, and the task was to think of a missing member and suggest it. I'd look up at the board and say to myself, "Let's see now. Which ones aren't up there yet? Hmm. We still don't have 'What are their customs?' or 'What's their religion?'" We gave Mrs. McKenzie the "questions" she was after. There was purpose in our utterances; but it was not inquiry's purpose. We were engaging in a teacher-pleasing exercise. It was only a game. We were not engaging in inquiry, for there was nothing we were curious about, no information or explanation we were seeking or trying to confirm, nothing we were wondering about. Our turns were complete, giving Mrs. McKenzie something to respond to, but they did not turn toward a partner in puzzlement or curiosity. As competent eight-year-olds, we were linguistically skilled enough to place the right kind of *sentence structures* into the spaces Mrs. McKenzie provided. However, we were not engaging in *communication acts* that carried out inquiry's purpose, although Mrs. McKenzie did not know this.

Here is another game that sometimes gets confused with inquiry in both classrooms and research studies. The teacher (or researcher) holds up a picture and says to the children, "Ask me any questions you can think of about this picture, something that begins with *where, when, why, what, who,* or *how.*" But there is nothing the children want to know about the picture, nothing they wonder about in regard to it. If there were, they would have asked. But this makes no difference. The questions come.

"Where were they before they came where they are in the picture?"
"What are they gonna do next?"
"Why does he have that thing in his hand?"

The teacher nods and smiles in response to each offering—may even say, "Good"—which isn't at all the way we respond to people's real acts of inquiry, of course. When people ask us something for real, we answer it or say we don't know or ask them for clarification or suggest a way to find out or . . . But the teacher's response of smile, nod, "good" is OK with the children because they know this event is not inquiry at all and so they really do not expect the teacher to respond as she would if someone really had inquired. Worse yet, it could be that this strange teacher response gets no particular reaction from the children for, although the ritual makes no sense, the children have come to accept rituals that do not make sense as being part of school. And I cannot help thinking of my own inquiries that, more often than not, don't begin with *where, what, why* at all: "Help me understand X," I say to a student, or "Tell me about Y," or "I wonder if . . ." And so it is with children's inquiries also: they do not necessarily announce themselves with where, what, when, why, how, who—which may partly explain why they are sometimes difficult to recognize in a classroom.

Twenty Questions is another classroom favorite that sometimes gets confused with inquiry. While visiting another university, I attended an undergraduate science methods course one day in which the instructor was demonstrating this game as one the students might want to use during their student teaching. The instructor produced a box and said, "Ask me twenty questions to see if you can find out what's in this box." I raised my hand, he called on me, and I did what any competent three-year-old would do: I asked, "What's in the box?" "Oh no, no, no," he said quickly. "You can only ask questions that can be answered yes or no." His response was the clearest possible indication that this activity was a guessing game, not an inquiry event (which he may have been fully aware of, I'm not sure). Now Twenty Questions is a great game and there may be some very good reasons to play it in a classroom. However, engaging children in an inquiry event is not one of them. When our children play Twenty Questions, they are not engaged in inquiry, just as they are not engaged in buying and selling real estate when they play Monopoly. If it is emergent inquiry that is our interest, then it must be inquiry acts, events, discourse that we engage the children in. And this means being able to hear in children's words the presence or the absence of inquiry's purpose.

For me that purpose is absent in these words: "What was uh, some kings were uh, about the kings?" (Apparently this student was attempting to ask, "Why is it that kings did not always make the best judges?") (Palincsar & Brown, 1984, p. 136). The words are spoken by Charles, a 7th grader who has been identified as a poor reader, specifically one who is an "adequate decoder" but a "poor comprehender" (though he is "*not* labeled as learning disabled or mentally retarded") (p. 126). Charles's words are puzzling. Why would a competent adolescent language user—a native speaker of English—produce such a "question"? Remember four-year-old Jill. She asks lots of questions and they do not sound anything like Charles's.

Context provides the answer to this puzzle. Charles was a subject in a training study designed to help him (and other similar poor readers) develop "comprehension-monitoring and comprehension-fostering" abilities. The training intervention, called reciprocal teaching, focused on "four strategies that were deemed to be ideal comprehension-fostering and comprehension-monitoring activities" (Palincsar & Brown, 1984, p. 168), namely *summarizing* (self-review), *questioning, clarifying,* and *predicting"* (p. 120). Pairs of subjects worked with the adult teacher (the investigator) every day for 15 days. The adult would introduce a new passage of expository text to the pair of students and assign one of them the role of "teacher" for the first text segment (typically a paragraph), which the pair would then read silently.

> Then the teacher [one of the two students] for that segment proceeded first to ask a question, then to summarize, and to offer a prediction or ask for a clarification when appropriate.
>
> The adult teacher provided the guidance necessary for the student teacher to complete the preceding activities through a variety of techniques: *prompting,* "What question did you think a teacher might ask?"; *instruction,* "Remember, a summary is a shortened version, it doesn't include detail" and *modifying the activity,* "If you're having a hard time thinking of a question, why don't you summarize first?" (p. 131, emphasis in original)

The students took turns being the teacher. Here are the results:

> Reciprocal teaching . . . led to a significant improvement in the quality of the summaries and questions . . . [and] to sizable gains on criterion tests of comprehension, reliable maintenance over time, generalization to classroom comprehension tests, transfer to novel tasks that tapped the trained skills of summarizing, questioning, and clarifying, and improvement in standardized comprehension scores. (p. 117)

And when, in a second study, the training procedure was carried out by two classroom teachers and two resource room teachers (instead of the investigator) working with their own "real" reading groups (of poor readers), the results were similar.

It is the "questioning" part of this procedure that is of special interest . . . which brings us back to Charles. "Questioning was not practiced as an isolated activity, but as a continuing goal of the whole enterprise—what main idea question would a teacher or test ask about that section of the text?" (Palincsar & Brown, 1984, p. 122). Charles was considered "a success story" (p. 154). It is easy to see why. On the first day of this training intervention, after reading a passage about poisonous snakes in the southeastern United States (including water moccasins, copperheads, rattlesnakes, and pit vipers), Charles asked, "What is found in the southeastern snakes, also the copperhead, rattlesnakes, vipers—they have. I'm not doing this right" (p. 138). The conversation goes on (Adult Teacher [the investigator in this case] and Charles):

*Teacher:* All right. Do you want to know about the pit vipers?
*Charles:* Yeah.
*Teacher:* What would be a good question about the pit vipers that starts with the word "why?"
*Charles:* (No response)
*Teacher:* How about, "Why are the snakes called pit vipers?"
*Charles:* Why do they want to know that they are called pit vipers?
*Teacher:* Try it again.
*Charles:* Why do they, pit vipers in a pit?
*Teacher:* How about, "Why do they call the snakes pit vipers?"
*Charles:* Why do they call the snakes pit vipers?
*Teacher:* There you go! Good for you. (p. 138)

But on Day 11, after Charles read a passage about the Venus Fly Trap, the conversation sounded very different:

*Charles:* What is the most interesting of the insect eating plants, and where do the plants live at?
*Teacher:* Two excellent questions! They are both clear and important questions. Ask us one at a time now. (p. 139)

And on Day 15, after Charles read a passage about the Southern Lights at the South Pole, he and the investigator had this conversation:

*Charles:* Why do scientists come to the South Pole to study?
*Teacher:* Excellent question. That is what this paragraph is all about.

There can be no doubt that Charles shows remarkable improvement. The question for me is, *improvement in what?* I know it is not inquiry because Charles did not want to know anything about pit vipers or Southern Lights or Venus's flytraps. I know it is not inquiry because the teacher responded to Charles' "questions" in a way we would never respond to an act of inquiry. I know it is not inquiry because if it were, Charles would have been able to formulate his utterances even at the outset of the study, just as four-year-olds do when they inquire. I know it is not inquiry because of what the participating adolescents said later about the study: "finding the good right question was the most difficult activity" (Palincsar & Brown, 1984, p. 167). Finding it? Inquiries come from within us, we do not "find" them. "*The* good right question"? Just one? Both "good and right"? Does an outsider judge the goodness and rightness of what I am trying to make sense of and the way I am going about it?

Charles and his peers were increasing their ability to be successful participants in an instructional event that occurs frequently in their classrooms. I think the researchers wanted to increase the students' success in these classroom events. But did they also intend to help these students do something more in their "questioning"? I think they did. My reading of this study suggests that they wanted to help these students develop as real readers, not just people who can play out a particular type of scripted classroom ritual. The researchers suggest that the strategies they focused on in their reciprocal teaching intervention "comprise a set of knowledge-extending activities that apply in a wide range of situations. . . . Mature learners question and elaborate their own knowledge and the content of the text" (Palincsar & Brown, 1984, p. 119).

> Reciprocal teaching . . . involves extensive modeling of the type of comprehension-fostering and comprehension-monitoring activities that are usually difficult to detect in the expert reader, as they are executed covertly. The reciprocal teaching procedure is a relatively natural forum for the teacher . . . to provide a model of what it is that expert readers do when they try to understand and remember texts. (p. 168)

This suggestion prompted me to pull from my library shelf a text that I had recently been working very hard to understand: Bakhtin's (1986) *Speech Genres and Other Late Essays.* I knew that I had filled the margins with my scrawled comments, questions, and emotings ("Ah!" "Nice!" "What a wonderful way to say this!"). Compared with Charles, I am an "expert reader." And so I wondered,

in the absence of reading partners, when I ask questions (of myself? of the author?) in the margins of the text I am trying to understand, do I ask "main idea questions that a teacher or test might ask?" If so, then reciprocal teaching would indeed demonstrate what an expert reader does covertly.

Here are a few of the questions that I had written in the margins on pages 86–92.

> Utterances are very intentional, in this view. Does this connect in any way with chap. 1 of *Acts of Meaning?*— Bruner's focus on intentionality?
>
> What IS inquiry (discourse) to Bakhtin? Is it a "plan" (i.e., purpose/intention)? Is it a genre? (I don't think so, for it doesn't fit his examples, yet it does involve a relatively stable combination of forms).
>
> [Is there] Such a thing as individual inquiry style?
>
> Is there anything to be gained by trying to define "question" as a particular type of conversational turn that evokes particular type of action response position in listener? What happens if you try to define question from listener's (instead of speaker's) point of view? As what is *understood,* rather than what is intended?
>
> Is this why children's questions express what they DO know more than what they don't know?

These questions make very little sense even to me taken out of context this way, for they are contingent on Bakhtin's written text. (He and I were having quite a conversation here.) But the point is that they do not sound at all like main-idea questions that a teacher or test might ask. And that is because they are not such "questions": they are *inquiries,* my own attempts to go beyond my present understanding, and in the absence of a physically present partner, I addressed these questions to . . . well, I'm not sure really. To the author? To my "otherized" self? These are my own inquiries, my own wonderings. "Questions" like those in the reciprocal teaching dialogues can belong to someone else. They can be produced on demand to satisfy someone else's requirements. But inquiries can only belong to the inquirer. These questions of mine—but even more, my impression of my own general behavior as a reader trying to understand challenging text—make me skeptical of Palincsar and Brown's (1984) suggestion that the kinds of "questions" practiced in the reciprocal teaching intervention "model . . . what it is that expert readers do when they try to understand and remember texts" (p. 186). I think that expert readers engage in *acts of inquiry,* not in the production of "teacherlike questions." It makes sense to me that—if inquiry is what real readers do—then inquiry is what teachers will demonstrate and engage their students in. Which is exactly what Karen Smith does.

## AN EXAMPLE OF AUTHENTIC INQUIRY

Karen Smith's students are fifth- and sixth-grade Mexican American children from low-income families. They are emergent readers, considered by some (though not, I think, by Karen) to be "at risk." In the following example, six of these students (three fifth-grade girls and three sixth-grade girls) join Karen in literature study discussion (K. Smith, 1990b). These six students have become a (temporary) group because they all chose to read and study the same book, *Dicey's Song,* by Cynthia Voigt (1982). They spent a week reading the book on their own, and the next week, on three successive days, they discussed the book together. The story, in brief, is this: Dicey, 12 years old, is the oldest of four (fatherless) children who find their way from Boston to their maternal grandmother's home in Maryland after their mother is hospitalized with what appears to be a complete mental breakdown. After some months, several letters come to the grandmother from the Boston hospital, informing her of the mother's worsening condition, information that the grandmother keeps from the children. One day the hospital notifies the grandmother that her daughter is dying, and Gram and Dicey go to Boston. Dicey's mother dies, and Gram has the body cremated. Dicey and her grandmother return home to Maryland with the ashes.

## Text No. 4: *Dicey's Song*

(The following excerpts come from videotape transcripts of the students' three discussions. Student, below, is any one of the six students.)

*1. Student:* There's a part I wanted to ask when, uh, you know when they said they buried the mom in the yard?

*2. Teacher:* Uh-huh.

*3. Student:* I'm trying to figure out is that right what I read, because you know how they bury people in like the cemetery.

*4. Teacher:* Cemetery.

*5. Student:* You know it's weird if when they buried her inside the yard.

*6. Student:* It would be kinda scary.

*7. Student:* I know, to go by—

*8. Teacher:* To have it there?

*9. Student:* Yeah. Like having everybody's dead body.

*10. Teacher:* OK. Do you understand they cremated her? They burned her body? Maybe that's what was confusing you. What they did, you know, usually people—well not usually—there's two ways—you either put the body like in a casket and they bury the whole body, or they take them and they cremate them, which means they burn the body, so all you have left is like some ashes. So they cremated her mother and they put the ashes in that wooden box. So that's what she was carrying on the train—you know the wooden box on the train?

*11. Student:* Uh-hm.

*12. Teacher:* She was carrying her mother's ashes. From her being cremated. (pause) So it wasn't a body.

*13. Student:* I thought it was a body.

*14. Teacher:* No. . . .

*15. Student:* This is the part—this is what I don't get when, remember when the mom died?

*16 Teacher:* Uh-hm.

*17. Student:* And then the grandma said, um, she didn't tell her nothing, they just kept on going on sitting and tell her nothing. Until she seen her mom.

*18. Teacher:* That she was dying?

*19. Student:* Uh-huh.

*20. Teacher:* And that surprised you?

*21. Student:* Yeah. I wonder why she didn't tell her.

*22. Student:* I thought that that would have [inaudible] was hiding when those letters were coming and she asked her what did they say and she say, "Nothing."

*23. Teacher:* Yeah, I wonder why the grandma was so secretive about that, 'cause she did that with the letters and then she did that on the bus, didn't tell her.

*24. Student:* Sometimes I thought it was 'cause, um, she didn't want them to find about her mom's [inaudible] 'cause she, um, liked them, not so she could adopt them or something?

*25. Teacher:* Well sometimes it's—I think she knew that Dicey knew a lot of that. Seems like she made it harder on Dicey by not telling her. 'Cause it seemed like Dicey'd handled a lot of hard things in her life, she could have handled what was in those letters.

*26. Student:* Well maybe she, maybe the grandma couldn't handle it that her last daughter died.

*27. Teacher:* So you think maybe it was the grandma feeling it more than worrying about Dicey's feelings. Hmmm. . . .

*28. Student:* It was pretty sad.

*29. Teacher:* It sure is sad. You know, there's some controversy about writing for adolescents or children, that a lot of people think you shouldn't put death in books like this. That you, kids your age can't deal with that or it's too hard. What do you, what do you think about that?

30. *Student:* This book [*Homecoming,* the preceding book in the *Dicey* series] was real hard too, when the mom left them.

31. *Student:* Uh-huh.

32. *Student:* But basically you have to look at the way their struggle is, in this book. How they get to give Grandma—get to know her—

33. *Teacher:* Do you think it was too much to ask you to cope with death and the hard things that they were doing?

34. *Student:* I think we learn faster [inaudible].

35. *Teacher:* In what ways?

36. *Student:* 'cause um, this shows how to deal with it in a much better way than just start crying crying, 'cause crying doesn't do much [inaudible].

37. *Student:* I think, I think that if the author shows you that, that if you ever run away or something if you don't have nobody around you or something that shows you how the way their struggle is there, and like if you're on your own, they show you the way, like, what would you do and stuff.

38. *Teacher:* It's not gonna be that easy, is it? Just show you that it is a struggle, that tension, and that death is hard. It's really hard.

I do not hear a scripted conversation here. I hear this group doing what expert readers do: engaging with one another and with text as they go beyond their present understanding. This is inquiry, and because this is the overarching purpose of this event, inquiry acts dominate the discussion.

The teacher's and children's inquiry utterances reflect and also further the exploratory purpose the participants are playing out as they construct this oral text together. Karen *demonstrates* inquiry, with comments such as:

"That surprised you?"
"I wonder why"
"So you think maybe"
"What do you think about that?"
"In what ways [do you learn faster]?"

Notice Karen's tentative stance, a crucial part of her inquiry demonstration (maybe, I wonder, I think, seems like, could have). Karen is demonstrating the language of conjecture here, bringing a reflective cast to the discourse that she and the students are creating. Not that she is conscious of doing this necessarily. She is simply being who she is (an active inquirer) doing what she does (engaging with the au-

thor and with others to extend and deepen her understanding of the book). This is demonstration.

The participants have come together, understanding that they will share their responses to the book they have read, by way of deepening their understanding (as they have done before in similar literature discussions). Their discussion actualizes this going-beyond purpose, but not in a prescripted way: Their discussion evolves as their probing evolves, going in directions and using expressive means that neither Karen nor the students could have anticipated. I think that Karen's demonstration "tells" these students much about ways of responding to others in collaboratively constructing inquiry events such as this one. In her responses, she works

to signal her attention (#2, #16, #31)
to understand the point the student is making (#18, #20, #27, #35)
to grasp points of confusion—the problems the students are having with the text (#8, #10)
to clarify misunderstanding (#10, #12)
to support students' observations (#29, #38)

Karen is working hard here, and this work may provide the most important demonstration of all: inquiry is important. She would not work this hard, marshaling this kind of focused attention, unless she valued the inquiry activity in which she and her students are engaged. And indeed, it is clear that inquiry *is* that activity for her students as well as herself:

"There's a part I wanted to ask . . ."
"I'm trying to figure out . . ."
"This is what I don't get . . ."
"I thought it was . . ."
"I wonder why . . ."
"Well maybe . . ."
"I think that . . ."

The students sound very like Karen in the tentativeness of their talk, in their closely connected responses to one another, and in their commitment to the work they are doing. I wonder what their talk was like before they were so experienced in literature discussion.

The talk in the reciprocal teaching event sounds very different from the talk in the literature discussion. Of course. The two events are different in a number of ways, such as in the number and roles and grade levels of the participants, and the kinds of text the participants are focusing on (efferent or aesthetic) (Rosenblatt, 1978). But the most important difference—the one that exerts the greatest influence on the nature of the utterances within the interaction—is, I think, the overarching purpose of each event. The participants in these two events understand themselves to be carrying out quite different purposes. In the reciprocal teaching event, I believe that the adult and students understand the purpose to be that the students will learn to manage challenging text in ways that demonstrate "comprehension" as this is defined and performed in their classroom. Demonstration and engagement happen toward this end, for example, explicit clarification of the strategies, guided practice toward formulating questions and summary statements, supportive and encouraging responses to students' attempts, commitment to the work being done in these episodes.

It is not surprising that the sound of working to perfect a skill will be very different from the sound of working to explore a text. And yet initially it may seem surprising that the talk of working to perfect a skill includes so many questions, whereas the talk of exploring text includes so few. Surprising initially, perhaps, but not on reflection. These two contrasting events bring into sharp focus the difference between Bakhtin's sentence (unit of grammar) and utterance (unit of communication). The reciprocal teaching event abounds in "questions," that is, sentence structures that we label *interrogative*. But these are not inquiry utterances, that is, they are not speakers' attempts to go beyond present understanding with the help of another. They are, rather, the practice of a particular skill. In contrast, the literature-discussion transcript includes relatively few interrogatives, but is heavy in inquiry utterances. In each event, the utterances (whatever their form) contribute to the framing purpose of the event.

Palincsar and Brown (1984) make an observation that underscores the interrogative form/inquiry utterance distinction. They point out that "documentation of students' difficulties generating questions on what they are reading is legion, and . . . the problem is particularly acute for the slower student" (p. 121). The contrast between this well-documented difficulty (evident in Charles's behavior) and the apparent ease with which Karen's students inquire in these discussions, underscores the difference between the two events and the utterances that comprise them: the first is not an inquiry event and the "questions" within it are not inquiries; the second is an inquiry event, inevitably dominated by inquiry acts (most of which are not in question form). It is indeed difficult to "generate questions" to satisfy someone else; but it is not difficult to generate your own inquiries.

Notice that the students' (and Karen's) utterances in the literature discussion are not perfectly formed. Neither were Charles's early questions. But Charles's early questions and the discussion group's utterances are ill formed in quite different ways: Charles's early questions are quite bizarre for a 12-year-old, whereas Karen's and her students' utterances retain imperfections that are characteristic of normal conversation (uh, like, I mean). Notice, too, that Charles's later questions are flawless in form, whereas the utterances of the discussion group remain imperfect in form. This is because Charles participates in a practiced script, whereas Karen and her students participate in creating an exploratory text that is ever in rough draft. It makes sense that inquiry utterances are often imperfectly formed—even downright messy sometimes, for they are acts of going beyond, not acts of having arrived. It is important to hear the difference.

## CLASSROOM CHALLENGES

Obviously, inquiry is not all we need to be doing in classrooms. There are other important kinds of work (and play) to do also. But surely inquiry is central. To say this is only to recognize the depth of inquiry purposes in every human life, and to appreciate the child's early and continuing inquiry orientation, as well as his achievement of quite sophisticated linguistic means of carrying it out. How strange it would be if inquiry did not occupy a central place in classroom life.

It is fine for inquiry purposes and other purposes to coexist in a classroom. But it is not fine for noninquiry purposes and events to substitute for inquiry events. What about Twenty Questions? If we play this game with our students and recognize that we are playing a game—if we mark this event as a game, enjoy this event as a game—fine. But it is not so fine if we see and treat this event as one that supports inquiry's emergence.

More troubling for me is the substitution of classroom games that (unlike Twenty Questions) are themselves suspect. For me these include Mrs. McKenzie's "please-the-teacher-question-event," the "what-where-why-questions-about-the-picture game," or—possibly the most pervasive of all—the whole-group "discussion" that is actually a public performance ritual masquerading as an exploration of ideas. If such interactions stand in place of inquiry events, then we are telling our students, "*This* is inquiry." And this is to tell them something that is not so.

It is easier, I think, to recognize inquiry acts when they are in interrogative form than when they are in other forms. The student says, "'I'm trying to figure out is that right what I read, because you know how they bury people on like the cemetery." She is trying to engage another in her attempt to understand. Thus her words voice inquiry's intention.

But it would perhaps be easier to recognize this had she said, "Is it right that they buried her in the yard instead of in a cemetery?" Later in the discussion Karen says, "Seems like she made it harder on Dicey by not telling her." Another inquiry act, but one we might more readily recognize as an inquiry if she had said, "Didn't she make it harder on Dicey by not telling her?" The challenge is to hear through the words to the intention that lies behind them and gives birth to them. I am glad that this teacher and student said what they did, choosing expressive forms other than interrogative sentences, because the greater the range of inquiry expression that the participants incorporate in their discussion, the greater the possibilities for every participant's development of a rich repertoire of expressive possibilities—which is, after all, what emergent inquiry is about. The presence of these harder-to-hear (nonprototypic) inquiry utterances in this meaningful, meaning-making event enhances emergent inquiry for these students and their teacher.

It also seems to me that inquiry acts of wondering are more difficult to recognize than inquiry acts of information-seeking. Wondering acts: invitations to others to join in playing with possibilities.

"I wonder why she didn't tell her . . ."
"I wonder why the grandma was so secretive . . ."
"Maybe the grandma couldn't handle it . . ." (instead of "Was it because the grandma couldn't handle it?")

These wondering acts contrast with the information-seeking utterances of the transcript:

"Do you understand they cremated her?"
"That surprised you?"
"Do you think it was too much to ask you to cope with death?"

How facile these participants are in moving back and forth between seeking information and wondering. With each type of inquiry act, the speaker turns to others differently, takes a different stance toward the topic and toward the participants, brings a different tone to the discourse. In their responses, the participants move to the speaker and take on her stance. In #1–14, the participants engage in clarifying a confusion. In #1 and #3, the confusion is identified, and in #5, #6, #7, and #9, several students elaborate the problem. In #10 and #12 Karen provides the clarification the students seek. The participants know that this is a clarification agenda, not a wondering agenda. The goal is to resolve an issue and they join in doing that. And when Karen poses her own inquiry in #29 and #33, the students work

to provide an answer for her. But the agenda is different in #15–27. Here the purpose is not to clarify confusion or provide information, but rather to reflect, to play with possibilities, to wonder. Both the inquiry acts and others' responses to them indicate that these participants know what the agenda is and what kind of inquiry discourse they are in. They shift stances as appropriate, moving in and out of information-seeking and wondering orientations.

If acts of wondering are more difficult to recognize than are acts of information-seeking, would it help to actually name these acts in classroom discourse? What if we responded to students' wondering utterances (not always, of course, but sometimes) with a comment such as, "Hm. So you're wondering about . . ." or "I sometimes wonder about that too." Would our use of the word *wonder* help to make wondering acts more visible—to our students and to ourselves? Naming something has a way of doing that. We cannot have a word for something without there being something there for the word to represent. A word alerts us to the presence of a particular something and helps us form a concept. But beyond rendering wondering acts more visible (audible?), would our generous use of the word *wonder* also legitimize this type of language act as one that is valued in the classroom? I really don't know; I am of two minds here. Surely we would want to avoid substituting contrived talk for authentic talk. The point is not to sprinkle the word *wonder* through class discussion at regular and frequent intervals, reminiscent of the vocabulary control of basal readers. But perhaps as we ourselves become more aware of acts of wondering, the word that names these acts might naturally become more prominent in our talk. (See Copenhaver, 1993, Seifert, forthcoming; and Whitin & Whitin, 1997 for examples of teachers intentionally incorporating children's wondering into their curriculum.)

Not only are wondering acts more difficult to hear than are information-seeking acts; they are also more difficult to provide for in a classroom. In many schools, efficiency and accountability drive the educational endeavor. In such a school, wondering will not score any points: It takes time. It does not improve test scores. It does not meet sequenced curricular objectives. It does not result in a product—you have nothing to show for it. It gives students and teachers nothing helpful to say in response to another's question, "What did you do in school today?" The answer "We wondered a lot" is not helpful.

In such schools and classrooms, wondering may be especially difficult to recognize because there is so little of it.

Perhaps the inquiry acts that are the most difficult of all to hear are those that are expressed in ways culturally unfamiliar to us—when the sounds that inquiry makes are different from those we are used to hearing in our own social group. The group that nurtured us taught us its inquiry ways. So, too, did the social groups that nurtured the students we teach. It is unlikely that there exists a community in which children do not engage in inquiry. It is equally unlikely that there exists a community in which these ways are not culturally distinctive.

During the past several decades, we have increasingly come to recognize, to understand, and to value the culturally distinctive "ways with words" that children bring to the classroom. (See Baugh, 1983; Edelsky, 1991; Heath, 1982, 1983; Lindfors, 1986, 1987; Smitherman, 1977.) And increasingly we have responded by modifying our ways of instruction—how we incorporate, respond to, and build on children's various ways with oral and written language. (See Au, 1980; Hudelson, 1989, 1994; Rigg & Allen, 1989.) This culturally oriented interest has not focused specifically on children's ways of inquiry. And so the bad news is that we currently know far less about cultural variation in children's inquiry than we would like to. But there is good news too. We are perhaps more ready to listen for it than we have been at any time in the past. Being more aware of the presence of language variation in our classrooms, we may be more attuned to its presence in inquiry acts specifically. We can listen, knowing that we will hear it, believing that it is there. The question that orients our listening is not "How come this child doesn't express curiosity about anything?" but rather "How does this child express his curiosity? How does he engage others in his own going-beyond?" Researchers have described children from social groups that especially value listening (sometimes more than speaking) (Philips, 1972, 1983) or that expect deference from children as a sign of respect in adult-child interactions.

Such children's interactive ways may pose special challenges for teachers from a mainstream background that tends to value overtly expressive, highly initiating behavior in children. We may need to hear the "sounds of silence," to recognize inquiry acts expressed nonverbally or in peer interaction.

Perhaps the best news of all is that classrooms have never been better places than they are today for hearing inquiry's many voices. This is because classrooms are increasingly about voice: about *having* it, about *using* it. We are no longer surprised to find many classroom events that resonate with student voices—interactive writing, learning logs, writing workshop, cross-age tutoring, literature discussions like Karen's, individual student projects, interactions with others beyond the classroom via the Internet . . . the list is long, but these kinds of classroom experiences no longer surprise us. All these activities share two features that should help us hear inquiry's different voices. First, they all empower students: there is power sharing between student and teacher. Mrs. McKenzie did not share power with me and my third-grade peers. She set the agenda, she gave the assignments, she provided the scripts; we carried them out and did so on her terms. Thus she did not hear *our* voices, but only her own played back in our "What do Eskimos eat for breakfast?" But in classroom events like those above, which increasingly characterize today's classrooms, students shape agendas, projects, discourse. Second, these classroom events all involve students in interaction that is abundant, diverse, and authentic. Student empowerment and student interaction in classrooms work well for culturally diverse inquiry, for in such classrooms inquiry can *speak* in many voices—voices both culturally and personally distinctive; and so, in such classrooms, inquiry's many voices can be *heard*.

# Sociocultural and Personal Perspectives

# Whose Standard? Teaching Standard English

## Linda Christensen

### EDITOR'S INTRODUCTION

Language often functions as a gatekeeper in our society. High school teacher Linda Christensen explores ways to help her students understand the power of their own language patterns and also learn "the Standard" without humiliation. She takes them inside language so they understand its rules, examining social patterns at the same time they are studying English.

When I was in the ninth grade, Mrs. Delaney, my English teacher wanted to demonstrate the correct and incorrect ways to pronounce the English language. She asked Helen Draper, whose father owned several clothing stores in town, to stand and say "lawyer." Then she asked me, whose father owned a bar, to stand and say "lawyer." Everyone burst into laughter at my pronunciation.

What did Mrs. Delaney accomplish? Did she make me pronounce lawyer correctly? No. I say attorney. I never say lawyer. In fact, I've found substitutes for every word my tongue can't get around and for all the rules I can't remember.

For years I've played word cop on myself. I stop what I'm saying to think, "Objective or subjective case? Do I need I or me here? Hmmmm. There's a lay coming up. What word can I substitute for it? Recline?"

And I've studied this stuff. After all, I've been an English teacher for almost 20 years. I've gone through all of the Warriner's workbook exercises. I even found a lie/lay computer program and kept it in my head until I needed it in speech and became confused again.

Thanks to Mrs. Delaney I learned early on that in our society language classifies me. Generosity, warmth, kindness, intelligence, good humor aren't enough—we need to speak correctly to make it. Mrs. Delaney taught me that the "melting pot" was an illusion. The real version of the melting pot is that people of diverse backgrounds are mixed together and when they come out they're supposed to look like Vanna White and sound like Dan Rather. The only diversity we celebrate is tacos and chop suey at the mall.

## UNLEARNING "INFERIORITY"

It wasn't until a few years ago that I realized grammar was an indication of class and cultural background in the United States and that there is a bias against people who do not use language "correctly." Even the terminology "standard" and "nonstandard" reflects that one is less than the other. English teachers are urged to "correct" students who speak or write in their home language. A friend of mine, whose ancestors came over on the Mayflower, never studied any of

*Source:* "Whose Standard? Teaching Standard English" by L. Christensen, 1994. In *Rethinking Our Classrooms* (pp. 142–145), B. Bigelow, L. Christensen, S. Karp, B. Miner & B. Peterson, Eds., Milwaukee: Rethinking Schools Limited.

173

the grammar texts I keep by my side, but she can spot all of my errors because she grew up in a home where Standard English was spoken.

And I didn't, so I've trained myself to play language cop. The problem is that every time I pause, I stop the momentum of my thinking. I'm no longer pursuing content, no longer engaged in trying to persuade or entertain or clarify. Instead I'm pulling Warriner's or Mrs. Delaney out of my head and trying to figure out how to say something.

"Ah, but this is good," you might say. "You have the rules and Mrs. Delaney to go back to. This is what our students need."

But it doesn't happen that way. I try to remember the rule or the catchy phrase that is supposed to etch the rule in my mind forever like "people never get laid," but I'm still not sure if I used it correctly. These side trips cost a lot of velocity in my logic.

Over the years my English teachers pointed out all of my errors—the usage errors I inherited from my mother's Bandon, Oregon dialect, the spelling errors I overlooked, the fancy words I used incorrectly. They did this in good faith, in the same way, years later, I "corrected" my students' "errors" because I wanted them to know the rules. They were keys to a secret and wealthier society and I wanted them to be prepared to enter, just as my teachers wanted to help me.

And we should help kids. It would be misleading to suggest that people in our society will value my thoughts or my students' thoughts as readily in our home languages as in the "cash language" as Jesse Jackson calls it. Students need to know where to find help, and they need to understand what changes might be necessary, but they need to learn in a context that doesn't say, "The way you said this is wrong."

## WHEN FEAR INTERFERES

English teachers must know when to correct and how to correct—and I use that word uneasily. Take Fred, for example. Fred entered my freshman class last year unwilling to write. Every day during writing time I'd find Fred doodling pictures of *Playboy* bunnies. When I sat down and asked him why he didn't write, he said he couldn't.

I explained to him that in this class his writing couldn't be wrong because we were just practicing our writing until we found a piece we wanted to polish, in the same way that he practiced football every day after school, but only played games on Fridays. His resistance lasted for a couple of weeks. Around him, other students struggled with their writ-

ing, shared it with the class on occasion and heard positive comments. Certainly the writing of his fellow students was not intimidating.

On October 1st, after reading the story, "Raymond's Run" by Toni Cade Bambara, about trusting people in our lives, Fred wrote for the first time:

*I remember my next door neighbor trusted me with some money that she owed my grandmother. She owed my grandmother about 25 dollars.*

Fred didn't make a lot of errors. In the first piece of writing it looked like he had basic punctuation figured out. He didn't misspell any words. And he certainly didn't make any usage errors. Based on this sample, he appeared to be a competent writer.

However, the biggest problem with Fred's writing was the fact that he didn't make mistakes. This piece demonstrates his discomfort with writing. He wasn't taking any risks. Just as I avoid lawyer and lay, he wrote to avoid errors instead of writing to communicate or think on paper.

When more attention is paid to the way something is written or said than to what is said, students' words and thoughts become devalued. Students learn to be silent, to give as few words as possible for teacher criticism.

## VALUING WHAT WE KNOW

Students must be taught to hold their own voices sacred, to ignore the teachers who have made them feel that what they've said is wrong or bad or stupid. Students must be taught how to listen to the knowledge they've stored up, but which they are seldom asked to relate.

Too often students feel alienated in schools. Knowledge is foreign. It's about other people in other times. At a conference I attended recently, a young woman whose mother was Puerto Rican and whose father was Haitian said, "I went through school wondering if anyone like me had ever done anything worthwhile or important. We kept reading and hearing about all of these famous people. I remember thinking, 'Don't we have anyone?' I walked out of the school that day feeling tiny, invisible, unimportant."

As teachers, we have daily opportunities to affirm that our students' lives and language are unique and important. We do that in the selections of literature we read, in the history we choose to teach, and we do it by giving legitimacy to our students' lives as a content worthy of study.

One way to encourage the reluctant writers who have been silenced and the not-so-reluctant writers who have found a safe and sterile voice is to encourage them to recount their experiences. I sometimes recruit former students to share their writing and their wisdom as a way of underscoring the importance of the voices and stories of teenagers. Rochelle, a student in my senior writing class, brought in a few of her stories and poems to read to my freshmen. Rochelle, like Zora Neale Hurston, blends her home language with Standard English in most pieces. She read the following piece to open up a discussion about how kids are sometimes treated as servants in their homes, but also to demonstrate the necessity of using the language she hears in her family to develop characters:

> *"I'm tired of washing dishes. Seems like every time our family gets together, they just got to eat and bring their millions of kids over to our house. And then we got to wash the dishes."*
>
> *I listened sympathetically as my little sister mumbled these words.*
>
> *"And how come we can't have ribs like the grownups? After all, ain't we grown?"*
>
> *"Lord," I prayed, "seal her lips while the blood is still running warm in her veins."*
>
> *Her bottom lip protruded farther and farther as she dipped each plate in the soapy water, then rinsed each side with cold water (about a two second process) until she felt the majority of suds were off.*
>
> *"One minute we lazy women that can't keep the living room half clean. The next minute we just kids and gotta eat some funky chicken while they eat ribs."*
>
> *. . . Suddenly it was quiet. All except my little sister who was still talking. I strained to hear a laugh or joke from the adults in the living room, a hint that all were well, full and ready to go home. Everyone was still sitting in their same spots, not making a move to leave.*
>
> *"You ought to be thankful you got a choice."*
>
> *Uh-oh. Now she got Aunt Macy started. . . .*

After reading her work, Rochelle talked about listening to her family and friends tell their stories. She urged the freshmen to relate the tales of their own lives—the times they were caught doing something forbidden, the times they got stuck with the dishes, the funny/sad events that made their freshman year memorable. When Rochelle left, students wrote more easily. Some. Some were afraid of the stories because as Rance said, "It takes heart to tell the truth about your life."

But eventually they write. They write stories. They write poems. They write letters. They write essays. They learn how to switch in and out of the language of the powerful as Rochelle does so effortlessly in her "Tired of Chicken" piece.

## SHARING LESSONS

And after we write, we listen to each other's stories in our read-around circle where everyone has the opportunity to share, to be heard, to learn that knowledge can be gained by examining our lives. . . . In the circle, we discover that many young women encounter sexual harassment, we learn that store clerks follow black students, especially males, more frequently than they follow white students, we find that many of our parents drink or use drugs, we learn that many of us are kept awake by the crack houses in our neighborhood.

Before we share, students often understand these incidents individually. They feel there's something wrong with them. If they were smarter, prettier, stronger, these things wouldn't have happened to them. When they hear other students' stories, they begin to realize that many of their problems aren't caused by a character defect. For example, in Literature in U.S. History, the class I teach with Bill Bigelow, a young man shared a passionate story about life with his mother who is a lesbian. He loved her, but felt embarrassed to bring his friends home. He was afraid his peers would think he was gay or reject him if they knew about his mother. After he read, the class was silent. Some students cried. One young woman told him that her father was gay and she'd experienced similar difficulties, but hadn't had the courage to tell people about it. She thanked him. Another student confided that his uncle had died from AIDS the year before. What had been a secret shame became an opportunity for students to discuss sexual diversity more openly. Students who were rigidly opposed to the idea of homosexuality gained insights into their own homophobia—especially when presented with the personal revelations from their classmates. Those with homosexual relatives found new allies with whom they could continue their discussion and find support.

Sharing also provides a "collective text" for us to examine the social roots of problems more closely: Where do men/women develop the ideas that women are sexual objects? Where do they learn that it's OK for men to follow women or make suggestive remarks? Where is it written that it's the woman's fault if a man leers at her? How did these roles develop? Who gains from them? Who loses? How could we make it different? Our lives become a window to examine society.

## LEARNING THE "STANDARD" WITHOUT HUMILIATION

But the lessons can't stop there. Fred can write better now. He and his classmates can feel comfortable and safe sharing their lives or discussing literature and the world. They can even understand that they need to ask "Who benefits?" to get a better perspective on a problem. But still when they leave my class or this school, some people will judge them by how their subjects and verbs line up.

So I teach Fred the rules. It's the language of power in this country, and I would be cheating him if I pretended otherwise. I teach him this more effectively than Mrs. Delaney taught me because I don't humiliate him or put down his language. I'm also more effective because I don't rely on textbook drills; I use the text of Fred's writing. But I also teach Fred what Mrs. Delaney left out.

I teach Fred that language, like tracking, functions as part of a gatekeeping system in our country. Who gets managerial jobs, who works at banks and who works at fast food restaurants, who gets into what college and who gets into college at all, are decisions linked to the ability to use Standard English. So how do we teach kids to write with honesty and passion about their world and get them to study the rules of the cash language? We go back to our study of society. We ask: Who made the rules that govern how we speak and write? Did Ninh's family and Fred's family and LaShonda's family all sit down together and decide on these rules? Who already talks like this and writes like this? Who has to learn how to change the way they talk and write? Why?

We make up our own tests that speakers of Standard English would find difficult. We read articles, stories, poems written in Standard English and those written in home language. We listen to videotapes of people speaking. Most kids like the sound of their home language better. They like the energy, the poetry, and the rhythm of the language. We determine when and why people shift. We talk about why it might be necessary to learn Standard English.

Asking my students to memorize the rules without asking who makes the rules, who enforces the rules, who benefits from the rules, who loses from the rules, who uses the rules to keep some in and keep others out, legitimates a social system that devalues my students' knowledge and language. Teaching the rules without reflection also underscores that it's OK for others—"authorities"—to dictate something as fundamental and as personal as the way they speak. Further, the study of Standard English without critique encourages students to believe that if they fail, it is because they are not smart enough or didn't work hard enough.

---

### Language Prison

All day words
run past my tongue

words tumble and fall
and you catch
the wrong ones
and count them back to me

All day I watch
my tongue

for words
that slip
down the slope of my
neighborhood

words that separate
me from you

words that you catch
and hold against me

All day I watch
for words misshapen
or bent
around my too thick tongue

run-down at the heel words
thin soled words

words that slip
from my tongue

words that tell of mops
and beer
and bent backs

words that shape my world
against a different map
than yours

All day I watch my tongue
for words

—*Linda Christensen*

They learn to blame themselves. If they get poor SAT scores, low grades on term papers or essays because of language errors, fail teacher entrance exams, they will internalize the blame; they will believe they did not succeed because they are inferior instead of questioning the standard of measurement and those making the standards.

We must teach our students how to match subjects and verbs, how to pronounce lawyer, because they are the ones without power and, for the moment, have to use the language of the powerful to be heard. But, in addition, we need to equip them to question an educational system that devalues their life and their knowledge. If we don't, we condition them to a pedagogy of consumption where they will consume the knowledge, priorities, and products that have been decided and manufactured without them in mind.

It took me years to undo what Mrs. Delaney did to me. Years to discover that what I said was more important than how I said it. Years to understand that my words, my family's words, weren't wrong, weren't bad—they were just the words of the working class. For too long, I felt inferior when I spoke. I knew the voice of my childhood crept out, and I confused that with ignorance. It wasn't. I just didn't belong to the group who made the rules. I was an outsider, a foreigner in their world. My students won't be.

# American Sign Language: "It's Not Mouth Stuff— It's Brain Stuff"

## Richard Wolkomir

**EDITOR'S INTRODUCTION**

In this article, Richard Wolkomir explains recent research on how deaf people communicate—the cultural and mental processes, body motions and facial expressions involved in American Sign Language. This work helps shed new light on the origins of language as well as the connections between language and culture.

In a darkened laboratory at the Salk Institute in San Diego, a deaf woman is signing. Tiny lights attached to her sleeves and fingers trace the motions of her hands, while two special video cameras whir.

Computers will process her hands' videotaped arabesques and pirouettes into mathematically precise three-dimensional images. Neurologists and linguists will study these stunning patterns for insight into how the human brain produces language.

Sign has become a scientific hot button. Only in the past 20 years have linguists realized that signed languages are unique—a speech of the hand. They offer a new way to probe how the brain generates and understands language, and throw new light on an old scientific controversy: whether language, complete with grammar, is innate in our species, or whether it is a learned behavior. The current interest in sign language has roots in the pioneering work of one renegade teacher at Gallaudet University in Washington, D.C., the world's only liberal arts university for deaf people.

When Bill Stokoe went to Gallaudet to teach English, the school enrolled him in a course in signing. But Stokoe noticed something odd: among themselves, students signed differently from his classroom teacher.

## "HAND TALK": A GENUINE LANGUAGE

Stokoe had been taught a sort of gestural code, each movement of the hands representing a word in English. At the time, American Sign Language (ASL) was thought to be no more than a form of pidgin English. But Stokoe believed the "hand talk" his students used looked richer. He wondered: Might deaf people actually have a genuine language? And could that language be unlike any other on Earth? It was 1955, when even deaf people dismissed their signing as "slang." Stokoe's idea was academic heresy.

It is 37 years later. Stokoe—now devoting his time to writing and editing books and journals and to producing video materials on ASL and the deaf culture—is having lunch at a café near the Gallaudet campus and explaining how he started a revolution. For decades educators fought his idea that signed languages are natural languages like

*Source:* "American Sign Language: 'It's Not Mouth Stuff—It's Brain Stuff'" by R. Wolkomir, 1992, *Smithsonian, 25*(4), pp. 30–41.

English, French and Japanese. They assumed language must be based on speech, the modulation of sound. But sign language is based on the movement of hands, the modulation of space. "What I said," Stokoe explains, "is that language is not mouth stuff—it's brain stuff."

It has been a long road, from the mouth to the brain. Linguists have had to redefine language. Deaf people's self-esteem has been at stake, and so has the ticklish issue of their education.

"My own contribution was to turn around the thinking of academics," says Stokoe. "When I came to Gallaudet, the teachers were trained with two books, and the jokers who wrote them gave only a paragraph to sign language, calling it a vague system of gestures that looked like the ideas they were supposed to represent."

Deaf education in the '50s irked him. "I didn't like to see how the hearing teachers treated their deaf pupils—their expectations were low," he says. "I was amazed at how many of my students were brilliant." Meanwhile, he was reading the work of anthropological linguists like George Trager and Henry Lee Smith Jr. "They said you couldn't study language without studying the culture, and when I had been at Gallaudet a short time, I realized that deaf people had a culture of their own."

When Stokoe analyzed his student's signing, he found it was like spoken languages, which combine bits of sound—each meaningless by itself—into meaningful words. Signers, following similar rules, combine individually meaningless hand and body movements into words. They choose from a palette of hand shapes, such as a fist or a pointing index finger. They also choose where to make a sign; for example, on the face or on the chest. They choose how to orient the hand and arm. And each sign has a movement—it might begin at the cheek and finish at the chin. A shaped hand executing a particular motion creates a word. A common underlying structure of both spoken and signed language is thus at the level of the smallest units that are linked to form words.

Stokoe explained his findings on the structure of ASL in a book published in 1960. "The faculty then had a special meeting and I got up and said my piece," he says. "Nobody threw eggs or old vegetables, but I was bombarded by hostility." Later, the university's president told Stokoe his research was "causing too much trouble" because his insistence that ASL was indeed a *language* threatened the English-based system for teaching the deaf. But Stokoe persisted. Five years later he came out with the first dictionary of American Sign Language based on linguistic principles. And he's been slowly winning converts ever since.

## "WHEREVER WE'VE FOUND DEAF PEOPLE, THERE'S SIGN"

Just as no one can pinpoint the origins of spoken language in prehistory, the roots of sign language remain hidden from view. What linguists do know is that sign languages have sprung up independently in many different places. Signing probably began with simple gestures, but then evolved into a true language with structured grammar. "In every place we've ever found deaf people, there's sign," says anthropological linguist Bob Johnson, "but it's not the same language. I went to a Mayan village where, out of 400 people, 13 were deaf, and they had their own Mayan Sign—I'd guess it's been maintained for thousands of years." Today at least 50 native sign languages are "spoken" worldwide, all mutually incomprehensible, from British and Israeli Sign to Chinese Sign.

Not until the 1700s, in France, did people who could hear pay serious attention to deaf people and their language. Religion had something to do with it. "They believed that without speech you couldn't go to heaven," says Johnson.

For the Abbé de l'Epée, a French priest born into a wealthy family in 1712, the issue was his own soul: he feared he would lose it unless he overcame the stigma of his privileged youth by devoting himself to the poor. In his history of the deaf, *When The Mind Hears,* Northeastern University psychologists Harlan Lane notes that, in his 50s, de l'Epée met two deaf girls on one of his forays into the Paris slums and decided to dedicate himself to their education.

The priest's problem was abstraction: he could show the girls a piece of bread and the printed French word for "bread." But how could he show them "God" or "goodness"? He decided to learn their sign language as a teaching medium. However, he attempted to impose French grammar onto the signs.

"Methodical signing," as de l'Epée called his invention, was an ugly hybrid. But he did teach his pupils to read French, opening the door to education, and today he is a hero to deaf people. As his pupils and disciples proliferated, satellite schools sprouted throughout Europe. De l'Epée died happily destitute in 1789 surrounded by his students in his Paris school, which became the National Institution for Deaf-Mutes under the new republic.

Other teachers kept de l'Epée's school alive. And one graduate, Laurent Clerc, brought the French method of teaching in sign to the United States. It was the early 1800s; in Hartford, Connecticut, the Rev. Thomas Hopkins Gallaudet was watching children at play. He noticed that one girl, Alice Cogswell, did not join in. She was deaf. Her father, a surgeon, persuaded Gallaudet to find a European teacher and create the first permanent school for the deaf in the United States. Gallaudet then traveled to England, where the "oral" method was supreme, the idea being to teach deaf children to speak. The method was almost cruel, since children born deaf—they heard no voices, including their own—could have no concept of speech. It rarely worked. Besides, the teachers said their method was "secret." And so Gallaudet visited the Institution for Deaf-Mutes in Paris and persuaded Laurent Clerc to come home with him.

During their 52-day voyage across the Atlantic, Gallaudet helped Clerc improve his English, and Clerc taught him French Sign Language. On April 15, 1817, in Hartford, they established a school that became the American School for the Deaf. Teaching in French Sign Language and a version of de l'Epée's methodical sign, Clerc trained many students who became teachers, too, and helped spread language across the country. Clerc's French Sign was to mingle with various "home" signs that had sprung up in other places. On Martha's Vineyard, Massachusetts, for example, a large portion of the population was genetically deaf, and virtually all the islanders used an indigenous sign language, the hearing switching back and forth between speech and sign with bilingual ease. Eventually, pure French Sign would blend with such local argots and evolve into today's American Sign Language.

After Clerc died, in 1869, much of the work done since the time of de l'Epée to teach the deaf in their own language crumbled under the weight of Victorian intolerance. Anti-Signers argued that ASL let the deaf "talk" only to the deaf; they must learn to speak and to lip-read. Pro-Signers pointed out that, through sign, the deaf learned to read and write English. The Pros also noted that lipreading is a skill that few master. (Studies estimate that 93 percent of deaf schoolchildren who were either born deaf or lost their hearing in early childhood can lip-read only one in ten everyday sentences in English.) And Pros argue correctly that the arduous hours required to teach a deaf child to mimic speech should be spent on real education.

"Oralists" like Horace Mann lobbied to stop schools from teaching in ASL, then *the* method of instruction in all schools for the deaf. None was more fervent than Alexander Graham Bell, inventor of the telephone and husband of a woman who denied her own deafness. The president of the National Association of the Deaf called Bell the "most to be feared enemy of the American deaf." In 1880, at an international meeting of educators of the deaf in Milan, where deaf teachers were absent, the use of sign language in schools was proscribed.

After that, as deaf people see it, came the Dark Ages. Retired Gallaudet sociolinguist Barbara Kannapell, who is cofounder of Deafpride, a Washington, D.C. advocacy group, is the deaf daughter of deaf parents from Kentucky. Starting at age 4, she attended an "oral" school, where signing was outlawed. "Whenever the teacher turned her back to work on the blackboard, we'd sign," signs Kannapell. "If the teacher caught us using sign language, she'd use a ruler on our hands."

Kannapell has tried to see oralism from the viewpoint of hearing parents of deaf children. "They'll do anything to make their child like themselves," she signs. "But, from a deaf adult's perspective, I want *them* to learn sign, to communicate with their child."

In the 1970s, a new federal law mandated "mainstreaming." "That law was good for parents, because they could keep children home instead of sending them off to special boarding schools, but many public schools didn't know what to do with deaf kids," signs Kannapell. "Many of these children think they're the only deaf kids in the world."

Gallaudet's admissions director, James Tucker, an exuberant 32-year-old, is a product of the '70s mainstreaming. "I'd sit in the back, doing work the teacher gave me and minding my own business," he signs. "Did I like it? Hell no! I was lonely—for years I thought I was an introvert." Deaf children have a right to learn ASL and to live in an ASL-speaking community, he asserts. "We learn sign for obvious reasons—our eyes aren't broken," he signs. Tucker adds: "Deaf culture is a group of people sharing similar values, outlook and frustrations, and the main thing, of course, is sharing the same language."

Today, most teachers of deaf pupils are "hearies" who speak as they sign. "Simultaneous Communication," as it is called, is really signed English and not ASL. "It looks grotesque to the eye," signs Tucker, adding that it makes signs too "marked," a linguistic term meaning equally stressed. Hand movements can be exaggerated or poorly executed. As Tucker puts it: "We have zealous educators trying to impose weird hand shapes." Moreover, since the languages have entirely different sentence structures, the effect can be bewildering. It's like having Japanese spoken to English-speaking students with an interpreter shouting occasional English words at them.

New scientific findings support the efforts of linguists such as Bob Johnson, who are calling for an education system for deaf students based on ASL, starting in infancy. Research by Helen Neville, at the Salk Institute, shows that children *must* learn a language—any language—during their first five years or so, before the brain's neural connections are locked in place, or risk permanent linguistic impairment. "What suffers is the ability to learn grammar," she says. As children mature, their brain organization becomes increasingly rigid. By puberty, it is largely complete. This spells trouble because most deaf youngsters learn language late; their parents are hearing and do not know ASL, and the children have little or no contact with deaf people when young.

Bob Johnson notes that more than 90 percent of all deaf children have hearing parents. Unlike deaf children of deaf parents, who get ASL instruction early, they learn a language late and lag educationally. "The average deaf 12th-grader reads at the 4th-grade-level," says Johnson. He believes deaf children should start learning ASL in the crib, with schools teaching in ASL. English, he argues, should be a second language, for reading and writing: "All evidence says they'll learn English better." It's been an uphill battle. Of the several hundred school programs for the deaf in this country, only six are moving toward ASL-based instruction. And the vast majority of deaf students are still in mainstream schools where there are few teachers who are fluent in ASL.

Meanwhile, researchers are finding that ASL is a living language, still evolving. Sociolinguist James Woodward from Memphis, who has a black belt in karate, had planned to study Chinese dialects but switched to sign when he came to Gallaudet in 1969. "I spent every night for two years at the Rathskeller, a student hangout, learning by observing," he says. "I began to see great variation in the way people signed."

Woodward later concentrated on regional, social and ethnic dialects of ASL. Visiting deaf homes and social clubs in the South, he found that Southerners use older forms of ASL signs than Northerners do. Southern blacks use even more of the older signs. "From them, we can learn the history of the language," he says.

Over time, signs tend to change. For instance, "home" originally was the sign for "eat" (touching the mouth) combined with the sign for "sleep" (the palm pillowing the cheek). Now it has evolved into two taps on the cheek. Also, signs formerly made at the center of the face migrate toward its perimeter. One reason is that it is easier to see both signs and changes in facial expressions in this way, since deaf people focus on a signer's face—which provides crucial linguistic information—taking in the hands with peripheral vision.

Signers use certain facial expressions as grammatical markers. These linguistic expressions range from pursed lips to the expression that results from enunciating the sound "th." Linguist Scott Liddell, at Gallaudet, has noted that certain hand movements translate as "Bill drove to John's." If the signer tilts his head forward and raises his eyebrows while signing, he makes the sentence a question: "Did Bill drive to John's?" If he also makes the "th" expression as he signs, he modifies the verb with an adverb: "Did Bill drive to John's inattentively?"

Sociolinguists have investigated why this unique language was for so long virtually a secret. Partly, Woodward thinks, it was because deaf people wanted it that way. He says that when deaf people sign to the hearing, they switch to English-like signing. "It allows hearing people to be identified as outsiders and to be treated carefully before allowing any interaction that could have a negative effect on the deaf community," he says. By keeping ASL to themselves, deaf people—whom Woodward regards as an ethnic group—maintain "social identity and group solidarity."

## A KEY LANGUAGE INGREDIENT: GRAMMAR

The "secret" nature of ASL is changing rapidly as it is being examined under the scientific microscope. At the Salk Institute, a futuristic complex of concrete labs poised on a San Diego cliff above the Pacific, pioneer ASL investigator Ursula Bellugi directs the Laboratory for Cognitive Neuroscience, where researchers use ASL to probe the brain's capacity for language. It was here that Bellugi and associates found that ASL has a key language ingredient: a grammar to regulate its flow. For example, in a conversation a signer might make the sign for "Joe" at an arbitrary spot in space. Now that spot stands for "Joe." By pointing to it, the signer creates the pronoun "he" or "him," meaning "Joe." A sign moving toward the spot means something done *to* "him." A sign moving away from the spot means an action *by* Joe, something "he" did.

In the 1970s, Bellugi's team concentrated on several key questions that have been of central concern ever since MIT professor Noam Chomsky's groundbreaking work of the 1950s. Is language capability innate, as Chomsky and his followers believe? Or is it acquired from our environments? The question gets to the basics of humanity since our language capacity is part of our unique endowment as a species. And language lets us accumulate lore and pass it on to succeeding generations. Bellugi's team reasoned that if ASL is a true language, unconnected to speech, then our penchant for language must be built in at birth, whether we express it with our tongue or hands. As Bellugi (above) puts it: "I had to keep asking myself, 'What does it mean to be a language?'"

A key issue was "iconicity." Linguistics has long held that one of the properties of all natural languages is that their words are arbitrary. In English, to illustrate, there is no relation between the sound of the word "cat" and a cat itself, and onomatopoeic words like "slurp" are few and far between. Similarly, if ASL follows the same principles, its words should not be pictures or mime. But ASL does have many words with transparent meanings. In ASL, "tree" is an arm upright from the elbow, representing a trunk, with the fingers spread to show the crown. In Danish Sign, the signer's two hands outline a tree in the air. Sign languages are rife with pantomimes. But Bellugi wondered: Do deaf people *perceive* such signs as iconic as they communicate in ASL?

One day a deaf mother visited the lab with her deaf daughter, not yet 2. At that age, hearing children fumble pronouns, which is why parents say, "Mommy is getting Tammy juice." The deaf child, equally confused by pronouns, signed "you" when she meant "I." But the sign for such pronouns is purely iconic: the signer points an index finger at his or her own torso to signify "I" or at the listener to signify "you." The mother corrected the child by turning her hand so that she pointed at herself. Nothing could be clearer. Yet, as the child chattered on, she continued to point to her mother when she meant "I."

Bellugi's work revealed that deaf toddlers have no trouble pointing. But a pointing finger in ASL is linguistic, not gestural. Deaf toddlers in the "don't-understand-pronouns" stage do not see a pointing finger. They see a confusing, abstract word. ASL's roots may be mimetic, but—embedded in the flow of language—the signs lose their iconicity.

By the 1980s, most linguists had accepted sign languages as natural languages on an equal footing with English, Italian, Hindi and others of the world. Signed languages like ASL were as powerful, subtle and intricately structured as spoken ones.

The parallels become especially striking in wordplay and poetry. Signers creatively combine hand shapes and movements to create puns and other humorous alterations of words. A typical pun in sign goes like this: a fist near the forehead and a flip of the index finger upward means that one understands. But if the little finger is flipped, it's a joke meaning one understands a little. Clayton Valli at Gallaudet has made an extensive study of poetry in ASL. He finds that maintenance or repetition of hand shape provides rhyming, while meter occurs in the timing and type of movement. Research with the American Theater of the Deaf reveals a variety of individual techniques and styles. Some performers create designs in space with a freer movement of the arms than in ordinary signing. With others, rhythm and tempo are more important than spatial considerations. Hands may be alternated so that there is a balance and symmetry in the

structure. Or signs may be made to flow into one another, creating a lyricism in the passage. The possibilities for this new art form in sign seem bounded only by the imagination within the community itself.

The special nature of sign language provides unprecedented opportunities to observe how the brain is organized to generate and understand language. Spoken languages are produced by largely unobservable movements of the vocal apparatus and received through the brain's auditory system. Signed languages, by contrast, are delivered through highly visible movements of the arms, hands and face, and are received through the brain's visual system. Engagement of these different brain systems in language use makes it possible to test different ideas about the biological basis of language.

The prevailing view of neurologists is that the brain's left hemisphere is the seat of language, while the right controls our perception of visual space. But since signed languages are expressed spatially, it was unclear where they might be centered.

To find out, Bellugi and her colleagues studied lifelong deaf signers who had suffered brain damage as adults. When the damage had occurred in their left hemisphere, the signers could shrug, point, shake their heads and make other gestures, but they lost the ability to sign. As happens with hearing people who suffer left-hemisphere damage, some of them lost words while others lost the ability to organize grammatical sentences, depending on precisely where the damage had occurred.

Conversely, signers with right-hemisphere damage signed as well as ever, but spatial arrangements confused them. One of Bellugi's right-hemisphere subjects could no longer perceive things to her left. Asked to describe a room, she reported all the furnishings as being on the right, leaving the room's left side a void. Yet she signed perfectly, including signs formed on the left side. She had lost her sense of *topographic* space, a right-hemisphere function, but her control of *linguistic* space, centered in the left hemisphere, was intact. All of these findings support the conclusion that language, whether visual or spoken, is under the control of the left hemisphere.

One of the Salk group's current efforts is to see if learning language in a particular modality changes the brain's ability to perform other kinds of tasks. Researchers showed children a moving light tracing a pattern in space, and then asked them to draw what they saw. "Deaf kids were way ahead of hearing kids," says Bellugi. Other tests, she adds, back up the finding that learning sign language improves the mind's ability to grasp patterns in space.

# THINKING AND DREAMING IN SIGNS

Salk linguist Karen Emmorey says the lab also has found that deaf people are better at generating and manipulating mental images. "We found a striking difference in ability to generate mental images and to tell if one object is the same as another, but rotated in space, or is a mirror image of the first," she says, noting that signers seem to be better at discriminating between faces, too. As she puts it: "The question is, does the language you know affect your other cognitive abilities?"

Freda Norman, formerly an actress with the National Theater of the Deaf and now a Salk research associate, puts it like this: "English is very linear, but ASL lets you see everything at the same time."

"The deaf *think* in signs," says Bellugi. "They *dream* in signs. And little children sign to themselves."

At McGill University in Montreal, psychologist Laura Ann Petitto recently found that deaf babies of deaf parents babble in sign. Hearing infants create nonsense sounds like "babababa," first attempts at language. So do deaf babies, but with their hands. Petitto watched deaf infants moving their hands and fingers in systematic ways that hearing children not exposed to sign never do. The movements, she says, were their way of exploring the linguistic units that will be the building blocks of language—their language.

Deaf children today face a brighter future than the generation of deaf children before them. Instruction in ASL, particularly in residential schools, should accelerate. New technologies, such as the TDD (Telecommunications Device for the Deaf) for communicating over telephones, relay services and video programs for language instruction, and the recent Americans with Disabilities Act all point the way to a more supportive environment. Deaf people are moving into professional jobs, such as law and accounting, and more recently into computer-related work. But it is not surprising that outside of their work, they prefer one another's company. Life can be especially rewarding for those within the ASL community. Here they form their own literary clubs, bowling leagues and gourmet groups.

As the Salk laboratory's Freda Normal signs: "I love to read books, but ASL is my first language." She adds, smiling: "Sometimes I forget that the hearing are different."

# An Interview with Hang Nguyen

## Suzanne Stiel

Hang Nguyen came to the United States in 1983 as one of the "boat people" from Vietnam. Her family constructed their own boats and organized their own escape. Her father came in the first boat with seven of Hang's brothers and sisters. Hang came in the second boat with her sister, her husband, and her daughter who was four years old. Her mother and grandmother came to the United States in 1992. Hang's parents, grandmother, and nine brothers and sisters are living in Pennsylvania. She has one sister who escaped by boat to Australia and still lives there today. Hang and her family were immersed in a new language and culture when they fled Vietnam to seek sanctuary in the United States. She shares with Suzanne Stiel first-hand experiences they endured at school and the effect on her daughter's self-esteem when she was asked to make choices between the languages of home and school. Hang lives in Portland, Oregon, with her daughter Thu, and works as a multicultural specialist for Portland Public Schools.

Susanne Stiel interviewed her; Hang's comments follow.

There are many things that are disappointments. I guess the trend now is changing a little bit, more toward multiculturalism. I think the problem I faced then was that my daughter wasn't treated as if she was an entity, as if she was a person who could speak, who could learn, who could understand, because she didn't speak English. The teachers in school tended to treat parents of minority kids like they're stupid idiots, savage and uncivilized. So when they talk to you they are always patronizing, always give you a phrase like "You are very nice, and your daughter is very nice," but never any comment like "she's very smart," or "she's very quick," or "she's intelligent." Nothing! It's always "She's very nice in class and behaves." That's the thing that really bugged me all those years.

Another thing is when there was a fight in school because my daughter didn't speak English. She wanted to play, but she didn't know the rules and the other kids started getting mad and fighting. The teacher came out and pulled my daughter in and was pointing at her, "You behave yourself! You don't do this here! This is not Vietnam!" I thought that remark was really stupid! The town we lived in was very conservative. All white. It seemed like everything their way was fine, but my way was not.

First thing when my daughter came home she said "I'm not supposed to speak Vietnamese at home, Mom, because I have to learn English. My teacher said to go home and practice English." That was the message she got when she was five and six years old. And that is the thing that really made me angry. When she told me that I was just astounded. I was appalled. I asked her, "Who told you that?" And she said "My teacher did; she said that I'm supposed to go home and speak English, so I can get used to it and use it because I live here." That was the first disappointment that I got in this country.

After that every time I went to the conference I always heard "Oh, you are very nice," but never anything like "Do you need some help?" or "Do you think I can help you with anything?" or anything related to my daughter actually learning. They always made comments about how very nice I am, meaning I may be an idiot, but I'm smiling and I'm polite! When I asked pointed questions like "What about my daughter's math score? I want to know her score. I want to see her work," they tell me "She's doing fine, just fine," which means that they don't know if she's doing fine or not. But at the conference I am the parent and they have to treat me like other parents, but they don't want to bother. It had only been five minutes and they were saying "It was very nice to meet you. I have another parent waiting outside." That parent went in and I hung around to see, and that parent was there for half an hour and all kinds of work was brought out! Since that day, in my mind, I would not come to the conference unprepared, and I would not leave until I'd seen my daughter's work. After that I made my point clear to every teacher when I went in for a conference.

Another disappointment that is related to this is how my daughter changed. She refused to learn the cultural way, the family way. She refused to learn Vietnamese. She refused to speak Vietnamese at home. Her excuse was "If I speak Vietnamese and think in Vietnamese I am going to get confused and I will not be able to get ahead here." That's the message she's received since she was in first grade until now. It was a continual message. She was allowed in the ESL program for one year and then she had to be out in the mainstream classes. The worst thing that happened to my daughter is that she feels inferior, that she doesn't fit in. She tried very hard to belong, and she tried very hard to deny who she is. That attitude and that mentality were created the day she started school and continued until now. She just started coming around about six months ago saying "I want to know about the Vietnamese way," and "I will speak more Vietnamese at home now, Mom," and "I'm proud to be Vietnamese." But before, when I would go to the conference and would speak Vietnamese to her, she would say "Don't speak Vietnamese here." She would whisper in my ear. She was ashamed of it. Even when she was in seventh and eighth grade I would speak Vietnamese with her before we went into the conference and she would turn away. It was like she was saying "I don't know that language. Don't speak that language here because nobody speaks that language." Do you see how wrong it is to make a kid feel like she's not one of the group, and how wrong it is to make her turn away from her family? If they don't live the way the family lives how can they understand what is valuable and what is not? Do the parents have any way with them at all? When they say something, like disciplining them, the kids will not respect their parents because most parents don't speak English and don't live the American way. The kids go home and are disrespectful to their parents and totally ignore them. They don't see that their parents fit in with anything. They are ashamed. That's the problem.

My daughter has some friends who don't speak Vietnamese. They don't know how because they grew up here. I guess my daughter's interest in her culture started when I did the Asian Youth Leadership conference at Portland State University. I did one session called *Story of Who We Are.* I had a hundred kids in there and I was telling them a Vietnamese folktale. I read it in Vietnamese and then I read it in English, and then I asked them how they felt about it. Some understood it, and some didn't. Some remembered it, and some didn't. My message to them was to feel proud of who they are and where they're from, and not to forget that everyone has roots and traditions and culture. Then when it was in the newspaper I cut that section out and I showed it to my daughter. Some of her friends from school had gone to that conference and they told her how nice it was to hear that language, and to see, among millions of Americans, how suddenly your language was there and your story was told. I guess it gave my daughter an awakening call.

My daughter is bilingual, but only half bilingual because she doesn't know how to read and write. She only speaks Vietnamese. She can just guess. She can try to put words together and read them, but she is guessing, and she's not able to write them. She was four years old when we came over, and she started kindergarten early. So since she was five years old until just recently she has been continuously bombarded with the ideas "You live here. You have to speak the language. You have to learn the way to live here. Your language is not important. Your language is an embarrassment. If you learn your language you will not be able to learn English. English is the main language here." That's the message that she got. It was not always obvious, but she would be told "You need to go home and practice your English. You need this . . . you need that . . . ," and I think that was enough to poison her mind against what she stands for.

Sometimes my daughter asks me about Vietnam, and I tell her, but it doesn't seem to interest her at all. At some point maybe she will go back and ask for more details. I told her what happened, and how we came over here. She's just not interested. I think it's very difficult for parents coming here. They are too old. They're already rooted in the old culture and the old way of life, and the society was so different. You come over here and suddenly you see you are given rights, and there's no limit. And there's television, peers, the media, and all kinds of things that your kids are exposed to everyday.

Another hard thing for parents is they have to work. They cannot live on welfare. They cannot get charity. They've got too many kids. If they don't work they won't have anything. Because both parents have to work, sometimes long hours to get enough money, they don't have time for their kids at home. That very much affects how they grow up. They don't see their parents, and when they do their parents are so tired. They lie to their parents about this and that. The attitude of the parents is "I trust you. If you tell me you do so, then I believe that you do so." They were lying to get what they wanted. They were by themselves too much. When you're by yourself at a young age you want to explore. You won't stay home. Even though you want to please your parents, you would be gone when they're gone, and come back before they get home, so that you wouldn't make them feel bad. In the meantime you go out and explore.

And what do they explore? Things that they are never allowed to have at home, and are never allowed to do at home, such as smoking, drinking, going dancing and to the movies, hanging out and talking dirty, seeing this and that. That's what they're not allowed at home. So in between the times they see their parents, when the parents are absent, they will go do those things. In front of their parents they are very nice, so if anyone tries to tell their parents that their son or daughter are doing these things, they will not believe it. I may be wrong in my estimation, but I would say that a very high number of Vietnamese families here, maybe seventy-five to eighty percent, have this problem. Their kids will lie to them. They will turn away from them, and will do things that we would call rebellious. They rebel against their culture, and against the beliefs that the parents really stand for.

In Vietnam you have this, but you also have what we call a collective culture. You have your aunts and uncles, the whole family surrounding you. In Vietnam the biggest thing is the family pride. Whatever you do contributes to that pride. You don't do something and get credit for yourself. Your family, your parents, your grandparents get the credit. You will hear "Her grandson did this or that," and that makes the family feel proud because it gives them honor. Over here you don't see this. Over here, for example, if you graduated you would get the credit for that yourself, but over there people would be talking about so-and-so's granddaughter or so-and-so's niece graduating and it would reflect on every member of the family. The family reputation relies on every single member of the family. That's what keeps the kids in line. If you are shunned by your family because you have done something bad, no one would take you in because they are all protecting what I call the social order. If one family says that you're bad, your own family would disown you. You must be really bad. It's hard for kids over there to get out of line. It's also unfair in some ways. Families are too strict. But one thing compensates for another. Over here you take credit for what you do yourself. Your parents are in the background. Over there it's because of your parents that you are successful, because they have contributed, they've been supportive, everything. So when kids come over here they start seeing this.

First they go to school and say "I'm going to get all A's so my parents will be proud." Then when they get the awards and recognition, their name's up on the board, nothing is sent home to the parents. In Vietnam they would send everything home to the parents, and the parents would see the work of their child. Here, the child's name is on the board in school, and whose parent is going to see that? Only the other students are going to see that. It is very much individualized. That makes it very difficult for Vietnamese parents to reinforce the family tradition. My daughter saw it right away. In Vietnam I would not live so far away from my parents. I could have my own house, but very close to theirs. I would still go back and forth, and rely on them for help. Over here she can see it. We moved across the country and we're here by ourselves. Do I rely on my family? No. Does my family rely on me? No. Everybody has their own life to take care of. The young people see it right away. They have their own life. Especially when they are coming over at sixteen and seventeen, they know that in a year or two they are going to get out. So who's going to listen to their parents?

# Narrative, Literacy, and Face in Interethnic Communication

## Ronald Scollon and Suzanne Scollon

### EDITOR'S INTRODUCTION

Ronald and Suzanne Scollon are researchers who have spent many years studying the language and culture of the Athabaskan Indians, a tribe located primarily in Alaska and the Northern Canadian territories. In this excerpt from their study, *Narrative, Literacy and Face in Interethnic Communication,* the Scollons consider the subtle ways differences in communication styles across cultures can cause misunderstanding.

## THE DISTRIBUTION OF TALK

When two or more people talk together, it takes a lot of coordination to keep things going smoothly. Although it does not seem like it, in ordinary conversation the various speakers are careful not to talk all at once or to interrupt or to fail to answer if there is a question. This cooperation takes a good bit of work and common understanding. In interethnic communication there are often differences in the systems of the speakers, so that mistakes happen that lead to further misunderstandings. We will look in this section at how conversationalists decide who speaks first, how topics are controlled, how turns at talking are exchanged, and how conversations are ended.

### Who Speaks First

When an Athabaskan and a speaker of English talk to each other, it is very likely that the English speaker will speak first. Many people have observed this. It is not hard to see why the English speaker will speak first if we consider what was said about the presentation of self. The Athabaskan will feel it is important to know the relationship between the

two speakers before speaking. The English speaker will feel talking is the best way to establish a relationship. While the Athabaskan is waiting to see what will happen between them, the English speaker will begin speaking, usually asking questions in fact, to find out what will happen. Only where there is a longstanding relationship and a deep understanding between the two speakers is it likely that the Athabaskan will initiate the conversation.

### Control of Topic

It might not seem very important at first glance who speaks first in a conversation. Studies of conversation have shown, however, that the person who speaks first also controls the topic of conversation. Schegloff (1972) found that the person who spoke first took the role of the summoner. His speech in effect asks the other speaker for the right to talk. The second speaker answers but in a very open way. The

*Source:* Excerpt from *Narrative, Literacy, and Face in Interethnic Communication* (pp. 22–28) by R. Scollon and S. Scollon, 1983, Norwood, NJ: Ablex.

answer of the second speaker gives the first speaker the right to go ahead and talk. The first speaker then introduces the topic of the conversation to which the second must then reply. If the second speaker wants to introduce his own topic he must wait for a chance to introduce it later, after they have talked about the first speaker's topic.

These general rules seem so obvious and trivial that it is hard to believe how strictly we hold to them. It is easy to see how strong these rules are, though, by trying to break them. If someone calls on the phone (the phone ring is the first speaker), and if you answer by talking about what you want to talk about, both you and the caller will feel something very strange has happened. During their study, one of Schegloff's colleagues was being troubled by obscene phone calls. She found that if she picked up the phone but did not say anything, the caller would not go on to say any obscenities. He was following the conversational rules that would only allow him to speak after the second speaker answered. He followed conversational rules even though he was violating the moral rules of the same society.

In another study Scollon (1976) found that a one-year-old child learned these conversational rules before she was two years old. A one-year-old has very little she can say easily. The child in that study, Brenda, found that if she was the first speaker she could talk about what she wanted to talk about. She used one word, "here," as a summons. She would give a piece of paper or trash or almost anything to someone else and say, "here." The other person would take it and say "thank you." Then Brenda would say whatever she wanted to say.

Sometimes an adult would try to speak to Brenda first. She would refuse to answer. If the adult persisted she would say "here" and hand him something. That would make her the first speaker and ultimately give her the right to introduce her topic. Brenda had learned how to use speaking first to keep control of the topic of conversation by the time she was two years old.

We have said that in Athabaskan-English conversations the English speaker almost always speaks first. This has the consequence of allowing him to introduce his own topic and of making it very difficult for the Athabaskans to introduce any other topic. The general result of these two facts is that in interethnic communications between Athabaskans and English speakers topic of conversation is almost always the English speaker's topic, not the Athabaskan's.

Another complication is introduced by the fact that at least some Athabaskans use a conventional greeting that gives the answerer the right to introduce the topic. At Fort Chipewyan, Alberta, it is common to greet people with ?ɛdlánioen "what are you thinking?" The appropriate response is an open-ended introduction of the answerer's topic if he should choose to say something.

Here as before these discourse problems lead to stereotyping. The Athabaskan starts to feel that his ideas are always being ignored. At the same time he feels that the English speaker is either egocentric or ethnocentric. He feels that the English speaker only wants to talk about his own ideas. From the English speaker's point of view it seems either that the Athabaskan does not have any ideas of his own or that when they are introduced these ideas are off the topic. By putting together the assumptions about the presentation of self that Athabaskans and English speakers hold and a quite mechanical rule of conversational interchange, we get a situation in which one speaker is always in control of what the participants talk about.

## The Exchange of Speaking Turns

We have said that at least in English conversation one speaker begins, a second answers, the first introduces the topic, and the second continues on that topic. Of course, conversations can be more complicated than that. There may be more than two speakers, for one thing. But to keep this discussion from getting too complex, we will just talk about two-person conversation.

As the conversation goes on the speakers continue to take turns in speaking. They do not normally both speak at the same time. In fact, simultaneous speech is usually a good sign that something has gone wrong. When the timing goes off so far that both speakers start speaking together it usually takes some time to smooth things out again. Usually after one speaker finishes the other can take a turn. If the other one does not say anything, then the first speaker can take another turn if he wishes. If the other comes in too soon it feels as if he is interrupting.

Problems start to come up when two speakers have different systems for pausing between turns. Generally speaking, Athabaskans allow a slightly longer pause between sentences than do English speakers. The difference is probably not more than half a second in length, but it has an important effect on interethnic communication. When an English speaker pauses he waits for the regular length of time (around one second or less), that is, *his* regular length of time, and if the Athabaskan does not say anything, the English speaker feels he is free to go on and say anything else he likes. At the same time the Athabaskan has been waiting his regular length of time before coming in. He does not want to interrupt the English speaker. This length of time we think is around one and one-half seconds. It is just enough longer that by the time the Athabaskan is ready to speak the English speaker is already speaking again. So the Athabaskan waits again for the next pause. Again, the English speaker begins just enough before the Athabaskan was going to speak. The net result is that the Athbaskan can never get a word in edgewise (an apt metaphor in this case), while the English speaker goes on and on.

The Athabaskan point of view is that it is difficult to make one's whole point. The length of pause that the Athabaskan takes while expecting to continue is just about the length of pause the English speaker takes in exchanging turns. If an Athabaskan has in mind a series of sentences to say, it is most likely that at the end of the first one the English speaker will think that he has finished because of the length of the pause and will begin speaking. The Athabaskan feels he has been interrupted and the English speaker feels the Athabaskan never makes sense, never says a whole coherent idea. Much of this misunderstanding is the result of something like a one-half second difference in the timing of conversational pauses, but it can result in strong stereotypical responses to the opposite ethnic group.

A second factor in the exchange of speaking turns that only increases the difficulty we are looking at here is that there are different expectations about how long a speaker should be allowed to speak at one turn. Generally Athabaskans expect that a speaker will take as long as necessary to develop an idea. The ideal situation is that of an older speaker, a person in a clear superordinate position, narrating a traditional story. Although this idea may not often be practiced, there is nevertheless an expectation that something like a monologue is the normal speaking turn. The role of other speakers is that of an audience that by frequent traffic signal responses indicates that it is following. English speakers, on the other hand, treat monologues as exceptions, with the norm being the dialogue in which speakers exchange more or less equal turns.

In Athabaskan-English interethnic communication, the expectation that English speakers have is rarely fulfilled. True dialogue rarely occurs. The reason for this has been given. The exchange of turns works toward the English speaker's continually regaining the floor and against the Athabaskan's being able to hold the floor for more than a brief speaking turn. Where an Athabaskan may expect to get his turn after a long English monologue, he rarely gets more than a brief statement before another English monologue begins. The result is again stereotyping of the English speaker as egocentric and the Athabaskan as having no ideas of his own.

## Departure Formulas

It is safe to say that an Athabaskan-English conversation will usually begin with the English speaker speaking first. It is almost as certain that it will end with the Athabaskan making no formal close. On the surface the explanation seems simple enough. Most of the formulas for ending conversation refer to the future. Athabaskans feel it is bad luck to make predictions about the future. This applies even to such routine statements as "I'll see you later" or "I'll see you tomorrow." Where the English speakers feel these are simple closing statements, ways of saying "Now our talk is ended," they carry an overtone of bad luck for the Athabaskan and thus are avoided.

The impression of these closing formulas from the Athabaskan point of view again confirms the English speaker's bravado regarding his good luck and future. From the English speaker's point of view, the lack of closings gives a feeling that something has gone wrong in the communication. As we have reason to believe now, that is very likely to be true; but it may be misleading. The conversation may have been very compatible and yet leave the English speaker feeling that something went wrong because of the lack of a close.

We need to look a bit closer at departures to understand this problem. As Goffman (1974) has said, departures do much more than bring a conversation to a close. They set up the conditions for future conversations. English speakers feel it is essential at the end of each encounter to be clear just where you stand with the other speaker. The closing formula is the way this is done. Something as simple as "It's been nice talking to you" suggests that you expect to do more of it in the future. As we depart we prepare the future, and it is this aspect of the formula that for the English speaker fits in well with the general negotiation of intersubjective reality. The departure is the final check on where you have gotten to in the negotiation that has taken place. It cements this into place so that the negotiation can be resumed at the next opportunity.

This preparation of the future through the departure formula is directly contrary to the Athabaskan prohibition on speaking strongly of the future. If one enjoyed a conversation, it would be bad luck indeed to say so and that you hoped it would happen again. So in closing a conversation as in beginning it, the Athabaskan is careful not to display carelessness or to present himself in too favorable a light. The English speaker who has begun the conversation as a way of getting to know the other closes the conversation with an indirect but important summary of how things have gone. Perhaps the worst outcome from the English point of view is a complete rupture of the relationship. This would be shown by a violation of discourse conventions, including the convention of a formulated departure. The Athabaskans, being careful of courting bad luck, may quite unknowingly signal to the English speaker the worst possibility, that there is no hope of getting together again to speak.

## The Importance of Discourse and Cultural Factors

In interethnic communication between English speakers and Athabaskans, talk is distributed so that the English speaker is favored as first speaker, as controller of topic, as principal speaker, and yet in the end he may not have any conclusive idea of what went on. For the Athabaskan speaker it is difficult to get the floor, to bring the conversation around to his own topic, and in the end to feel he has had much effect on the outcome. This situation is prepared by cultural expectations about the presentation of self. It works through the mechanics of a slight difference in pausing systems and the general mechanics of turn taking in human communication. The result is a considerable potential for difficulty in interethnic communication. It is important to point out now that we have not yet mentioned any factors that have to do with the grammatical or lexical structure of language directly. The potential difficulties and misunderstandings that we have discussed are the same whether the communication is carried on in English, Athabaskan, so-called Village English, or any combination of these. As long as the discourse patterns and the presentation of self are clearly Athabaskan in origin on the one hand and English in origin on the other these possibilities of problems will arise.

At first it will seem ironic that the situation in which there is the greatest potential for problems is where the language being used by the two speakers is the most similar. We are so accustomed to thinking that communication is a matter of grammar and vocabulary that if the grammar and vocabulary are the same or similar for two speakers it is difficult to believe that there might be trouble. Yet, as we have said earlier, these discourse patterns and cultural expectations are learned very early in life and change slowly. Even where someone learns to speak a new language later in life, it is very likely that he will speak it using the discourse patterns of his early language training. In present-day Alaska and Canada, many people who do not speak any Athabaskan language have nevertheless learned Athabaskan discourse patterns which are essential for effective communication within the village, even though the language used may be English. We want to be careful then not to think that understanding will be automatic just because two speakers do not differ greatly in grammar or vocabulary. Assumptions about the presentation of self and the distribution of talk in interethnic communication lie at the bottom of many communicative conflicts.

## REFERENCES

Goffman, E. (1974). *Frame analysis.* New York: Harper & Row.

Schegloff, E. (1972). Sequencing in conversational openings. J. Gumperz and D. Hymes (Eds.). *Directions in sociolinguistics.* New York: Holt, Rinehart and Winston.

Scollon, R. (1976). *Conversations with a one-year-old: A case study of the developmental foundation of syntax.* Honolulu: University Press of Hawaii.

# English con Salsa

## Gina Valdés

### EDITOR'S INTRODUCTION

Growing up bilingual often also means living two lives and learning the rules of two cultures. Gina Valdés' poem "English con Salsa" (on p. 194) celebrates the experiences, rhythms, and sounds of that double life.

## GLOSSARY FOR "ENGLISH CON SALSA"

*inglés con chile y cilantro:* English with spice

Benito Juárez: President of Mexico from 1857 to 1863 and from 1867 to 1872

Xochicalco: small town in Mexico

*dólares and dolores:* dollars and pains

Teocaltiche: town in Mexico

English *refrito:* refried English

English *con sal y limón:* English with salt and lemon
    *requinto* from Uruapán: small guitar from the town of Uruapán

*mezcal* from Juchitán: a strong liquor made from cactus, in this case from the city of Juchitán

*amigos del sur:* friends from the south

Zapotec: a specific tribe of Mexican Indians

Nahuatl: the Aztecan language

*duendes:* goblins or ghostly spirits

Santa Tristeza: Saint Sadness

Santa Alegría: Saint Happiness

Santo Todolopuede: Saint All-Powerful

*pollo loco:* literally, crazy chicken

*chapulines:* small children

Mixtec: an adjective describing something particular to the Mexican indigenous people known by the same name

*la tierra:* the earth

*Source:* "English con Salsa" by Gina Valdés is reprinted with permission from the publisher of *The Americas Review* Vol. 21 No. 1 (Houston: Arte Publico Press—University of Houston, 1994).

Welcome to ESL 100, English Surely Latinized,
inglés con chile y cilantro, English as American
as Benito Juárez. Welcome, muchachos from Xochicalco,
learn the language of dólares and dolores, of kings
and queens, of Donald Duck and Batman. Holy Toluca!
In four months you'll be speaking like George Washington,
in four weeks you can ask, More coffee? In two months
you can say, May I take your order? In one year you
can ask for a raise, cool as the Tuxpan River.

Welcome, muchachas from Teocaltiche, in this class
we speak English refrito, English con sal y limón,
English thick as mango juice, English poured from
a clay jug, English tuned like a requinto from Uruapán,
English lighted by Oaxacan dawns, English spiked
with mezcal from Juchitán, English with a red cactus
flower blooming in its heart.

Welcome, welcome, amigos del sur, bring your Zapotec
tongues, your Nahuatl tones, your patience of pyramids,
your red suns and golden moons, your guardian angels,
your duendes, your patron saint, Santa Tristeza,
Santa Alegría, Santo Todolopuede. We will sprinkle
holy water on pronouns, make the sign of the cross
on past participles, jump like fish from Lake Pátzcuaro
on gerunds, pour tequila from Jalisco on future perfects,
say shoes and shit, grab a cool verb and a pollo loco
and dance on the walls like chapulines.

When a teacher from La Jolla or a cowboy from Santee
asks you, Do you speak English? You'll answer, Sí,
yes, simón, of course. I love English!

                              And you'll hum
        a Mixtec chant that touches la tierra and the heavens.

# Silencing in Public Schools

## Michelle Fine

### EDITOR'S INTRODUCTION

Other authors have explored what is possible when talk in schools is nurtured. Michelle Fine takes a look at the flip side, when adolescents' voices are silenced in schools. The following article looks closely at one of the findings from her disturbing high school ethnography. She examines what happens when students are excluded from the discussion and learn a passive role, burying their own voices.

> *Lying is done with words and also with silence.*
> Adrienne Rich, *On Lies, Secrets and Silence.*

Demands for silencing signify a terror of words, a fear of talk. This essay examines these demands as they echoed through a comprehensive public high school in New York City. The silencing resounded in words and in their absence; the demands emanated from the New York City Board of Education, book publishers, corporate sponsors, religious institutions, administrators, teachers, parents, and students. In the odd study of *what's not said* in public schools, one must be curious about whom silencing protects, but vigilant about how silencing students and their communities undermines fundamentally the vision of education as empowerment (Freire 1985; Shor 1980).

This essay examines what doesn't get talked about in schools and how "undesirable" talk is subverted, appropriated, and exported. In this essay silencing constitutes a process of institutionalized policies and practices which obscure the very social, economic, and therefore experimental conditions of students' daily lives, and which expel from written, oral, and nonverbal expression substantive

and critical "talk" about these conditions. Silencing orchestrates the paradoxical life of institutions such as schools, which are marked as *the* opportunity for mobility when indeed groups are unevenly "mobilized" by the same educational credential, and even more unevenly disabled by its absence. Further, in a city such as New York, dropouts from the wealthiest neighborhoods are systematically more likely to be employed than high school graduates from the poorest neighborhoods (Tobier 1984). Yet simple, seamless pronouncements of equal opportunity and educational credentials as the primary mode of mobility are woven through the curriculum and pedagogy of urban high school classes. Silencing constitutes the process by which contradictory evidence, ideologies, and experiences find themselves buried, camouflaged, and discredited.

*Source:* "Silencing in Public Schools" by M. Fine, 1987, *Language Arts 64* (2), pp. 157–174. Copyright 1987 by the National Council of Teachers of English. Reprinted with permission.

While schools are replete with countertensions, including the voices of exposure and critique, the press for silencing pervades low income urban schools. The centralized and tiered structure of educational administration, books used, curriculum generated, pedagogy applied, administrative withholding of data, "objective" mechanisms for evaluating teachers and students, and strategies for excluding parents/guardians and community activists compromise the means by which schools establish themselves as fortresses against low-income communities; students are subverted in their attempts to merge school and home, and conversations are aborted.

Silencing, I would guess, more intimately informs low-income, public schooling than relatively privileged situations. To question from above holds intellectual promise; to question from below forebodes danger. In low-income schools both the process of inquiry into students' lived experience, and the content to be unearthed are assumed to be, a priori, unsafe territory.

Silencing sustains the belief in schooling as the mechanism for social mobility, with contradictory evidence barred. And silencing diverts critique away from the economic, social, and educational institutions which organize class, race, and gender hierarchies. But the silencing process bears not only ideological or cosmetic consequence. These very demands permeate classroom life so primitively as to make irrelevant the lived experiences, passions, concerns, communities, and biographies of low-income, minority students. In the process the very voices of students and their communities that public education claims to nurture, shut down.

This essay focuses on silencing primarily at the level of classroom and school talk in a low-income, "low-skill" school. The corporate, institutional, and bureaucratic mandates from which demands for silencing derive, while acknowledged, remain relatively immune from the present analysis. This is not to locate blame inside classrooms nor with individual teachers, but merely to extract from these interactions the raw material for a critical view of silencing. The data derive from a year-long ethnography of a high school in Manhattan, attended by 3,200 students, predominantly low-income blacks and Hispanics from Central Harlem, and run primarily by black paraprofessionals and aides, white administrators and teachers, with some Hispanic paraprofessionals and teachers (see Fine 1985, 1986).

The analysis seems important for two reasons. First, there is substantial evidence that many students in this school, considered low in skill and motivation, were eager to choreograph their own learning, to generate a curriculum

of lived experience and to engage in a participatory pedagogy. Every attempt, intended or not, to undermine their educational autobiographizing, by teachers or administrators, sacrificed another chance to connect with students and their communities (Bastian, Fruchter, Gittell, Greer & Haskins 1985; Connell, Ashenden, Kessler & Dowsett 1984; Lightfoot 1978). While not overstating the academic energy spontaneously displayed by these adolescents, I would stress that those administrators, teachers, and paraprofessionals sufficiently interested and patient did generate classrooms of relatively "alive" participants. More overwhelming to the observer, however, silencing engulfed life inside the classrooms and administrative offices.

This loss of connection bears significant consequence for low-income, minority students who are fundamentally ambivalent about the educational process and its credentials (Carnoy & Levin 1985). As confident as they were that "you can't get nowhere without a diploma," most were also mindful that "the richest man in my neighborhood didn't graduate but from eighth grade." And, of course, they were not wrong. Each of these two beliefs withstands tests of empirical validity, measured in labor force statistics, as well as experiential validity, confirmed daily on their streets. "Within democratic society, . . . contradictions between the rhetoric of equality and the reality of domination must be obscured" (Cummins 1986, p. 25). And so the process of silencing camouflaged such contradictions, advancing ironically the cynicism of the latter student belief, eroding the idealism of the former.

The silencing process is but one aspect of what is often, for low-income students, an impoverished educational tradition. Infiltrating administrative "talk," curriculum development, and pedagogical technique, the means of silencing establish impenetrable barriers between the worlds of school and community life.

## THE IMPULSE TO SILENCE: FEARS OF NAMING

In June of 1984 I decided to spend the following fall and spring conducting an ethnography inside this high school, watching specifically for the production and reproduction of high school graduates and dropouts, not yet interested in anything I would later consider silencing (see Fine 1985, 1986).[1] To my request for entree to his school, the principal greeted me as follows:

---

[1]This research was made possible by a grant from the W. T. Grant Foundation, New York City, 1984 through 1985.

*Field Note, June 1984.*

*Mr. Stein:* Sure you can do your research on dropouts at this school. With one provision. You can not mention the words "dropping out" to the students.

*MF:* Why not?

*Stein:* I firmly believe that if you say it, you encourage them to do it.

My field notes continue, "When he said this, I thought, adults should be so lucky, that adolescents wait for us *to name* dropping out, or sex, for them to do it." From September through June I witnessed daily life inside classrooms, deans' and nurses' offices, the attendance room, and the lunchroom. Over time it struck me as even more naive that the school administrator would believe that what adults say engenders teenage compliance. With so little evidence that adult talk promotes any adolescent compliance, how could one continue to believe that if an authority says it, students will conform; that naming is dangerous and not naming is safe?

As the year transpired, what became apparent was not naivete but a systematic, school-based fear of talk; a special kind of talk which might be called *naming*. Naming gives license to critical conversation about social and economic arrangements, particularly inequitable distributions of power and resources, by which these students and their kin suffer disproportionately. The fear of naming provoked the move to silence.

One can only speculate on this inferred fear of naming. By no means universal, it was, by every measure, commonplace. Let us assume that urban teachers and administrators seek to believe that schooling can make a significant difference, collectively or individually, in the lives of these adolescents. Given that they have little authority to create what they might consider the necessary conditions (see Carnegie Forum on Education and the Economy 1986; Holmes Group 1986), "choices" are undoubtedly made about how to make sense of their work and their presumably limited effectiveness. Not naming fits essentially with how one structures meaning of the work of public education.

With one strategy administrators and teachers viewed most of these students as unteachable, following the logic of social studies teacher Mr. Rosaldo, "If I reach 20 percent, if we save 20 percent, that's a miracle. Most of these kids don't have a chance." While the incidence of this belief remains to be documented, compelling correlational evidence suggests that those teachers who feel most disempowered in their institutions are also most likely to subscribe to such a notion, to agree that "These kids can't be helped" (Fine 1983). Perhaps these teachers have themselves been

silenced over time. For them, *naming* social equities in the classroom could only expose social circumstances they believed to be basically self-imposed and diminish the distance between "them" and "us." When I presented the data to the faculty at the end of the year and suggested, for example, that the level of involuntary "discharges" processed through this school would never be tolerated in the schools attended by the faculty's children, I was reminded by a faculty member, "That's an absurd comparison. The schools my kids go to are nothing like this—the comparison is itself sensationalism!" The social distance between "them" and "us" was reified and naturalized.

Other teachers subscribed loyally to beliefs in a color-blind meritocracy. They merely dismissed the empirical data which would have had to inform the process of naming. Here they followed the logic of science teacher Ms. Tannenbaum, "If these students work hard, they can really become something. Especially today with Affirmative Action." They rejected or avoided counterevidence: e.g., that black high school graduates living in Harlem are still far less likely to be employed than white high school dropouts living in more elite sections of New York (Tobier 1984). Enormous energy must be required to sustain beliefs in equal opportunity and the color-blind power of credentials, and to silence nagging losses of faith when evidence to the contrary compels on a daily basis. Naming in such a case would only unmask, fundamentally disrupting or contradicting one's belief system.

But some educators did actively engage their students in lively, critical discourse about the complexities and inequities of prevailing economic and social relations. Often importing politics from other spheres of their lives, the feminist English teacher, the community activist who taught grammar, or the Marxist historian wove critical analysis into their classrooms with little effort. These classrooms were permeated with the openness of naming, free of the musty tension which derives from conversations-not-had.

Most educators at this school, however, seemed to survive by not naming or analyzing social problems. They taught the curricula and pedagogical techniques they hoped would soothe students and smooth social contradictions. Many would probably have not considered conversation about social class, gender, or race politics relevant to their courses, or easily integrated into their curricula. One could have assumed, therefore, that they had benignly neglected these topics.

Evidence of *fear,* however, rather than neglect, grew salient when students (activated by curiosity or rebellion) raised topics which were rapidly shut down. A systemic expulsion of dangerous topics permeated the room. I would posit that, to examine power differentials, the very conditions which contribute to insidious social class, racial, ethnic, and gender divisions in the U.S., when the teacher is relatively privileged by class usually and race often, introduces for educators fantasies of danger. Such conversations *problematize* what seem like 'natural' social distinctions, such as the distinction between where one teaches and where one sends one's children to be taught. Such conversations threaten to erode teachers' authority. While usually not by conscious choice, teachers and administrators engaged in diverse strategies to preempt, detour, or ghettoize such conversations. *Not naming,* as a particular form of silencing, was accomplished creatively. Often with good intentions, not naming bore equally devastating consequences.

Naming may indeed be dangerous to beliefs often promoted in public schools; it is for that very reason *essential* to the creation of an empowered and critical constituency of educated social participants (Aronowitz & Giroux 1985). To *not name* bears consequences for all students, but more so for low-income, minority youths. To not name is to systematically alienate, cut off from home, from heritage and from lived experience, and ultimately to sever from their educational process. Following the lead of Adrienne Rich in the opening quote, silencing is examined below through what was said and what was not said in this public school across the academic year 1984–1985, beginning with the obvious, if redundant occurrence of administrative silencing.

## ADMINISTRATIVE SILENCING: WHITE NOISE

*Field Note: September 1985*

We are proud to say that 80 percent of our high school graduates go on to college.

Principal, Parents' Association meeting, September 1985

At the first Parent's Association meeting, Mr. Stein, the principal, boasted an 80 percent "college-bound" rate. Almost all graduates of this inner city high school head for college; a comforting claim oft repeated by urban school administrators in the 1980s. While accurate, the pronouncement fundamentally detoured the conversation away from the fact that in this school, as in others, only 20 percent of incoming ninth graders of 1978–1979 were headed for college by 1985. The "white noise" promoted by the administration reverberated silence in the audience. Not named, and therefore not problematized, was retention. No questions were asked.

Not naming signifies an administrative craft. The New York City Board of Education, for example, refuses to monitor retention, promotion, and educational achievement statistics by race and ethnicity for fear of "appearing racist" (Personal Communication 1984).[2] As a result huge discrepancies in educational advancement, by race and ethnicity, remain undocumented in Board publications. Likewise dropout calculations may include students on register when they have not been seen for months; may presume that students who enroll in GED programs are not dropouts, or that those who produce "working papers" are about to embark on careers (which involves a letter, for example, from a Chicken Delight clerk assuring that José has a job, so that he can leave school at sixteen). Such procedures insidiously contribute to not naming the density of the dropout problem.

While administrative silencing is unfortunately almost a redundant notion, the concerns of this essay are primarily focused on classroom- and school-based activities of silencing. Examining the processes of not naming pedagogically and within the public school curriculum, the essay ends with the most dramatic embodiment of silencing, the academically mute bodies of those young black teenage girls who say nothing all day, who have perfected the mask of being silenced, who are never identified as a problem.

The remainder of the essay moves from pedagogy to curriculum to discipline as discrete moments in the silencing process.

## CLOSING DOWN CONVERSATIONS

*Field Note: October 17, Business Class*

*White teacher:* What's EOE?

*Black male student:* Equal over time.

*White teacher:* Not quite. Anyone else?

*Black female student:* Equal Opportunity Employer.

*Teacher:* That's right.

*Black male student (2):* What does that mean?

*Teacher:* That means that an employer can't discriminate on the basis of sex, age, marital status, or race.

*Black male student (2):* But wait, sometimes white people only hire white people.

*Teacher:* No, they're not supposed to if they say EOE in their ads. Now take out your homework.

---

[2]Personal communication with employee in the High Schools' Division, New York City Board of Education, in response to inquiry about why New York City does not maintain race/ethnicity-sensitive statistics on dropping out and school achievement.

Later that day:

*MF:* Why don't you discuss racism in your class?
*Teacher:* It would demoralize the students, they need to feel positive and optimistic—like they have a chance. Racism is just an excuse they use not to try harder.

What enables some teachers to act as if students benefit from such smoothing over (Wexler 1983)? For whose good are the roots, the scars and the structures of class, race, and gender inequity obscured by teachers, texts and tests (Anyon 1983)? Are not the "fears of demoralizing" a projection by teachers of their own silenced loss of faith in public education, and their own fears of unmasking or freeing a conversation about social inequities?

At the level of curriculum, texts, and conversation in classrooms, school talk and knowledge were radically severed from the daily realities of adolescents' lives and more systematically allied with the lives of teachers (McNeil 1981). Routinely discouraged from critically examining the conditions of their lives, dissuaded from creating their own curriculum, built of what they know, students were often encouraged to disparage the circumstances in which they live, warned by their teachers: "You act like that, and you'll end up on welfare!" Most were or have been surviving on some form of federal, state or city assistance.

"Good students" managed these dual/duel worlds by learning to speak standard English dialect, whether they originally spoke black English, Spanish, or Creole. And more poignant still, they trained themselves to speak and produce in two voices. One's "own" voice alternated with an "academic" voice which denied class, gender, and race conflict; reproduced ideologies about hard work, success, and their "natural" sequence; and stifled the desire to disrupt.

In a study conducted in 1981, it was found that the group of South Bronx students who were "successes"—those who remained in high school—when compared to dropouts, were significantly *more* depressed, *less* politically aware, *less* likely to be assertive in the classroom if they were undergraded, and *more* conformist (Fine 1983)! A moderate level of depression, an absence of political awareness, the presence of self-blame, low-assertiveness, and high conformity may tragically have constituted evidence of the "good" urban students at this high school. They learned not to raise, and indeed to help shut down, "dangerous" conversation. The price of "success" may have been muting one's own voice.

Other students from this school resolved the "two voices" tension with creative, if ultimately self-defeating, strategies. Cheray reflected on this moment of hegemony

after she dropped out: "In school we learned Columbus Avenue stuff and *I* had to translate it into Harlem. They think livin' up here is unsafe and our lives are so bad. That we should want to move out and get away. That's what you're supposed to learn."[3]

Tony thoroughly challenged the academic voice as ineffective pedagogy: "I never got math when I was in school. Then I started sellin' dope and runnin' numbers and I picked it up right away. They should teach the way it matters."

Alicia accepted the academic voice as the standard, while disparaging with faint praise what *she* knew: "I'm *wise,* not *smart.* There's a difference. I can walk into a room and I knows what people be thinkin' and what's goin' down. But not what he be talkin' about in history."

Finally many saw the academic voice as exclusively legitimate, if inaccessible. Monique, after two months out of school, admitted, "I'm scared to go out lookin' for a job. They be usin' words in the interview like in school. Words I don't know. I can't be askin' them for a dictionary. It's like in school. You ask and you feel like a dummy."

By segregating the academic voice from one's own, schools contribute to controversy not only linguistic in form (Zorn 1982). The intellectual, social, and emotional substance which constitutes minority students' lives was routinely treated as irrelevant, to be displaced and silenced. Their responses, spanning acquiescence to resistance, bore serious consequence.

## CONTRADICTIONS FOLDED: THE PEDAGOGICAL CREATION OF DICHOTOMIES

If "lived talk" was actively expelled on the basis of content, contradictory talk was basically rendered impossible. Social contradictions were folded into dichotomous choices. Again, one can only speculate on whom this accommodates, but the creation of dichotomies and the reification of single truths does much to bolster educators' control, enforcing an explicit distance between those who *know* and those who don't; discrediting often those who *think* (McNeil 1981).

In early spring, a social studies teacher structured an in-class debate on Bernard Goetz—New York City's "subway vigilante." She invited "those students who agree with Goetz to sit on one side of the room, and those who think he was wrong to sit on the other side." To the large residual group

---

[3]Columbus Avenue, on the upper West Side, has recently become a rapidly gentrified, elite neighborhood in Manhattan, displacing many low-income, particularly black and Hispanic residents.

who remained midroom the teacher remarked, "Don't be lazy. You have to make a decision. Like at work, you can't be passive." A few wandered over to the "pro-Goetz" side. About six remained in the center. Somewhat angry, the teacher continued: "Ok, first we'll hear the pro-Goetz side and then the anti-Goetz side. Those of you who have no opinion, who haven't even thought about the issue, you won't get to talk unless we have time."

Deidre, a black senior, bright and always quick to raise contradictions otherwise obscured, advocated the legitimacy of the middle group. "It's not that I have no opinions. I don't like Goetz shootin' up people who look like my brother, but I don't like feelin' unsafe in the projects or in my neighborhood either. I got lots of opinions. I ain't bein' quiet 'cause I can't decide if he's right or wrong. I'm talkin'."

Deidre's comment legitimized for herself and others the right to hold complex, perhaps even contradictory positions on a complex situation. Such legitimacy was rarely granted by faculty—with clear and important exceptions including activist faculty and paraprofessionals who lived in central Harlem with the kids, who understood and respected much about their lives.

Among the chorus of voices heard within this high school, then, lay little room for Gramsci's (1971) contradictory consciousness. Artificial dichotomies were understood as received and natural: right and wrong answers, good and bad behavior, moral and immoral people, dumb and smart students, responsible and irresponsible parents, good and bad neighbors. Contradiction and ambivalence, forced underground, were experienced often, if only expressed rarely.

I asked Ronald, a student in remedial reading class, why he stayed in school. He responded with the sophistication and complexity the question deserved, "Reason I stay in school is 'cause every time I get on the subway I see this drunk and I think 'not me.' But then I think 'bet he has a high school degree.'" The power of his statement lies in its honesty, as well as the infrequency with which such comments were voiced. Ronald explained that he expected support for his position neither on the street nor in the school. School talk filled youths with promises that few believed, but many repeated: the promises of hard work, education, and success; warnings about welfare. Street talk belied another reality, described by Shondra, "They be sayin, 'What you doin' in school? Could be out here scramblin' [selling drugs] and makin' money now. That degree ain't gonna get you nothing better.'"

When black adolescent high school graduates, in the October following graduation, suffered a 56 percent unemployment rate and black adolescent high school dropouts suffered a 70 percent unemployment rate, the very contradictions which remained unspoken within school were amplified in the minds and worries of these young men and women (Young 1983).

## CONVERSATIONS PSYCHOLOGIZED: THE CURRICULUM SPLITS THE PERSONAL AND THE SOCIAL

Some conversations within the schools were closed; others were dichotomized. Yet a few conversations, indeed those most relevant to socioeconomic arrangements and inequities, remained psychologized. The topics were managed exclusively as personal problems inside the offices of school psychologists or counselors. The lived experiences of *all* adolescents, and particularly those surviving city life in poverty, place their physical and mental well-being as well as that of their kin in constant jeopardy. And yet conversations about these were conditions of life, about alcoholism, drug abuse, domestic violence, environmental hazards, gentrification, and poor health—to the extent that they happened at all—remained confined to individual sessions with counselors (for those lucky enough to gain hearing with a counselor in the 800–1 ratio, and gutsy enough to raise the issue) or, if made academic, were raised in hygiene class (for those fortunate enough to have made it to twelfth grade when hygiene was offered). A biology teacher, one of the few black teachers in the school, actually integrated creative writing assignments such as "My life as an alcoholic" and "My life as the child of an alcoholic" into her biology class curriculum. Her department chairman reprimanded her severely for introducing "extraneous materials" into her classroom. Teachers, too, were silenced.

The prevalence of health and social problems experienced by these adolescents, and their curricular marginalization, exemplified a rigid academic unwillingness to address these concerns, in social studies, science, English, or even math. A harsh resistance to name the lived experiences of these teens paralleled the unwillingness to integrate these experiences as the substance of learning. Issues to be avoided at all costs, they were addressed only once they dramatically pierced the life of an adolescent who sought help.

The offices of school psychologists or counselors therefore became the primary sites for addressing what were indeed social concerns, should have been academic concerns, and were most likely to be managed as personal and private concerns. The curricular privatizing and psychologizing of public and political issues served to reinforce the alienation of students' lives from their educational experiences, made worse only by those conversations never had.

## CONVERSATIONS NEVER HAD

A mechanistic view of teachers terrorized of naming and students passively accommodating could not be further from the daily realities of life inside a public high school. Many teachers name and critique, although most don't. Some students passively shut down, but most remain alive and even resistant. Classrooms are filled with students wearing Walkmans, conversing among themselves and with friends in the halls, and some even persistently challenging the experiences and expertise of their teachers. But the typical classroom still values silence, control, and quiet, as John Goodlad (1984), Theodore Sizer (1985), Jean Anyon (1983), and others have documented. The insidious push toward silence in low-income schools became most clear sometime after my interview with Eartha, a sixteen-year-old high school dropout.

*MF:* Eartha, when you were a kid, did you participate a lot in school?
*Eartha:* Not me, I was a good kid. Made no trouble.

I asked this question of fifty-five high school dropouts. After the third responded as Eartha did, I realized that for me, participation was encouraged, delighted in, and a measure of the "good student." For these adolescents, given their contexts of schooling, "participation" signified poor discipline and rude classroom behavior.

Students learned the dangers of talk, the codes of participating and not, and they learned, in more nuanced ways, which conversations were never to be initiated. In Philadelphia a young high school student explained to me: "We ain't allowed to talk about abortion. They tell us we can't discuss it no way." When I asked a School District Administrator about this policy, she qualified: "It's not that they can't talk about it. The teacher, if the topic is raised by a student, can define abortion, just not discuss it beyond that." This distinction between *define* and *discuss* makes sense only if education signifies teacher authority, and control implies silence. Perhaps this is why classroom control often feels so fragile. Control through omission *is* fragile, fully contingent on students' willingness to collude and "play" at not naming. While it ostensibly postures teacher authority, it actually betrays a plea for student compliance.

Silence comes in many forms. Conversations can be closed by teachers, or forestalled by student compliance. But other conversations are expressly subverted, never had. A policy of enforced silencing was applied to information about the severe economic and social consequences of dropping out of high school. This information was systematically withheld from students who are being discharged. When students were discharged in New York State—a "choice" available to few middle-class, particularly white students—they were guaranteed an exit interview, which, in most cases, involved an attendance officer who asked students what they planned to do, and then requested a meeting with a parent/guardian to sign official documents. The officer handed the student a list of GED/outreach programs. The student left, often eager to find work, get a GED, go to a private business school, or join the military. Informed conversations about the consequences of the students' decision are not legally mandated. As they left, these adolescents *did not learn:*

- that over 50 percent of black high school dropouts suffer unemployment in cities like New York City (U.S. Commission on Civil Rights 1982);
- that 48 percent of New Yorkers who sit for the Graduate Equivalency Diploma test fail (New York State Department of Education 1985);
- that private trade schools, including cosmetology, beautician, and business schools have been charged with unethical recruitment practices, exploitation of students, earning more from students who drop out than those who stay, not providing promised jobs and having, on average, a 70 percent dropout rate (see Fine 1986);
- that the military, during "peacetime," refuses to accept females with no high school degree, and only reluctantly accepts such males, who suffer an extremely high rate of less-than-honorable discharge within six months of enlistment (Militarism Resource Project 1985).

Students were thereby denied informed consent if they left high school prior to graduation. These conversations-not-had failed to correct and therefore nurtured powerful beliefs that "the GED is no sweat, a piece of cake"; that "you can get jobs, they promise, after goin' to Sutton or ABI"; or that "in the Army I can get me a GED, skills, travel, benefits. . . ."

## MAINTAINING SILENCE THROUGH DEMOCRACY AND DISCIPLINE

Means of maintaining silences and assuring no dangerous disruptions know few bounds. One institutionalized strategy involves the appropriation of internal dissent, framed as democracy for parents and students. This strategy is increasingly popular in this era of rhetorical "empowerment."

At this school the Parents' Association executive board was comprised of ten parents: eight black women, one black man, and one white woman. Eight no longer had children attending the school. At about midyear teachers were demanding smaller class size. So too was the President of the Parents' Association at this Executive meeting with the Principal.

*President:* I'm concerned about class size. Carol Bellamy (City Council President) notified us that you received monies earmarked to reduce class size and yet what have you done?

*Mr. Stein:* Quinones (Schools Chancellor) promised no high school class greater than 34 by February. That's impossible! What he is asking I can't guarantee unless *you* tell me how to do it. If I reduce class size, I must eliminate all specialized classes, all electives. Even then I can't guarantee. To accede to Quinones, that classes be less than 34, we must eliminate the elective in English, in social studies, all art classes, eleventh year math, physics, accounting, wordprocessing. We were going to offer a Haitian Patois bilingual program, fourth year French, a museums program, bio-pre-med, health careers, coop and pre-coop, choreography and advanced ballet. The nature of the school will be changed fundamentally. We won't be able to call this an academic high school, only a program for slow learners.

*Woman (1):* Those are very important classes.

*Stein:* I am willing to keep these classes. Parents want me to keep these classes. That's where I'm at.

*Woman (2):* What is the average?

*Stein:* Thirty-three.

*Woman (1):* Are any classes over forty?

*Stein:* No, except if it's a *Singleton* class—the only one offered. If these courses weren't important, we wouldn't keep them. You know we always work together. If it's your feeling we should not eliminate all electives and maintain things, OK! Any comments?

*Woman (1):* I think continue. Youngsters aren't getting enough now. And the teachers will not any more.

*Woman (3):* You have our unanimous consent and support.

*Stein:* When I talk to the Board of Education, I'll say I'm talking for the parents.

*Woman (4):* I think it's impossible to teach forty.

*Stein:* We have a space problem. Any other issues?

An equally conciliatory student council was constituted to decide on student activities, prom arrangements, and student fees. They were largely pleased to meet in the principal's office.

At the level of critique, silence was guaranteed by the selection of and then democratic participation of individuals within "constituency-based groups."

If dissent was appropriated through mechanisms of democracy, it was exported through mechanisms of discipline. The most effective procedure for silencing was to banish the source of dissent, tallied in the school's dropout rate. As indicated by the South Bronx study referred to above (Fine 1983), and the research of others (Elliott, Voss & Wendling 1966; Felice 1981; Fine & Rosenberg 1983), it is often the academic critic resisting the intellectual and verbal girdles of schooling who "drops out" or is pushed out of low-income schools. Extraordinary rates of suspensions, expulsions, and discharges experienced by black and Hispanic youths speak to this form of silencing (Advocates for Children 1985). Estimates of urban dropout rates range from approximately 42 percent for New York City, Boston, and Chicago Boards of Education to 68–80 percent from Aspira, an educational advocacy organization (1983).

At the school which served as the site for this ethnographic research, a 66 percent dropout rate was calculated. Two-thirds of the students who began ninth grade in 1978–79 did not receive diplomas nor degrees by June 1985. I presented these findings to a collection of deans, advisors, counselors, administrators, and teachers, many of whom were the sponsors and executors of the discharge process. At first I met with total silence. A dean then explained, "These kids need to be out. It's unfair to the rest. My job is like a pilot on a hijacked plane. My job is to throw the hijacker overboard." The one black woman in the room, a guidance counselor, followed: "What Michelle is saying is true. We do throw students out of here and deny them their education. Black kids especially." Two white male administrators interrupted, chiding the "liberal tendencies" of guidance counselors, who, as they put it, "don't see how really dangerous these kids are." The meeting ended.

Dissent was institutionally "democraticized," exported, trivialized, or bureaucratized. These mechanisms made it unlikely for change or challenge to be given a serious hearing.

## WHISPERS OF RESISTANCE: THE SILENCED SPEAK

In non-elite public high schools organized around control through silence, the student, teacher, or paraprofessional who talks, who tells or who wants to speak, transforms rapidly into the subversive, the trouble maker. The speaking student, unless she or he spoke in an honors class or affected the academic mode of imputing nondangerous topics and benign words, unless protected by wealth, influential parents, or an unusual capacity to be both critic *and* good student, emerged as provocateur. Depending on school, circumstance, and style, the students' response to silence varied. She may have buried herself in mute isolation. He may have been promoted to resist or organize other students. But most of these youths, for complex reasons, were ultimately propelled to flee prior to graduation. Some then sought "alternative contexts" in which their strengths, their competencies, and their voices could flourish on their own terms:

*[Hector's a subway graffiti artist:]* It's like an experience you never get. You're on the subway tracks. It's 3:00 A.M., dark, cold and scary. You're trying to create your best. The cops can come to bust you, or you could fall on the electric third rail. My friend died when he dropped his spray paint on that rail. It exploded. He died and I watched. It's awesome, intense. A peak moment when you can't concentrate on nothin', no problems, just creation. And it's like a family. When Michael Stewart [graffiti artist] was killed by cops, you know he was a graffiti man, we all came out of retirement to mourn him. Even me, I stopped 'cause my girl said it was dangerous. We came out and painted funeral scenes and cemeteries on the #1 and the N [subway lines]. For Michael. We know each other, you know an artist when you see him: It's a family. Belonging. They want me in, not out like at school.

*Carmen pursued the Job Corps when she left school:* You ever try plastering, Michelle? It's great. You see holes in walls. You see a problem and you fix it. Job Corps lost its money when I was in it, in Albany. I had to come home, back to Harlem. I felt better there than ever in my school. Now I do nothin'. It's a shame. Never felt as good as then.

*Monique got pregnant and then dropped out:* I wasn't never good at nothing. In school I felt stupid and older than the rest. But I'm a great mother to Chita. Catholic schools for my baby, and maybe a house in New Jersey.

*Carlos, who left school at age twenty, after a frustrating five years since he and his parents exiled illegally from Mexico hopes to join the military:* I don't want to kill nobody. Just, you know how they advertise, the Marines. I never been one of the Few and the Proud. I'm always 'shamed of myself. So I'd like to try it.

In an uninviting economy, these adolescents responded to the silences transmitted through public schooling by pursuing what they considered to be creative alternatives. But let us understand that for such low-income youths, these alternatives generally *replaced* formal schooling. Creative alternatives for middle-class adolescents, an after-school art class or music lessons, privately afforded by parents, generally *supplement* formal schooling.

Whereas school-imposed silence may be an *initiation* to adulthood for the middle-class adolescent about to embark on a life of participation and agency, school-imposed silence more typically represents the *orientation* to adulthood for the low-income or working-class adolescent about to embark on a life of work at McDonald's, in a factory, as a domestic or clerk, or on Aid to Families with Dependent Children. For the low-income student, the imposed silence of high school cannot be ignored as a necessary means to an end. They are the present *and* they are likely to be the future (Ogbu 1978).

Some teachers, paraprofessionals, and students expressly devoted their time, energy, and classes to exposing silences institutionally imposed. One reading teacher prepared original grammar worksheets, including items such as "Most women in Puerto Rico (is, are) oppressed." A history teacher dramatically presented his autobiography to his class, woven with details on the life of Paul Robeson. An English teacher formed a writers' collective of her multilingual "remedial" writing students. A paraprofessional spoke openly with students who decided not to report the prime suspect in a local murder to the police, but to clergy instead. She recognized that their lives would be in jeopardy, despite "what the administrators who go home to the suburbs preach." But these voices of naming were weak, individual, and isolated.

What if these voices, along with the chorus of dropouts, were allowed expression? If they were not whispered, isolated, or drowned out in disparagement, what would happen if these stories were solicited, celebrated, and woven into a curriculum? What if the history of schooling were written by those high school critics who remained in school and those who dropped out? What if the "dropout problem" were studied in school as a collective critique by consumers of public education?

Dropping out instead is viewed by educators, policy makers, teachers, and often students as an individual act, an expression of incompetence or self-sabotage. As alive, motivated, and critical as they were at age seventeen, most of the interviewed dropouts were silenced, withdrawn, and depressed by age twenty-two. They had tried the private trade schools, been in and out of the military, failed the GED exam once more, had too many children to care for, too many bills to pay, and only self-blaming regrets, seeking private solutions to public problems. Muting by the larger society had ultimately succeeded, even for those who fled initially with resistance, energy, and vision (Apple 1982).

I'll end with an image which occurred throughout the year, repeated across classrooms and across urban public high schools. As familiar as it is haunting, the portrait most dramatically captures the physical embodiment of silencing in the urban schools.

*Field Note: February 16*

Patrice is a young black female, in eleventh grade. She says nothing all day in school. She sits perfectly mute. No need to coerce her into silence. She often wears her coat in class. Sometimes she lays her head on her desk. She never disrupts. Never disobeys. Never speaks. And is never identified as a problem. Is she the student who couldn't develop two voices and so silenced both? Is she so filled with anger, she fears to speak? Or so filled with depression she knows not what to say?

Whose problem is Patrice?

## POSTSCRIPT ON RESEARCH AS EXPOSING

The process of conducting research within schools to identify words that could have been said, talk that should have been nurtured, and information that needed to be announced, suffers from voyeurism and perhaps the worst of post hoc arrogance. The researcher's sadistic pleasure of spotting another teacher's collapsed contradiction, aborted analysis, or silencing sentence was moderated only by the ever-present knowledge that similar analytic surgery could easily be performed on my own classes.

And yet it is the very 'naturalness' of not naming, of shutting down or marginalizing conversations for the 'sake of getting on with learning' that demands educators' attention. Particularly so for low-income youths highly ambivalent about the worth of a diploma, desperately desirous of and at the same time discouraged from its achievement.

If the process of education is to allow children, adolescents, and adults their voices—to read, write, create, critique, and transform—how can we justify the institutionalizing of silence at the level of policies which obscure systemic problems behind a rhetoric of "excellence" and "progress," a curriculum bereft of the lived experiences of students themselves, a pedagogy organized around control and not conversation, and a thoroughgoing psychologizing of social issues which enables Patrice to bury herself in silence and not be noticed?

A self-critical analysis of the fundamental ways in which we teach children to betray their own voices is crucial.

## REFERENCES

Advocates for Children. *Report of the New York Hearings on the Crisis in Public Education.* New York, 1985.

Anyon, J. "Intersections of Gender and Class: Accommodation and Resistance by Working Class and Affluent Females to Contradictory Sex Role Ideologies." In *Gender, Class and Education,* edited by S. Walker and L. Barton. London: Falmer Press.

Anyon, J. "School Curriculum: Political and Economic Structure and Social Change." *Social Practice,* (1980): 96–108.

Apple, M. *Cultural and Economic Reproduction in Education.* Boston: Routledge & Kegan Paul, 1982.

Aronowitz, S., & Giroux, H. *Education under Siege.* South Hadley, Massachusetts: Bergin & Garvey, Inc., 1985.

Aspira, *Racial and Ethnic High School Dropout Rates in New York City: A Summary Report.* New York, New York, 1983.

Bastian, A., Fruchter, N., Gittell, M., Greer, C., and Haskins, K. "Choosing Equality: The Case for Democratic Schooling." *Social Policy,* (1985): 35–51.

Carnegie Forum on Education and the Economy. *A Nation Prepared: Teachers for the 21st Century.* New York: Carnegie Foundation, 1986.

Carnoy, M., & Levin, H. *Schooling and Work in the Democratic State.* Stanford: Stanford University Press, 1985.

Connell, R., Ashenden, D., Kessler, S., & Dawsett, G. *Making the Difference.* Sydney, Australia: George Allen & Unwin, 1982.

Cummins, J. "Empowering Minority Students: A Framework for Intervention." *Harvard Education Review,* 56 (1986).

Elliott, D., Voss, H., & Wendling, A. "Capable Dropouts and the Social Milieu of High School." *Journal of Educational Research,* 60 (1966): 180–186.

Felice, L. "Black Student Dropout Behaviors: Disengagement from School Rejection and Racial Discrimination." *Journal of Negro Education,* 50 (1981): 415–424.

Fine, M. "Perspectives on Inequity: Voices from Urban Schools." In *Applied Social Psychology Annual IV,* edited by L. Bickman. Beverly Hills: Sage, 1983.

Fine, M. "Dropping out of High School: An Inside Look." *Social Policy,* (1985): 43–50.

Fine, M. "Why Urban Adolescents Drop into and out of Public High School." *Teachers College Record,* 87 (1986).

Fine, M., & Rosenberg, P. "Dropping Out of High School: The Ideology of School and Work." *Journal of Education,* 165 (1983): 257–272.

Freire, P. *The Politics of Education.* South Hadley, Massachusetts: Bergin & Garvey Publishers, 1985.

Goodlad, J. *A Place called School: Prospects for the Future.* New York: McGraw Hill, 1984.

Gramsci, A. *Selections from Prison Notebooks.* New York: International, 1971.

Holmes Group. *Tomorrow's Teachers.* East Lansing, Michigan, 1986.

Lightfoot, S. *Worlds Apart.* New York. Basic Books, 1978.

McNeil, L. "Negotiating Classroom Knowledge: Beyond Achievement and Socialization." *Curriculum Studies,* 13 (1981): 313–328.

Militarism Resource Project. *High School Military Recruiting: Recent Developments.* Philadelphia, PA, 1985.

New York State Department of Education. Memo from Dennis Hughes, State Administrator on High School Equivalency Programs. December 4, 1985. Albany, NY.

Ogbu, J. *Minority Education and Caste: The American System in Cross-cultural Perspective.* New York: Academic Press, 1978.

Rich, A. *On Lies, Secrets and Silence.* New York. Norton Books, 1979.

Shor, I. *Critical Teaching and Everyday Life.* Boston: South End Press, 1980.

Sizer, T. *Horaces Compromise: The Dilemma of the American High School.* Boston: Houghton Mifflin, 1985.

Tobier, E. *The Changing Face of Poverty: Trends in New York City's Population in Poverty, 1960–1990.* New York, New York: Community Service Society, 1984.

U.S. Commission on Civil Rights. *Unemployment and Underemployment among Blacks, Hispanics and Women.* Washington, D.C., 1982.

U.S. Department of Labor. *Time of Change: 1983 Handbook of Women Workers.* Washington, D.C., 1983.

Wexler, P. *Critical Social Psychology.* Boston: Routledge & Kegan Paul, 1983.

Young, A. Youth Labor Force Marked Turning Point in 1982. U.S. Department of Labor. Bureau of Labor Statistics, Washington, DC., 1983.

Zorn, J. "Black English and the King Decision." *College English,* 44 (1982).

# It Begins at the Beginning

## Deborah Tannen

### EDITOR'S INTRODUCTION

Analyzing everyday conversations and investigating their effects on relationships has been the focus of Deborah Tannen's work as a sociolinguist. In *You Just Don't Understand,* she explores the ways conversation patterns for men and women develop differently, making conversation between the genders often seem like cross-cultural communication. This brief excerpt serves as an introduction to Tannen's influential work.

Even if they grow up in the same neighborhood, on the same block, or in the same house, girls and boys grow up in different worlds of words. Others talk to them differently and expect and accept different ways of talking from them. Most important, children learn how to talk, how to have conversations, not only from their parents but from their peers. After all, if their parents have a foreign or regional accent, children do not emulate it; they learn to speak with the pronunciation of the region where they grow up. Anthropologists Daniel Maltz and Ruth Borker summarize research showing that boys and girls have very different ways of talking to their friends. Although they often play together, boys and girls spend most of their time playing in same-sex groups. And, although some of the activities they play at are similar, their favorite games are different, and their ways of using language in their games are separated by a world of difference.

Boys tend to play outside, in large groups that are hierarchically structured. Their groups have a leader who tells others what to do and how to do it, and resists doing what other boys propose. It is by giving orders and making them stick that high status is negotiated. Another way boys achieve status is to take center stage by telling stories and jokes, and by sidetracking or challenging the stories and jokes of others. Boys' games have winners and losers and elaborate systems of rules that are frequently the subjects of arguments. Finally, boys are frequently heard to boast of their skill and argue about who is best at what.

Girls, on the other hand, play in small groups or in pairs; the center of a girl's social life is a best friend. Within the group, intimacy is key: Differentiation is measured by relative closeness. In their most frequent games, such as jump rope and hopscotch, Nick and Sue tried to get what they wanted by involving a third child; the alignments they created with the third child, and the dynamics they set in motion, were fundamentally different. Sue appealed to Mary to fulfill someone else's desire; rather than

*Source:* Excerpt from *You Just Don't Understand* (pp. 43–47) by Deborah Tannen, 1990. New York: William Morrow and Company. Copyright 1990 by Deborah Tannen, Ph.D. Used by permission of William Morrow & Company, Inc.

saying that *she* wanted the pickle, she claimed that Lisa wanted it. Nick asserted his own desire for the pickle, and when he couldn't get it on his own, he appealed to Joe to get it for him. Joe then tried to get the pickle by force. In both these scenarios, the children were enacting complex lines of affiliation.

Joe's strong-arm tactics were undertaken not on his own behalf, but chivalrously, on behalf of Nick. By making an appeal in a whining voice, Nick positioned himself as one-down in a hierarchical structure, framing himself as someone in need of protection. When Sue appealed to Mary to relinquish her pickle, she wanted to take the one-up position of serving food. She was fighting not for the right to *have* the pickle, but for the right to *serve* it. (This reminded me of the women who said they'd become professors in order to teach.) But to accomplish her goal, Sue was depending on Mary's desire to fulfill others' needs.

This study suggests that boys and girls both want to get their way, but they tend to do so differently. Though social norms encourage boys to be openly competitive and girls to be openly cooperative, different situations and activities can result in different ways of behaving. Marjorie Harness Goodwin compared boys and girls engaged in two task-oriented activities: The boys were making slingshots in preparation for a fight, and the girls were making rings. She found that the boys' group was hierarchical: The leader told the others what to do and how to do it. The girls' group was egalitarian: Everyone made suggestions and tended to accept the suggestions of others. But observing the girls in a different activity—playing house—Goodwin found that they too adopted hierarchical structures:

The girls who played mothers issued orders to the girls playing children, who in turn sought permission from their play-mothers. Moreover, a girl who was a play-mother was also a kind of manager of the game. This study shows that girls know how to issue orders and operate in a hierarchical structure, but they don't find that mode of behavior appropriate when they engage in task activities with their peers. They do find it appropriate in parent-child relationships, which they enjoy practicing in the form of play.

These worlds of play shed light on the world views of women and men in relationships. The boys' play illuminates why men would be on the lookout for signs they are being put down or told what to do. The chief commodity that is bartered in the boys' hierarchical world is status, and the way to achieve and maintain status is to give orders and get others to follow them. A boy in a low-status position finds himself being pushed around. So boys monitor their relations for subtle shifts in status by keeping track of who's giving orders and who's taking them.

These dynamics are not the ones that drive girls' play. The chief commodity that is bartered in the girls' community is intimacy. Girls monitor their friendships for subtle shifts in alliance, and they seek to be friends with popular girls. Popularity is a kind of status, but it is founded on connection. It also places popular girls in a bind. By doing field work in a junior high school, Donna Eder found that popular girls were paradoxically—and inevitably—disliked. Many girls want to befriend popular girls, but girls' friendships must necessarily be limited, since they entail intimacy rather than large group activities. So a popular girl must reject the overtures of most of the girls who seek her out—with the result that she is branded "stuck up."

# A Love of Language, a Love of Research, and a Love of Teaching: A Conversation with Deborah Tannen

## Ruth Shagoury Hubbard

Deborah Tannen has brought her original and complex analyses of language to a wider public, helping spark national debates about communication—and miscommunication—between the sexes, cross-culturally, in the workplace, and in the home. University Professor and Professor of Linguistics at Georgetown University, Dr. Tannen is the author of *That's Not What I Meant!: How Conversational Style Makes or Breaks Relationships; You Just Don't Understand: Women and Men in Conversation;* and, most recently, *Talking from 9 to 5: How Women's and Men's Conversational Styles Affect Who Gets Heard, Who Gets Credit, and What Gets Done at Work,* as well as many other articles and scholarly books.

In our conversation, Deborah Tannen shared how her love of language merges into all her work, from her teaching to her research, to the many kinds of writing that fill her life. Besides her nonfiction work, Tannen is a poet and playwright currently putting the final touches on a new play which will be produced this spring in Washington, D.C.

At the core of her rich life is her teaching, which she emphasized to me is her foundation and her mooring. Her profound respect for her students shines through in this interview, providing inspiration for all of us as we sort out the complicated conversation patterns in our classrooms.

*Ruth Hubbard: Could you begin by sharing a little about what got you started studying language?*

*Deborah Tannen:* There are always so many different possible answers to a question like that, and they would all be true. I would have to say that I have always been a lover of language, fascinated by language. I think that's true of a lot of people. I wrote from the time I was very young; at 6 or 7, I was already writing stories and poems at home.

*RH: Was that encouraged by your family?*

*DT:* I think they were indifferent. My father encouraged me to read, but I don't recall being urged to write. They were very impressed and supportive when I did it, but I don't think it was especially encouraged. My parents were born in Europe. My mother graduated from high school and that's all. My father is a lawyer, but never graduated from high school. You could do it back then. He came to this country when he was 12 and he had no father; he had a mother and a sister and as soon as he was able to go to work and support them, he did. He quit high school after one year and went to work full time to support the family—while constantly dodging the truant officer. But he was very smart. He took high school equivalency tests and went right into law school, which you could do at the time. He went to St. John's Law School at night. It was designed for this kind of student. So, he held down a full time job, went to law school, and got both a law degree and a master's degree in law.

*RH: So, your parents spoke English as a first language?*

*DT:* No, my father was born in Poland and grew up speaking Polish and Yiddish and my mother was born in Russia and grew up speaking Yiddish. They were apparently speaking fluent English in six months or so.

*RH: Certainly, a facility with languages is in your family.*

*DT:* Yes, my father had an aptitude for language, definitely. An interest in language, a love of language, an aptitude for it. I suppose I could say I picked it up from him. I always remember him reading and commenting on how people spoke and using "big" words.

*RH: Did you grow up speaking or understanding either Polish or Yiddish?*

*DT:* No.

*RH: It's kind of sad, isn't it?*

*DT:* I think so, and I gave my parents a real argument at one point. They said, "Well, who thought about it?"

*RH: It's sad to me, too. My dad is Syrian and English is a second language for him, but I never learned to speak Arabic, and it was never encouraged for us. And I feel sort of cheated for not having that background.*

*DT:* I feel the same way. I suppose our parents were part of the same era when immigrants wanted to become Americans and didn't think of the native language as anything really necessary. So, that was that.

*RH: Did you start right out in college knowing that you were going to major in linguistics or study language?*

*DT:* I came to linguistics late. I was almost 30 when I went back to graduate school. But English was always my love. I got a B.A. in English literature and then I went off and lived in Greece for a couple of years, and I think that had a lot to do with my interest in cross-cultural communication.

*RH: I think your love of literature comes through in the way you write: You write like a novelist, and there are so many stories within, and also the wonderful references that you make to short stories and to novels.*

*DT:* Which some people love and some people are irritated by. I do think that the fact that I studied literature and write fiction and poetry myself probably does come through.

*RH: So, before you went back to school, were you teaching?*

*DT:* Yes, I went to Greece where I taught English as a second language. I taught ESL in Greece for about a year and a half. Then I came back to the States, got a masters in English at Wayne State, and taught ESL there while working on my masters. Then I got a job at Mercer County Community College in Trenton, NJ, which I had for a year. I taught ESL there because by this time I was an experienced ESL teacher and nobody else had much experience at that time. I even developed an ESL program for them. Then I got a job at Lehman College of the City in New York, where I taught remedial writing for three years. After a summer linguistic institute in 1973, I decided to study linguistics. I went to Berkeley, where I got a Ph.D. in linguistics, and supported myself by teaching ESL at Berkeley.

*RH: You have a pretty strong background in teaching English as a second language. It sounds like teaching is an important part of your life.*

*DT:* I love teaching. That's the simple answer. It's also my foundation, my mooring. I miss it when I don't teach. In fact, I have had quite a bit of leave in the last few years. Right after the publication of *You Just Don't Understand,* of course, my whole life turned upside down. And I had a year and a half where I didn't teach, and I really missed it. I never feel that I do very well when I'm not teaching. This term, I will be teaching my two courses in linguistics.

*RH: Do you find that you are able to merge your life and your research interests into your classroom work?*

*DT:* Yes, I always do. When I did the research on gender, it made me look at my classroom differently. One class I taught was in analyzing conversation, so it was natural to turn the classroom into a lab. I had the class break down into small groups, which I often did, but I had the added element that I varied the groups according to conversational style and gender and then had them look at their interaction in the various groups and take field notes on it. It was fascinating. And the results were very enlightening for me and the students. It was back and forth between the teaching and the research, then going back to the classroom and doing more research.

*RH:* Which ends up really enriching your teaching, and when your students are involved in it with you, it invites them to try on the lenses of researchers, too.

*DT:* Yes, and I always try to do that. It's a natural because I teach analyzing talk and what we do in class is talk. So, it is a natural thing for the class talk to be the object of analysis also.

*RH:* Do you have any advice for some of the beginning teacher researchers who are just starting to analyze the language in their classrooms? What are some of the things that would help them get started?

*DT:* I think tape recording is a very helpful aid, if they feel comfortable and if their students feel comfortable. I think it's important to involve the students as researchers as well. And it's important to keeping running field notes. I would emphasize note-taking and tape recording, because if you just try to notice what's going on, and write it down later, you're apt to miss a lot. I'd invite the students to be observers and keep running field notes of observations about classroom interactions. Sometimes students are in a better position to notice things—for example, someone's hand is up and hasn't been called on. Whose topics become the basis for further discussion? Whose questions are answered more fully?

The question of what you're actually going to look at is a vexing one, because there's always so much one could look at. I tell my students you can start by looking for things that trouble you because they don't sit right and you think there's a problem, or you can start by trying to understand things that really go well. You might think, "This was just a great moment; this was a wonderful conversation we were having here." You could look at that and see what it was that made it so great.

*RH: So, either a tension or something that you know is working well, but you don't know why.*

*DT:* You can always, too, think about something you've read and test that in your own classroom. I know there's so much work done now about gender equity in the classroom. You could look at your own speaking patterns in the classroom along those lines. But it's very important not to become simple-minded about this. I get discouraged when I see people do things like just count features or words.

*RH: Right. As your research has shown, if you just count interruptions, that's not going to really tell you what kind of interruptions, or if they are interruptions that people are comfortable with.*

*DT:* Exactly. So, even if you count something, you need to look at it closely and ask what's being done here. What's the intent and what's the effect?

*RH: As I was reading your most recent book,* Talking from 9 to 5, *I kept thinking of your workplace findings in terms of the group work that so many of us do in our classrooms, and how maybe some of the same problems with negotiation are going on. It seems a more in-depth look at the impact gendered conversation styles might be having in schools could be helpful. Much more than just the straight counting.*

*DT:* Yes, I think that in many ways a classroom is a lot like a workplace, from the perspective that you're being judged. This is one of the key things that came out when I was looking at the workplace as compared to private conversation. The same thing goes for a classroom. On the one hand, you say things in class—both the teacher and the students—because you want the information out, but you're also going to be evaluated. Anything you say becomes the basis for judging you.

*RH: And there's certainly the same hierarchy with the teachers having so much power.*

*DT:* Anthropologists write about the participant structure which reflects the hierarchy. In schools, the teacher is the person who determines who speaks when—and often, physically, the teacher is up at the front, and the students look up at the teacher. All kinds of things like that. And there are hierarchies among the students, of course—the high-status kids and the low-status kids. A lot of which the teachers don't even know about.

Also, the organization of the classroom is really closer to the participant structure of boys' social groups than girls' because girls tend to talk one on one or in small groups. The boys' groups tend to be larger, and self-display is expected of boys so that they can get high status in the group. This is a lot closer to what they are usually expected to do in classrooms: show what they are good at and know, take center stage—all things that girls are resistant to do in the girls' social group, because maybe the other girls won't like them: "She's bossy. Who does she think she is?"

*RH: Do you think of any other suggestions for teacher-researchers?*

*DT:* I want to stress again that students really enjoy taping and transcribing. Transcribing makes you listen in a new way. I think the power of narrative is very useful. Kids are already very skilled at telling stories and that is something they can do—transcribe stories that are told in conversation and compare them to written stories and discover their structure. I'd also stress again the power of keeping field notes, which encourages people to be researchers.

*RH: And having that written record helps you see patterns you wouldn't see otherwise.*

*DT:* I think so, and also keeping a written record allows you to see how much you've learned: what you didn't know last week and you do know this week. It can feel like you always knew what you know now.

*RH: Can you name some of the linguists or researchers or writers who have been important to you?*

*DT:* Well, in the field, it would be three people I worked with at Berkeley: Robin Lakoff, Wallace Chafe, and John Gumperz. I also mention often Alton Becker—he's a professor emeritus at Michigan, a linguist. I got into linguistics that first summer in 1973 at the Linguistic Institute and I was lucky; I had Introduction to Linguistics with him. I managed to stay in touch with him for the rest of my career and now I count him as one of my closest friends. His approach to linguistics is very humanistic, and he writes about the aesthetics of language. He's quite anthropological, and has really helped me very much.

*RH: His approach has clearly had an effect on you.*

*DT:* Yes, first it resonated with interests that were there, but having his support has been very important. In addition, as colleagues, Fred Erickson and Shirley Brice Heath, whose work I respect enormously.

*RH: What's next for you in your research?*

*DT:* Believe it or not, what I'm actually doing right now is writing plays.

*RH: That seems like a perfect tie-in: dialogue, conversation . . .*

*DT:* Right. I'll need to finish the play I'm working on now very soon. Actually, I've written a first and a second draft and it's in the hands of the director. The play will be produced in the spring.

*RH: What's it about?*

*DT:* Well, it's about my family. Last fall, I had written a short play that was about my father and his childhood in Poland and the trip we made together to Poland. This spring they decided to give it a full production, but requested a second one to go with it. So, I wrote another one that leads up to the trip to Poland that I made with my father. I'm trying to get away from the completely autobiographical approach, but it is still largely based on my experiences. I guess it's about the sense in which parents are often completely different parents to each child. Although each child is born into the same family, it's quite a different family for each one. The play also explores each of our relationships to Judaism. That's what I've been doing most recently.

*RH: What a change for you, but how much fun it must have been!*

DT: I love it, yes. Of course, the last big project was *Talking from 9 to 5,* which I finished pretty recently. I'm not yet sure what my next big project will be.

*RH: There is certainly a lot of current debate around the issues of language standards and the place of different languages, cultures, and dialects in the classroom. What do you believe teachers need to know or do in terms of these issues in their classrooms?*

DT: That is so complicated. Of course, as a sociolinguist, I'm inclined to say all language is a dialect, makes sense, and serves a purpose. I'm aware of the history of this particular conflict. There was a movement, perhaps largely sparked by sociolinguists, that defended certain dialects: One example would be Black English, as it was then called, the language of African-Americans in cities. Teachers were told that they should understand the structure of the language that the kids were using and that they would likely even learn better if they were taught in their own language. And I know that that was interpreted by many African-American parents as, "You're trying to hold my kids back." "You wouldn't let your kids talk that way; how come it's all right for my kids?" So, I know that all these things are very complicated. I suppose realistically, one has to accept what those black parents were getting at: If a certain "standard English" is what is expected for advancement in the world, and you want schools to give kids the best chance, then ideally, they should give kids the tools to speak standard English.

But it's hard to say to kids, "Well, it's really okay for you to talk as you do, only I'm going to teach you a different way for different situations." They hear it as, "It's not okay." As I say, I think it's pretty complicated.

*RH: Any suggestions for teachers to help them deal with it better?*

DT: I would hope that teachers would not speak in terms of right and wrong. There's certainly no point in telling kids the way they are speaking is "wrong" when they know this is an effective way to speak. I think awareness would certainly be helpful. Robin Lakoff has commented that Oprah Winfrey, for example, uses vernacular Black English very effectively. She switches into it. She'll be speaking a variation of standard English, then slip in expressions in Black English, and it's very effective. So, maybe that's another way that kids could be researchers—watch Oprah, and notice how she does that.

*RH: And, I suppose, notice how they do it themselves, that we all speak differently in different situations and to different people.*

DT: So, maybe the general principle that I think everybody would recognize is that you don't talk the same way to everybody just as you don't dress the same way in every situation. It would be useful to think of it in those terms rather than this is the right way, this is the wrong way. Also, I hope that teachers would always speak to children with respect, and respect their ways of speaking as well as everything else about their cultures.

# Teacher Research Extension: "I'm Not Sittin' by No Girl!"

## Jill Ostrow
## Grades 1–3 Multiage Teacher

"I'm not sittin' by no girl!" whined Austin on the first day of school. He was a fourth grader joining our newly formed grades 4–6 multiage class. The majority of this class were students that were in my grades 1–3 multiage classes in previous years. Some of these students had been with me since first grade. But this upper elementary multiage class was a unique experience for all of us—part of a brand new program. How incredibly wonderful it was to have a group of older students, most of whom I knew and had taught in the past!

The majority of these kids knew me well. They knew how the room worked, and were comfortable and familiar with the way it was set up. The new students seemed excited by the classroom environment. They were elated with the couches set prominently in the middle of the room, and with the wooden tables instead of desks.

The kids who had worked with me before took for granted the freedom of movement around the room. There are no seating charts; the kids make their own choices as to where to sit. At times I will put them into groups; at other times they are free to choose their own. They assume that they will have experience working with all the students in our class community because they know that the foundation of our classroom is the idea of community and respect.

On that first day, the kids came in and sat on the couches; that's how we've always begun our school day. There were the usual comments about the uniqueness of our classroom; I was expecting these, but I was not expecting Austin's loud protest. It caught me off guard. Still, I knew I could sit back and let the other kids who have been a part of our community challenge his words.

"Austin, just let her sit there. It doesn't matter—geez!" was Dave's frustrated response to his comment. Kyle rolled his eyes at Austin and shook his head at me and said under his breath, "I can't believe he just said that" Carly, a girl in the class, looked hurt by such a comment, and Tiffany giggled that a girl would want to sit by a boy.

*Source:* Ostrow, Jill "I'm Not Sittin' by No Girl," from *We Want to Be Known: Learning from Adolescent Girls,* (Hubbard, Barbieri, and Power, eds.) pp. 45–52. Copyright 1998 by Stenhouse Publishers: Portland, ME. Reprinted with permission.

I began to wonder how there could be such a contrast between these students. What would make one boy move away from a girl and another one not even notice? Did it have to do with what went on in their homes, or was it more complicated than that?

This was a pretty homogeneous group. The cultural differences and socioeconomic levels of the families varied only slightly, 98 percent were middle-class white suburban children. Why then were their experiences with gender in the classroom so different? We were considered an "alternative" to the traditional classroom. The sixth graders were not attending the middle school; they were spending the year in a self-contained multiage class. The parents of these students were all fairly progressive educational thinkers who chose to place their children in my class.

When I shared Austin's response with a friend, she said, "Oh, welcome to fourth-grade boys! It's just normal." Normal? Is it normal to be rude and disrespectful to girls just because you're a fourth-grade boy? I have heard comments like this ever since I was in college working toward my teaching degree over sixteen years ago: girls and boys dislike each other when they reach a certain age; they aren't interested in each other. I can accept the fact that boys and girls typically go their separate ways for some years during their development, but should rudeness and disrespect be accepted as normal?

What if Austin had said, "I'm not sitting next to no black kid!"? Would that be acceptable? After all, Austin lives in an all white neighborhood; he doesn't have any exposure in his immediate outside world with African Americans. Would it be "normal" that because of his age and lack of experience it should be accepted that he be a little racist? No, of course not. Why then is it so readily accepted in classrooms to let negative comments slide by as "normal" when they deal with gender?

"Oh, it's just the age," is a comment I detest. It's an excuse to accept behaviors and attitudes without confronting them. There are physical characteristics that go along with age, and so certain stages of development are anticipated and expected. For instance, this year I made sure I had a package of sanitary pads in a cabinet just in case one of my sixth-grade girls began menstruating. Physical changes occur in girls at or around sixth grade. Having your period isn't an attitude; it isn't a learned behavior. I believe it is wrong to say that when boys are rude, it is normal and healthy and should be expected and left alone.

Children should be given choices. If a boy wants to play with his boy friends, he should be free to do so. But I think there is a danger in allowing boys and girls to get away with statements like, "I'm not letting her play, she's a girl!" I remember watching a play-ground supervisor accept such a comment from a group of boys playing soccer in the field. Yet when a group of girls were excluding another girl from playing with them, the super-visor told the group they weren't being very nice and should include the lone girl. The very comment "no, she's a girl" was acceptable for excluding a girl from a boys' play group.

I can't speak for Austin's experience in school before fourth grade because that was his first year with me. But I have been in classrooms where comments about gender have been tossed aside as "normal" or acceptable. It was the students who had been with me that spoke in protest to his comment. I don't think this was a coincidence. I believe children's attitudes stem from their history in their school community.

The students who had been a part of our community were accustomed to openness when talking about equality and diversity. Learning about diversity wasn't something we did in November as a theme; it was a constant and continual discussion interwoven with all that we did. When we talk about another culture we don't just learn what foods people eat or what clothes they wear. I try to have the children imagine what it is like to be in a minority group. I ask them to imagine how it feels to be disliked because you have the "wrong" color skin or the "wrong" religion. If kids can begin to imagine what it is like for someone else, it opens the door for empathy and understanding.

Many schools now make multiculturalism a part of their curriculums. Learning about different cultures and diversity is important, but so is learning about racism, religious freedom, and gender inequalities.

A few years ago, my 1–3 multiage class was studying the 1940s and World War II. The kids were learning about the injustices of the war in Europe and how Jews, Gypsies, and other minority groups were being terribly persecuted, especially in Germany. We didn't just discuss why that was wrong, but tried to imagine what life must have been like for those people and talked about other groups of individuals who have been persecuted, in the past and today. After our studies, the students were asked to begin a project in which they were to hide a family in Europe—either Jewish or Gypsy; they decided they also wanted to hide a Japanese American family in this country.

"Jill, our family is going to be called Nomo. They're Japanese Americans and we want to hide them from going to the internment camps. Is that okay?" asked Kyle. I was fascinated by the connection he was making. I stopped the class as they were working in their groups and called them over to the couches.

"Kyle, can you share your family with everyone?" I asked.

"Yeah, sure. We're hiding a Japanese American family instead," he began.

"Were there Japanese Americans in Europe?" interrupted Mark.

"No," Kyle laughed, "But, we want to hide one so they won't have to go to one of the internment camps."

"Did American people hide Japanese Americans?" Chris asked.

"I don't think so, Chris. I've never read anything about it," I answered.

"How come?" And so began a conversation about why certain groups were helped and protected and others weren't. They had associated the persecution of Japanese Americans in this country with the Jews in Europe—a sophisticated link for young children to make. Making connections between minority groups in elementary, middle, and high schools is crucial. And gender connections fit right in.

Emil, who came to our class as a new second grader, had trouble accepting girls as part of his daily school life. After one group experience where he refused to work with Caitlin because she was a girl, I decided to bring up the incident not as a gender issue but as a community problem.

"How did your groups do this morning? Who wants to share first? Caitlin?" I asked.

"Well, we couldn't get anything done because Emil wouldn't help do anything," Caitlin shared.

"Uh-oh, what happens when not everyone in a group helps out?" I asked the class.

"The work won't get done!" chanted the entire class.

"Can anyone explain to Emil why it is important that he help out?" I asked.

"Emil, if you don't help out, the stuff you want to get done won't get done," Ross chimed in.

"Plus," said Megan, "It isn't fair that Caitlin do all the work herself."

"Emil, do you hear what Ross and Megan are telling you?" I asked him.

"Yeah," he said, looking down.

"Can you give Emil some advice as to how he can help out more and can you also give Caitlin some advice as to how she can help Emil so she doesn't get so frustrated?" I asked the class.

"Emil, just do what you need to do. Ask Caitlin questions if you forget. And, Caitlin, if I were you, I'd just do my half and then give the rest to Emil and don't worry about it. Don't do all of it," Kyle offered.

"Emil, do you want to add anything?" I asked him.

"Sorry, Caitlin, I'll work more better, but you need to let me do some of it too," he said to Caitlin.

"You just won't work because I'm a girl and it isn't fair!" Caitlin said angrily.

"Is that true, Emil?" I questioned.

"Man, Emil, that isn't very good for the community. How do you think the world would work if the boys didn't help the girls? It doesn't matter if you work with a girl or not. You just need to work and help," Kyle told him.

"Emil, what is it about working with a girl that makes it hard to work? Is it just hard to work with Caitlin, or all girls?" Megan asked him.

"I don't know," he said.

"Maybe you should think about Megan's question, Emil," I said, and then went on and let someone else share. He did begin to think about his behavior because we challenged it. He saw that the other kids in the class were not only confused but frustrated with his reaction to working with Caitlin. Throughout the year, as he had more experience with working in our community, his negative attitudes about girls began to lessen.

I made a conscious decision to talk about this with the class as opposed to pulling Emil off to the side and discussing it with him. Gender issues are not individual problems; they are cultural issues that affect the classroom community and should be discussed openly in the community.

After the incident this year when Austin commented about sitting next to a girl, I asked the class during our morning meeting, "If an African American child came and sat down next to you right now would you get up and move away?"

"*No!* Man, Jill, that would be sick!" said Dave. Most reactions were similar to his.

"Okay, what about someone who is Jewish?" More nos.

"What about someone who is Chinese? Someone who is blind? Someone who is younger than you?" The kids looked disgusted and confused by my questions. Good. That's what I wanted. "Why then, do you think it's okay to get up and move away from a girl or a boy?" Stunned faces. Silence. They couldn't answer because there was no answer.

"Tell me, what's the difference? Why is it wrong to yell comments about a person's color or religion at them, but it's okay to make nasty comments about a person's gender?" I knew that bluntness was what was needed. Instead of avoiding the issue, I went head on into it and the result was worth it. The new kids began to realize that we were more than just a class of boys and girls; we were a community who, in order to function as one, needed to be respectful of each other.

I have some guiding principles that I bring to the classroom to help my children confront gender issues.

First, I discuss issues openly and treat comments about gender with importance. I don't accept being disrespectful to those of the other gender in our class, no matter what the age of the student. I consider gender issues to be social issues of our classroom community that must be addressed as a whole group.

Second, we discuss issues and comments that come up as a group, and I don't pull children aside. No matter what grade level I teach, open discussion has become imperative for building a respectful community.

Third, I don't call on students, but allow children to share their own work. The emphasis is on the work and on equal sharing of work and responsibility. Research says that teachers call on boys more often than girls during math classes. I don't put myself in the position of needing to choose either a boy or a girl to call on. My room just isn't set up that way. The class is responsible for ensuring everyone has equal time in sharing their ideas together.

It's important that children be responsible for their comments early on in school. The reason why fourth-grader Kyle was so frustrated with Austin's lack of respect for girls is because he has been discussing gender inequalities ever since first grade.

Austin's attitude toward girls changed dramatically over the year. He came to be much more respectful of who a person is, not what a person is. A parent who had helped out in our classroom shared a story with me about how Austin came to the defense of her daughter.

"It was Becca's birthday and Carl, Austin's younger brother, was making a huge scene because he had to share a seat belt with her. She felt horrible. Austin stepped in and told Carl to move over and be quiet. He then told Becca he'd share a seat belt with her. It was so wonderful. What a change."

Austin was still a fourth-grade boy when that incident happened. He hadn't outgrown his old attitude toward girls—he had outlearned it through working in our classroom community. It's not an age thing; it's a respect thing.

# Yada-Yada-Yada: The Babbling Period Between Four and Eight Months of Age

**Roberta Michnick Golinkoff and Kathy Hirsh-Pasek**

## EDITOR'S INTRODUCTION

Why do babies babble in the first place? In this fascinating article, the authors explore the link between babbling and later speech. They argue that babbling is not just play; it helps babies practice forming the sounds of their own language, modulating the volume, rhythms, and intonation. Much of our success in communicating with each other rests on our manipulation of these variables.

## BABIES DO BABBLE

Heidi, a six-month-old baby, is lying on her back in her crib, having been put down for a nap by her father. She holds her little hands up in the air and forms little gestures with them as she laughs quietly to herself. In another few minutes, Heidi is asleep.

Rachel, also a six-month-old, has also just been put down for her nap. She rolls over onto her back and makes little noises like "babababababa" and "nuhnuhnuh-nuh" until she drifts off to sleep.

What do these babies have in common? On the surface, it looks like their age, sex, and circumstance—that is, they're both awaiting the arrival of the sandman. But Heidi is a deaf child who has been born to parents who are also profoundly deaf and who speak in sign language. Rachel is a hearing child who was born to hearing parents who talk to her almost incessantly when she is awake, although they don't really expect her to reply in kind. For Rachel's parents, even a burp from Rachel is an acceptable conversational contribution.

What these babies have in common is that they are both babbling. You have no trouble believing that about Rachel—

after all, she is producing the usual combinations of meaningless vocalizations associated with babbling. But Heidi? How can she be said to be babbling? Dr. Laura Pettito of McGill University in Montreal has some fascinating research on babies born to deaf and hearing parents. Although all babies move their hands (and feet) in novel ways, only the infants of deaf parents use their hands in ways that approximate the sign language of the deaf. Just as hearing babies produce vocalizations that sound like language but are meaningless, deaf babies produce hand shapes that look like sign language but convey no meaning. Dr. Pettito's results suggest that language is almost irrepressible in the human species. Language seems to burst forth through any available avenue.

In this chapter, we look at babies' burgeoning language skills. They didn't say much in the first three months, but that is about to change. Between four and eight months, we

*Source:* "Yada-Yada-Yada: The Babbling Period Between Four and Eight Months of Age" In *How Babies Talk: The Magic and Mystery of Language in the First Three Years of Life.* Roberta Michnick Golinkoff and Kathy Hirsh-Pasek, 1999, Dutton.

can chart the typical course of sound making that babies go through before they say their first word. Not surprisingly, the change in the baby's abilities to produce sounds is tied to biological changes in her sound-producing apparatus: This partly answers the implicit question that many may have had when reading about babies in the first three months: If babies are so capable, why don't they talk sooner? Researchers have found that the infant vocal tract is not simply a miniature version of an adult's. Rather, it resembles the vocal tract of nonhuman primates. This prevents babies from using the mouth as an instrument in the ways necessary for speech. Not until the end of the first year of life, when the oral cavity has lengthened and expanded, are babies able to produce language sounds.

After looking at the early precursors of language production through babbling, we go on to ask just what babies are hearing. Even if they can't talk to us, we do a superb job of talking to them! How do we talk to them and what do they hear from our chatter? This chapter goes beyond the young children's meager productions to their comprehension of language in the world around them. Do babies understand what we say? A wonderful Gary Larson cartoon suggests one answer. A dog owner might say: "Okay, Ginger, I've had it! You stay out of the garbage! Understand, Ginger?" *What the dog hears* might be more like this: "blah, blah Ginger blah blah blah blah blah blah blah blah blah blah blah Ginger." Does this cartoon capture the human experience as well?

One thing is for sure: Most middle-class American parents talk to their babies all the time. Babies don't have to say a single word for parents to take every opportunity to share gobs of useless information with them. Listen in for a moment as Rachel's mother comments on her newfound interest in the thermometer that hangs outside the kitchen door:

Ooooooooooh, Rachel found the thermometer. Yes, that tells Mommy how hot or cold it is outside so I know how to dress Rachel. Does Rachel want to go outside later? Well, when that little arrow goes above thirty-two degrees, we can go out. Would you like that, Rachel?

As Rachel's mother does, we all talk in a very different way to our babies (and to our pets) than to our friends and acquaintances. We talk in a high-pitched, singsong way that seems to grab the infant's attention. This "baby talk" is not only used by hearing parents, but by deaf parents who use sign language as well. We'll look more closely at how we talk to our children and how we modify our speech in this chapter.

But is all this talk useless? Do babies hear only strings of sounds in a stream of speech? Do they just hear blah blah blah? In this chapter, we'll discover that babies listen carefully and figure out things about their native language's unique properties. They are analyzing and comparing adult language in ways that are preparing them for their dramatic entrance into language. Rachel and Heidi are like little scientists, using their mothers' talk and other language that comes their way as grist for their language-learning mill.

Even though Heidi is deaf and Rachel can hear, they have a tremendous amount in common as they enter the dawn of language learning. What lies beneath the surface of our language (be it oral speech or visual signs) is a rich system that is at the very core of what it means to be human. When the coos and gurgles of the first three months give way to babbles in months four to eight, the system really starts to take off.

## How Babies Talk to Us

In the beginning, babies like Rachel (and Heidi) make sounds reflexively, to express their feelings. Fussing noises as well as vegetative sounds associated with eating make up their repertoire. In the first month speech-like sounds are rare. Instead, as any new parent can report, cries are the most frequent expression. By the time Rachel is three months old, her parents can look forward to some relief: the amount of crying seriously declines. Rachel is awake more and her vocal apparatus is growing, so she can now make sounds that have variously been called "gooing" or "cooing." Roughly in the second month, she produces open-mouth vowel-like sounds as in "gooooooo" or "gaaaaah." She also develops a hearty laugh. It may not be language, but there is nothing more delightful than hearing a four-month-old laugh irrepressibly.

With these developments as a backdrop, let's look at Rachel's progression in vocal play between roughly four and eight months of age. At four months, Rachel now sounds as if she is manipulating her vocal apparatus purposefully—sometimes shouting, sometimes whispering. She is clearly having fun making noises. It is in this period that children first produce raspberries and snorts. Vocal play occurs both when Rachel is alone and when she is interacting with an adult. Studies show, however, that Rachel's vocal responses sound *more* like language when she is interacting with an adult than when she is alone. Perhaps she is listening to the adult's sounds and attempting to match or reproduce some of the qualities of what she hears.

If research shows that four-month-old babies vocalize more when an adult is present, what is the crucial factor that stimulates this vocalization? Eye gaze! When an adult looks

Rachel in the eye, she babbles more. This research goes on to show just how conversational Rachel is. If the adults around Rachel talk to her by *following* her vocalizations rather than by speaking *during* her vocalizations, the pattern of her babbling changes. When Rachel is interrupted, she tends to vocalize in bursts. When we wait until Rachel has finished and then start our part of the conversation, she pauses, looks attentively at the adult, smiles after the adult's vocalization, and then starts the cycle again. Although Rachel doesn't understand the meaning of what is being said to her, she vocalizes only after the adult is finished. By just four months of age, Rachel already enjoys talking to adults and taking conversational turns.

### Try This: Conversations from the crib?

Test these conversational abilities in your own baby by trying an experiment. When your baby is alert and making sounds, hold the baby facing you but do not make eye contact. (The fact that this is terribly hard to do shows what compelling conversational partners babies are.) Now listen to see how much the baby "talks." In the next step, change your strategy by looking into your baby's eyes. You'll probably find that your baby starts to talk even more. See if you notice the difference. You should also notice that your baby talks more when he can see you than when you are out of view.

If you are an adventurous parent, you can try to replicate the research on turn-taking that we just discussed. While looking into your baby's eyes, wait for him to talk and then add your own commentary when he is finished. Now try to interrupt him by talking when he is "talking." Do you get a different pattern of vocalizing? Does your baby look happier when you wait until he has finished what he wanted to say?

## From Coos and Goos to Babbling

A four-month-old's coos and gurgles represent only the beginning. Starting about six or seven months of age, infants around the world begin to make real, language-like sounds. They begin to sound somewhat like Bam Bam in *The Flintstones*. When this occurs, parents are sure they hear patterns that approximate the first words. What parents are hearing is *babbling*. This kind of sound making heralds a big step forward in the progression to language. Indeed, babbling in this period sounds like standard syllables repeated over and over again. "Dadadada" and "mamama" are premier examples. Before calling all the relatives to say that Rachel

or Heidi has produced her first words, however, parents need to observe when these sounds are made. If Rachel says "dada" whether her father is present or not, it is unlikely that she means dada. It is striking, however, when true babbling begins because it does so suddenly. Even babies like Heidi will babble orally at this stage. Amazingly, deaf babies babble in both oral speech (as if exercising their vocal cords) and through their hands. Without any feedback from their own speech, however, Heidi's oral babbling quickly drops off in favor of visually rewarding signed babbling.

Toward the end of this period, around eight months of age, Rachel engages in a different, even more advanced kind of babbling. She no longer produces merely the same syllables over and over (as in "mamama") but begins using different syllables strung together, such as "mada" or "dele." The technical name for this kind of babbling is "variegated," since the parts of any given babble vary. Some children even string together long "sentences" of babbles, with the rhythm and intonation of real English sentences. Rachel produces "jargon," as it is called, and it is hilarious to hear. She sounds as though she is really talking, but she makes absolutely no sense. She even ends some of her "sentences" with the intonation of a question, making the adults around her feel compelled to respond. It is as if babies who use jargon (and not all do) are imitating the way entire sentences sound even before they know that sentences have meaning.

Researchers used to assume that children went through a period of babbling, variegated babbling, and jargon, and then became silent just before they uttered their real first word. Extensive observational research, however, has shown that babbling, jargon, and real words exist side by side. Rachel can babble away while introducing what may sound like some real words into her jargon. Parents often give babies the benefit of the doubt, although at this age it's wishful thinking to think that these are real words.

### Try This: Are "Mama" and "Dada" real words or just arbitrary sounds?

During the early babbling period, chart the kinds of babbling patterns your baby uses by writing down the sounds your baby makes and also the context in which you hear these sounds used. Are any found regularly—are certain sounds used more often in certain kinds of situations?

When do you hear the first "mamama" or "dadada"? Are these true words for the baby or just sound play? If the baby says "Mama" mostly when Mommy is present, or "Dada" mostly when Daddy is present, you might be hearing real words. More probably, babies are just engaging in sound play at this stage. By keeping records, you will see for yourself how the baby begins to use the vocal instrument of the mouth and how certain syllables are practiced over and over again. You will probably discover why languages around the world have chosen the sounds of "mmm" and "dddd" to represent Mom and Dad. Languages seem to have capitalized on the sounds that babies can produce in abundance early on.

## Many Babies Babble

All this talk about babbling raises a curious question. Why do babies babble in the first place? If they can make the sounds, why not move directly to words? And what is the link, if any, between babbling and later speech? Perhaps the way to think about this is to remember back to when we were children and struggled to put a puzzle together. Grown-ups around us would have called our activity "play" and relegated it to a category of things less important than, say, brushing one's teeth or learning to say "please" and "thank you." Yet consider what a child is doing when he puts that same puzzle together over and over. He is practicing the skills of finding pieces that fit into the puzzle, of seeing spatial relationships, and of comparing and contrasting puzzle pieces that look very much alike.

Babbling is analogous to putting a puzzle together over and over. Just as children learn a good deal about how puzzle pieces differ in small but significant ways, so do babies learn how to manipulate the pieces of sound that make up the puzzle of language. Rachel is learning how to move her lips and tongue to replicate the sounds she hears around her. She is learning that placing her tongue in a slightly different position has the effect of producing a slightly different sound. She is learning as well how to modulate her voice—how to yell and how to whisper.

How do we know that babbling helps babies practice forming the sounds of language or modulating the volume and intonation of their voices? Every now and then a child who can hear perfectly well is unable to babble because of medical problems. John Locke of Harvard University found a child he referred to as "Jenny" who had a tube inserted into her trachea (windpipe), which bypassed her larynx (voice box) because she had various respiratory abnormalities. The tube was not always present but inserted intermittently. Jenny was normal in all other ways. When the tube was removed for good, she was 17 months old. Her vocalizations immediately increased in number when the tube was removed. However, the quality of her vocalizations was not up to par. Even by the end of her 21st month, Jenny had still

not begun to produce well-formed syllables in her babbling. Furthermore, Jenny produced only five different sounds. Children who have had an opportunity to practice their babbling produce nearly *thirty* unique sounds by 18 months of age. Jenny also produced sounds in a quiet monotone with very little variation in volume and tone. This too is far from typical. Since Jenny was normal in all other ways, the only explanation for the poor quality of her sound production is that she had missed out on hearing herself make playful babbling sounds.

So babbling is not just play. If a baby cannot hear herself make noise, she will eventually lag behind in the quality of the sounds she makes. She will produce fewer true consonant-vowel-consonant or consonant-vowel syllables. The baby will also lose the opportunity to practice "playing" with the volume and intonation of language. Much of how we communicate with each other rests on our manipulation of these variables. Volume can transmit urgency, anger, or interest, among other emotions. Intonational changes can give an entirely different meaning to the same exact words. Try saying "I love your tie" as though you mean it and then say it sarcastically. Babies who can't babble (like Jenny) or hear themselves babble (like Heidi) lose out on important practice in being able to manipulate these factors to suit their communicative needs.

Proof that babies are practicing the sounds of their language when they babble comes from much careful research. One way to test if babies' babbles resemble the language they hear around them is to have native speakers of a language—people who are not linguists—make judgments from audiotaped recordings. That's exactly what several French scientists decided to do. They appointed judges who were asked to listen to 15-second segments of babble before deciding whether the babies were French or not. By and large, the judges *could* identify which babies were French just from their babbling. How did they do this? The researchers determined that the judges' decisions were based on the *sounds* the babies used along with the *rhythm* and *intonation* of the babbles. For instance, English-reared babies babble mostly with a falling intonation. That is, their voices go down at the end of a string of babbles, just as an adult's voice does at the end of many sentences. The babble of French babies, however, end on an up note about half the time, just as sentences in French often end in a rising intonation. This finding shows us that the intonation pattern of a language is one of the first aspects babies identify.

Researchers have also found that babies produce different *proportions* of the same sounds when they are reared in different countries. For example, Rachel, hearing English, produces more vowels like the *i* in "ice" and the *e* in "easy" while Jing, a Chinese baby, produces more vowels like the *a* in "ask" and the *u* in "use." By ten months of age, just as a baby is on the verge of producing words, his variegated babbles come to take on the sound patterns of the language in which he is being reared. It's almost as if the syllables a baby produces in variegated babbling are frames that are being set up to accept what will soon be real words. But even after real words are used, babbling will persist into the first year of life.

# Everyone Has an Accent

## Walt Wolfram

**EDITOR'S INTRODUCTION**

How people speak—our patterns of language use—is called dialect by linguists. Walt Wolfram discusses the ways that "dialect discrimination" affects people's perceptions of each other. The examples in this article show how learning about dialect can help all students in their acquisition of Standard English, at the same time they learn to appreciate their own regional patterns of talk.

Tanya's family has finally settled in. Now, after the long trek across the country, she faces one more hurdle—the first day of school. Tanya takes a deep breath as she enters a new 5th grade classroom, full of unfamiliar faces and voices.

The teacher senses her awkward isolation and steps forward. "Class, we have a new student who moved here over the summer." He smiles at Tanya. "Would you like to tell us a little bit about where you're from?"

Tanya begins to speak, but a buzz erupts in the classroom before she has finished her first sentence.

"You have a funny accent!"

"Where did you learn to talk?"

"Did you hear how she said her name?"

Even the teacher can hardly keep from chuckling at the way Tanya speaks, though he hushes the others quickly. No one seems to notice Tanya's bewilderment or her withdrawal at the assault on her speech. And no one bothers to acknowledge or address the prejudice reflected in the responses.

Tanya's experience is repeated every day in classrooms across the country. The Appalachian child from Kentucky who moves to Detroit, the urban child from Boston who moves to rural Texas, the Native American child from the Navajo reservation who moves to Tucson—all are subject to charges that they "talk funny."

Everyone notices dialects, and lots of people seem to be fascinated by them. But is it simply a matter of curiosity? What really lies beneath the laughter and the impetuous comments people make about how others speak?

## The Dialect Game

Linguists use the term *dialect* to denote patterns in the way people use language. These patterns include pronunciation (or "accent"), vocabulary and grammatical structures that reflect the user's cultural and regional background. Dialect is not limited to spoken language; users of American Sign Language employ variations that reflect their regional and social backgrounds as well.

*Source:* "Everyone Has an Accent: *A North Carolina professor advocates teaching respect for dialects*" by Walt Wolfram, 2000, *Teaching Tolerance 18*, pp. 18–23.

The lingering firestorm over Ebonics in the Oakland, Calif., schools a few years ago suggests that there is a lot at stake when it comes to dialect differences, in education and elsewhere. Pay attention to the labels used to describe "accents" or dialects in the media, in the classroom, and in social gatherings everywhere—*funny, thick, bad, foreign, hick, weird, corrupt.* A moment's reflection exposes the level of judgment and prejudice about dialects and, by extension, their speakers. Consider the following recorded examples:

- "They hear this Brooklyn accent, they think you grew up in the slum, hanging out on the corner."

- "Wisconsin people, they're really bad, they sound like they're Norwegian."

- "It's ignorant, it sounds ignorant, they gonna hear this and say, 'Look at them two beautiful girls; if they'd keep their mouth shut they'd be great.'"
  *—from the video* American Tongues

- "What makes me feel that Blacks tend to be ignorant is that they fail to see that the word is spelled A-S-K, not A-X."
  *—from "The Oprah Winfrey Show"*

The societal norm seems to be that attitudes about language differences don't even have to be disguised. Well-intentioned people who would be hesitant to make overt statements about race, gender or class openly mock and disparage language differences. In *English with an Accent* (see Resources), author Rosina Lippi-Green says that dialect discrimination is "so commonly accepted, so widely perceived as appropriate, that it must be seen as the last back door to discrimination. And the door stands wide open."

A recent column published in newspapers across the United States responded to the recognition of dialect differences with the headline, "There's a word for it; the word is 'wrong.'" Some people would like to stamp out dialects, imagining the development of a homogenized "standard"-English devoid of any local character. But present studies of dialects in the United States actually show that, despite forceful efforts to rid students of their variant speech patterns, some dialects are becoming more, rather than less, distinctive.

## TRUTH AND FICTION ABOUT DIALECTS

There is a popular belief that dialects are simply corruptions of "real" or "good" English that reflect basic ignorance of well-known grammar rules. But the truth is that dialect structures are in themselves quite natural and neutral. Their social impact comes solely from their association with different groups in our society. If people belong to a socially oppressed group, they can count on having their language stigmatized; if they belong to a prestigious group, their language will carry prestige value.

Most people are unaware that a few centuries ago, the pronunciation of *ask* as *ax* was perfectly acceptable among the socially elite classes of England. And early masters of English literature, including Chaucer, routinely used the "double negative"—as in *They didn't go nowhere*—without any fear of sounding illogical or conveying unintended meanings. Contrary to the common belief that standards of language are fixed forever, they respond, like any other aspect of culture, to the dynamics of social change.

Within this fluid state, all dialects involve intricate, detailed patterning governed by the scientific laws of language structure. The western Pennsylvanian who says *The house needs painted,* the Southerner who pronounces *pin* and *pen* the same but *bit* and *bet* differently, and the urban African American who says *They always be acting nice,* all follow specifically detailed patterns of their dialect that can be captured and described in terms of specific "rules" or "laws" of language.

Variation in speech is at the core of social and historical identity, interwoven into the fabric of cultural differences. Would the isolated Appalachians really be as Appalachian without the lingering voices of their Scots-Irish heritage? Would urban African American preachers be as effective with their congregations if they used only the structures of standard English in uninterrupted monologues? Would young Northern Californians seem as urbane without the sentence intonation that makes their statements sound like questions?

Some English dialects are more readily recognizable than others and evoke more comment, but the fact remains: *It is impossible to speak English without speaking some dialect of the language.* Skilled dialectologists trained to detect the nuances of language variation affirm that the notion of a "pure" English, safeguarded in dictionaries and grammar books, evaporates as soon as we open our mouths to speak.

The misinformation and misunderstanding about dialects in our society is not simply a matter of innocent folklore. People's intelligence, capability and character are often judged on the basis of a sentence, a few phrases or even a single word. Studies show that children as young as 3 to 5 years of age show strong preferences—and prejudices—based on dialect variations among speakers. Teachers sometimes classify students' speech as "deficient" when it is simply different from the testing norm. In the workplace, perfectly capable workers who speak non-mainstream dialects may be denied occupational opportunity because they "just don't sound right for the job."

It gets more personal: Views about dialects also affect how we feel about ourselves. As one speaker from New York City put it, "It's not them feeling superior, it's me feeling inferior, and I hate when I feel like that. And when I speak, uh, horribly, I feel stupid and don't have confidence in myself, and it's holding me back." If someone has been told enough times that she speaks badly, it's just a matter of time before she starts believing that she is as worthless as her speech.

## WHAT'S THE SOLUTION?

For over a decade now, a small group of linguists and educators have been piloting programs specifically designed to instruct students about dialect. The goal of these "dialect awareness" programs is straightforward: to provide accurate information about the nature of dialect differences and promote understanding of the role of dialects in American society.

---

**Activity**
Levels of Dialect

---

Language is organized on several different levels. One level of organization is **pronunciation,** which concerns how sounds are used in speech. Different dialects may use sounds in quite different ways. Sometimes this is referred to simply as *accent.* For example, some people from New England pronounce the words *car* and *far* without the *r.* Also, some people from the South may say *greasy* with a *z* sound in the middle of the word, so that they pronounce it *greazy.* On Ocracoke Island, the way some people say *hoi toide* for *high tide* is an example of distinctive pronunciation.

Another level of language organization is **grammar.** Grammar concerns the particular ways in which speakers arrange sentences and words. Different dialects may arrange words and sentences in different ways. For instance, when someone in western Pennsylvania says *The car needs washing,* we have an example of **dialect grammar.**

A third level of language involves how different words are used, called the **vocabulary** or **lexicon** of the language. Speakers of different dialects use different words to mean the same thing. For example, New Englanders may use *frappe* and Outer Banks residents *cabinet* to denote what is more widely known as a *milk shake.* In other cases, a common word might be used with different meanings across dialects. Thus, a speaker of African American dialect might use the verb *stay* to signify residing in a particular place, whereas speakers of other dialects might use the verb *live.*

### What Kind of Difference Is It?

In the sentences given below, decide whether the difference in each pair is at the pronunciation, grammar or vocabulary level. Place a **P** for *pronunciation,* a **G** for *grammar* or a **V** for *vocabulary* in the blank provided beside each pair.

1. ___ That *feller* sure was tall.
   That *fellow* sure was tall.

2. ___ She needed a *rubberband.*
   She needed a *gumband.*

3. ___ They usually *be doing* their homework.
   They usually *do* their homework.

4. ___ I *weren't* there yesterday.
   I *wasn't* there yesterday.

5. ___ She drank a *milk shake.*
   She drank a *cabinet.*

6. ___ I asked him *if he was going over the beach.*
   I asked him *if he was going to the beach.*

7. ___ The *skeeters* are bad in August.
   The *mosquitoes* are bad in August.

8. ___ That meal was *good-some.*
   That meal was *good.*

9. ___ They caught two hundred *pound* of flounder.
   They caught two hundred *pounds* of flounder.

10. ___ They went *hunting and fishing.*
    They went *a-hunting and a-fishing.*

---

*Adapted from* Dialects in Schools and Communities *(see Resources).*
*Answers: 1-P, 2-V; 3-G; 4-G; 5-V; 6-G; 7-P; 8-G; 9-G; 10-G.*

Learning about dialects is hardly at odds with the acquisition of standard English grammar. In fact, part of the education process involves mastering appropriate styles of speech for different occasions, including those situations where standard English is required. At the same time, growing evidence supports the conclusion that respect for and knowledge of a student's community dialect aids rather than hinders the acquisition of standard English.

The social and educational ramifications of dialect awareness programs can be far-reaching, as students as well as teachers confront stereotypes, prejudices and misconceptions about dialects. In pilot classrooms ranging from 4th grade through secondary schools, in locations as diverse as central Baltimore and isolated Ocracoke Island on North Carolina's Outer Banks, these programs teach students the truth—and the consequences—of dialect differences.

Since nothing is more central to education and human behavior than language, dialect awareness programs should not be a tangential adjunct to so-called "core" knowledge. In light of pervasive misunderstandings about dialects—as well as the illusion of a homogeneous "broadcast English"—it is essential to provide instruction specifically targeting language diversity at the local, regional and national levels. It is a curious and even dangerous omission when the unique sounds of a culture are silenced.

The current pilot programs on dialects are interwoven with social studies, language arts, history and science. In each of these subject areas, some of the most central issues of social equity are associated with variation in language use. Teachers can readily adapt some of the dialect awareness strategies to their existing curricula, emphasizing the need for understanding and tolerance.

One important theme in dialect awareness programs, particularly in social studies and language arts, is the "naturalness" of dialect variation. As students listen to a range of representative regional, class and ethnic speech samples, comparing them with each other and with their own dialects, they can appreciate the reality of diverse speech traditions. In the pilot programs, students view vignettes of real-life situations from the popular video documentary *American Tongues* (see Resources), exposing them not only to dialect differences but also to some of the raw prejudices about dialects.

Teachers then raise questions for discussion: "What do you know about dialects?" "How do you feel about them?" "How are dialects portrayed in the media?" Such discussion often causes students to confront the stereotypes and prejudices that often surround specific speech patterns. It is not surprising that an evaluation of the dialect awareness curriculum on Appalachian English conducted a few years ago in Western Carolina showed that the most-cited learning experience was concern for the "unfairness" of dialect prejudice. As one 8th grader put it, "It's not right for people to make fun of the way people speak, and I will try to do that less."

## Activity
### Community Dialect Survey

Put together a list of 10 dialect words from your community. Often, words for different foods and refreshments are among the dialect words; for example, *soda, pop, cola* and *soft drink* are all used for the same type of carbonated drink in different regions. Now, figure out a way to ask people about each of these words without saying the word itself. For example, you may say, "When people are hot and thirsty, they may get a _____ from the machine" in order to get a person to name the carbonated drink.

Conduct the questionnaire with individuals who represent different groups in your community, such as older people, younger people, various racial or ethnic groups, and people who come from outside the community, as well as longtime residents.

After getting the responses, create a chart that tallies each group's responses to your words.

• What kinds of trends do you see in the use of the words?

• What does the survey show about the different groups of people?

• Does the community dialect seem to be changing with respect to the use of these words? If so, how?

Another important theme concerns the patterning of dialect. In order to identify and classify detailed dialect patterns, students must use cognitive skills and techniques of inquiry that link language arts with the science curriculum. For example, a dialect awareness lesson might require students to analyze sets of dialect data—such as information about words and phrases for the second person plural pronoun (e.g., *yous, you'ns* and *y'all*).

On the basis of the data sets presented or collected, students must determine the specific language pattern, or "rule," that describes precisely the patterning of the structure. In the process, they formulate a hypothesis about the language "law" and confirm or disconfirm it on the basis of its generality and predictability—the cornerstone of scientific inquiry.

Other dialect awareness activities focus on specific structures in a range of regional and ethnic dialects to illustrate these regular patterns—such as the use in Appalachia of the *uh* sound (usually transcribed as *a-*) before words ending in *ing (She's a-fishing today),* the use of *be* in urban African American English to denote habitual activities *(She be fishing all the time),* or the absence of the plural *-s* inflection (as in *four mile*) in rural Southern dialects.

To discover how natural and inevitable dialect differences are—and how they change over time and place—young dialectologists can collect examples of distinctive speech in their own environment. For example, virtually all communities have some local and regional names for over-the-counter foods *(sub, hoagie, hero)* and drinks *(soda, pop, cola).* From such a simple starting point, the inquiry can take on wider dimensions as students interview parents, grandparents, friends and others about local words and work together in documenting, organizing and analyzing the findings.

Students begin to grasp the inner workings of dialects most effectively when they get a chance to observe and analyze their own speech patterns alongside those of others. Urban African American children revel in the patterning of Appalachian forms while learning about the use of *be* in their own dialect. At the same time, students in isolated Southeastern coastal communities learn new respect for the use of *be* in urban African American English while learning about their own use of *weren't* for *wasn't,* as in *I weren't there* or *She weren't ready.*

The opportunity to compare and contrast dialects offers students much more than a lesson in grammar. As an 8th grader from the unique Ocracoke dialect area of North Carolina's Outer Banks put it, "I never realized that our dialect rules were so complex. It makes me proud that I learned about my dialect."

For her teacher, Gail Hamilton, dialect studies have opened a new window on old assumptions. "I didn't realize there was a pattern," she says. "As an English teacher, when they would talk I would cringe at what I considered 'bad grammar.' Showing me that there is a specific pattern, a method of speech, is something that now I'm proud they know."

# RESOURCES

*Dialects in Schools and Communities* ($24.95), by Walt Wolfram, Carolyn Adger and Donna Christian, gives more specific details about the role of dialects in the acquisition of educational skills such as reading, writing and learning spoken standard English. It also includes more examples of dialect awareness activities and a useful list of vernacular dialect structures for a full range of American English dialects.

**Lawrence Erlbaum Associates**
**10 Industrial Ave.**
**Mahwah, NJ 07430-2262**
**(800)926-6579**
**www.erlbaum.com**

*Spoken Soul: The Story of Black English* ($24.95) is a highly readable account of the history, structure and current controversy about Ebonics. The description shows how this unique dialect is effectively used by writers, orators, comedians, singers and rappers at the same time it is condemned in public commentary.

**John Wiley & Sons**
**1 Wiley Dr.**
**Somerset, NC 08875-1272**
**(800) 225-5945**
**www.wiley.com**

*English with an Accent: Language, Ideology, and Discrimination* $21.99) presents a sobering account of the manifestation of language prejudice and discrimination in American society. The book demonstrates how pervasive and subtle language discrimination can be in venues that range from animated films to the legal and educational system.

**Routledge Customer Service**
**7625 Empire Dr.**
**Florence, KY 41042**
**(800) 634-7064**
**cserve@routledge-ny.com**

Slang, code-switching and word migration are just a few of the topics that make *Spreading the Word: Language & Dialect in America* ($12.50) such a helpful guide to classroom communication. By placing dialects of English within a dynamic global context, the author opens new avenues for both sharpening language skills and appreciating expressive differences.

**Heinemann**
**88 Post Rd. W.**
**Westport, CT 06881**
**(800) 793-2154**
**www.heinemann.com**

*American Tongues* is an award-winning video documentary on American dialects for high school level and up. It combines an entertaining presentation of American speech patterns with the reality of dialect prejudice in a way that encourages audiences to openly discuss their attitudes. A 40-minute high school version ($150) and a 56-minute adult version ($285) are available.

**CNAM Film Library**
**22-D Hollywood Ave.**
**Hohokus, NJ 07423**
**(800) 343-5540**
**www.cnam.com**

The Web site of the Center for Applied Linguistics *(www.cal.org)* is a good place to start for information on the practical application of linguistic knowledge to social and educational problems. The dialect/ebonics link provides helpful resources and references on dialects, as well as detailed information about the Ebonics controversy.

The Web site of the North Carolina Language and Life Project *(www.ncsu.edu/linguistics/llp.htm)* offers lots of audio examples and video clips of documentaries on dialects. North Carolina is one of the richest dialect areas in the United States, with Appalachian, Southern, Outer Banks, Native American and African American dialects, among others.

# A Linguistic Big Bang

## Lawrence Osborne

### EDITOR'S INTRODUCTION

The world's newest language, Nicaraguan Sign Language, is giving linguists a window into how children generate language. This language was created "out of thin air" in Managua when a group of deaf children were enrolled in school and began to build on each other's invented signs. A decade later, a new language has blossomed, providing intriguing insights.

When the Greek historian Herodotus was traveling in Egypt, he heard of a bizarre experiment conducted by a King named Psammetichus. The inquisitive monarch, wrote Herodotus, decided to wall up two baby boys in a secluded compound. Whatever came out of the boys' mouths, reasoned the King, would be the root language of our species—the key to all others. Herodotus tells us that eventually the children came up with the Phrygian word for bread, *bekos*. In addition to demonstrating the superiority of the Phrygian tongue, the King's inquiry proved that even if left to their own devices, children wouldn't be without language for long. We are born, Herodotus suggested, with the gift of gab.

Ever since, philosophers have dreamed of repeating Psammetichus's test. If children grew up isolated on a desert island, would they develop a bona fide language? And if so, would it resemble existing tongues? Yet only someone with the conscience of a Josef Mengele would carry out such an experiment. Then, in the mid-1980's, linguists were confronted with an unexpected windfall. Psammetichus's experiment was repeated, but this time it came about unintentionally. And not in Egypt but in Nicaragua.

Following the 1979 Sandinista revolution, the newly installed Nicaraguan Government inaugurated the country's first large scale effort to educate deaf children. Hundreds of students were enrolled in two Managua schools. Not being privy to the more than 200 existing sign languages used by hearing-impaired people around the world, Managua's deaf children started from ground zero. They had no grammar or syntax—only crude gestural signs developed within their own families. These pantomimes, which deaf kids use to communicate basic needs like "eat," "drink" and "ice cream," are called *mimicas* in Spanish.

Most of the children arrived in Managua with only a limited repertory of mimicas. But once the students were placed together, they began to build on one another's signs. One child's gesture solidified into the community's word. The children's inexperienced teachers—who were having paltry success communicating with their profoundly deaf students—watched in awe as the kids began signing among themselves. A new language had begun to bloom.

A decade later, the children's creation has become a sensation of modern linguistics. Nicaraguan Sign Language (known to experts as I.S.N., for *Idioma de Signos Nicaragüense*) has been patiently decoded by outside scholars, who describe an idiom filled with curiosities yet governed by the same "universal grammar" that the linguist Noam

Source: " A Linguistic Big Bang" by L. Osborne. October 24, 1999, pp. 84-88. © 1999 by New York Time Magazine.

Chomsky claims structures all language. Steven Pinker, author of "The Language Instinct," sees what happened in Managua as proof that language acquisition is hard-wired inside the human brain. "The Nicaraguan case is absolutely unique in history," he maintains. "We've been able to see how it is that children—not adults—generate language, and we have been able to record it happening in great scientific detail. And it's the first and only time that we've actually seen a language being created out of thin air."

Managua's deaf children were stranded in school, not on a desert island. Spanish-speaking teachers were there to guide them. Yet it turns out that Nicaraguan Sign Language doesn't resemble Spanish at all. Indeed, the Managua teachers say they left hardly an imprint on the children's improvised language—largely because their lack of experience led them to adopt poor pedagogy. When the schools first opened, the Sandinista education officials were misguidedly urged by Soviet advisers to adopt "finger spelling," which uses simple signs to limn the alphabets of spoken languages. This approach was a disaster. Because the students had no prior concept of words (let alone letters), it proved fruitless to try to communicate in this fashion. The children remained linguistically disconnected from their teachers.

This failure to adopt a workable teaching strategy, paradoxically, gave the Nicaraguan children an opportunity to erect a linguistic structure of their own. Indeed, the frustrated Managua teachers began to notice that although the children could barely communicate with their instructors, they were beginning to communicate well among themselves, using a sign system that no teacher recognized. But what, exactly, was it?

In June 1986, the Nicaraguan Ministry of Education contacted Judy Kegl, an American sign-language expert at Northeastern University. They invited her to visit the deaf schools in Managua and see if she could shed some light on the enigma. Armed with notebooks and a Pentax camera—and a vague tenderness for the revolution—the 33-year-old Kegl set off for Managua.

Her first stop was Villa Libertad, a vocational school for deaf teen-agers. Kegl, now a professor at the University of Southern Maine in Portland, set out to make a rudimentary dictionary of the signs being used by a small group of adolescent girls in a hairdressing workshop. Some signs were obvious enough: objects like "eyebrow tweezers" and "rolling curlers" were signed by more or less imitating the things themselves. But one day, a student playfully tested a more intricate sign on her. She first laid out her left palm flat; then, using her right hand, she traced a line from the middle finger to the base of the palm, turning her right hand over afterward and pointing below her belt. As a result of the

girl's giggling, Kegl guessed that the sign meant "sanitary napkin." She had learned her first word in what seemed to be a simple form of communication.

After a few days, Kegl figured out the sign for "house" and could combine it with a typical Nicaraguan gesture for "What's up?"—a strong wrinkle of the nose—to ask the deaf students where they lived. The students' responses, however, were baffling. Each student would produce a series of complex but apparently meaningless hand wriggles. Only later would Kegl figure out that these wriggles were in fact precise descriptions of Managua's labyrinthine bus routes. Indeed, the grammar underlying this enigmatic sign system completely eluded her. "I felt like I was failing as a linguist," she recalls. "I couldn't find any consistent regularities. It seemed to be complete chaos."

Three weeks later, however, Kegl moved on to the primary school, known as San Judas, where younger children were being taught. On the first day, she observed a young girl named Mayela Rivas signing in a courtyard. Her gestures were rapid and had an eerie rhythmic consistency. Kegl sensed that Mayela was not just making crude mimicas or the kind of signed pidgin practiced by the older students at Villa Libertad.

"I looked at her, and I thought to myself, Holy cow, that girl is using some kind of rule book," she says. Ann Senghas, a former assistant of Kegl's who is now a professor at Barnard College, shares her wonder. "It was a linguist's dream," she says. "It was like being present at the Big Bang."

To crack the code used by the younger San Judas children, Kegl had them retell stories of Mr. Koumal, a popular Czech cartoon character. To relate the contents of a Koumal picture book, the children would need a variety of syntactic constructions and verb senses. In "Mr. Koumal Flies Like a Bird," for example, the adventurous Czech makes wings for himself by stealing chicken feathers. But after he crashes into a mountainside, Mr. Koumal uses the feathers to make Indian headdresses he can sell to children. By having the children reconstruct these stories in their own tongue, telltale regularities emerged that, bit by bit, provided Kegl with clues to the language's grammar.

It was noticeable at once that the younger children used signs in a more nuanced way than the older students. For example, the teenage pidgin signers at Villa Libertad had a basic gesture for "speak"—opening and closing four fingers and a thumb in front of the mouth. The younger children used the same sign, but modulated it, *opening* their fingers at the position of the speaker and *closing* them at the position of the addressee. To Kegl, this apparently small difference had enormous implications. "This was verb agreement," she says, "and they were all using it fluently." Similarly, in retelling the Koumal story, the younger kids could express what linguists call "spatial agreement" with their verbs. When they used the verb "to fall"—as in "Mr. Koumal falls down the mountain"—they made a link between Mr. Koumal's falling and what he was falling down. These nuanced signers would first lift one hand in the air to signify "mountaintop" and then begin the sign for "fall" from this height, flipping the hand back and forth while moving it down an imaginary slope.

What explained this difference between the younger and older signers? Kegl's theory, which has been disseminated in various linguistic journals, is that an original group of home signers came up with an elemental pidgin among themselves, known to linguists as *Lenguaje de Signos Nicaraguense.* This was the comparatively crude signing she had observed among the older students. Then, very young children of 5 or 6 had come into the school system. Quickly mastering the pidgin from their elder peers, they had then taken it, quite unconsciously, to a far higher level. This second version was the fast, elegantly orchestrated language that Kegl had seen flying from the little fingers of Mayela Rivas. This was what would become known as the *idioma,* or Nicaraguan Sign Language. These three quite distinct levels—home signs, the *lenguaje* and the *idioma*—represent phases of evolution, from pantomime to pidgin to language. "Real language in this case," she says, "only emerged with young children first exposed to a signed pidgin."

But how did Nicaraguan Sign Language evolve in the first place? Kegl likens the process to a field of stones waiting to be made into a fence. The "stones" in this case came from the gesture system that speaking Nicaraguans use in daily life. Hence, the first deaf signs for "eat" and "drink" were close to those used by hearing speakers: a flat hand with the fingers bending back and forth before the mouth for "eat"; a thumb gesturing toward the mouth for "drink."

"What happens," Kegl explains, "is that these gestures become gradually richer and more varied. But we can't see the leap between them and the first signs of language because the grammar is inside the child. It manifests itself only as the child is exposed to this ever-richer mix of odds and ends." This ability to organize a heap of stones into a fence lies within the brain itself, and is apparently stimulated by interaction with other children.

"We see these children coming to some kind of unconscious consensus about which signs to use and which ones to drop," she continues. "But we can't explain it fully; we can just witness the outcome. There's an element of mystery in the way in which each child adapts to and then changes the language." The very youngest children, Kegl theorizes, filter the linguistic jumble around them differently and then transmit their inventions, deformations and additions back to the larger group. In this way, new words enter the lexicon. "Yet there's no dominant alpha speaker who leads the way," she adds. "Each child gives birth to a kind of individual dialect, which is then pooled among the others according to a process that we don't fully understand."

After more than a decade of study, Kegl and Ann Senghas have mapped out an idiom striking in its flexibility. Verbs, for example, can be stretched like a rubber band to include all kinds of nouns and prepositions. In the story "Mr. Koumal Flies Like a Bird," children line up to give the wily Czech an egg each in exchange for one of his Indian headdresses. This action is expressed by a single verb sign in which the hand turns up in an egg shape, bounces twice away from the body and then turns sharply upward. This one sign would be literally translated in English as "each person in a row of individuals gives an egg-shaped object to an adult." Even more oddly, prepositions in Nicaraguan Sign Language function much like verbs. Hence, where an English speaker would say, "The cup is on the table," a Nicaraguan signer will sign something like, "Table cup ons." Verbs and prepositions are therefore protean in a way that resembles only a few spoken languages, like Navajo.

With all of these idiosyncrasies, it is easy to forget that Nicaraguan Sign Language is but the accidental creation of children. Indeed, adult-engineered idioms like Esperanto seem pallid by comparison. As Kegl marvels, "No linguist could create a language with half the complexity or richness that a 4-year-old could give birth to."

Little Yuri Mejía is 9 years old and has been deaf from birth. Under the mango trees of the Parque Reyes in Bluefields, a remote port city on Nicaragua's Mosquito Coast, she peers down into an ornamental pool filled with tiny baby alligators. She is neatly dressed in her pressed navy skirt and symmetrical pigtails. With facial expressions and hand gestures working simultaneously, she turns out crisp, twinkling sentences at lightning speed. Her face slips and slides, moving from clownlike frowns to delicate nose wrinkles. Yuri is one of the youngest pupils at the Escuelita de Bluefields, an experimental school that Judy Kegl and her husband, James Shepard-Kegl, have been running since 1995.

Because she was educated so early, Yuri signs with a fluent grace. "When are the alligators going to wake up?" she signs to me through James Shepard-Kegl, who has agreed to act as my translator. "Every time I come to the park they're asleep."

With Shepard-Kegl's help, I ask her if she likes school.

"At home," she signs back quickly, "I'm bored. I live with my grandmother. It's way over there in the barrio. We sit around, and we're bored all the time. We do a lot of laundry. But at school, everyone's deaf, so I can talk to them. And I can read a book about Babar."

Bursting with curiosity, she then asks me where I live. The one Nicaraguan sign I have mastered on my second day in Bluefields is the one for New York. You put your forefinger against your forehead three times to imitate the tiara spikes of Lady Liberty and then raise your arm in a fist.

"Do you live with your grandmother, too?" Yuri asks.

"No."

"Do you know who Babar is?"

"Yes, of course."

"His mommy was killed in the forest, and he came to the town and went up an elevator." She nods wisely. "Babar went up and down in the elevator," she signs.

To make the sign for Babar, Yuri holds up four fingers (the sign for "B"), touches her nose with her thumb and quickly dips the hand down to describe an elephant's trunk. To convey the elevator's movement, she forms a platform with her left hand upon which she plants two fingers of her right hand in an inverted V: a person standing on an elevator floor. She then moves the "elevator" up and down.

Yuri and I head to the school's dormitory on the waterfront. The pink house sits on a winding alley of cracked paving stones from which the moody Bluefields lagoon can be seen. Inside, 15 students between the ages of 10 and 25 relax on homemade bunk beds, entertained by a television set with the sound turned off. There, I meet the Bluefields family one by one. The students range from Daphney, a freckled 15-year-old who recently broke her leg turning cartwheels, to 11-year-old Barney, a vivacious boy with shells twisted into his hair who began signing the language as a baby.

Immediately curious about the newcomer, they cast about for a name sign for me. Sign-language names are not phonetic but visual. One boy raised his hand to signify height. (I am 6 foot 5, gigantic by Nicaraguan standards.) Another offered a personalized twist on the sign for "journalist": a miming of a microphone passing from mouth to mouth. Finally, however, by dinnertime the matter was settled otherwise. One girl put a finger vertically against her chin, and amid a burst of laughter, I was christened "Dimple."

Many of these whimsical name signs are perceptive. The one for Daniel Ortega, Nicaragua's former Sandinista President, for example, is one hand tapping the opposing wrist to signify Ortega's flashy Rolex watch, a loud symbol for a poor deaf child. Fidel Castro is a wagging, sermonizing finger combined with a V-sign near the mouth to suggest smoking a cigar. Signs for many nouns are similarly expressive: a wriggling hand for "fish" or fingers shooting like pistols for "Texas." Verbs, by contrast, can seem elegantly esoteric. To say "to look for," the left hand is first held flat with the palm facing downward; then the pinkie, index finger and thumb of the right hand are extended while the two remaining fingers brush the back of the left hand repeatedly.

The Bluefields schoolhouse is a simple, one-room building with maize-yellow walls. The curriculum varies from elementary word recognition for the tots to mathematics and geography for the older signers. In addition, the students are working to translate Nicaraguan Sign Language onto the written page. (They use a Danish symbolic system for transcribing signs into a written phonemic code: there is a symbol for wrinkling one's nose, for example, and another for clenching one's right fist.) One of the first books to be translated is "The Story of Babar," explaining why the innocent elephant has become a constant reference point for the children. The school's dictionary now totals 1,600 words, and the children have begun preparing a heavily truncated version of "Moby-Dick." One thing that is not taught at Bluefields, however, is a more established sign system like American Sign Language. In order to preserve what Nicaragua's deaf have created, Kegl does not want to encourage the adoption of other idioms—even if that leaves the students unable to communicate with other deaf communities. "We don't want to kill indigenous language," she says.

Toward the end of my first day in school, the class is interrupted by a troupe of clowns who for some reason have decided to test their act on the deaf children. The students head outside to the garden to watch. The clowns then put on a show of Fellini-esque ineptitude, dropping their bowling pins and failing to turn their somersaults. Finally one of them gets it right, and I decide it is time for applause. I begin clapping furiously. There is utter silence. A little put out, I turn to see the entire class raising their hands above their heads and wiggling their fingers with deadpan expressions.

Impressed by this silent form of applause, I decide that from now on I will do the same, and so I raise my hands, wriggling my fingers. The class laughs and all simultaneously put their fingers to their chins. Dimple is catching on.

The sign languages of deaf children have been of central interest to linguists for a quarter century. Underlying this interest is a quest to find a linguistic "bioprogram": that is, an innate human ability to generate all the fundamental characteristics of language, from word creation to grammar—without the help of auditory or vocal cues.

In 1978, Heidi Feldman, Susan Goldin-Meadow and Lila Gleitman published a seminal paper on the linguistic propensities of deaf children, based on a group of Philadelphia kids who used simple home signs to communicate with their hearing parents. The researchers found that a deaf child making crude home signs would, in time, begin bending them into languagelike patterns without knowing what he was doing and without being taught. The mothers of these home signers, the scholars revealed, knew far fewer signs than the children themselves. (As trained linguists, they were able to determine the full extent of the children's vocabularies.) And while the parents used the home signs erratically, the deaf children deployed their home signs in a more consistent order.

"Even deaf children grammaticize, regularize—yet they can't have learned it anywhere," Lila Gleitman says. She sees the Nicaraguan case as buttressing her own work. "In Managua, the children formed a continuing community that allowed their nascent language to grow in grammatical and semantic structure. It's a magnificent example of a whole language emerging with incredible richness."

Yet for all its triumphs, the scholarship on Nicaraguan Sign Language makes clear that a precise line between nature and nurture is difficult to establish. Language is the product of a shadowy collusion between biological predisposition and social stimuli. The bioprogram, in other words, is triggered into action by a language community. "It would be hard to find language acquisition in a vacuum," says Gleitman.

Jill Morford, a linguist at the University of New Mexico in Albuquerque, argues that home signers are stuck in a limbo between gesture and language. "Home signing," she says, "is cognitively similar to language, but it doesn't have a grammar as such. It's in between. The beauty of the Nicaraguan children is that they show dramatically how we need both sides of the coin, the social and the innate working together."

To see the limitations on home signing for myself, I take a trip with James Shepard-Kegl by motorboat to the Pearl Lagoon, one hour north of Bluefields. There, a few deaf children still live in almost total isolation deep in the forests. If Bluefields seems remote, then the Pearl Lagoon resembles another planet. Dreamy estuaries snake through bromeliad-sprinkled rain forest that is almost empty except for a handful of farmers living in tiny settlements connected only by river.

In a hamlet called Haulover, where huts are ringed with paths of oyster shells, I meet a 10-year-old deaf boy named Winston. He has never been to school. A kind of Pearl Lagoon Huck Finn, he's about as isolated a home signer as we could possibly hope to find anywhere. He spends all his days fishing with his homemade lines and has a small if appropriate repertory of fishing signs. Excited to have visitors from the big city of Bluefields, he shows us some pigeons he shot with his sling. As we sit in rocking chairs on the porch, his mother tells us that she and Winston can "talk just fine." Winston goes into long bouts of head-rocking laughter and shows us his limited stock of signs. It is clear that he communicates with his family on some level, but there is no rhythm, no fluidity, to his speech.

"Did you catch fish?" I ask. His mother translates.

"Catch," he signs back.

"How?"

He makes a whacking gesture.

Winston cannot express things like "today" or "later," and he rarely if ever puts three signs together to make something that one could call a sentence. Whereas Bluefields children somersault through complex sentences, Winston lumbers along slowly, one sign at a time.

As he walks Shepard-Kegl and me back to the jetties of Pearl Lagoon, Winston shows me a few signs. "Tree." "River." "House." His hand motions are slow, and there is a curious monotony in his expression that somehow belies his exuberance.

I take his picture, and he shows me his fishing line and his knife. "Big," he adds. "Tasty. Catch. Eat."

"It's sad," says Shepard-Kegl as we walk away. "But Winston's family doesn't want him to come to the school, and so he'll remain at this level all his life. He'll never develop a real language."

On the terrace of the Tía Irene, a waterfront hotel in Bluefields, I sit with 20-year-old Anselmo Alemán playing chess while rain pounds on the thatched roof. The lagoon is shadowed; the rusted fishing boats rock violently in the downpour. We are eating a plate of pale purple star apples. The slender Alemán is a charming chess companion, apart from being impossible to beat. Like Winston, he grew up in the deep rain forest, but unlike him, Alemán came to Bluefields.

Suddenly moving his bishop into check-mate position, he smiles. "It's like war," he signs. "You must concentrate or you lose."

Alemán learned Nicaraguan Sign Language at 15, a relatively late age. Intelligence and hard work, however, have enabled him to master the idiom with almost total fluency. "I couldn't learn the language earlier," he signs, "because I grew up in the forest. It was during the war, too, and since my father was a contra, we were always hiding, being hunted down by Sandinistas. So I remember guns, fear, hiding. When I came to Bluefields I was amazed. I was like"—he pauses for a moment—"Babar in the big city going in the elevator for the first time."

Alemán tells me a long, complicated story about his being hit by a firetruck when he was little, sprinkling his account with small scenes and characters. "I can remember my childhood," he signs, "but I can also remember not having any way to communicate. Then, my mind was just a blank." He makes a poignant sign for this emptiness, the palm wiping his forehead to suggest someone erasing a blackboard.

But Alemán will never return to the blank slate. He stands at the center of a young, dynamically evolving language that is now devolving into dialects and variations. Like all living languages, Nicaraguan Sign Language is plastic, mercenary and gleefully derivative—picking up idioms, slang and even basic nouns wherever it fancies. There is even a "street" dialect that diverges in sometimes salacious ways from the official version sanctioned by the Nicaraguan National Association of the Deaf.

The precise intellectual import of Nicaraguan Sign Language is still being hammered out by linguists. Noam Chomsky, who calls what has happened in Nicaragua "a remarkable natural experiment," has for decades propounded the theory that there is a "biology of grammar" embedded in our brains. (It is no accident, he has argued, that every language from English to Zulu has subjects and verbs.) But he is wary of saying that Kegl's research settles the issue. "These children may have shown us something remarkable, if in-

deed they came up with this language with little or no input from outside," he says. "If that's the case, it's a very intriguing situation indeed."

But the meditations of world-famous linguists do not mean much to Alemán as we stroll down to the Parque Reyes. As we sit under the coconut palms amid rusting pieces of farm machinery, decorative rubber tires and a dilapidated bust of the Nicaraguan poet Ruben Darío, the park seems to be at the end of the world. Seeing us signing together, a group of Miskito Indian women stare at us in amazement and are soon joined by the local sorbet vendor.

"I can't imagine," Alemán signs, genuinely mystified, "why you came all this way to hear us talk. It's just our language. What's the big deal?"

I tell him that many people are curious to know how a few deaf children invented the world's youngest language.

"I never thought of it that way," he signs.

"It's a pretty language, too," I try to sign back. I hold both palms toward my chest, moving my hands up and down to signify "sign language." Then I join the index finger and thumb of my right hand to make an oval—almost like the American sign for "O.K."—and glide it away from my chest to say "pretty."

"Is it?" Alemán replies. Then he beams with an undisguised pleasure. "Yes," he says, "I suppose it is."

# Life As We Know It

## Michael Berube

**EDITOR'S INTRODUCTION**

In his very personal essay, Michael Berube tells the story of the early years of his son James, born with Down's Syndrome. Berube eloquently explores what he calls a "crucial characteristic" of our common humanity: the desire to communicate, to understand and to be understood.

In my line of work I don't think very often about carbon or potassium, much less about polypeptides or transfer RNA. I teach American and African-American literature; Janet Lyon, my legal spouse and general partner, teaches modern British literature and women's studies. Nothing about our jobs requires us to be aware of the biochemical processes that made us—and, more recently, our children—into conscious beings. But in 1985–86, when Janet was pregnant with our first child, Nicholas, I would lie awake for hours, wondering how the baseball-size clump of cells in her uterus was really going to form something living, let alone something capable of thought. I knew that the physical processes that form dogs and drosophilas are more or less as intricate, on the molecular level, as those that form humans; but puppies and fruit flies don't go around asking how they got here or how (another version of the same question) DNA base-pair sequences code for various amino acids. And though humans have been amazed and puzzled by human gestation for quite a while now, it wasn't until a few nanoseconds ago (in geological time) that their wonder began to focus on the chemical minutiae that somehow differentiate living matter from "mere" matter. The fact that self-replicating molecules had eventually come up with a life-form that could actually pick apart the workings of self-replicating molecules . . . well, let's just say I found this line of thought something of a distraction. At the time, I thought that I would never again devote so much attention to such ideas. I figured the miracle of human birth, like that of humans landing on the moon, would be more routine than miracle the second time around. It wasn't.

Five years later, in September 1991, Janet was pregnant again, another fall semester was beginning, and I was up late writing. At 2:00 A.M., Janet asked when I was coming to bed. At 4:00 A.M., she asked again. "Soon," I said. "Well, you should probably stop working now," she replied, "because I think I'm going into labor." At which point she presented me with an early birthday present, a watch with a second hand.

That was the first unexpected thing: James wasn't due for another two weeks. Then came more unexpected things in rapid succession.

Eight hours later, in the middle of labor, Janet spotted a dangerous arrhythmia on her heart monitor. The only other person in the room was an obstetrics staff nurse; Janet turned to her and barked, "That's V-tach. We need a cardiologist in here. Get a bolus of lidocaine ready, and get the crash cart." (Being an ex-cardiac-intensive-care nurse comes in handy sometimes.) Pounding on her chest and forcing herself to cough she broke out of what was possibly a lethal heart rhythm. Labor stalled. Janet and I stared at each other for an hour. Suddenly, at a strange moment when she and I were the only people in the room, James's head presented. I hollered down the hall for help. James appeared within minutes, an unmoving baby of a deep, rich, purple hue, tangled in his umbilical cord. "He looks Downsy around the eyes," I heard. Downsy? He looks stillborn, I thought. They unwrapped the cord, cut it, gave him oxygen. Quickly, incredibly, he revived. No cry, but who cared? They gave him an Apgar score of 7, on a scale of 1 to 10. I remember feeling an immense relief. My wife was alive, my second child was alive. At the end of a teeth-grating hour during which I'd wondered if either of them would see the end of the day, Down syndrome somehow seemed like a reprieve.

Over the next half hour, as the nurses worked on James, and Janet and I tried to collect our thoughts, I realized I didn't know very much about Down's, other than that it meant James had an extra chromosome and would be mentally retarded. I knew I'd have some homework to do.

But what kind of homework were we talking about? Would we ever have normal lives again? We'd struggled for eight years on salaries that left us able to peer at the poverty line only if one of us stood on the other's shoulders. A mere three weeks earlier, the university had hired Janet, thus making us one of the extremely rare dual-career academic couples working in the same department; we knew how lucky we were, and we thought we were finally going to be "comfortable." But now were we going to spend the rest of our days caring for a severely disabled child? Would we have even an hour to ourselves? Christ, we'd only just finished paying off the bills two months earlier for *Nick's* birth, and now were we facing the kind of catastrophic medical debt that fills the op-ed pages? These were selfish thoughts, and the understanding that such thoughts are "natural" didn't make them any less bitter or insistent.

We went over the past few months. The pregnancy had been occasionally odd but not exactly scary. We'd decided against getting an amniocentesis, on the grounds that a sonogram would pick up nearly any serious problems with the fetus *except* Down syndrome, and the chances of having a child with Down syndrome at Janet's age, thirty-six, were

roughly equal to the chances of an amniocentesis-induced miscarriage (1 in 225 and 1 in 200, respectively). Later, there were some hitches: reduced fetal movements, disproportionate fetal measurements on sonograms, low weight gain, and so on. Our worries were vague but persistent.

Back in the present, over on his table in the birthing room, James wasn't doing very well. He still wasn't moving, he had no sucking reflex, and he was getting bluer. It turned out that the fetal opening in his heart hadn't closed fully. You and I had the same arrangement until around the time of birth, when our heart's ventricles sealed themselves off in order to get us ready to start conducting oxygen from our lungs into our bloodstream. But James still had a hole where no hole should be, and wasn't oxygenating properly.

There was more. Along with his patent ductus arteriosus and his trisomy 21, there was laryngomalacia (floppy larynx), jaundice, polycythemia (an abnormal increase in red blood cells), torticollis, vertebral anomaly, scoliosis, hypotonia (low muscle tone), and (not least of these) feeding problems. That's a lot of text to wade through to get to your kid.

Basically, James was in danger. If he made it through the night he would still be a candidate, in the morning, for open-heart surgery *and* a tracheostomy. Because of the laryngomalacia, which isn't related to Down's, he couldn't coordinate sucking, swallowing, and breathing, and his air supply would close off if he slept on the wrong side. The vertebral problems, we learned, occur in roughly one of six kids with Down's; his first three vertebrae were malformed, his spinal cord vulnerable. And his neck muscles were abnormally tight (that's the torticollis), leaving him with a 20-degree head tilt to the left. He was being fed intravenously and had tubes not only in his arm but in his stomach as well, run neatly through his umbilical artery, still viable from the delivery. Our first Polaroid of him shows a little fleshy thing under a clear plastic basin, lost in machinery and wires. I remember thinking, it's all right that they do all this to him now because he'll never remember it. But it can't be a pleasant introduction to the world.

Within days things got better, and one anxiety after another peeled away: Jamie's duct closed, and as I entered the intensive-care unit one morning I found that the staff had erased from his chart the phone number of the emergency helicopter service that would have flown him to Peoria for heart surgery. His blood-oxygen levels reached the high 90s and stayed there, even as he was weaned from 100 percent oxygen to a level just above the atmospheric norm. A tracheoscopy (that is, a viewing of his throat with an eyepiece at the end of a tube) confirmed that he didn't need a tracheostomy. He still wasn't feeding, but he was opening an eye now and then and looking out at his brother and his parents.

I got hold of everything I could on genetics, reproduction, and "abnormal" human development, dusting off college textbooks I hadn't touched since before Nick was born. At one point a staff nurse was sent in to check on *our* mental health; she found us babbling about meiosis and monoploids, wondering anew that Jamie had "gotten" Down syndrome the second he became a zygote. When the nurse inadvertently left behind her notes, Janet sneaked a peek. "Parents seem to be intellectualizing," we read. "Well," Janet shrugged, "that seems accurate enough."

Looking over the fossil record, I really don't see any compelling logic behind humans' existence on the planet. I'm told that intelligence has obvious survival value, since organisms with a talent for information processing "naturally" beat out their competitors for food, water, and condos, but human history doesn't convince me that *our* brand of intelligence is just what the world was waiting for. Thus I've never believed we were supposed to survive the Ice Age, or that some cosmic design mandated the cataclysmic collision in the late Cretaceous period that gave us an iridium layer in our soil and may have ended the dinosaurs' reign. Bacteria and horseshoe crabs unmodified for aeons are still with us, but what has become of *Eusthenopteron*, introduced to me by then-five-year-old Nicholas as the fish that could walk on land? If you were fighting for survival 350 million years ago, you'd think you'd have had a leg up on the competition if you developed small bones in your fins, enabling you to shimmy onto shore. But you'd be wrong: these days, *Eusthenopteron* is nothing more than a card in Nick's "prehistoric animals" collection, alongside the Ankylosaur, the mastodon, and the jessehelms. I figured we were here thanks to dumb luck, and though we have managed to understand our own biochemical origins and take neat close-up pictures from the far side of Saturn, we also spend much of our time exterminating ourselves and most other species we meet. And nothing in Nick's cards says we too won't wind up in nature's deck of "prehistoric" animals.

Still, it wasn't until I got to college and started thinking about sex and drugs in rather immediate ways that I began to realize that the workings of chance on the molecular level are even more terrifying than on the evolutionary plane. Of course, the molecular and the evolutionary have everything to do with each other; it's just the minutiae of mitosis are more awe-inspiring to me than the thought of random rocks slamming into my home planet every couple of hundred million years. For those who don't feel like cracking open old textbooks, Richard Power's novel *The Gold Bug Variations* offers some idea of what's involved in cell division: "seven feet of aperiodic crystal unzips, finds complements of each of its billion constituents, integrates them perfectly without tearing or entangling, then winds up again into a fraction of a millimeter, all in two minutes." And this is just the ordinary stuff your cells are doing every moment. Sex, as always, is a little more complicated.

So let's talk about sex. Of the 15 percent of pregnancies that end in miscarriage, more than half are the result of chromosomal abnormalities, and half of these are caused by trisomy—three chromosomes where two should be. Of the myriad possible genetic mistransmissions in human reproduction, excluding anomalies in the sex chromosomes, it appears that only three kinds of trisomies make it to term: people with three thirteenth chromosomes (Patau's syndrome), three eighteenth chromosomes (Edwards' syndrome), and three twenty-first chromosomes (Down syndrome). About one in four or five zygotes with Down's winds up getting born, and since Down's accounts for one of every 600 to 800 live births, it would appear that trisomy 21 happens quite often, maybe on the order of once in every 150 to 250 fertilizations. Kids with Edwards' or Patau's syndrome are born severely deformed and profoundly retarded; they normally don't live more than a few months. That's what I would expect of genetic anomaly, whatever the size of the autosome: though the twenty-first chromosome is the smallest we have, James still has extra genetic material in every single cell. You'd think the effects of such a basic transcription error would make themselves felt pretty clearly.

But what's odd about Down's is how extraordinarily subtle it can be. Mental retardation is one well-known effect, and it can sometimes be severe, but anyone who's watched Chris Burke in TV's *Life Goes On* or "Mike" in McDonald's commercials knows that the extent of such retardation can be next to negligible. The *real* story of Down's lies not in intelligence tests but in developmental delays across the board, and for the first two years of James's life the most important of these were physical rather than mental (though thanks to James I've come to see how interdependent the mental and physical really are). His muscles are weaker than those of most children his age, his nasal passages imperceptibly narrower. His tongue is slightly thicker; one ear is crinkly. His fingers would be shorter and stubbier but for the fact that his mother's are long, thin, and elegant. His face is a few degrees flatter through the middle, his nose delicate.

Down's doesn't cut all children to one mold; the relations between James's genotype and phenotype are lacy and intricate. It's sort of like what happens in Ray Bradbury's short story "A Sound of Thunder," in which a time traveler accidentally steps on a butterfly while hunting dinosaurs 65 million years ago and returns home to find that he's changed the conventions of English spelling and the outcome of the previous day's election. As he hit the age of two, James was very pleased to find himself capable of walking; by three, he had learned to say the names of colors, to count to ten, and to claim that he would *really* be turning four. Of all our genetic nondisjunctions (with the possible exception of hermaphroditism), only Down syndrome produces so nuanced, so finely articulated a variation on "normal" reproduction. James is less mobile and more susceptible to colds than his peers, but—as his grandparents have often attested—you could play with him for hours and never see anything "wrong."

And then there's a variant form of Down's, called mosaicism, which results from the failure of the chromosome to divide not *before* fertilization but immediately *after,* during the early stages of cell division. Only one in a hundred people with Down's are mosaics, but it's possible for such folks to have some normal cells and some with trisomy 21; there's something about the twenty-first, then, that produces anomalies during either meiosis *or* mitosis. Now, that's truly weird. There's also translocation, in which the twenty-first chromosome splits off and joins the fourteenth or fifteenth, producing people who can be called "carriers"; they can give birth to more translocation carriers, normal children, or translocation kids with Down's. And although everyone knows that the incidence of Down's increases with maternal age, almost no one knows that three quarters of all such children are born to mothers under thirty-five, or that fathers are genetically "responsible" for about one fifth of them. *Parents seem to be intellectualizing.* And why not?

There has never been a better time than now to be born with Down syndrome—and that's really saying something, since it has recently been reported in chimpanzees and gorillas. Because our branch of the evolutionary tree split off from the apes' around 15 to 20 million years ago, these reports would seem to suggest that we've produced offspring with Down syndrome with great regularity at every point in our history as hominids—even though it's a genetic anomaly that's not transmitted hereditarily (except in extremely rare instances) and has no obvious survival value. The statistical incidence of Down's in the current human population is no less staggering: there may be 10 million people with Down's worldwide, or just about one on every other street corner.

But although *Homo sapiens* (as well as our immediate ancestors) has always experienced some difficulty dividing its chromosomes, it wasn't until 1866 that British physician J. Langdon Down diagnosed it as "mongolism" (because it produced children with almond-shaped eyes reminiscent, to at least one nineteenth-century British mind, of central Asian faces). At the time, the average life expectancy of children with Down's was under ten. And for a hundred years thereafter—during which the discovery of antibiotics lengthened the life span of Down's kids to around twenty—Down syndrome was formally known as "mongoloid idiocy."

The 1980 edition of my college genetics textbook, *The Science of Genetics: An Introduction to Heredity,* opens its segment on Down's with the words, "An important and tragic instance of trisomy in humans involves Down's syndrome, or mongoloid idiocy." It includes a picture of a "mongoloid idiot" along with a karyotype of his chromosomes and the information that most people with Down's have IQs in the low 40s. The presentation is objective, dispassionate, and strictly "factual," as it should be. But reading it again in 1991, I began to wonder: is there a connection between the official textual representation of Down syndrome and the social policies by which people with Down's are understood and misunderstood?

You bet your life there is. Anyone who has paid attention to the "political correctness" wars on American campuses knows how stupid the academic left can be: we're always talking about language instead of reality, whining about "lookism" and "differently abled persons" instead of changing the world the way the real he-man left *used* to do. But you know, there really is a difference between calling someone "a mongoloid idiot" and calling him or her "a person with Down syndrome." There's even a difference between calling people "retarded" and calling them "delayed." Though these words may appear to mean the same damn thing when you look them up in Webster's, I remember full well from my days as an American male adolescent that I never taunted my peers by calling them "delayed." Even from those of us who were shocked at the frequency with which "homo" and "nigger" were thrown around in our fancy Catholic high school, "retard" aroused no comment, no protest. In other words, a retarded person is just a retard. But *delayed* persons will get where they're going eventually, if you'll only have some patience.

One night I said something like this to one of the leaders of what I usually think of as the other side in the academic culture wars. Being a humane fellow, he replied that although epithets like "mongoloid idiot" were undoubtedly used in a more benighted time, there have always been persons of goodwill who resisted such phraseology. A nice thought, but it just ain't so. Right through the 1970s, "mongoloid idiot" wasn't an epithet; it was a *diagnosis.* It wasn't uttered by callow, ignorant persons fearful of "difference" and central Asian eyes; it was pronounced by the best-trained medical practitioners in the world, who told families of kids with Down's that their children would never be able to dress themselves, recognize their parents, or live "meaningful" lives. Best to have the child institutionalized and tell one's friends that the baby died at birth. Only the most stubborn, intransigent, or inspired parents resisted such advice from their trusted experts. Who could reasonably expect otherwise?

It's impossible to say how deeply we're indebted to those parents, children, teachers, and medical personnel who insisted on treating people with Down's as if they *could* learn, as if they *could* lead "meaningful" lives. In bygone eras, parents who didn't take their children home didn't really have the "option" of doing so; you can't talk about "options" (in any substantial sense of the word) in an ideological current so strong. But in the early 1970s, some parents did bring their children home, worked with them, held them, provided them physical therapy and "special learning" environments. These parents are saints and sages. They have, in the broadest sense of the phrase, uplifted the race. In the 15-million-year history of Down syndrome, they've allowed us to believe that we're finally getting somewhere.

Of course, the phrase "mongoloid idiocy" did not cause Down syndrome any more than the word "homo" magically induces same-sex desire. But words and phrases are the devices by which we beings signify what homosexuality, or Down syndrome, or anything else, will mean. There surely were, and are, the most intimate possible relations between the language in which we spoke of Down's and the social practices by which we understood it—or refused to understand it. You don't have to be a poststructuralist or a postmodernist or a post-*anything* to get this; all you have to do is meet a parent of a child with Down syndrome. Not long ago, we lived next door to people whose youngest child had Down's. After James was born, they told us of going to the library to find out more about their baby's prospects and wading through page after page of outdated information, ignorant generalizations, and pictures of people in mental institutions, face down in their feeding trays. These parents demanded the library get some better material and throw out the garbage they had on their shelves. Was this a "politically correct" thing for them to do? Damn straight it was. That garbage has had its effects *for generations.* It may look like words, but perhaps the fragile little neonates whose lives were thwarted and impeded by the policies and conditions of institutionalization can testify in some celestial court to the power of mere language, to the intimate links between words and social policies.

Some of my friends tell me this sounds too much like "strict social constructionism"—that is, too much like the proposition that culture is everything and biology is only what we decide to make (of) it. But although James is pretty

solid proof that human biology "exists" independently of our understanding of it, every morning when he gets up, smiling and babbling to his family, I can see for myself how much of his life depends on our social practices. On one of those mornings I turned to my mother-in-law and said, "He's always so full of mischief, he's always so glad to see us—the only thought I can't face is the idea of this little guy waking up each day in a state mental hospital." To which my mother-in-law replied, "Well, Michael, if he were waking up every day in a state mental hospital he wouldn't *be* this little guy."

As it happens, my mother-in-law doesn't subscribe to any strict social constructionist newsletters; she was just passing along what she took to be good common sense. But every so often I wonder how common that sense really is. Every ten minutes we hear that the genetic basis of something has been "discovered," and we rush madly to the newsweeklies: Disease is genetic! Homosexuality is genetic! Infidelity, addiction, obsession with mystery novels—all genetic! Such discourses, it would seem, bring out the hidden determinist in more of us than will admit it. Sure, there's a baseline sense in which our genes "determine" who we are: we can't play the tune unless the score is written down somewhere in the genome. But one does not need or require a biochemical explanation for literary taste, or voguing, or faithless lovers. In these as in all things human, including Down's, the genome is but a template for a vaster and more significant range of social and historical variation. Figuring out even the most rudimentary of relations between the genome and the immune system (something of great relevance to us wheezing asthmatics) involves so many trillions of variables that a decent answer will win you an all-expenses-paid trip to Stockholm.

I'm not saying we can eradicate Down's—or its myriad effects—simply by talking about it more nicely. I'm only saying that James's intelligence is doing better than it would in an institution, and people who try to deny this don't strike me as being among the geniuses of the species. And every time I hear some self-styled "realist" tell me that my logic licenses the kind of maniacal social engineering that produced Auschwitz, I do a reality check: the people who brought us Auschwitz weren't "social constructionists." They were eugenicists. They thought they knew the "immutable laws" of genetics and the "fixed purpose" of evolution, and they were less interested in "improving" folks like Jamie than in exterminating them. I'll take my chances with the people who believe in chance.

And yet there's something very seductive about the notion that Down syndrome wouldn't have been so prevalent in humans for so long without good reason. Indeed, there are days when, despite everything I know and profess, I catch myself believing that people with Down syndrome are here for a specific purpose—perhaps to teach us patience, or humility, or compassion, or mere joy. A great deal can go wrong with us in utero, but under the heading of what goes wrong, Down syndrome is among the most basic, the most fundamental, the most common, *and* the most innocuous, leavening the species with children who are somewhat slower, and usually somewhat gentler, than the rest of the human brood. It speaks to us strongly of design, if design may govern in a thing so small.

After seventeen days in the ICU, James was scheduled for release. We would be equipped with the materials necessary for his care, including oxygen tanks and an apnea monitor that would beep if his heart slowed, became extremely irregular, or stopped. To compensate for his inability to take food orally, James would have a gastrostomy tube surgically introduced through his abdominal wall into his stomach. Janet and I balked. James had recently made progress in his bottle feeding; why do preemptive surgery? We nixed the gastrostomy tube, saying we'd prefer to augment his bottle feedings with a nasal tube and we'd do it ourselves. James stayed three more days in the ICU, and came home to a house full of flowers and homemade dinners from our colleagues.

For the most part, I've repressed the details of that autumn. But every once in a while, rummaging through the medicine closet for Ace bandages or heating pads, I come across the Hypafix adhesive tape with which we attached James's feeding tube to the bridge of his nose, or the strap we wrapped around his tiny chest for his apnea monitor. It's like discovering evidence of another life, dim but indelible, and you realize that once upon a time you could cope with practically anything. Running a small tube through your baby's nose to his stomach is the worst kind of counterintuitive practice. You have to do it carefully, measuring your length of tubing accurately and listening with a stethoscope to make sure you haven't entered the lung. Whenever James pulled out his tubes, we had to do the whole thing over again, in the other nostril this time, lubricating and marking and holding the tube while fumbling with the world's stickiest tape. It's a four-handed job, and I don't blame the staff doctors for assuming we wouldn't undertake such an enterprise alone.

But slowly we got James to bottle feed. After all, for our purposes, Jamie's nasal tube, like unto a thermonuclear weapon, was there precisely so that we *wouldn't* use it. Each week a visiting nurse would set a minimum daily amount for Jamie's milk intake, and whatever he didn't get by bottle would have to go in by tube. So you can see the incentive at work here. Within a month we began to see glimpses of what James would look like sans tube. Then we stopped giving him oxygen during the night, and gradually his tiny nostrils found themselves a lot less encumbered. He still didn't have a voice, but he was clearly interested in his new home and very trusting of his parents and brother.

In the midst of that winter James began physical therapy and massages. We stretched his neck every night, and whenever we could afford it we took him to a local masseuse who played ambient music, relaxed us all, and worked on James for an hour. His physical therapist showed us how everything about James was connected to everything else: His neck, if left uncorrected, would reshape the bones of his face. The straighter his neck, the sooner he'd sit up, the sooner he'd walk. If he could handle simple solid foods with equal facility in both sides of his mouth, he could center himself more easily; and the sooner he could move around by himself, the more he'd be able to explore and learn. In other words, his eating would affect his ability to walk, and his thighs and torso would impinge upon his ability to talk. I suppose that's what it means to be an organism.

Not only did we realize the profound interdependence of human hearts and minds; we also discovered (and had to reconfigure) our relations to a vast array of social practices and institutions. "Developmental" turns out to be a buzzword for a sprawling nexus of agencies, state organizations, and human disabilities. Likewise, "special needs" isn't a euphemism; it's a very specific marker. We're learning about the differences between "mainstreaming" and "inclusion," and we'll be figuring out the Americans with Disabilities Act for the rest of our lives. Above all else, we know that James is extremely lucky to be so well provided for; when every employer is as flexible as ours, when parental leave is the law of the land, when private insurers can't drop families from the rolls because of "high risk" children, when every child can be fed, clothed, and cared for—*then* we can start talking about what kind of a choice "life" might be.

Because, after all he's been through, James is thriving. He's thrilled to be here and takes a visible, palpable delight in seeing his reflection in the oven door as he toddles across the kitchen, or hearing his parents address him in the voices of the *Sesame Street* regulars, or winging a Nerf ball to his brother on the couch. He knows perfectly well when he's doing something we've never seen before, like riding his toddler bicycle down the hall into the laundry room or calling out "Georgia" and "Hawaii" as he flips through Nick's book of the fifty states. He's been a bibliophile from the moment he learned to turn pages. His current favorite is Maurice Sendak's classic *Where the Wild Things Are,* surely a Great Book by any standard; he began by identifying with Max and then, in one of those "oscillations" described by reader-response criticism and feminist film theory, switched over to identifying with the wild things themselves—roaring his terrible roar and showing his terrible claws.

He has his maternal aunts' large deep eyes, and a beautiful smile that somehow involves his whole body. He's not only an independent cuss, but he also has an attention span of about twenty minutes—eighteen minutes longer than the average American political pundit. He's blessed with a preternaturally patient, sensitive brother in Nick, who, upon hearing one of his classmates' parents gasp "Oh my God" at the news that Jamie had Down's, turned to her and said with a fine mixture of reassurance and annoyance, "He's perfectly all *right.*" Like Nick, James has a keen sense of humor; the two of them can be set agiggle by pratfalls, radical incongruities, and mere sidelong looks. He's just now old enough to be curious about what he was like as a baby: as he puts it, all he could do was go "waaah" (holding his fists to his eyes). Barring all the contingencies that can never be barred, James can expect a life span of anywhere from thirty-five to fifty-five years. For tomorrow, he can expect to see his friends at day care, to put all his shapes in his shapes box, and to sing along with Raffi as he shakes his sillies out and wiggles his waggles away.

Before James was born I frankly didn't think very highly of appeals to our "common humanity." I thought such appeals were well intentioned but basically inconsequential. Clearly, Muslim and Christian do not bond over their common ancestor in *Australopithecus.* Rwandan Hutu and Rwandan Tutsi do not toast to the distinctive size of their cerebral cortices. The rape of Bosnia, and Bosnian women, does not stop once Serbian soldiers realize that they too will pass from earth.

And yet we possess one crucial characteristic: the desire to communicate, to understand, to put ourselves in some mutual, reciprocal form of contact with one another. This desire hasn't proven any better at disarming warheads than any of the weaker commonalities enumerated above, but it stands a better chance nonetheless. For among the most amazing and hopeful things about us is that we show up, from our day of birth, programmed to receive and transmit even in the most difficult circumstances; the ability to imagine mutual communicative relations is embedded in our material bodies, woven through our double-stranded fibers. Granted, it's only one variable among trillions, and it's not even "fundamentally" human—for all we know, dolphins are much better at communication than we are. And the sociohistorical variables of human communication will always be more significant and numerous than any genetic determinism can admit. All the same, it's in our software somewhere, and, better still, it's a program that teaches itself how to operate each time we use it.

Whether you want to consider reciprocal communication a constant or a variable, though, the point remains that it's a human attribute requiring other people if it's going to work. Among the talents we have, it's one we could stand to develop more fully. It's only natural: among our deepest, strongest impulses is the impulse to mutual cuing. Nothing will delight James so much as the realization that you have understood him—except the realization that he has understood *you,* and recursively understood his own understanding and yours. Perhaps I could have realized our human stake in mutual realization without James's aid; any number of other humans would have been willing to help me out. But now that I get it, I get it for good. Communication is itself self-replicating. Sign unto others as you'd have them sign unto you. Pass it on.

# Name Index

# Subject Index